Presumed Equal

What America's Top Women Lawyers Really Think About Their Firms

Presumed Equal

What America's Top Women Lawyers Really Think About Their Firms

By
Suzanne Nossel
and
Elizabeth Westfall

CAREER PRESS
3 Tice Road
P.O. Box 687
Franklin Lakes, NJ 07417
1-800-CAREER-1
201-848-0310 (NJ and outside U.S.)
FAX: 201-848-1727

Presumed Equal

ISBN 1-56414-313-9, $24.99

ISBN 1-56414-320-1, $50.00

Cover design by Suzanne Bennett

Printed in the U.S.A. by Book-mart Press

To order this title by mail, please include price as noted above, $2.50 handling per order, and $1.50 for each book ordered. Send to: Career Press, Inc., 3 Tice Road, P.O. Box 687, Franklin Lakes, NJ 07417.

Or call toll-free 1-800-CAREER-1 (NJ and Canada: 201-848-0310) to order using VISA or MasterCard, or for further information on books from Career Press.

Library of Congress Cataloging-in-Publication Data

Nossel, Suzanne, 1969-
    Presumed equal : what America's top women lawyers really think about their firms / by Suzanne Nossel and Elizabeth Westfall.
        p.   cm.
    ISBN 1-56414-320-1 (hc).
    ISBN 1-56414-313-9 (pbk.)
    1. Women lawyers--United States.   2. Sex discrimination against women--Law and legislation--United States. 3. Job satisfaction--United States.   I. Westfall, Elizabeth, 1968- .   II. Title.
KF299.W6N67   1998
340'.082--dc21   97-39595
                                                                            CIP

Acknowledgments

First and foremost, we wish to thank the more than 1,200 women who took the time to share their thoughts and insights in response to our survey. We also wish to express appreciation to the staff at Career Press. Our deepest gratitude goes to Francesca Bignami, Meredith Fuchs, Jared Goldstein, Deborah Hamilton, Nancy Letsinger, Amanda Maisels, Christopher Meade, Dena Ringold, Judith Rosenberg, Kathleen Ryan, Amy Sherff, Catherine Stetson, Justin Smith, Elliot Thomson, and Cora Tung, for their gracious and cheerful assistance with this project. We are extremely grateful to Preetal Bansal, Robert Stack, and Susan Crawford for their advice and counsel. We also thank both of our families, and Elizabeth's friends and colleagues at Wilmer, Cutler & Pickering and Suzanne's friends and colleagues at the United States Court of Appeals for the District of Columbia Circuit for their encouragement and support. Finally, we wish to extend a special thanks to Elizabeth's husband, Scott Wiener, for his enthusiasm, patience, and assistance at every stage of this project.

This expanded edition of *Presumed Equal* follows publication of a first edition of *Presumed Equal* by the Harvard Women's Law Association in 1995. We reiterate our gratitude to all of the supporters of the first edition, particularly Professor Laurence Tribe.

Suzanne F. Nossel

Elizabeth S. Westfall

Contents

Introduction

The impetus for *Presumed Equal* arose more than two years ago when, as second-year law students at Harvard contemplating jobs at large firms, we were alerted to the complex set of issues and conflicts facing women in private legal practice. During interviews for summer associate positions at large firms across the country, we and our friends caught arresting glimpses of the difficulties women attorneys face in shaping their careers, balancing work and home life, and confronting the perceptions of colleagues and clients about women's professional abilities.

One summer job interview was postponed for nearly half an hour as the candidate listened to a panic-stricken attorney make arrangements to cover for a sick nanny. At another firm, a lawyer recounted the ultimatum issued by her husband who had grown impatient with her long working hours—"Quit your job or I am leaving you." A corporate associate confided that she had simply stopped making plans to see family or friends because she inevitably had to break them. After a 15-minute conversation, a classmate of ours was told by a male interviewer that although she seemed like a "real nice lady," she was not tough enough to make it at a large corporate firm.

These and similar tales caught us and many of our women classmates off guard. The concerns they generated stemmed from the fact that, having spent most of our young adulthoods on university campuses during the late 1980s and early 1990s, most of us were unaware that being a woman could hinder our future success or achievement. Because we had all won acceptances to college and law school, received good grades, and had opportunities for campus leadership positions, barriers to the advancement of women seemed like things of the past. In addition, because very few of us had children, the challenges of combining career and family were known to us only in the abstract.

What we heard from women in firms was a rude awakening, signaling that the treatment we took for granted might change once we entered the workplace. As members of the Women's Law Association, we decided to seek ways to inform law students about what they might encounter at large law firms, and to ensure that women's employment choices took into account issues that, although remote to us as students, figured profoundly in determining the levels of satisfaction of practicing women attorneys.

Having found that women in firms were eager to talk about their lives and that—if our classmates were any indication—law students were eager to listen, we decided to conduct a survey of women at firms nationwide to canvass their experiences on advancement, gender discrimination, work and family, and diversity. Our efforts were further motivated by an awareness that many women in firms feel too isolated and vulnerable to raise issues of concern, and as members of the Harvard Women's Law Association, we were positioned to act where others could not.

Cobbling together funds from faculty members and alumni, we mailed out the first *Presumed Equal* survey to women at 57 firms across the country in July 1995. We were surprised and gratified when more than 600 women responded, many writing detailed and personal accounts of their working lives.

In the fall of 1995, we compiled the surveys into the first edition of Pres*umed Equal*, which we printed ourselves under the Women's Law Association banner. With no marketing, no publicity, and a distribution scheme that consisted of filling orders from the Women's Law Association office in between our classes, *Presumed Equal* sold more than 1,000 copies and received media coverage in *The Wall Street Journal, Washington Post, Los Angeles Times, New York Post,* on National Public Radio, and in numerous legal journals and newspapers.

More importantly, students from Harvard and other law school campuses thanked us for providing them with an uncensored account of women's experiences at the firms they considered joining, and women attorneys around the country reported that the findings in *Presumed Equal* served as a stimulus for their firms to pay greater attention to the issues confronting women attorneys.

Soon after the first edition of *Presumed Equal* was released, students and attorneys urged us to update the study periodically to draw attention to and monitor the status of women in private practice. Because our successors at the Harvard Women's Law Association had moved on to new projects after graduating from law school, we decided to prepare a second edition for a commercial publisher who could ensure wider distribution. In this edition of *Presumed Equal*, we have increased our coverage from 57 to 77 firms, and our response more than doubled from approximately 600 to approximately 1,225.

From the outset, *Presumed Equal* has attracted questions from students, professors, and practicing attorneys. Answering these queries has helped us refine our vision of the project, and by sharing our answers, we hope to offer readers a clear understanding of what this book aims to accomplish.

One of the first questions raised was, "Why big law firms?" Although our interest in the status of women in the legal workplace extends beyond private practice in law firms, our study focuses on firms in part because we recognize that at law schools, private firms are virtually the only employers that actively compete to woo students, rather than the other way around. We concluded, therefore, that by disseminating information about firms, we could not only assist students in making employment choices, but also provide an impetus for firms to address women attorneys' concerns in order to make themselves more attractive to prospective recruits. Our decision to focus on large firms—in most cases, those with 50 or more women attorneys—was motivated primarily by the desire to provide data for the largest hiring pool, as well as to protect the anonymity of respondents.

The choice to focus on large law firms was also rooted in a recognition that they exert a significant influence on the broader legal community in a variety of ways. Large law firms, because of their prominence and the respect they command, often set the standard for their smaller counterparts. Lawyers in every branch of government and every sphere of practice—both private and public—have spent time working in large law firms. Because individuals are shaped by the institutions with which they are affiliated, advancing the position of women within law firms may ultimately have a ripple effect that is felt throughout the legal practice.

A second question raised relates to the elite focus of this project. If we are interested in the progress of women, why look only at those whose skills and income place them at the pinnacle of professional advancement? Our choice of focus stems from a belief that social change, in the women's movement and more broadly, must proceed on multiple fronts simultaneously. No single battle can be fought to the exclusion of—or at the expense of—all others. Within multipronged initiatives, there is value to having groups and individuals put pressure on the levers that are most firmly within their grasp.

When we started this project as members of the Harvard Women's Law Association, we recognized that our organizational affiliation was well-suited for a project directed at law firms. In repeating the survey, we seek to build upon a foundation already in place. Although our initiative is very modest, we suspect that the problems uncovered in large law firms may be characteristic of professional work settings throughout the economy, and we hope that progress within the legal profession may ultimately set a standard against which the business world and other sectors can be judged.

One of the strongest criticisms that we have encountered relates to our focus on "women's issues." Several survey respondents stressed, in some cases with consternation, that their answers to questions concerning work and family issues or diversity applied equally to male and female attorneys. Some critics suggested that our findings are of limited value because we have not compared women's experiences to men's.

We reject the premise upon which this criticism is based—namely, that men are a kind of control group in the legal profession, and that women's experiences can only be evaluated against what is normal or ordinary for men. Our intent in writing *Presumed Equal* is to give women an idea of what life in particular firms is like for other *women*. This information is relevant less because of what it may suggest about the differences between women and men, more because of the light it might shed on how women's experiences can vary based upon where they work. Moreover, when studies are conducted on overwhelmingly male pools of scientists, politicians, or CEOs, they are rarely criticized for failure to measure their findings against comparably situated women.

Others have commented that many of the issues examined in *Presumed Equal*, particularly work-family concerns, apply to men as well as women. We could not agree more. Our decision to refer to women's issues arises from the recognition that women continue to perform the vast majority of caretaking, child-rearing, and homemaking functions in our society. We look forward to a time when these responsibilities are fulfilled in equal proportions by women and men. In addition to liberating women, such a dispensation would introduce more men to the joys and rewards of a life in which work and professional achievement are just one among a set of absolute priorities in life. With that in mind, we expect that the findings reported in *Presumed Equal* will be of interest to men who are themselves struggling with work and family issues, and with the other concerns addressed in the survey.

Some lawyers have also challenged what they perceive as the premise of *Presumed Equal*, the assumption that female law students will make their employment choices based solely on women's issues. As one law firm partner put it, "When I looked for a job, I wanted to know what kind of work I would do and how much responsibility I would get."

The answer here is obvious. Of course women are deeply interested in firms' practice areas, clients, and in the assignments associates receive. For good reason, law students are veritably showered with this information in firm resumes and portfolios, recruitment letters,

career services offices, and during interviews. We view this guidebook as one volume amidst a library of important resources for students researching firms. Further, we look forward to the day when a woman candidate's professional interests can form the sole basis upon which she chooses a firm, and when women need no longer conclude, "The work sounds great, but I've heard it's just not the place to go if you want a family."

The majority of our survey respondents, however, seem to agree that the profession is not yet at a point where women's levels of long-term professional satisfaction are determined solely by the substance of their work. Because, at least for the time being, gender bias, the availability of childcare, part-time options, and other women's issues play an important role in shaping women's experiences, we offer this guide as a source of information that may bear directly on women's experiences at firms, information that is difficult, if not impossible, to garner in interviews or from recruitment materials.

Perhaps the concern that has given us greatest pause relates to the subjective nature of the information presented here. What we report is personal and anecdotal and reflects the views of a relatively small group of women attorneys. We received responses from varying percentages of the women at firms, and in some cases, the numbers were concededly small. In some instances, we had no way of knowing whether the sentiments conveyed by respondents from particular firms were reflective of widespread views.

This concern must be recognized by the reader. Our decision to make the information available, even when the sample of respondents was small, was based on the recognition that obtaining empirically comprehensive data on the highly qualitative questions covered in the survey would be virtually impossible. If all perceptions were required to be scientific in nature, information on the matters addressed in this guide might never become available. In our opinion, the alternative is far less attractive: Telling students they should rely on accidental exposure to particular individuals in their attempt to discover "what they're really in for." Our goal is to assist in "risk assessment."

Although the responses with respect to most firms are a mixed bag, it is possible to identify a few "rotten apples" where large numbers of responses are consistently negative and where respondents give the same reasons for their dissatisfaction. By the same token, there is every reason to believe that firms that received consistently positive ratings on particular axes must be doing something right.

Upon reading the results of this year's survey, we were pleased to learn that in some instances, the firms that fared the worst in 1995 used *Presumed Equal* as a starting point to launch comprehensive efforts aimed at understanding and remedying the problems identified in the survey. We applaud these efforts and note that they were taken even though the 1995 results were based on a much smaller sample size than we now offer. With the understanding that the information provided here may not be incontrovertible or definitive, we hope and believe that it will still provide a lever for debate and change.

On a related note, some law firm leaders have voiced concern that the only attorneys who would spare the time to respond to our survey are those who are disgruntled. This assumption is contradicted by the fact that we received at least a few very positive responses from most firms surveyed, and that quite a few firms covered in the study came across overall as very hospitable places for women. The fact that many women partners took the time to respond further indicates that the survey is of interest to more than just a select group of dissatisfied attorneys.

The reverse could also be argued. In the cover letter accompanying the survey, we made clear that the results might be consulted by students during the recruitment season. From the tenor of their comments, it could be argued that some respondents, particularly partners, chose to focus exclusively on the positive aspects of firm life in an effort to buoy their firm's position in the eyes of potential recruits. Thus, although we cannot claim that the perspectives we relay are objective or definitive, by reporting our precise methodology and response rates, we seek to give readers a chance to draw their own conclusions about what weight to place on the information we convey.

In presenting the information, we have sought to be as faithful as possible to our respondents. We have been careful to indicate when a quotation reflects views expressed by several associates, and when it was a lone opinion. When there was even one dissenter about a particular issue, we made an effort to include remarks that ran counter to the prevailing consensus, whether that dissent was positive or negative. Most important, we attempted to be *fair*—to give a reasonable and measured summary of *all* the surveys received.

We are confident that our readers will recognize that firms differ dramatically in structure, size, goals, and geographic location and that, for this reason, direct comparisons are not always meaningful. The rating we offer of firms is based on the charts that appeared on the second page of our survey, and is designed to offer readers a rough notion of how firms stack up against one another, rather than to posit that particular firms are actually the "best" or the "worst."

One survey respondent wrote that she and her colleagues were shocked to learn that their firm was number one in our 1995 edition, because it was far from an ideal place for women. (It fares worse in the current survey.) With that in mind, we ask that readers not view the numerical tallies as gospel, and instead look carefully at the specifics of what women had to say about each particular firm.

Some lawyers we have consulted expressed concern about whether this project is "constructive." Our interest in *Presumed Equal* stems entirely from a hope that this study will promote the advancement of women in the profession. Our objective was not to offer an extensive prescriptive list of things that firms should do to change. Rather, in our view, the most constructive development that can emerge from this project is the initiation of a dialogue between law firm leaders and the women who work with them. The survey responses indicate unmistakably that women have a great deal to say about the questions we asked. Firms should

not, however, expect individual women to come forward about their concerns if doing so makes them feel spotlighted or vulnerable. Instead, difficult though it may be, firms must create opportunities for these issues to be debated openly, with a concerted effort made to minimize, if not eliminate, any threat of reprisal.

Finally, we wish to address an issue related to our respondents' confidentiality that was brought to our attention by survey respondents. We asked respondents to name the firm where they are employed, but not to identify themselves by name. The survey was done anonymously because we believe that this is the only way to get significant numbers of women to respond frankly to the questions posed.

After the 1995 edition was circulated, we received disturbing reports of efforts to identify the attorneys who had made particular comments included in the study—"witch hunts," as respondents called them. As compilers of the study, we are deeply concerned about this troubling development. It is difficult to imagine that any firm that purports to be a hospitable place for women would try to ferret out those who are most unhappy in order to chide or stigmatize them for the comments they made on the survey. Virtually all of the concerns and issues raised by respondents are, to a large extent, general rather than personal in nature, and invite solutions that should be directed at all women.

Although we have attempted to verify factual information contained in the firm profiles, it was not always possible to obtain formal confirmation from law firms of facts reported by respondents. For example, although we made an effort to ascertain the accuracy of statements concerning the attrition rates of female attorneys, several firms we contacted were not willing or able to provide us with data on this subject. Thus, while we have included statements made by respondents concerning attrition and other issues, we ask readers to bear in mind that it was not always possible for us to get official confirmation of the accuracy of such information.

The Findings

Among the most striking findings of our study is the fact that there is no single "woman's" experience at any firm. The attorneys at each of the firms surveyed varied considerably in terms of their impressions of their workplaces. That women diverge in their accounts of what individual firms are like is not surprising. Women attorneys come from diverse backgrounds and have varying priorities and expectations. Attitudes and tones that make some women feel right at home can make others very uncomfortable. Assignment systems that give some women tremendous opportunity can leave others feeling underutilized and frustrated. Differences in perceptions may be attributable to distinct personalities, different hopes in terms of professional satisfaction, or varying levels of talent, drive, and stamina.

That women are not unanimous in what they expect and want from firms does not mean that firms cannot identify steps that can be taken to increase women's levels of job satisfaction and performance overall. Rather, it means that such steps must be grounded upon a clear understanding of the spectrum of women's concerns, rather than on a simplified understanding of a single, essential "woman's" experience.

Amidst the variations in women's responses to our questionnaire, several strong themes emerged. From our perspective, women's accounts of their lives at large law firms help shed light on the potential and limitations of "formal equality," a system wherein formal rules do not differentiate between individuals on the basis of gender. Women have had a large presence in the private legal profession for almost two decades; women lawyers are hired by firms for the same positions as their male counterparts and, at least in the junior ranks, they are given equal pay. Women enter firms with educational backgrounds equal to those of men. The elimination of entry barriers for women into private legal practice has brought with it considerable change. While 50 years ago very few firms were willing to interview top women law school graduates, most respondents now report that their firms are "comfortable" places for women and that harassment and sexism are rare.

Despite marked progress, survey respondents reported difficulties in every area covered in the questionnaire. On the whole, respondents did not think that the problems they faced would be remedied over time through existing approaches and attitudes. Instead, respondents commented that systemic forces hold back women's progress and will continue to do so until institutional and societal changes are made. The following is a brief, nonexhaustive summary of the responses we received.

Advancement: At the firms that received the highest ratings in this regard, women reported that their chances of being promoted to partner equal those of men, provided they are willing and able to put in the long hours and enormous energy. Almost without exception, mentoring was cited as central to advancement and, at many firms, women were reported to be less likely to be mentored than men. As numerous respondents observed, men far outnumber women in firm partnerships, and because people are more likely to take under their wing young colleagues with whom they personally identify, informal relationships tend to favor male associates.

Respondents reported that this has a harmful effect on women's career prospects. There are too few female mentors to go around, and women partners are often not senior enough to exert the force necessary to help propel a young attorney's career. Respondents indicated that formal, firm-initiated mentor programs, although they do not always succeed in creating ongoing relationships, can provide a useful point of entry for junior lawyers seeking to forge relationships with more senior colleagues.

Assignment quality also matters for advancement, and women can be at a disadvantage in this regard, as well. Some respondents reported full satisfaction with the level of work they have been assigned, but others suggested that women litigators do research and writing while men do depositions and court appearances, and women corporate lawyers work on due diligence while their male peers are negotiating deals. In some cases, the disparity was attributed to partners' perceptions of women's capabilities and their ability to win the confidence of clients.

Numerous respondents observed that failure to secure increasingly complex

and challenging assignments will doom an attorney's prospects for advancement. With regard to assignment systems, while some women seem to fare very well when left to their own devices to drum up work, other respondents reported that these informal systems tend to favor associates who can form strong personal bonds with senior attorneys. These respondents indicated that more structured assignment systems can help ensure greater equity in the distribution of assignments at junior levels and can enable women attorneys to earn the respect of senior colleagues who might not otherwise have gravitated toward them.

At more senior levels, respondents commented that business generation is often a critical factor for promotion to partner and for advancement within partnership ranks. Women are reported to be at a disadvantage in this regard for several reasons: Older male CEOs and corporate counsels may be less inclined to put their trust in women law partners; related to the uneven mentoring pattern, male partners are said to be more likely to pass clients on to younger male protégés; and women who shoulder family responsibilities often have little time to devote to client cultivation activities.

Some firms have taken the positive step of supporting women partners' efforts at business generation. Some successful rainmaking initiatives have brought together women attorneys and women CEOs, although, as several women pointed out, to compete for partnership and leadership slots female attorneys must gain greater access to business from both male and female clients.

One development that generated much more discussion in this survey than it did in 1995 is the growth of two-tiered partnership structures divided between income and equity partners. Some respondents applauded such arrangements for offering women with outside responsibilities a secure, prestigious, long-term position entailing significant responsibility but less pressure to generate business. Others derided income partnership positions as glorified associateships that end up as permanent plateaus for women. At the few firms in our survey that have multilevel partnership structures, women partners seem to be concentrated at the lower ranks, with the jump to equity partnership proving elusive for most. At some firms, distinctions within partnership ranks can also disfavor women in terms of compensation.

Finally, attrition continues to be perceived as a widespread problem among women associates, with ramifications not only in terms of the number of women making partner but also in a shortage of senior women associates to provide mentoring and guidance for more junior associates. The most oft-cited reason why women leave firms relates to the difficulty of sustaining a law firm career once one has children. Further, it appears women tend not to wait around to be rejected by firms where they perceive their chances at partnership to be slim because of a lack of mentoring and desirable assignments, as well as heavy emphasis on business generation. Instead, women depart in large numbers, leaving those behind to wonder whether it's in the firm's interest to invest its resources to train such large numbers of junior associates, most of whom leave within a few years.

Attitudes and atmosphere: The good news is that most women feel fairly comfortable at their firms on a day-to-day basis. Very few instances of sexual harassment or ugly work environments were reported. Very often, women's levels of comfort tended to be higher in departments with large percentages of women and/or with women in partnership positions. Where women work together in significant numbers, they seem to form support networks that can significantly enhance quality of life. In contrast, women in virtually all-male corporate and litigation departments seem to encounter the most difficulty.

Instances of exclusion most frequently cited by respondents relate to firm-sponsored client development outings. Some respondents reported that their firms sponsor outings involving cigar smoking, drinking, and golf, and that women tend to learn about these excursions only after the fact. As many attorneys point out, women's exclusion from gatherings of this sort deprives them of opportunities to cultivate clients and to forge close bonds with powerful (male) partners.

In some cases, respondents said, the reluctance of male partners to socialize with female associates stems from the desire to avoid an appearance of impropriety. In the case of group events, however, respondents pointed out that there is no legitimate reason why female colleagues should be left out. In some cases, the absence of women at after-hours functions is by choice. Women with family commitments said that they tend to be less available for drinks, dinners, and weekend outings. They believed that declining these social opportunities for time with spouses or children can place women at a disadvantage.

Although most respondents spoke favorably of their relationships with male colleagues, some reported that certain unacceptable behaviors persist. (Although there were many egregious allegations from respondents that we chose *not* to include in the text.) At some firms, women reported that comfort levels are contingent upon personality. In some, assertive, outspoken women are shunned, whereas elsewhere, more quiet women are written off as meek and lacking in intellectual force.

Work and family: Balancing family with big-firm legal practice is never easy, but some firms do far more than others to help make it possible. Firm-sponsored emergency day-care service appears to be more widely available now than it was at the time of the first *Presumed Equal* survey. In addition, several firms were strongly praised for providing attorneys with laptops and e-mail hookups to enable them to telecommute and spend more time with their families.

As women with families begin to reach partnership positions in greater numbers, some firms seem to be recognizing that having a child does not in itself signify a lessening of commitment to work. At many firms, however, attorneys reported that those who have achieved partnership are overwhelmingly single and childless, and that chances of advancement appear to shrink dramatically once an associate has children.

The fact remains that, particularly at partnership level, many men in firms have wives who do not have careers outside the home and can assume primary responsibility for child rearing. These men enjoy peace of mind and

freedom from guilt, which is elusive even for women who have excellent childcare arrangements. Only a few female partners around the country are said to have "Mr. Mom" husbands. Short of that, although women in firms have careers that are typically at least as demanding as those of their spouses, they still shoulder the overwhelming burden of family-related responsibilities.

Working the double shift at home and at a law firm can be made easier by colleagues who openly acknowledge attorneys' outside responsibilities. Some women reported that a male counterpart's leaving work at midday to watch a daughter's dance performance is viewed as sweet and endearing, whereas women who do the same are criticized for lack of commitment and unreliability. At firms where family responsibilities are openly respected and where getting the work done on schedule is more important than "face time," women report that with creativity and stamina, it *is* possible to do it all.

One downside of a firm climate that is receptive to family responsibilities and affords flexibility to working parents is that single lawyers may bear an added burden because their need for personal time and a predictable schedule is regarded as less pressing.

Several partner respondents wrote that some men are beginning to follow women out of firms because they feel that the long hours leave them insufficient time with their families.

Flexibility of work arrangements: A growing number of firms appear to be offering part-time options, although drawbacks still abound. At some firms, part-time arrangements are made available on an *ad hoc* (case-by-case) basis, meaning that junior attorneys feel the need to curry favor with their higher-ups if they hope to take advantage of such policies in the future.

Respondents agreed that flexibility on the part of both the lawyer and the firm is the touchstone of a viable part-time arrangement, and that communicating the availability of part-time and formalizing a part-time policy can lessen the uncertainty for attorneys while still leaving room for individualized arrangements. Numerous respondents reported that part-time work is more tenable in some practice areas (e.g., tax and real estate) than in others (e.g., litigation and corporate). Nevertheless, although some respondents concluded that a part-time schedule is incompatible with a fast-paced litigation or corporate practice, others reported that part-timers do play vital roles even on high-profile cases and deals.

Regardless of whether a formal part-time policy exists, personal viewpoints of the partners can influence the lot of part-timers. Where part-time work is viewed as a legitimate, respected option, part-timers tend to be highly motivated and to see themselves as valued members of the team. Where part-timers are viewed as less committed and on their way out of the firm, they get less desirable assignments and feel stigmatized. At firms where part-time is available on paper but not respected by the partners, those who are supposedly on reduced schedules can end up working as many hours as full-time attorneys. In some instances, "part-time" attorneys who have put in hours that are above-average for full-timers have been denied their requests to be compensated for the extra time worked. Thus, at many firms,

part-time is said to entail the same amount of work for less pay.

At partnership level, the availability of part-time options seems to be expanding slowly. Many firms are said to be grappling with the question of how part-time work should affect advancement prospects. Often, the policy is that by taking part-time status, an attorney goes permanently "off track," meaning that it is understood she will never make partner. Increasingly, firms are moving away from this approach and recognizing that a woman's desire to spend more time at home does not mark her permanently unfit for partnership. Growing numbers of firms now permit women to go back "on track" once they return to full-time status after a part-time stint.

The arrangement that respondents found most fair for all concerned involves affording part-timers partial "credit" for time spent on a reduced schedule, meaning that partnership consideration is delayed until they have clocked roughly the same amount of total work time as those who remained steadily on a full-time schedule. Although some women are very grateful to have made partner "on time" with their class after a part-time stint, others fear that giving full credit for periods of part-time work may leave women at a disadvantage in terms of skills and experience when they come up for partnership.

Generally speaking, a greater number of firms is recognizing that the fast track to partnership need not be the only model for a career in private legal practice. Although of-counsel positions and junior partnerships are frustrating plateaus for some, for others these arrangements can be ideal ways to enjoy job security and challenging work without the demands and stresses of partnership.

Diversity: Respondents appeared to have much less to say on this topic than on others, and their responses were generally less revealing. Most respondents wrote that their firms showed some commitment to recruiting lawyers from diverse backgrounds, but had had little success in actually achieving a racially or ethnically diverse workforce.

Retention rates for minority attorneys tend to be poor, and the absence of minority lawyers at senior levels in most firms means that junior minority lawyers can feel isolated and unsupported.

In contrast, numerous firms were reported to be supportive environments for gay and, to a lesser extent, lesbian attorneys.

Women in leadership positions: We asked about this issue for the first time in this year's survey and found the answers quite revealing. Although the number of women partners at most firms is on the rise, very few women are said to be actual powerbrokers within their firms. Women's lack of influence within partnership ranks is attributable in part to the difficulties they face with respect to business generation. At most firms, leadership positions are tied to rainmaking abilities, meaning that women are often shut out of the management or policy committees that make major firm decisions. Where women do hold leadership positions, they tend to be in "softer" areas such as the personnel or recruitment committees. Similarly, where women chair firm practice groups, they tend to be in smaller departments such as trusts and estates, health care, or environmental, rather than corporate or litigation.

The responses from women associates revealed a high level of expectations of—and often disappointment with—the role the women partners in their firms play. In some instances, women associates reported that their colleagues in the partnership were very supportive in terms of mentoring and helping to promote opportunities and quality of life for women, yet numerous respondents reported that the senior women at their firm seem to feel that because they had made tremendous sacrifices along the way, others must do the same. In some cases, women remarked that because many of the most influential women partners do not have children themselves, they are not always sensitive to the needs of associates trying to combine work and family.

The remarks of junior associates often reflected a keen awareness that the women who have achieved the greatest success in their firms did so at considerable personal cost. In some instances, women associates described female partners in terms that seemed harsh and cruel, such as "barracudas" or "men in women's clothing."

We felt some reluctance about printing these comments, mainly out of concern that they would fuel negative stereotypes about powerful women. When reading these responses, we reminded ourselves that the challenges described in *Presumed Equal* about law firm life in the 1990s were far more pronounced for women who entered law firms in the 1960s, 70s, and 80s, and that then, as now, there was no simple or ideal way of responding to these obstacles. Some women did so by becoming, in the eyes of others, "just like men"; others developed tough, forceful exteriors that instill fear in subordinates; still others did so by cultivating personas that have won them universal respect and acclaim.

We have included negative as well as positive comments about senior female partners on the rationale that the way women perceive their firms hinges in part on the way they perceive themselves and one another, and that opening debate on these issues is the only way they will ultimately be resolved.

Many partners observed—and some associates acknowledged—that there is another side to the story of female partners who decline to assist junior female attorneys. Women partners are extremely busy with work and outside responsibilities and may have little time to spare for mentoring. Heavy involvement in mentoring or recruiting women takes away time from work, family responsibilities, and client-development activities. Still, in firms where women partners do reach out to associates in one-to-one relationships, through social events or on women's forums or committees, associates reported deep appreciation.

Challenges Ahead

Based on the survey responses and the portrait they give of firm life for women, we wish to pose a series of challenges to the majority of firms covered in our survey. First, there are wide disparities in the sorts of policies different firms deem viable. Many respondents reported that at their firms, the prevalent view is that part-time and other flexible work options, and in some cases even full-time work by mothers with significant family responsibilities, are incompatible with the nature of large-firm practice and the pace of client demands. On the other hand, a growing number of firms have succeeded in enabling women with major outside responsibilities to play leadership roles with clients and in firm management.

On-site childcare facilities and telecommuting are credited with helping working parents to achieve a balance in their lives, and allowing firms to get the most from women attorneys. The firms that have pioneered these innovations, like all those included in the survey, are large, prestigious, and serve major Fortune 500 clients. Their experience is powerful evidence that altering institutional arrangements to make it easier for women to contribute their talents and expertise to firm practice need not come at the expense of client service or profits. Firms that contend that such adaptations are impossible or would undermine the level of client service must be challenged to explain their failure to follow the example of more family-friendly firms.

A second challenge our findings pose relates to the need to both institutionalize efforts that are responsive to the needs of women in the work place, and to ensure that such efforts take root firm-wide.

Concerning business generation, women are generally left to their own devices to cultivate clients, even though they often lack the mentors and connections necessary to make such efforts succeed. On the flip side, while formalized policies are a vital step, firms that consider themselves committed to the advancement of women must take a hard look at how policies, procedures, and attitudes interact to affect women.

Careful attention must be paid to what goes on in the interstices between written policies and formal directives—the allocation of assignments, the interactions at luncheons and social events, and the comments made about women who take time off to have or care for children. Having a great part-time policy on paper may mean nothing if individual partners look down on part-timers and give them consistently inferior work. Even if they are invited to client gatherings, women may still feel at a disadvantage if the activities center around golf, cigar smoking, or other pastimes in which women may have less interest or experience.

Next, we ask firms to recognize that professional growth for lawyers retains echoes of the traditional system of apprenticeship wherein more senior attorneys took responsibility for launching their subordinates' careers. Women at almost all firms we surveyed stressed the importance of mentoring as a source of support for young attorneys, and as an indispensable ticket to advancement. The forces that lead senior male attorneys to mentor men more frequently than they do women are understandable. Yet, this pattern perpetuates the subordination of women lawyers and must thus be reexamined if firms are serious about ensuring equal opportunity for women.

Overall, our findings make clear that offering women jobs and salaries commensurate with men's represents only the first tentative steps on the journey to making the legal profession an arena where women can thrive and contribute throughout the duration of their working lives. The challenges that lie ahead are posed not only to law firms, but also to women lawyers and law students. Individual women in firms are in a tough position. If they are perceived as instigators, their advancement potential, or even their jobs, may be threatened. For many, the easiest solution to the dilemmas and sacrifices described by respondents is to leave the law, or at least give up large-firm practice. While this may be a wise choice for individuals, as a group, women must not withdraw from seeking leadership roles in this large and powerful sphere of the profession, or from trying to effect change within law firm corridors.

Law students in particular have entire careers ahead of them, during which they can help shape legal practice in an image that suits their goals and expectations. While individual women may feel vulnerable or trapped, as a collective, women are far from powerless. We constitute almost 50 percent of entering associate classes at many large law firms, we have allies in partnership positions, and, as students, we are essential to firms' futures.

Advocacy efforts take time and energy—resources that are in short supply for women in law firms. Such efforts, however, also depend heavily on intelligence, drive and courage—resources with which women lawyers abound.

Elizabeth Westfall is currently an associate at Wilmer, Cutler & Pickering. The views expressed in Presumed Equal *are those of the authors and not the views of Wilmer, Cutler & Pickering.*

Although we mailed surveys to women at Wilmer, Cutler & Pickering, it was decided to omit the firm's profile in order to avoid any appearance of conflict.

Methodology

Survey: The information contained in *Presumed Equal* was compiled using a two-page written survey, a copy of which is included in the Appendix. The survey was mailed to women attorneys, along with a cover letter, which is also included in the Appendix. (To facilitate response, postage-paid reply envelopes were provided.) The survey and cover letter were drafted by us based on those used in the 1995 *Presumed Equal* survey.

Firms covered: The majority of firms covered in the study are located in Atlanta, Boston, Chicago, Houston, Los Angeles, New York, San Francisco, and Washington, D.C. Several firms from other cities were also included. The choice of firms was based on size and on a rough assessment of interest the firms generate nationally in the student recruitment process. Because of space constraints, the survey was sent to main offices of firms only. The survey was originally sent to attorneys at 105 firms, 27 of which were excluded from the book because of insufficient responses.

Attorneys approached: We obtained lists of attorneys employed at the selected firms using West's Legal Directory on the Internet. In some cases, the directory may not have been entirely up-to-date, meaning that first-year and other new attorneys may not have received the survey. We examined the lists to determine which attorneys had women's names. This system was obviously not foolproof. As a result, some women did not receive the survey, and some men wrote back to us to say that they had received it in error. Approximately 7,000 surveys were mailed.

Responses: The surveys were mailed in late April 1997, and the initial due date was May 5, 1997. Shortly after the surveys were sent, we wrote letters to recruitment coordinators at the firms requesting they circulate memoranda or e-mail encouraging women attorneys to respond, and also to offer a copy of the survey to anyone who had not received one. This was done in an attempt to improve our response rate and to help ensure that the responses we received reflected the views of a spectrum of attorneys, not merely those who were either disgruntled or overjoyed about life at their firms.

After the surveys were returned to us, we identified the firms from which we had received a low number of responses and then recontacted the recruitment coordinators to request their assistance in distributing the survey and encouraging additional responses. We extended the deadline for these firms and ultimately received a total of approximately 1,225 surveys. At that point, we divided the surveys according to law firm and summarized the results. The charts included at the end of each entry reflect the responses we received to check-answer questions contained on the last page of the survey.

Ratings: Each respondent, in addition to supplying prose answers to specific questions (which comprise much of the text), was asked to check whether she agreed or disagreed with nine specific statements. Respondents could *Strongly* agree, Agree, Disagree, or *Strongly* disagree. In order to calculate a firm's rating, we assigned the following points to each category: Strongly agree (4), Agree (3), Disagree (2), and Strongly disagree (1). We totaled all the scores for each question, which gave us the firm's "raw score."

Example: Suppose we received 12 surveys from a firm (which means there was a potential total of 108 check marks—nine questions on each survey). Suppose further, simply for the sake of illustration, that these check marks were evenly distributed, i.e., 27 marks in Strongly agree, 27 in Agree, 27 in Disagree, and 27 in Strongly disagree. The firm's initial tally would, therefore, be:

27 x 4 (for Strongly agree) =   108
27 x 3 (for Agree) =   81
27 x 2 (for Disagree) =   54
27 x 1 (for Strongly disagree) = <u>27</u>
                                 270 (actual raw score)

This tally is not the rating that the firm received.

Rather, we next calculated the maximum possible score that the firm *could* have received if all respondents "Strongly agreed" to all statements. In this case, our firm's maximum score would have been 432 (12 surveys multiplied by nine questions multiplied by four points for all Strongly agree answers).

The rating we gave each firm was simply the raw score divided by the maximum potential score. In our example, the firm would have received a rating of 62.50 (270 divided by 432). Therefore, this rating is clearly a percent—a characterization, if you will, of how closely its raw score approached its highest potential score.

The maximum possible rating, therefore, is 100—a case in which a firm's raw score was identical to its highest potential score. The minimum possible rating was 25, which a firm would have achieved if all of its survey respondents checked Strongly disagree for every statement.

In some instances, survey respondents did not receive or failed to complete the chart on page two of the survey. Accordingly, there are a few cases where the number of respondents exceeded the number of responses tallied on the charts.

The gavels that appear at the beginning of each profile were assigned by listing all firms in the order of the ratings they received, and then dividing this list into five categories, with the highest scoring firms receiving five gavels, the lowest scoring firms receiving one gavel, etc.

In some cases, we were surprised to note significant disparities between the comments in the narrative sections of the surveys and the numerical rating calculated by tallying the check marks. In the interests of objectivity, however, we relied exclusively on the numerical ratings in determining our firm ratings. As with all other material contained in this directory, readers should use their judgment in determining the weight properly accorded to the information we offer.

We gratefully acknowledge the 1997-1998 National Directory of Legal Employers, a publicaiton of the National Association of Law Placement, for the data included at the beginning of the profiles and the data on diversity.

The firms listed below were surveyed, but their responses were too few in number to justify a write up. They are listed here in alphabetical order:

Akin, Gump, Strauss, Hauer & Feld LLP, Washington, DC

Alston & Bird, Atlanta, GA

Anderson Kill & Olick, P.C., New York, NY

Andrews & Kurth LLP, Houston, TX

Cahill Gordon & Reindel, New York, NY

Chapman and Cutler, Chicago, IL

Foley & Lardner, Milwaukee, WI

Foster, Pepper & Shefelman, Seattle, WA

Gibson, Dunn & Crutcher LLP, Los Angeles, CA

Hopkins & Sutter, Chicago, IL

Kelley Drye & Warran LLP, New York, NY

Kramer, Levin, Naftalis & Frankel, New York, NY

LeBoeuf, Lamb, Greene & Macrae LLP, New York, NY

Lord, Bissell & Brook, Chicago, IL

Manatt, Phelps & Phillips, LLP, Los Angeles, CA

McCutchen, Doyle, Brown & Enersen LLP, San Francisco, CA

Mitchell, Silberberg & Knupp, Los Angeles, CA

Munger, Tolles & Olson LLP, Los Angeles, CA

Orrick, Herrington & Sutcliffe LLP, San Francisco CA

Patton Boggs LLP, Washington, DC

Paul, Hastings, Janofsky & Walker LLP, Los Angeles, CA

Piper & Marbury LLP, Baltimore, MD

Shaw, Pittman, Potts & Trowbridge, Washington, DC

Sheppard, Mullin, Richter & Hampton LLP, Los Angeles, CA

Sullivan & Worcester LLP, Boston, MA

Thompson Coburn, St. Louis, MO

Wachtell, Lipton, Rosen & Katz, New York, NY

Williams & Connolly, Washington, DC

Elizabeth Westfall is currently an associate at Wilmer, Cutler & Pickering. Although we mailed surveys to women at Wilmer, Cutler & Pickering, Washington, DC, it was decided to omit the firm's profile in order to avoid any appearance of conflict.

Profiled Firms (by Rating)

⟨⟨⟨⟨⟨

1. Sonnenschein Nath & Rosenthal = 88.20
2. Bracewell & Patterson LLP = 87.79
3. Foley, Hoag & Eliot LLP = 87.70
4. Dechert Price & Rhoads = 87.36
5. Venable, Baetjer and Howard LLP = 87.05
6. Covington & Burling = 86.96
7. Choate, Hall & Stewart = 86.64
8. Troutman Sanders = 85.87

⟨⟨⟨⟨

9. Davis Wright Tremaine = 84.09
10. Ropes & Gray = 83.79
11. Bingham Dana & Gould = 83.33
12. Hogan & Hartson LLP = 82.91
13. Hale and Dorr LLP = 82.33
14. Palmer & Dodge LLP = 82.30
15. Heller Ehrman White & McAuliffe = 82.23
16. Sutherland, Asbill & Brennan LLP = 81.13
17. Duane, Morris & Heckscher = 81.10
18. Sidley & Austin = 80.90
19. Schulte, Roth & Zabel LLP = 80.04

20. Arnold & Porter = 79.70

21. Ballard Spahr Andrews & Ingersoll = 79.55

22. Schnader Harrison Segal & Lewis = 79.33

23. Vinson & Elkins LLP = 78.68

24. Rudnick & Wolfe = 78.52

25. Baker & Daniels = 78.36

26. Debevoise & Plimpton = 78.01

27. Mintz, Levin, Cohn, Ferris, Glovsky and Popeo, P.C. = 77.34

28. Morrison & Foerster LLP = 77.33

29. Crowell & Moring LLP = 77.27

30. Sullivan & Cromwell = 76.73

31. Patterson, Belknap, Webb & Tyler LLP = 76.25

32. Goodwin, Procter & Hoar = 75.98

33. Mayer, Brown & Platt = 75.71

34. Irell & Manella LLP = 75.63

35. Powell, Goldstein, Frazer & Murphy = 75.56

36. Stoel Rives LLP = 75.40

37. Davis Polk & Wardwell = 75.00

38. Katten Muchin & Zavis = 74.70

39. Willkie Farr & Gallagher = 74.53

40. Baker & Botts LLP = 73.95

41. Hughes Hubbard & Reed LLP = 73.82

42. Cleary, Gottlieb, Steen & Hamilton = 73.58

43. Howrey & Simon = 73.50

44. Jenner & Block = 73.31

45. Steptoe & Johnson LLP = 73.28

46. Milbank, Tweed, Hadley & McCloy = 71.84

47. Skadden, Arps, Slate, Meagher & Flom LLP = 71.25

48. Faegre & Benson LLP = 70.79

49. Cravath, Swaine & Moore = 70.63

50. Pillsbury, Madison & Sutro LLP = 70.53

51. Hunton & Williams = 70.28

52. Wilson Sonsini Goorich & Rosati = 69.89
53. Arent Fox Kintner Plotkin & Kahn = 69.80
54. Weil, Gotshal & Manges LLP = 69.34
55. Proskauer Rose LLP = 68.97
56. Dickstein Shapiro Morin & Oshinsky = 68.53
57. White & Case = 68.10
58. Dewey Ballantine = 67.74
59. Kirkland & Ellis = 67.69
60. Testa, Hurwitz & Thibeault LLP = 67.59
61. King & Spalding = 66.95
62. Baker & McKenzie = 66.73
63. Wolf, Block, Schorr and Solis-Cohen = 65.65
64. Jones, Day, Reavis & Pogue = 65.01
65. Chadbourne & Parke LLP = 65.00
66. Shearman & Sterling = 64.50
67. Fried, Frank, Shriver, Harris & Jacobson = 63.96
68. Kaye, Scholer, Fierman, Hays & Handler LLP = 63.93
69. Fulbright & Jaworski LLP = 62.30
70. McDermott, Will & Emery = 61.46

71. Winston & Strawn = 58.92
72. Latham & Watkins = 58.77
73. Rogers & Wells = 57.60
74. Morgan, Lewis & Bockius LLP = 56.48
75. Simpson Thacher & Bartlett = 55.68
76. Brobeck, Phleger & Harrison LLP = 55.00
77. Paul, Weiss, Rifkind, Wharton & Garrison = 51.90

Profiled Firms (by City)

Atlanta
King & Spalding = 66.95
Powell, Goldstein, Frazer
  & Murphy = 75.56
Sutherland, Asbill & Brennan
  LLP = 81.13
Troutman Sanders = 85.87

Baltimore
Venable, Baetjer and Howard
  LLP = 87.05

Boston
Bingham, Dana & Gould LLP = 83.33
Choate, Hall & Stewart = 86.64
Foley, Hoag & Eliot LLP = 87.70
Goodwin, Procter & Hoar = 75.98
Hale and Dorr LLP = 82.33
Mintz, Levin, Cohn, Ferris, Glovsky
  and Popeo, P.C. = 77.34
Palmer & Dodge LLP = 82.30
Ropes & Gray = 83.79
Testa, Hurwitz & Thibeault
  LLP = 67.59

Chicago
Baker & McKenzie = 66.73

Jenner & Block = 73.31
Katten Muchin & Zavis = 74.70
Kirkland & Ellis = 67.69
Mayer, Brown & Platt = 75.71
McDermott, Will & Emery = 61.46
Rudnick & Wolfe = 78.52
Sidley & Austin = 80.90
Sonnenschein Nath
  & Rosenthal = 88.20
Winston & Strawn = 58.92

Cleveland
Jones, Day, Reavis & Pogue = 65.01

Houston
Baker & Botts LLP = 73.95
Bracewell & Patterson LLP = 87.79
Fulbright & Jaworski LLP = 62.30
Vinson & Elkins LLP = 78.68

Indianapolis
Baker & Daniels = 78.36

Los Angeles
Irell & Manella LLP = 75.63
Latham & Watkins = 58.77

Minneapolis
Faegre & Benson LLP = 70.79

New York
Chadbourne & Parke LLP = 65.00

Cleary, Gottlieb, Steen
& Hamilton = 73.58

Cravath, Swaine & Moore = 70.63

Davis Polk & Wardwell = 75.00

Debevoise & Plimpton = 78.01

Dewey Ballantine = 67.74

Fried, Frank, Shriver, Harris
& Jacobson = 63.96

Hughes Hubbard & Reed LLP = 73.82

Kaye, Scholer, Fierman, Hays
& Handler = 63.93

Milbank, Tweed, Hadley
& McCloy = 71.84

Patterson, Belknap, Webb
& Tyler LLP = 76.25

Paul, Weiss, Rifkind, Wharton
& Garrison = 51.90

Proskauer Rose LLP = 68.97

Rogers & Wells = 57.60

Schulte, Roth & Zabel LLP = 80.04

Shearman & Sterling = 64.50

Simpson Thacher & Bartlett = 55.68

Skadden, Arps, Slate, Meagher
& Flom LLP = 71.25

Sullivan & Cromwell = 76.73

Weil, Gotshal & Manges LLP = 69.34

White & Case = 68.10

Willkie Farr & Gallagher = 74.53

Palo Alto
Wilson Sonsini Goorich
& Rosati = 69.89

Philadelphia
Ballard Spahr Andrews
& Ingersoll = 79.55

Dechert Price & Rhodes = 87.36

Duane, Morris & Heckscher = 81.10

Morgan, Lewis & Bockius LLP = 56.48

Schnader Harrison Segal
& Lewis = 79.33

Wolf, Block, Schorr and
Solis-Cohen = 65.65

Portland
Stoel Rives LLP = 75.40

Richmond
Hunton & Williams = 70.28

San Francisco
Brobeck, Phleger & Harrison
LLP = 55.00

Heller Ehrman White
& McAuliffe = 82.23

Morrison & Foerster LLP = 77.33

Pillsbury, Madison & Sutro
LLP = 70.53

Seattle
Davis Wright Tremaine = 84.09

Washington, D.C.
Arent Fox Kintner Plotkin
& Kahn = 69.80

Arnold & Porter = 79.70

Covington & Burling = 86.96

Crowell & Moring LLP = 77.27

Dickstein Shapiro Morin
& Oshinsky = 68.53

Hogan & Hartson LLP = 82.91

Howrey & Simon = 73.50

Steptoe & Johnson LLP = 73.28

ARENT FOX KINTNER PLOTKIN & KAHN

Rating: 53

Arent Fox Kintner Plotkin & Kahn
1050 Connecticut Ave. NW
Washington, DC 20036
202-857-6000

No. of Attorneys: 191
No. of Women Attorneys: 55
No. of Partners: 98
No. of Women Partners: 15
No. of Survey Responses Received: 12

Respondent Profile: 4 partners, 7 associates, and 1 counsel responded—most did not indicate their practice area.

Summary: The experiences of women lawyers at Arent, Fox seem to be mixed, with the partners generally more positive than associates. Although the firm's ambiance is said to be largely pleasant, a significant minority of respondents (although only one partner) deemed women's prospects for advancement dimmer than men's, and part-time options, though available, are feared to be impractical for most attorneys.

Advancement: Reports were mixed on whether women are as likely as men to advance—associates were evenly split, while partners were more positive. Respondents who reported that women's prospects are dimmer attributed this phenomenon to widely different sources.

According to one associate, "Women may be slightly less likely than men to make partner, but the odds of *anyone* making partner today are much slimmer than in the past." A junior associate agreed: "No one seems to have any advancement potential." Another associate commented that she does not perceive a difference in the mentoring, assignments, or reviews of women as compared to men, but that "women's different career goals or family pressures [often keep them] from seeking advancement in the firm." Another lawyer said that, in her opinion, opportunities for women to advance seem "pretty dim." Given the "same amount of billable hours and essential service provided to the firm's clients," it was her opinion that "women are given less attribution or credit for work done to keep the client happy or work brought into the firm" and that more "visible and glamorous projects get assigned to men."

She added, "Among women partners who have made it earlier, they seem to be harsher to other women who may be coming up the ranks."

According to one midlevel associate, women's outside pressures often lead them to be "less willing or able to kill themselves on a particular case, leading to actual or perceived lesser work quality."

Rainmaking reportedly carries a great deal of weight at Arent, Fox, and some observed that this puts women at a disadvantage. A senior associate noted that the firm's criteria for partnership are objective, but that "you must be a busy attorney (1,900-plus hours billed per year) and have $400,000 in your own business." She reported that, although the firm may not intend it, this "objective criteria actually has a disparate impact on women, however, because I think it is more difficult for women to achieve $400,000 a year than men since most executives at clients are men."

Yet several partners stated that the advancement criteria applied at the firm are gender-neutral. According to one, what counts are "legal skills, oral skills, client generation potential, expertise in a 'hot' practice area, etc." She added that mentoring does help, "but with 15 female partners there are opportunities for same-sex mentoring."

Another partner's formula for advancement was somewhat different: "1) ability to keep partners satisfied/happy; 2) ability to keep clients satisfied/happy; 3) ability to make rain; 4) ability as a lawyer (no particular order). Also, it helps to work for partners who are powerful (i.e., on executive committees)."

According to one partner, women's opportunities equal those of men, "though it may be somewhat more difficult for a woman lawyer to be mentored by a male partner. I also do not believe that male partners fully understand the conflict and strains experienced by women lawyers with children." An associate reported that a mentoring program has recently been instituted, "the results of which remain to be seen."

"Vestiges of the 'boys' club' have been broken down over the years with the addition of more and more women partners."

Attitudes and atmosphere: A few respondents raved about Arent, Fox's atmosphere, and most offered at least nominally positive assessments of working at the firm on a daily basis. According to a first-year associate, the firm's atmosphere is "comparatively comfortable." A midlevel associate agreed, attributing the comfort level to "the sheer number of women at the firm."

One associate was very positive, describing the firm as "egalitarian and democratic, [in which] all attorneys' views are solicited and appreciated by management." And a partner remarked that men and women interact socially with ease and that "vestiges of the 'boys' club' have been broken down over the years with the addition of more and more women partners."

Two respondents expressed different views. One partner claimed that women at the firm are "still expected to be always supportive, friendly, cheerful, helpful, and never demonstrate male characteristics (bossy, demanding, gruff, etc.)." She added that there is *very little* social interaction between men and women."

A senior associate agreed: "There seems to be more natural social interactions between men in the firm. They discuss sports and off-color jokes and freeze when women join in the conversation."

"People working late and throughout the weekend get more recognition by the firm leadership because partners will talk about how hard they are working..."

Balancing work & family/personal life: One corporate associate with children, reflecting a consensus of the group, wrote that maintaining a balance is "possible—not easy, not difficult, but 'doable.' " She added that although she works many hours, she has "some flexibility about when and where I work them." A partner commented that this firm "runs like most law firms—like a business. You have to have a 'do it' personality to keep all the balls in the air."

One respondent, reflecting the views of others, wrote, "The hours are more reasonable than other big firms generally, but still are demanding." While another concluded, "The best way to have a life is to get in at 7:30 a.m." One attorney noted that although the working hours are relatively flexible, "people working late and throughout the weekend get more recognition by the firm leadership because partners will talk about how hard they are working and their billable hours," which are apparently heavily emphasized at the firm. One midlevel associate wrote that she finds the juggling tough as a single woman and observed that "other female attorneys do juggle family and work, but I think their work often suffers and this is noticed by the partnership."

Several attorneys reported that they have managed to strike a livable balance but attributed their success in part to being in practice areas in which the opportunities to do so are greater. According to an associate who is married with children, those who have reasonable family lives typically have spouses with less demanding jobs. One married partner wrote that it is possible to work normal hours in some of the regulatory practice areas, yet this is apparently difficult in litigation and in certain transactional areas. She added that all attorneys must have the flexibility to work full-time when necessary. An associate in a regulatory practice area agreed that the load in her department is manageable. She wrote that the pressure to bill is not "so great that a fairly good accommodation cannot be reached."

According to one partner with children, although she believes the firm does not support a balance, "many individual partners do." One partner in the international practice area wrote that despite being in a very demanding field that involves a great deal of international travel, she finds time to be with her children "by varying my schedule when I am in town, and the firm is accommodating in this respect."

The firm reportedly has emergency childcare available, although one respondent observed that there is "no on-site childcare. What a pity."

"Although it may be seen as 'reasonable' to turn down work because there 'aren't enough hours in the week,' turning down work because one is part-time simply isn't as acceptable."

Flexibility of work arrangements: Part-time arrangements are available, but most thought that, with the exception of a few, less-pressured practice groups, they were not practical.

One lawyer wrote it was her perception that opting for a part-time schedule is "definitely frowned on." Another associate characterized part-time as a "joke" and reported that she knew of one lawyer who had worked 2,000 hours and only received 80-percent pay. Another wrote that men "merely tolerate [part-time] as the women-thing" and that women resent it and believe that part-timers give other women "a bad name."

A partner agreed that it is "very difficult to work out part-time arrangements" and that, to her knowledge, it is "not encouraged and barely tolerated." Another partner seemed to disagree, however, reporting that part-time work arrangements are available at all levels, and "surprisingly, only one woman partner has elected to work part-time." Yet a senior associate opined that the part-timers are not "players in terms of partnership potential or power at the firm."

According to a midlevel associate, the firm's support for part-time exists "more in principle than in practice." She added that, based on the experience of some of her friends, part-timers face a "constant battle" to succeed. The pressure results, in this lawyer's view, from the fact that "although it may be seen as 'reasonable' to turn down work because there 'aren't enough hours in the week,' turning down work because one is part-time simply isn't as acceptable."

Several respondents wrote that the acceptance of part-time hinges on the practice area. One partner observed that in a "demanding atmosphere created in the litigation area, for example, it might be more difficult to maintain a part-time schedule." An associate in a regulatory practice group agreed that despite the availability of part-time arrangements, "taking advantage of them in reality may be another story."

> *Arent, Fox is "a very comfortable place for lawyers with diverse backgrounds, including women, minorities, and gays."*

Diversity: Despite the small number of minority attorneys at the firm, most respondents made positive remarks concerning its level of diversity. One associate wrote that although the firm "could do better on the racial/ethnic diversity front," it is good about political and lifestyle diversity. One partner reported that the firm's 15 female partners "are really a very diverse group—from the perspective of family, background, political leanings, etc."

Another partner characterized the firm as "a very comfortable place for lawyers with diverse backgrounds, including women, minorities, and gays." According to an associate, the firm has "a large number of homosexual attorneys whose partners are eligible for insurance benefits, and who consistently advance to partnership, if they meet the objective criteria."

One respondent was quite skeptical about the firm's dedication to diversity. Her perception was that "many women and minority women do not seem to last in the firm because they do not get the support and encouragement. Male partners take male associates under their wings to develop, but not women."

> *"[Most of the women] rainmakers are worse to work for than men: meaner, less understanding, more cruel."*

Women in leadership positions: Representation of women in power appears to be "fair, but not great," in the words of one. Many respondents noted the current absence of women on the firm's executive committee, which one termed "somewhat troubling." According to one partner, of the firm's five department managers, two are women. An associate reported that, until recently, the head of associate evaluation was a woman who was a good mentor and role model.

In the opinion of another partner, the firm's women partners are "concentrated" in the lower ranks of the hierarchy and play only minimal leadership roles. She added that business generation is the key factor in rising to a position of prominence within the firm.

A minority of respondents included harsh descriptions of the firm's most powerful female partners. According to one associate, these women "seem to be the first ones to sabotage other women—I don't see support coming from the women partners." Another associate opined that most of the women "rainmakers are worse to work for than men: meaner, less understanding, more cruel."

Arent, Fox, Kintner, Plotkin & Kahn No. of Responses: 12	Strongly agree	Agree	Disagree	Strongly disagree
Women's prospects for advancement at the firm are as strong as men's	3	4	4	1
I am satisfied with the firm's family and personal leave policies	2	6	4	
There are women in positions of power and influence in the firm	1	6	5	
Women are as likely as men to receive desirable work assignments	6	5		1
Women attorneys feel they can discuss family obligations openly	1	5	4	1
Women are as likely as men to be mentored by senior attorneys	2	6	2	1
Women attorneys enjoy a high level of job satisfaction	3	3	3	1
Women in the firm are supportive of their women colleagues	2	5		3
Firm management is receptive to the concerns of women attorneys	1	6	4	

ARNOLD & PORTER

Rating: 20

Arnold & Porter
555 12th St. NW
Washington, DC 20004
202-942-5000

No. of Attorneys: 277
No. of Women Attorneys: 78
No. of Partners: 133
No. of Women Partners: 24
No. of Survey Responses Received: 16

Respondent Profile: 8 partners and 8 associates responded. Practice areas included litigation, regulatory, antitrust, and corporate.

Summary: Arnold & Porter has set the standard for family-friendliness in the legal profession by offering its lawyers a range of childcare services and flexible work arrangements. Most partners and associates felt strongly that women's chances for advancement are favorable. While not as racially diverse as some would like, A & P is characterized as very hospitable to gay and lesbian attorneys.

Advancement: A majority of partners and associates thought women's chances for advancement at A & P were on par with men's.

One associate commented that women are as likely as men to make partner, and that the firm has "historically supported the advancement of women, hiring women and making them partners even at a time when this was not the standard and was even frowned upon." She noted, however, that mentoring is a problem for both men and women and that this "does hit women somewhat harder, since some older male partners are more comfortable working with men."

Seven of the eight partners who responded agreed that women's prospects for advancement at the firm are excellent. An antitrust partner noted that the percentage of women entering the partnership in recent years has been high

and that the firm has "an incredible commitment to this issue." A litigation partner asserted that women are just as likely to advance as men, and that in some years, women have made up the majority of newly elected partners. She added, however, "Women, like men, must be willing to step forward and assume leadership in the matters they are handling."

Several partners remarked that mentoring is critical, with one acknowledging, "Women may sometimes feel less opportunities for mentoring, but major efforts are being made to help remedy this."

The single dissenting partner took a dimmer view than her colleagues, remarking that the process of advancement at the firm suffers from gender bias, which does not disappear once one joins the partnership ranks. The firm, in her estimation, prefers to advance women who "contribute billable hours to clients for which male partners receive the billing credit." In addition, she reported that, in her experience, it is "very difficult for women to compete for associate resources needed to develop one's own practice," and that, in sum, "double standards apply."

One of two dissenting associates wrote, "The firm outwardly states that women have the same opportunities as men, but the reality doesn't seem to match." She added that the women partners "do not seem willing to reach out to the younger women and act as mentors." She further expressed a perception in the litigation group that men "get better assignments" and go to trial more often. However, because there are "so few women remaining in the litigation group," she concluded that the validity of these perceptions is difficult to test.

According to a senior associate, of the factors central to making partner, several are stacked against women with children: "quality work, long hours, ability to travel on little/no notice, working with many different partners, attendance at functions and luncheons."

> *The firm's leadership "sets a tone that is sensitive to gender and race issues and indicates intolerance for any discriminatory or harassing behavior."*

Attitudes and atmosphere: Many respondents reported a generally comfortable atmosphere at A & P. A partner said that it was "among the first of large corporate law firms to accept women into its ranks, and has continued its tradition of being hospitable to women." According to an associate, the firm's

leadership "sets a tone that is sensitive to gender and race issues and indicates intolerance for any discriminatory or harassing behavior." A litigation partner described the firm as "less stuffy than most large D.C. firms," and noted that men and women often socialize.

Again, a lone partner disagreed: "The 'boys' club' is firmly entrenched. I don't trust any of my male colleagues not to stab me in the back. There is a lot of immature, cliquish behavior, stealing of clients, not notifying women of important matters [or] developments affecting clients they serve."

According to a senior associate, "Women attorneys are still more often referred to as 'exaggerators,' or their comments are dismissed more quickly than those of male attorneys." Although one associate observed that the firm's environment "is *not* dominated by sports," another lawyer reported that "...conversations about sports are extremely prevalent, even at luncheons designed for training."

And an associate wrote, "Some secretaries...are not supportive of young, intelligent women whatsoever."

> *"The more senior you get, the more difficult it is, since you are required to demonstrate that you can do it all without the assistance of partners."*

Balancing work & family/personal life: Although the firm's progressive policies reportedly provide some relief, women lawyers still find it difficult to have a life outside the firm.

According to one partner, because of family-sensitive policies, "it is easier [here] than at almost any other firm with which I am familiar," though she conceded, it is "still a client-driven profession, and that difficulty cannot be eliminated."

One unmarried associate observed "an inordinate amount of pressure to work long hours" and a lack of "concern about whether you have a life." Another associate stated that many women wait until "late in the track" to have children. In addition, the pressure mounts as "the more senior you get, the more difficult it is, since you are required to demonstrate that you can do it all without the assistance of partners."

According to one associate, although the firm is better than most, "the practice of law in a large firm has become a dehumanizing experience. Personal satisfaction and happiness is traded for money and some perception of prestige."

In recognition of the firm's part-time, parental leave, childcare, and other benefits, **Working Mother** *magazine (in 1996) named it one of the country's 100* **best workplaces in America** *for working mothers.*

Flexibility of work arrangements: Arnold & Porter has distinguished itself from its peers by offering a range of childcare services and flexible work arrangements. It is said to have been the first firm in D.C. to offer an on-site, full-time childcare center with weekend coverage for attorneys and staff.

The firm has been a leader in offering part-time arrangements for working parents, according to one partner, although attorneys report that the practicality of a reduced schedule varies. One litigation partner described the firm as having "one of the most 'family-friendly' sets of

work policies and benefits available in a law firm." She reported that, in recognition of the firm's part-time, parental leave, childcare, and other benefits, *Working Mother* magazine (in 1996) named it one of the country's 100 best workplaces in America for working mothers. She added that she has utilized the childcare center frequently, and availed herself of part-time "or alternative schedules as necessary—never with any negative impact. I advanced to partnership on track and received excellent work assignments."

The success of part-time arrangements may vary. Some areas of work, according to one partner, are "inherently inconsistent with a part-time arrangement." For example, she reported that a part-timer "could not be given primary responsibility for a major case that is in litigation and on which the rest of the team is working seven days a week or out of town."

Part-time arrangements, although available for all, are reportedly usually taken advantage of by women. The part-time program is reportedly available at partnership level. According to a litigation associate, some feel the part-time options are fair, yet others feel "that they have been punished for going part-time or that their part-time status was not respected."

Another associate reported that, in order to remain on track, "you must work almost as much as [full-time]. If you exceed your part-time hours, which almost always happens, you are only compensated for that percentage over 10 percent. For example, if you work 80 percent (part-time) but actually put in 95 percent, you will [be] compensated for an additional 5 percent. (But the firm also allows a 10 percent swing, so you can also work under 10 percent without being penalized.)" A litigator observed that part-timers work long hours, leading her to "question just how part-time they are."

One partner reported that A & P provides generous maternity and paternity leave.

"We have people of all political persuasions, life-style choices, [and] sexual preferences at the partner and associate levels..."

Diversity: "Minorities, and particularly minority women, are severely under-represented at the firm," according to one lawyer, but the firm is widely reported to be a very hospitable place for gay and lesbian attorneys. One partner wrote, "We have people of all political persuasions, life-style choices, [and] sexual preferences at the partner and associate levels. We are not as racially diverse as we want to be."

A partner reported that the firm has committed to a "new 'diversity training program.'" Another maintained that the firm's support for diversity is demonstrated through its "affirmative action hiring policies, its sponsorship of diversity training for all lawyers and staff, its acceptance of openly gay male and female partners and associates, among other things."

Most concluded that the female partners are prominent and well-regarded.

Women in leadership positions: Although the "number of women in the upper ranks is small," the positions held by women include both appointed and elected posts, and A & P, according to one partner, was among the first firms to appoint a woman as executive director. One partner reported that three women sit on its management committee, one sits on its policy committee, four sit on its associate evaluation committee, and one sits on the billing and intake committee.

Nevertheless, another partner noted, and several agreed, "Women have yet to break into real leadership roles," although this is thought to be a matter of time. One partner observed that there are very few women with their own client bases.

An associate who defied the overwhelming positive consensus wrote, "There do not seem to be *any* powerful women at the firm," adding, "There was one—their shining example that they constantly held out to us—but she left."

With respect to supporting younger women, some women partners are better than others, according to several respondents. Most concluded that the female partners are prominent and well-regarded. A group of women partners apparently holds lunches and other less formal gatherings where issues of concern to women are discussed.

Disagreeing with the prevailing view, a senior associate stated, "The women partners here do not advocate for the younger women. They seem to have the attitude that they toughed it out, so we should too. We definitely could use (some) more mentoring here!" Another associate agreed that, in her estimation, there is a "fend-for-yourself policy" toward women attorneys.

Arnold & Porter No. of Responses: 16	Strongly agree	Agree	Disagree	Strongly disagree
Women's prospects for advancement at the firm are as strong as men's	8	5	2	1
I am satisfied with the firm's family and personal leave policies	11	4		
There are women in positions of power and influence in the firm	5	8		3
Women are as likely as men to receive desirable work assignments	5	9	1	
Women attorneys feel they can discuss family obligations openly	2	8	2	
Women are as likely as men to be mentored by senior attorneys	2	6	6	
Women attorneys enjoy a high level of job satisfaction	1	10	3	1
Women in the firm are supportive of their women colleagues	8	5	2	
Firm management is receptive to the concerns of women attorneys	10	4	1	

BAKER & BOTTS LLP

Rating: 40

◣◣◣

Baker & Botts LLP
One Shell Plaza
910 Louisiana
Houston, TX 77002
713-229-1234

No. of Attorneys: 212
No. of Women Attorneys: 57
No. of Partners: 89
No. of Women Partners: 9
No. of Survey Responses Received: 19

Respondent Profile: 4 partners and 15 associates responded. Practice areas represented included trial and corporate.

Summary: Baker & Botts offers women attorneys mentoring opportunities and challenging assignments, but brutal hours and less-than-generous alternative work arrangements could shorten women's stays at the firm. The part-time policy, although recently formalized, is feared by some associates to be a possible "kiss of death" for one's career at the firm. While associates tended to reach consensus on most questions, the four partners often disagreed, sometimes vehemently.

Advancement: Although well-aware of the small number of women in the partnership, most respondents were optimistic about the potential for advancement. "When you [allow for] women who leave because they have had children and prefer not to work at all or to work in a much less fast-paced environment, prospects for men and women are equal," wrote one associate. Some respondents noted that two of the four lawyers promoted to partnership this year were women, a development that one respondent found particularly encouraging, given that one was pregnant and both are mothers. She pointed out, however, that "both these women do heroic things to get the job done."

There was strong agreement that the hours required for success could be brutal.

One corporate associate said, "The general feeling is that, for any woman who wants more than a *career* out of life, they will have to move on." According to a senior associate, women make partner if they "meet superstar criteria— workaholic and if the firm feels like it needs to make one for appearances." A midlevel associate claimed that, in her opinion, more women are promoted in departments where there is more predictability in schedule. One partner observed that although the firm has a good record of providing equal opportunity to associates, in her experience, partners come up against a glass ceiling.

A large majority of respondents reported that they had enjoyed equal opportunities in terms of mentoring and work assignments. A corporate attorney wrote that she was aware of "a number of male partners who make an extra effort to mentor women because they want women to stay and make partner." One partner commented, "The firm has focused on recognizing good mentoring to be a valuable asset."

According to one senior litigation associate, however, the firm has no formal mentoring program, so associates generally seek advice from those for whom they work. She added, "Because there are fewer women partners, the mentors are more often men, and not all female associates will feel comfortable discussing issues with male partners."

One midlevel associate reported, "Families or not, we are expected to carry our fair share of the load, show initiative, and aggressively pursue 'visible' job assignments." She noted that during her three years at the firm, she has "been given *tremendous* opportunity and responsibility" and added that if "you prove yourself at B & B, you'll go far."

A colleague who is a senior associate in the trial department agreed: "Many of the older men in the firm take a very active role in mentoring women and in insuring that women trial attorneys are given substantial trial responsibility." For example, one of the very senior partners in the firm allowed a female associate to cross-examine all of the plaintiffs, as well as argue all pre- and post-trial motions. "Given the potential damages at stake and the 20 or more years of difference in levels of experience, he would certainly have been justified in giving [the associate] a more limited role." Instead, a respondent avowed, "he gave [her] a fabulous learning opportunity, not to mention a large boost in self-confidence."

A few associates regarded the small number of women in the partnership as daunting. "We have nine women and [80] men partners; that says it all for me," wrote one junior associate who added, "I'm not anticipating making a 'career' at this firm."

"There is no problem with harassment; there is, however, a problem of exclusion of women from informal social interactions both within the firm and with clients."

Attitudes and atmosphere: Most respondents described the firm's atmosphere as comfortable, although a large number noted that men in the firm are more likely to socialize with one another than with women, and several commented on the existence of a "boys' club" among the senior male partners.

A partner wrote, "There is no problem with harassment; there is, however, a problem of exclusion of women from informal social interactions both within the firm and with clients." Several respondents reported social segregation between men and women. Associates commented that it is rare for women to be included by men in social activities or lunches, unless recruiting is involved.

One trial associate wrote, however, that the firm has a group of people who run together at lunch, "mostly men, including senior partners, but women run with them as well." She added that the runners have encouraged others—both men and women—to join.

According to a corporate associate, although the firm "is very old guard and traditional, one of its central traditions is meritocracy. I have *not* seen here what my female friends at other firms complain about—male associates getting better work and more experience because they play golf with, talk about sports with, etc., the male partners."

A junior associate noted that although partners are receptive to her ideas and opinions, clients are "sometimes another story—especially the large institutional clients—but that's out of the firm's control." A partner agreed that the "only...gender discrimination comes from outside the firm—opposing counsel, judges, etc." A partner noted that despite the "infrequent joke or insensitive remark," Baker & Botts' leadership is "adamantly against overt or subtle discrimination." One trial associate reported that while she was reluctant to come to Baker "because I feared that a woman couldn't get ahead at a Texas firm," she has been "pleasantly surprised that the 'good ole boys,' though they haven't disappeared, certainly don't run this place."

"I would like to meet a woman who can raise an infant and bill 3,000 hours a year."

Balancing work & family/personal life: Most respondents were satisfied with the firm's policies and receptiveness to family issues. Nevertheless, some reported difficulty on this front, with several pointing out that expectations about billable requirements are extremely high.

One securities lawyer reported that hours in her department were "2,400 average last year, with eight associates over 2,500." In the transactional departments, hours "are phenomenal and approach 3,000 a year," according to one lawyer who exclaimed, "I would like to meet a woman who can raise an infant and bill 3,000 hours a year."

One junior corporate associate concluded that balancing work and personal life is impossible and that she could not "imagine having to take care of a child on this schedule." She added that, in her opinion, many women leave the firm for this reason. Another associate remarked that the firm "is still [one] that is being brought kicking and screaming into a world that allows for personal commitments as well as work."

An employment lawyer reported more varied hours, explaining that although she has had periods of working every weekend for two-month stretches, she is almost always home before 7 p.m. and has had months when she has worked no weekends at all. Still, she noted, "There is always pressure to bill."

"Face time," on the other hand, is unimportant, according to one partner: "You are not monitored too closely, so it is easy to leave to take care of family matters if the need arises and your work allows it." One lawyer who reported that she has maintained a life outside the firm "expects to be asked to leave eventually—billable hours are critical."

Although a solid majority of lawyers remarked that the firm is sensitive about family matters, one partner noted that neither men nor women talk openly about family responsibilities: "Instead of saying to everyone 'hey, I'm going to take my child to the doctor,' you just leave, do it, and come back to work later." Another partner reported that although the firm is "receptive to family issues, as a matter of reality it is extremely difficult to live up to the firm's and my own standards for practicing law, yet still protect my family needs."

Several lawyers, however, praised the firm's flexibility and accommodation of their personal needs. One lawyer reported that in order to care for a family member living in another city, she had taken some time off or worked from a different office and that her colleagues had been understanding and supportive.

One partner remarked that some associates may view part-time as "the kiss of death" for their careers.

Flexibility of work arrangements: The firm reportedly recently initiated a formal part-time policy, which was criticized by many respondents. One partner remarked that some associates may view part-time as "the kiss of death" for their careers. Several attorneys sensed that the partnership does not support the policy and said it was their impression that it is less favorable than that offered by comparable firms.

Under the policy, a respondent wrote, part-timers must work 75 percent of the hours worked by peers in their practice group and receive an unspecified amount, "less than 75 percent" in pay. The policy may be used for up to 12 months, with the possibility of a 12-month renewal. Part-timers are also reportedly required to be willing to travel. Associates reportedly receive one year of credit for every two years spent at the 75-percent load. The firm apparently must approve all requests for part-time work. Baker & Botts did return our calls and confirmed these details.

Respondents identified many shortcomings in the policy, as they perceived it, with one characterizing it as "insulting." Several commented that women who made individual arrangements prior to the issuance of the policy are in better

shape. According to one associate, the memo describing the new part-time policy gave her the impression that part-time work would not be helpful in trying to achieve partnership status. One lawyer reported that in deal-oriented departments, "unless one gets very comfortable saying no, she will find herself working full-time for part-time pay."

One partner remarked that the new policy is rigid, which in her view is a tradeoff for uncertainty about whether to ask under an informal policy, but it "clearly defines how to stay on partnership track." Another partner disagreed, asserting that part-time need not be a dead end as "some of the most well-respected associates have taken advantage of it."

"Moderate amounts of diversity [exist]—two or three blacks and two or three homosexuals."

Diversity: Baker & Botts is described as a traditional, conservative, firm that, according to one partner, has "a 'critical mass' problem—people who are different frequently don't want to come here because there are so few others like them here—they don't want to be pioneers." According to one senior associate, "Moderate amounts of diversity [exist]— two or three blacks and two or three homosexuals." Several lawyers left the diversity question blank or made comments to the effect that "I can't give first-hand feedback."

Several respondents questioned the firm's commitment to achieving racial and ethnic diversity, although one attorney suggested that because of a new hiring partner, this was starting to change. Most associates and partners at the firm are reportedly Republicans, although one lawyer observed that having different political leanings had not caused her problems. According to a midlevel associate, "color, political affiliation, or sexual orientation" are unimportant to the firm, "to the extent that these factors are neutral in an associate's ability to do good work, bill astronomical hours, and cultivate clients."

"We're not there yet—but it's only recently that women have been graduating from law school in such equal ratios to men."

Women in leadership positions: A majority of respondents—including all three partners who filled in the chart—did not believe there were women of power or influence at Baker & Botts. Nevertheless, according to one partner, women are "up and coming" and the firm is "a great place for strong, smart, savvy, reasonable women." She added, "We're not there yet—but it's only recently that women have been graduating from law school in such equal ratios to men."

Another partner completely contradicted her, declaring that she doesn't expect there to be any women in real power for the next several years.

A slim majority of associates agreed that of the women at the firm, none have real power. As for the women partners' level of supportiveness, one associate noted that while she had "good experiences with more senior women, who were generous with their time and advice," she was aware of some who find that the women partners are "no more supportive than men, or even less so."

Baker & Botts No. of Responses: 19	Strongly agree	Agree	Disagree	Strongly disagree
Women's prospects for advancement at the firm are as strong as men's	7	7	2	3
I am satisfied with the firm's family and personal leave policies	7	7	4	1
There are women in positions of power and influence in the firm	2	6	4	6
Women are as likely as men to receive desirable work assignments	12	4	2	1
Women attorneys feel they can discuss family obligations openly	3	8	5	1
Women are as likely as men to be mentored by senior attorneys	7	9	3	
Women attorneys enjoy a high level of job satisfaction	4	11	3	1
Women in the firm are supportive of their women colleagues	7	8	3	
Firm management is receptive to the concerns of women attorneys	5	7	5	2

BAKER & DANIELS

Rating: 25

Baker & Daniels
300 North Meridian St.
Suite 2700
Indianapolis, IN 46204
219-237-0300

No. of Attorneys: 151
No. of Women Attorneys: 48
No. of Partners: 116
No. of Women Partners: 12
No. of Survey Responses Received: 8

Respondent Profile: 2 partners and 6 associates responded. Practice areas included litigation, employee benefits, and utility.

Summary: For women who stay on track, opportunities for advancement at Baker & Daniels are apparently quite favorable. The firm is also reportedly discrimination-free. Part-time arrangements are widely used, although available only on a case-by-case basis. With one glaring exception, regarding "women of power or influence," respondents gave the firm uniformly high marks.

Advancement: The eight responding attorneys were unanimous in their assessment of advancement prospects for women at the firm.

A partner summed it up: "The prospects for advancement of women at Baker & Daniels are equal to the prospects for advancement for men. The patterns of advancement, however, are different for women because many women who have families opt for part-time or leave the firm for corporate counsel positions they perceive will be less demanding. Women who continue to work full-time are as likely as men to advance to partnership."

Another partner commented, "Many women have chosen to get 'off track.'" There was overwhelming agreement that the reasons for choosing this route relate to the time demands rather than any discrimination they face. According to one midlevel associate, for those who do request alternative work arrangements, such as reduced hours, "the opportunity to advance still exists, but timing of advancement is adjusted."

According to a senior associate, the key criteria for advancement include "having had a mentor throughout associateship who helps and promotes the woman," as well as getting assignments that demonstrate partnership ability, and being reviewed on criteria that demonstrates partnership ability.

> *"[Women tend to] hang with women and men with men, but no more so than if they were at a cocktail party of friends."*

Attitudes and atmosphere: Most respondents described Baker & Daniels as discrimination-free, with one partner commenting that she has witnessed no incidents of bias toward women during her decade-long stay at the firm. One partner characterized the atmosphere as "very collegial." Another described social interactions between attorneys as "fine." She added that women tend to "hang with women and men with men, but no more so than if they were at a cocktail party of friends."

A junior associate commented that although one-to-one interactions with her colleagues are "always comfortable," she believes that sometimes the "men are more afraid of offending me than they should be."

Another junior associate attributed Baker & Daniels' hospitality to women to the fact that the firm's male attorneys "are generally younger and more progressive/politically liberal," and noted that "many of their wives also hold down demanding jobs outside the home."

A midlevel associate commented, "There are still far more men than women attorneys [and] at certain functions this is very apparent." Another associate, however, reported that she has never been excluded from social activities because she's female.

One attorney surmised, "It may be easier for male attorneys to have client development opportunities with male partners because of the 'boys' club' mentality," which she described as "not structured, but it happens."

> *"The firm is sensitive to my 'mommy-track' desires in a very positive way."*

Balancing work & family/personal life: Although the firm reportedly shows sensitivity to its attorneys' attempts to balance work and home life, respondents pretty much agreed that women face a greater challenge to maintain a balance in light of greater family responsibilities.

One first-year associate commented that she is "prepared for 50-hour work weeks with a significant amount of pressure. I don't have kids yet and do not plan to be here when I do have them."

As with many other firms, respondents report that the ability to balance work and family varies between departments and according to the partners for whom one works. An employee benefits attorney remarked that the firm's sensitivity to family obligations varies greatly by "team," and that the most "family-friendly" teams are those "with partners who have families at home that they want to spend time with." A junior associate agreed: "Often, it is not the firm's attitude or sensitivity that drives the situation, but rather the other attorneys one works with."

According to a partner, "All people, including lawyers, are realizing quality of life counts." A part-time attorney said that for her it is very easy to sustain a "satisfying personal/family life. The firm is sensitive to my 'mommy track' desires in a very positive way."

> *"There are male and female partners who may value my employment less because of my part-time status, but not because I am a woman..."*

Flexibility of work arrangements: Part-time schedules are reportedly widely used at Baker & Daniels, even though one associate reported that the firm does not have a set policy concerning part-time and, thus, arrangements must be negotiated on a case-by-case basis. Another associate, based on her own long-term experience with part-time work, reported that she has not requested, "nor do I want, the responsibility of even part-time partnership." She wrote that she feels appreciated by all the attorneys with whom she works on a daily basis, but "there are male and female partners who may value my employment less because of my part-time status, but not because I am a woman. I do not work directly with these partners/associates, and consequently my perceptions may be unreasonable." She added that maybe "any devaluation is based on a dollars-and-cents estimate of my billable worth versus overhead—be it an accurate or inaccurate estimate."

Another respondent reported that she is "a percentage partner working on a reduced-hours basis" and that her experience has been positive.

A partner recounted that she decided to go part-time and that "at that time, part-time arrangements were permitted with the express understanding that part-time associates would not be considered for partnership. To the credit of firm management, however, it was decided that if lawyers are performing at partner-type levels, they should be made partner. I was made a partner with no push on my part."

While Baker & Daniels is "more diverse than it used to be, there remains room for a continued increase in diversity."

Diversity: Like many other firms, Baker & Daniels reportedly has difficulty attracting minority lawyers, and its commitment to the issue was questioned by some respondents. A partner commented that the firm has "a strong commitment to diversity and individuality," but has "experienced difficulty attracting and retaining minority, especially African-American, lawyers."

An associate added that the difficulty may lie in "finding minority candidates interested in working in Indianapolis." Another associate commented, however, that she has not "seen a big commitment to diversity through proactive steps. For example, [to my knowledge] management has never come out and said that diversity is a high priority for the firm."

One associate commented that although the firm is "more diverse than it used to be, there remains room for a continued increase in diversity."

There are "too few women partners to have enough women mentors."

Women in leadership positions: There is a concern that very few women have penetrated the upper ranks of influence at Baker & Daniels, according to a majority of our small sample of respondents. One associate claimed, "The power in the firm rests with the management and compensation committees," yet she professed that the firm "in recent years has not had any women on these committees." She attributed this, in part, to the fact that most of the female partners are "still too junior to influence the direction of the firm."

The firm has apparently never had a female managing partner, several respondents reported, and one commented that, in her estimation, "Right now we don't have a large pool of women with seniority in the partnership ranks from which to choose for leadership positions."

Most respondents reported that the small handful of women who serve as "team leaders" in various practice areas hold positions of power. According to one associate, although these partners are well-respected, "the true emotional leadership" of the overall firm clearly comes from the male partners. She added, "Women in power are positively perceived. However, the women associates who are obviously gunning for power are negatively perceived."

Another associate commented that one senior woman behaves "more like male attorneys, but she is also in a practice area that may demand this of her." According to a partner, although the number of women with "real power [is] small, the percentage of women with real power to all women is probably about the same as the percentage of men with real power to all men in the firm."

With perhaps one exception, the senior women at Baker & Daniels are said to do little to assist more junior attorneys. One associate reported that the partners have neither promoted nor denied opportunities or quality of life for other women in the firm, although she added that one partner has mentored her and "made my position here known as valuable and deserving of high status."

Another associate commented that she does not see most women in leadership doing very much to promote opportunities for women in the firm, with the exception of "one hard-working woman partner who often goes to bat for the part-time women associates on her team." She added that there are "too few women partners to have enough women mentors."

Baker & Daniels No. of Responses: 8	Strongly agree	Agree	Disagree	Strongly disagree
Women's prospects for advancement at the firm are as strong as men's	3	5		
I am satisfied with the firm's family and personal leave policies	2	4	2	
There are women in positions of power and influence in the firm	2	1	4	
Women are as likely as men to receive desirable work assignments	4	4		
Women attorneys feel they can discuss family obligations openly		6	1	
Women are as likely as men to be mentored by senior attorneys	3	4		
Women attorneys enjoy a high level of job satisfaction	2	4	1	
Women in the firm are supportive of their women colleagues	2	5	1	
Firm management is receptive to the concerns of women attorneys	1	5	1	

BAKER & McKENZIE

Rating: 62

Baker & McKenzie
One Prudential Plaza
Suite 3500
Chicago, IL 60601
312-861-8000

No. of Attorneys: 161
No. of Women Attorneys: 35
No. of Partners: 86
No. of Women Partners: 8
No. of Survey Responses Received: 15

Respondent Profile: 4 partners and 11 associates responded. Practice areas included trade, corporate, and employment.

Summary: A hefty majority of respondents (10 of 15) reported that Baker & McKenzie erects no formal barriers to women's advancement, yet many also said that the perceived impracticality of part-time options and the firm's inability to adequately address the particular concerns of working mothers may limit opportunities for advancement. As a result, many believe women partners are still few and far between.

Advancement: Most respondents reported few formal barriers (in fact, 10 of 15 were positive). Yet some perceived that Baker & McKenzie's failure to offer viable options to working mothers or to recognize the obstacles women face with respect to rainmaking may limit advancement opportunities for women. As one respondent put it, "Women are as likely as men to advance if they put in as many hours, put up with as much shit, and make the firm as much money as men."

One partner observed that women are not as likely as men to advance to partnership, "because of the absence of a demonstrated institutional commitment to allowing women to combine work and family." She added that "the compensation structure for attorneys at higher levels and partners is very market-oriented—rainmaking is essential."

An overwhelming majority of respondents (three of four partners and eight of nine associates) agreed that the quality and quantity of work assigned to men and women is equal. In the opinion of two associates, however, women are held to a higher standard. One respondent observed, "Women tend to need to prove themselves more than the men and, therefore, must work longer and harder hours to get to the same advancement opportunities." A junior associate said that, in her experience, "it seems women may need to be somewhat better qualified."

Respondents generally believed that women can only advance to partnership if they are willing to spend less time with family and children. One respondent observed that there is "very little recognition that women in the firm have two jobs—one at Baker and one outside

Baker." One associate, despite her current optimism, said, "I have no idea how I will be able to progress once I have children." A second associate agreed: "I could not possibly have children and hope to continue my career." An associate said that, in her opinion, there is apparently no precedent for women to take temporary part-time status. As a result, in growing numbers, talented women associates are feared to be leaving the firm.

Rainmaking is reportedly central to advancement, which is also perceived by some to put women at a marked disadvantage. As one associate observed, "There is no institutional recognition that women do not have the same access as men to the companies which are in the Baker & McKenzie market." She concluded, "If one realistically considers business development prospects, the outlook is fairly grim."

One associate advised that those seeking partnership should "find a sponsor— particularly a male one," and predicted that if they do so, their "career prospects will be much enhanced." Although woman-to-woman mentorship opportunities are reportedly limited, one associate reported that she has an excellent female mentor. A corporate associate remarked that what she observed to be the dismal numbers of women partners mean that "women may have a slight edge" because of "pressure on the partnership to have more female partners."

> **"[The firm] would be a more comfortable place for women to work if there were more women attorneys."**

Attitudes and atmosphere: Respondents reported that the firm is as comfortable for women as any male-dominated environment could be. In the opinion of one partner, "apart from a few dinosaurs and the fact that there are few women attorneys around, the atmosphere is not bad." A senior associate noted the firm "would be a more comfortable place for women to work if there were more women attorneys." A woman partner described being "warmly welcomed," and said she feels comfortable with the "collegial atmosphere."

Yet, at the associate level, there is a fear that the small percentage of women in the firm fosters certain attitudes and practices that can exclude and denigrate women. According to one lawyer, some male partners "need to learn to show respect for women." One associate advised that having "a thick skin/laugh-it-off ability is key," and added that she is "surprised at some of the instances of improper comments...even among some younger associates." Another associate agreed, observing, "The selection of venues for firm functions and off-the-cuff remarks regarding the commitment and anticipated tenure of various female associates demonstrate that there is room for making the firm a more comfortable place to work."

> **"Working at a large firm has its rewards, but don't expect a satisfying personal/family life to be among them..."**

Balancing work & family/personal life: It is feared that women routinely leave the firm when they have children, a source of discouragement to associates, many of whom said they expect to follow the same route once they become mothers. Moreover, one associate remarked that although she knows of no women attorneys who have children, in her estimation, "all the men do, though!!"

Another respondent commented that, in certain departments, there is a "willingness to accommodate the women attorneys' outside interests and obligations." Even for the few part-timers, "work pressure does not appear to have been abated," according to a partner's experience. In one associate's opinion, "there is not a receptive atmosphere for dual professional families."

Some attorneys have evidently accepted what they characterized as the gospel that work and family do not mix. One associate wrote that the impossibility of doing both is simply "the nature of the beast—to pay high salaries and maintain lavish offices and support, attorneys need to bring in a lot of money." She concluded, "Working at a large firm has its rewards, but don't expect a satisfying personal/family life to be among them. If this stinks, it stinks for everybody. Men have put up with this fact for years, and women who want to succeed must deal with it, as well."

One associate said, "As a single woman, I actually enjoy the work load," but added, "I do not plan on maintaining that life style once I have children."

One associate observed that the unavailability of part-time arrangements is, in her estimation, "probably Baker's biggest weakness."

Flexibility of work arrangements: Baker & McKenzie has yet to offer practical alternative work arrangements,

according to respondents' perceptions. One associate was quite adamant in her opinion: "No!! There are no part-time alternatives." More long-term alternative arrangements are also perceived as non-existent. One associate observed that the unavailability of part-time arrangements is, in her estimation, "probably Baker's biggest weakness."

Although one associate reported that the firm's handbook states that part-time may be permitted on a very limited basis, she said she heard that the firm cannot handle workloads effectively by allowing women to work part-time. A partner was concerned that "women working part-time have been made to feel 'guilty,' or sense an attitude of disapproval that results in [their] working more hours than intended and thus eventually giving up."

One associate commented that given her perception of the firm's attitude about part-time, she would feel uncomfortable even raising the possibility of a part-time schedule if she had children, and that she would "feel pushed into continuing to work full-time." One associate thought that her group would be open-minded about granting her part-time status, because her contributions are valued. But she says, "We have no pioneers to look to yet, and I feel somewhat in the dark."

At partnership level, respondents reported that there is no maternity leave policy, much less part-time options. According to one partner, the firm is in the process of developing a partner leave policy. Another partner, however, predicted, "Given the competitiveness and demand of work, I do not foresee that women partners can afford to have more flexible work arrangements."

> ***The firm's "reputation for both lack of diversity and racial/gender discrimination is undeserved."***

Diversity: Although several respondents, including one who is a member of the hiring committee, commented that the firm does seek diversity in recruiting, one associate commented that the firm's "reputation for both lack of diversity and racial/gender discrimination is undeserved," but sensed that it might scare people away. She added, "Cultural diversity is an integral part of the firm," as a result of the firm's international focus and the presence of many foreign-born attorneys.

Perceptions were somewhat divided as to whether the firm's leadership is seeking further diversity. One associate said that, in her opinion, there is no commitment to diversity. Another noted that although the firm makes offers to those with diverse backgrounds, in her estimation, the firm "could create a more comfortable and supportive environment." Nevertheless, according to an associate on the hiring committee, "We actively recruit female associates, particularly female associates of diverse backgrounds." The firm "has no problem with accepting women of diverse backgrounds," she said, "[but] such women tend to go elsewhere because they would prefer to be part of a larger, more established group with similar interests."

> ***[The more powerful women] "are respected among the attorneys but viewed as 'dragon ladies' by the staff."***

Women in leadership positions: Several women have occupied management positions and chair committees, but there are reportedly no female partners at all in the corporate and securities practice area, and, according to the firm, one "local" (lower-tier) woman partner in litigation. Several respondents asserted that the firm should do more to promote women to management posts. According to a partner's experience, "Women are vastly under-represented in firm leadership" and "the men tend to belittle their efforts." The successful women are said to be respected by many, but not to constitute a "particularly visible or cohesive force," according to one lawyer.

One associate mentioned a former administrative partner. Although this woman was respected by other women, the associate believed that male attorneys and the secretarial staff "viewed her 'harshly' because of the position she held." Another associate commented that the more powerful women "are respected [by] the attorneys but viewed as 'dragon ladies' by the staff."

One associate commented that the women in leadership positions "seem to extend their hand to other women" and another reported that she has had "only positive interactions with the women who are in positions of power at the firm."

Other respondents disagreed. Few women partners are said to participate in the monthly lunches for female attorneys. One associate, however, observed that they are probably too busy to attend as, in her estimation, "they have to work twice as hard as their male colleagues." Another associate wrote that the women in leadership roles are "perceived as playing no active or positive role in promoting the opportunities and quality of life of women attorneys in Chicago." She added that in contrast to the strong camaraderie among female associates, "the interaction between women associates and women partners outside their practice groups, in general, is lacking."

Baker & McKenzie No. of Responses: 15	Strongly agree	Agree	Disagree	Strongly disagree
Women's prospects for advancement at the firm are as strong as men's	2	8	5	
I am satisfied with the firm's family and personal leave policies		5	4	3
There are women in positions of power and influence in the firm	2	8	3	1
Women are as likely as men to receive desirable work assignments	3	8	2	
Women attorneys feel they can discuss family obligations openly	1	4	7	1
Women are as likely as men to be mentored by senior attorneys	3	4	7	
Women attorneys enjoy a high level of job satisfaction		5	10	
Women in the firm are supportive of their women colleagues	2	12	1	
Firm management is receptive to the concerns of women attorneys		8	5	

BALLARD SPAHR ANDREWS & INGERSOLL

Rating: 21

◄◄◄

**Ballard Spahr Andrews
& Ingersoll**
1735 Market St.
51st Fl.
Philadelphia, PA 19103
215-665-8500

No. of Attorneys: 189
No. of Women Attorneys: 99
No. of Partners: 117
No. of Women Partners: 23
No. of Survey Responses Received: 6

Respondent Profile: 2 partners, 3 associates, and 1 counsel responded. Practice areas included business, corporate, and trusts and estates.

Summary: All of our small sample of respondents agreed that women have an equal chance to advance at Ballard, though some believed it has yet to adopt the attitudes and policies that would make it possible for women at the associate level to achieve success without surrendering hopes for family life. Ballard offers an atmosphere that, with the exception of the litigation department, is viewed as fairly egalitarian. One respondent observed that the firm's female partners adhere to the "Thatcher Principle," meaning that they have little sympathy and no time for their junior colleagues.

Advancement: All respondents contended that women can and do make partner at Ballard, although some perceived that advancement is most attainable for those who are single and childless. One respondent observed, "It appears that women can advance to partnership in basically the same time frame as men, although in recent years the women who have made partner have almost all been without children—and indeed, without obvious 'life style issues.' The message seems to be that the closer you are to being one of the boys, the easier your ride will be."

Another associate feared that, although the firm does not prevent women from being promoted, "the problem is that partnership often coincides with the period in women's lives where they have young children. That creates a dilemma." One respondent observed that women are less likely to advance, "not because of [unfair treatment] but because of the nature of the current practice of law." She added that many women are "not willing to make the choices required to be (and stay) a partner," and that they are more likely to choose part-time work, in-house positions, "or other non-law firm environments." A partner agreed: "Associates (both male and female) typically leave for life style reasons and often choose in-house positions."

That said, in the opinion of one partner, women are "just as likely to advance as men." She reported, "In one year, recently, five of six persons becoming partner were women." Despite the absence of a formal mentoring system, according to one respondent, "most associates who are successful establish informal mentoring arrangements." A partner noted that assignments are allocated based upon "experience, availability, and practice diversification." An associate agreed that women's "assignments and reviews are equal to men's." According to one partner, however, this may be more true in some departments than in others. Nevertheless, she added, "advancement is not limited to those departments traditionally thought of as women's departments."

> **"Some cliques within the litigation department are pretty male-oriented, with a true 'boys' club' at a very high level."**

Attitudes and atmosphere: Most departments at Ballard are reportedly hospitable to women, though one attorney observed, "The litigation department tends to be a little more 'backward' in terms of bordering-on-inappropriate comments." She added that attitudes are better in the firm's corporate departments and that, in her opinion, "as a rule, the younger male lawyers tend to be much more comfortable treating women lawyers as equals."

A midlevel associate said it was her perception that "some cliques within the litigation department are pretty male-oriented, with a true 'boys' club' at a very high level." One partner stated that, despite the firm management's commitment to "gender-neutrality," some departments "are more hospitable than others, although changes are being made at the macro level."

Outside of the litigation group, women attorneys seem to enjoy a high comfort level. An associate observed, "Men and women seem to socialize in a very normal fashion, and the tone set by the leadership of the firm is very sensitive to avoiding even the appearance of discrimination." A partner in the corporate department reported that her practice group is "gender-neutral...Some lawyers have dated (some even married) over the years. Our firm does not have an anti-nepotism policy."

> **"One does not need to be seen consistently during business hours, and both men and women can and do choose to attend daytime family functions."**

Balancing work & family/personal life: Being a devoted parent and remaining on track for partnership at Ballard is perceived to be an either/or proposition. One attorney summarized her view of women's options: "Women here either do the full-time, partnership track 'work thing' or they decide that family is more important and—either formally or informally—take themselves out of the running for partnership." One alternative that some choose, in her opinion, is waiting until one is promoted to partnership before starting a family. For those who can defer familial inclinations until the brass ring of partnership is firmly in hand, she believed, "the choice is probably not so extreme, but a lot of women don't want to wait eight, nine, or 10 years."

Another associate was concerned that "working hours are long, there is pressure, no childcare,...and no real sensitivity" to family duties. One associate said, in her estimation, "It is difficult for 'on track' associates and partners to balance the necessary long working hours, billing pressures, etc., with a personal life (as it is for men, too)." She concluded that Ballard did not appear any less sensitive to family responsibilities "than any other [firm]."

Despite the demanding hours and pressure, Ballard reportedly affords its lawyers some leeway as to when and where work happens and does not place a premium on "face time." One associate reported, "There certainly is flexibility to attend to personal matters, as needed, as long as the work gets done." A partner confirmed, "One does not need to be seen consistently during business hours, and both men and women can and do choose to attend daytime family functions."

Another partner wrote that there are "many lawyers (men and women) who arrive at work later in the morning after their children have left for school."

Two partner respondents seemed to take the position that the firm need not take further steps to facilitate attorneys' ability to sustain a work-family balance. The viability of shouldering both sets of burdens, one wrote, "depends to a great degree on the efficiency and self-discipline of the individual. Each attorney is expected to carry their workload and be available to service clients." Another partner observed, "We do not provide childcare. I am not aware of problems lawyers have had with finding childcare."

> *The flexibility of hours is said to be "absolutely greater" at the partnership level.*

Flexibility of work arrangements: The firm reportedly offers part-time work arrangements at the associate and partner levels, though some perceived that opting for a flexible schedule takes one "off track" for promotions. One respondent reported, "In the last few years, the firm has increasingly recognized that women want a variety of alternative arrangements, and part-time work— while still relatively rare—is more common than ever before."

One attorney wrote that part-time and contract work arrangements are available to those with "established track records of competence at the firm." She added that, although she has been part-time for a large portion of her years at the firm, during years she has worked full-time on a contract basis she has been "treated equally with 'on track' associates. The firm has been very fair with me always."

The flexibility of hours is said to be "absolutely greater" at the partnership level. A partner reported that two partners work reduced hours. One partner said that she has been on a reduced schedule for some time, which has "been successful largely due to the support of my partners."

Another partner noted that in the transactional practice areas, reduced hours rather than a fixed part-time schedule tend to be more viable, in that flexibility concerning which hours are worked enables an attorney "to attract choice assignments" even though she is not always in the office. She said that, in her opinion, part-time attorneys have never been considered for partnership, although "a number of us (men and women)" want that to change.

> *One associate said it was her belief that when racial minorities first arrive at the firm, they are "often mistaken for (assumed to be) support staff."*

Diversity: Is Ballard diverse? Respondents were split on this question. In one lawyer's opinion, "Not really. It definitely pays to fit in." A partner observed: "This is a corporate firm and extreme behavior which impinges on the work environment would not be tolerated by anyone."

According to an associate, "There are very few lawyers of racial minority backgrounds." She added it was her belief that when racial minorities first arrive at the firm, they are "often mistaken for (assumed to be) support staff."

One respondent had a different view, commenting, "There are homosexual women, Democrats and Republicans, blacks and whites at all levels in the firm. I don't know that the firm has a 'commitment to diversity,' but there certainly are all types of ages, sexes and genders, and ethnic backgrounds working comfortably together here."

> *"The highest levels of power in the firm are all controlled by men."*

Women in leadership positions: According to a partner's perception, "Women are being given positions to demonstrate their talents, but no position of real power is yet filled by a woman." An associate observed that "the highest levels of power in the firm are all controlled by men." One associate commented that women have "real (but not top) power." One partner noted that there is an African-American woman on the firm's executive committee, and that women partners "are on, or have in the past been on, every committee of partners in the firm."

Several associates took a dim view of the efforts (or lack thereof) of senior women to help those lower down in the ranks. One associate observed that, in her opinion, there is a female partner at the firm who "is not supportive and has brought family leave policies backward, I believe."

Another associate answered only two questions in the survey but, with regard to the leadership issue, wrote, "The most important comment I want to make is that women who are in the 'front line,' i.e., the first to advance to partnership, are *not* helpful to the large group of women associates now moving up." She perceived that "these women partners are not interested in mentoring, helping, imparting wisdom on how to deal with a male-oriented profession, how to deal with balancing career and family." Dubbing the phenomenon the "Thatcher Principle," she observed: "I guess to get where they are now these women had to be tougher than the men around them." Noting that her colleagues within the associate ranks rally solidly around one another, she predicted that because the most senior female partners are, in her estimation, neither "admirable nor supportive," not until she and her peers advance toward and into partnership will "the practice of law really change."

One associate lauded the senior women for their efforts on behalf of their junior colleagues. This associate remarked, "Most of the influential women do work to promote opportunities, as they arise, for other women. They have women's dinners and get-togethers to talk about issues and to socialize."

Ballard Spahr Andrews & Ingersoll No. of Responses: 6	Strongly agree	Agree	Disagree	Strongly disagree
Women's prospects for advancement at the firm are as strong as men's	2	3		
I am satisfied with the firm's family and personal leave policies	2	1	1	1
There are women in positions of power and influence in the firm	1	3	1	
Women are as likely as men to receive desirable work assignments	3	2		
Women attorneys feel they can discuss family obligations openly	1	3	1	
Women are as likely as men to be mentored by senior attorneys	2	3		
Women attorneys enjoy a high level of job satisfaction	1	2	1	
Women in the firm are supportive of their women colleagues	3	2		
Firm management is receptive to the concerns of women attorneys	1	2	2	

BINGHAM, DANA & GOULD LLP

Rating: 11

🔨🔨🔨🔨

Bingham, Dana & Gould LLP
150 Federal Street
Boston, MA 02110
617-951-8000

No. of Attorneys: 188
No. of Women Attorneys: 47
No. of Partners: 76
No. of Women Partners: 10
No. of Survey Responses Received: 9

Respondent Profile: 3 partners, 5 associates, and 1 counsel responded. Practice areas included business and litigation.

Summary: Although one partner was scathingly negative, all other respondents were enthusiastic about Bingham's atmosphere, part-time policies, and opportunities for women's advancement. And the women at the top, who are said to provide guidance and support to their junior colleagues, received extremely warm praise.

Advancement: A solid majority of our respondents was optimistic about women's prospects for advancement at Bingham. One litigation associate declared her prospects for advancement to be equal to those of men, and another litigator commented that "the advancement opportunities appear favorable."

According to another partner in the litigation department, "The firm is eager to give women opportunities to succeed—both to make partner and to be successful as partners." One litigation associate noted that allocation of assignments appears to be done "on an equitable basis," since "the firm has been very busy for the past year and associates are in demand."

One associate in the business department perceived that women's prospects do not equal men's, which she attributed in part to the fact that women "are unwilling to work the number of hours required to be a strong candidate for partnership. Mentoring helps—it is easier to imagine yourself in that position knowing other women who have made it there." A first-year associate observed "no real disadvantage for women." She added, "If anything, this is a less caustic atmosphere than outside the firm. Advancement at B,D & G is merit-based."

A partner in the business department agreed that women can advance, "especially in those cases where family constraints don't reduce billable hours, etc. For women who have chosen to work part-time or otherwise reduce their workload, there have been trade-offs in terms of speed of advancement, but they generally are explainable. Working part-time does not seem to put you 'off track' forever here."

A partner, who did not list her practice area, suggested that advancement prospects for women are "in the corporate area, okay. In litigation, almost no chance at all, which becomes no chance *whatsoever* if one is so benighted as to have a family." (This partner was uniformly negative about every aspect of Bingham, in stark contrast to the generally positive perceptions of her colleagues.)

> *A partner wrote that in more than a decade with the firm, she has never experienced any gender discrimination.*

Attitudes and atmosphere: Most women are reportedly happy day-to-day at Bingham. One senior associate reported that she feels comfortable and respected at the firm, that there is "a lot of collegiality between women and men," and that she does not get "the 'second class' feeling I sometimes did at my last firm." A first-year associate concurred, writing that she "couldn't feel more at home here." A partner wrote that in more than a decade with the firm, she has never experienced any gender discrimination, and another reported that the "critical mass" of women at the firm means that "you don't feel like an outsider [and] there isn't a 'mold' you feel you need to fit."

The dissenting partner said that, in her assessment, some men "lunch only with other men, persist in talking sports, and treat any comments about kids with raised eyebrows and a troubled look."

> *According to a partner, the best evidence that the firm's environment is "pretty good" comes from the fact that so many of the women partners have children.*

Balancing work & family/personal life: "There is never enough time to do everything you want to do as well as you'd like to do it," observed one partner, although Bingham is reported to be responsive to this dilemma. This partner added, "No one is looking over your shoulder to see if you're out of the office for a meeting or a school event."

The firm reportedly has on-site emergency day care, and because a fair number of attorneys are shouldering both work and family demands, colleagues are not shocked when mini-crises hit. According to a partner, the best evidence that the firm's environment is "pretty good" comes from the fact that so many of the women partners have children. She added that she "feels completely comfortable saying 'I will be out of the office for a meeting at my kids' school, pediatrician's appointment, etc.'"

Once again, a single partner disagreed, saying it was her opinion that having an outside life is "impossible. A woman must choose one or the other. The only 'successful' women at the firm neglect their kids in order to be one of the guys. They, in turn, out of frustration, fail to support other women."

The associates joined the majority view. One woman who is part-time and describes herself as "on 'mommy track,'" wrote that her priority right now is at home, the firm knows it, and "the powers that be seem to admire my attitude, actually." A senior associate observed that despite the firm's demands of all lawyers, "those with childcare demands appear to manage both." A midlevel associate with children described the pace as "very amenable to a satisfying personal/family life."

Bingham seems to have found a way to be flexible and supportive of part-time arrangements.

Flexibility of work arrangements: Compared to many of the firms surveyed for this book, Bingham seems to have found a way to be flexible and supportive of part-time arrangements. One part-timer wrote that she works four days a week, receives four-fifths pay and 100-percent benefits. Despite having what sounds like a fairly generous policy relative to other firms, she commented that the firm "generally is supportive, but does not lavish money on me." She added that she also feels some pressure to return to work full-time.

Former part-timers have reportedly made partner. One respondent noted that a partner spent one year on a reduced schedule and described it as "great." Part-time work is accepted if not welcomed, according to one associate, but it requires "flexibility on the part of the women involved to work well, especially for women in a transactional practice." There is reportedly one partner currently on a reduced-hours arrangement.

The dissenting partner, not surprisingly, had a more negative perception, asserting that, although available in theory, part-time "absolutely does not work." Those who go part-time, she suggested, have seriously hurt their careers. Another respondent disagreed, stating that part-time options are legitimate and viable and merely slow the partnership track. An associate said it was her perception that, in addition to lengthening the track from associate to partner, shifting to part-time status "seems to slow the promotion to 'equity' (the second tier) of partnership."

One associate described the firm as being very diverse, yet another wrote that, in her opinion, there is "a dismal showing of minority hiring—summer and permanent."

Diversity: One associate described the firm as being very diverse, yet another wrote that, in her opinion, there is "a dismal showing of minority hiring—summer and permanent." According to an associate in the business department, the firm "demonstrates a commitment to judging its employees on their merits and the rest of it is fairly immaterial."

An associate remarked that in the past two years the firm has hired roughly equal numbers of men and women, "as well as a number of minorities."

One partner, however, observed that the firm is now making an active effort "not just to hire, but to help [minority lawyers] succeed over the long haul." According to the dissenting partner, the firm lacks diversity and, in her estimation, "wants a woman who is a man" and "who toes the party line."

An associate said it was her perception that the ranks of powerful women are actually thinning as "several prominent women partners have left to take positions as judges."

Women in leadership positions: According to two partners, women are just beginning to populate the corridors of power here, although most respondents clearly believed "the times, they are a-changin'," and gave senior women overwhelmingly positive reviews. A litigation partner reported that women are starting to "act as a serious force in the firm." She added that the women partners have been "involved in creating and recreating an ongoing Women's Mentoring Program with strong support from the managing partner."

Two women partners reported that several women in the firm have now developed substantial independent practices, "the real source of power in any firm," and that this promises to be the surest road to "a greater voice in policymaking decisions."

Although change may be in the works, one respondent maintained that "power is very centralized and is all male." Another respondent observed that although one woman heads up a practice group, it was her opinion that "she has power only because the guys have decided she is the token woman to hold up as the success story." An associate feared that the ranks of powerful women are actually thinning as "several prominent women partners have left to take positions as judges."

One senior attorney reported that the more powerful women in the firm "are perceived as accomplished and deserving of their positions." Another associate commented that there are "excellent female role models" at the firm, and a partner agreed that she and her partners are "quite supportive of women associates," and are "not afraid to speak [out] about issues of importance." A litigator remarked that the women partners "make an effort to mentor associates, both one-on-one and in a more comprehensive group structure."

Bingham, Dana & Gould No. of Responses: 9	Strongly agree	Agree	Disagree	Strongly disagree
Women's prospects for advancement at the firm are as strong as men's	5	1	2	1
I am satisfied with the firm's family and personal leave policies	4	3		1
There are women in positions of power and influence in the firm	3	5		1
Women are as likely as men to receive desirable work assignments	7	1	1	
Women attorneys feel they can discuss family obligations openly	6	1		1
Women are as likely as men to be mentored by senior attorneys	8			1
Women attorneys enjoy a high level of job satisfaction	4	4		1
Women in the firm are supportive of their women colleagues	5	3		1
Firm management is receptive to the concerns of women attorneys	3	4		1

BRACEWELL & PATTERSON LLP

Rating: 2

◤◤◤◤◤

Bracewell & Patterson LLP
South Tower Pennzoil Place
711 Lousiana
Suite 2900
Houston, TX 77002-2781
713-223-2900

No. of Attorneys: 149
No. of Women Attorneys: 44
No. of Partners: 69
No. of Women Partners: 12
No. of Survey Responses Received: 5

Respondent Profile: 3 partners and 2 associates responded. Practice areas included labor and employment, energy, and litigation.

Summary: According to our small sample of respondents, concerted efforts to support and integrate women lawyers at Bracewell & Patterson have paid off. Women's opportunities to advance are reportedly favorable, and the firm's environment appears to be hospitable. Although the feasibility of part-time arrangements and ability to sustain a home life were questioned, several respondents pointed to clients, not the firm, as the source of the problem.

Advancement: Our five respondents were unanimous that women's prospects for advancement at Bracewell & Patterson were as good as, if not better than, men's. A partner commented, "In the past few years, it appears that women have been advancing at a greater rate than the men." She attributed this to a growing number of women at the senior levels in the firm, which "has increased the comfort level" of more junior women. She added that her mentors and strongest supporters have been men.

A second partner agreed that women's chances are "better than men of equal qualifications." Another partner commented that women "have good prospects and are as likely as men to advance." The essential criteria, she added, are "being a top-notch lawyer, presenting yourself professionally [and] having a 'can-do' and 'take-charge' attitude to

both partners and clients." She added, however, "Good women lawyers leave because of life style choices. Clients are very demanding, making it difficult to balance work and family."

One associate commented that although prospects for advancement are good, to her knowledge, the transactional practice groups in the firm's Houston office have no women partners. (Although the firm noted there *are* women partners in the transactional groups at other offices.) She commented that women are "well-represented" in other practice areas and that her "hope is that, over time, we will reach a critical mass."

One associate said that male partners tend to find associate "buddies," forming relationships that she perceived "exclude women colleagues."

Attitudes and atmosphere: Focused efforts by the women at Bracewell to build networks and support one another contribute to a comfortable atmosphere at the firm.

One partner described an "increasing awareness of women networking with one another." She added that several groups, both formal and informal, focus on "women in the law and the firm." She characterized the firm's female lawyers as "very supportive of one another, particularly in assisting with balancing work and family and client development."

Another respondent reported that the firm's women attorneys have sponsored "several trips and significant social functions hosted by the women in the firm for women clients."

Respondents also reported that the firm sponsors a task force focusing on the development of women in the firm.

According to a partner, the firm's leadership, including the managing partner and the section heads, provides "lots of positive reinforcement" to women attorneys. She further noted that men and women at the firm enjoy "strong friendships."

Another respondent described the firm's leadership as "very open," and an associate reported that she finds the "partners, including male partners, more sensitive to potential gender bias than some of the male associates."

The single criticism made by one associate is that male partners tend to find associate "buddies," forming relationships that she perceived "exclude women colleagues."

> *Bracewell "has struggled on an ongoing basis to be as accommodating to women and family responsibilities as possible, but when the client calls and they want you, there is little the firm can do."*

Balancing work & family/personal life: Although the firm is reported to be sensitive to family responsibilities, several respondents commented that its clients are not. A partner opined that the firm is "generally family-friendly, but the work is not." She added that Bracewell "has struggled on an ongoing basis to be as accommodating to women and family responsibilities as possible, but when the client calls and they want you, there is little the firm can do."

Another partner reported that women with children "try, with some success, to be more focused during the workweek and allow more 'family time' on the weekends." Moreover, mothers at the firm apparently rely on each other for support. "We help one another out when childcare falls though, we share resources, and, if necessary, a shoulder to lean on," wrote one partner.

The two associates were slightly more guarded in their responses. One wrote that prospects for sustaining a thriving practice and a fulfilling family life are only "fair," although she concluded that this was "a hazard of our profession," rather than attributing it to the firm. The other concluded, "I don't know that any of us have a good solution."

> *"The marketplace is extremely demanding...and clients expect you to be at their beck and call whenever they need you."*

Flexibility of work arrangements:
Part-time arrangements "are legitimate," although there's a fear that they are not always viable for all Bracewell attorneys. Views as to the availability and use of part-time schedules varied between associates and partners.

According to one associate's perception, reduced schedules are "not readily available." A partner, on the other hand, remarked that "part-time and off-track positions [are] available and utilized." One partner reported that another partner has been working part-time "for several years."

The third partner observed that the success of the firm's part-time arrangements may not always be entirely within its control. This respondent wrote, "The trick in these situations is not dealing with the firm, but dealing with clients." She added, "The marketplace is extremely demanding on lawyers and their time and clients expect you to be at their beck and call whenever they need you."

> *The firm's partners publicly support "many political positions, [including] Democrats and Republicans, pro-choice and pro-life, etc."*

Diversity: Because only three of our respondents commented on this question, it was impossible to get a good sense of the firm's commitment to diversity. According to one partner, Bracewell is "an ethnically diverse group." She added that the firm has "allowed women partners [leave] to run for Congress," and that the firm's partners publicly support "many political positions, [including] Democrats and Republicans, pro-choice and pro-life, etc."

Another partner, however, said, "Women at the firm are not diverse from another." She added that as a group, women attorneys at the firm are "more liberal" than male attorneys.

An associate wrote that she was "not sure" whether the firm had a commitment to diversity, although "there is likely a willingness to employ women and men of diverse backgrounds; qualifications to 'do the job' are the primary criteria, however, as I believe they should be."

> *"Women are starting to advance and gain power in the partnership. Any lack of power is attributable, primarily, to seniority issues and a lack of extremely senior woman lawyers at the firm or in the community."*

Women in leadership positions: One woman reportedly serves as a section head at the firm, and other women sit on what one partner described as "critical committees like associate evaluation, long-range planning, etc."

The partner respondents were enthusiastic about the other women partners and long-term prospects for achieving more positions of power at the firm. One remarked, "Women are starting to advance and gain power in the partnership. Any lack of power is attributable, primarily, to seniority issues and a lack of extremely senior woman lawyers at the firm or in the community." According to another partner, "Our women are a closely knit group and mutually supportive. We admire one another's ability to juggle."

The two associates were a bit more guarded. One associate perceived that the senior women are "not really in 'real power'—at least from outside appearances." She added, however, that the women partners "are attempting to promote opportunities." The other associate wrote, "There are senior attorneys and partners who are women with clout. Some of them are active in their support and enthusiasm for female associates."

Bracewell & Patterson No. of Responses: 5	Strongly agree	Agree	Disagree	Strongly disagree
Women's prospects for advancement at the firm are as strong as men's	3	2		
I am satisfied with the firm's family and personal leave policies	4	1		
There are women in positions of power and influence in the firm	2	2	1	
Women are as likely as men to receive desirable work assignments	2	3		
Women attorneys feel they can discuss family obligations openly	3	1	1	
Women are as likely as men to be mentored by senior attorneys	3	1		
Women attorneys enjoy a high level of job satisfaction	2	2		
Women in the firm are supportive of their women colleagues	2	3		
Firm management is receptive to the concerns of women attorneys	3	2		

BROBECK, PHLEGER & HARRISON LLP

Rating: 76

Brobeck, Phleger & Harrison LLP
Spear Street Tower
One Market
San Francisco, CA 94105
415-442-0900

No. of Attorneys: 157
No. of Women Attorneys: 58
No. of Partners: 69
No. of Women Partners: 8
No. of Survey Responses Received: 6

Respondent Profile: 1 partner and 5 associates responded.

Summary: Our handful of respondents painted a picture of Brobeck, Phleger & Harrison as a firm that leaves much to be desired from the standpoint of its women lawyers. Women partners "tend to have sacrificed a family life to get here," and some respondents believed that once "at the top," they do little to help promote more junior women. Four out of five associates agreed that women's prospects for advancement were not as favorable as men's. The part-time policy, still in its infancy, is not perceived as being practical for those who aspire to partnership.

Advancement: Four of five responding associates agreed that women are at a disadvantage when it comes to partnership prospects. According to a litigator, "Brobeck certainly has a 'big-firm' environment, and men do advance more readily than women." This is true, in her opinion, not only with respect to partnership, but also as to "level of responsibility and trial experience." One associate concluded, "Women who pattern themselves in the traditional male" model have a better chance to succeed.

Associates also expressed dismay with the attrition of women lawyers and with the sacrifices that women must make in order to become partner. Women partners at the firm, in the words of one associate, "tend to have sacrificed a family life to get there."

Another associate remarked, "...even senior associates with kids are few and far between." According to one respondent, female associates drop out to work part-time, raise a family, or pursue a more family-friendly career. She added that, in her estimation, the firm "has not yet embraced alternative work schedules or telecommuting necessary for many (not all) women with families." As a result, she noted, there is a smaller pool of women eligible for partnership, and there are few women role models.

According to one associate, "Mentoring and review criteria do not differ for women," although she asserted that some departments within the firm are reputed to give men better assignments and more responsibility. According to another associate, when attorneys become more senior, it is expected that they do not need to be "fed" and can generate their own work, yielding billables of 1,950 hours per year.

Several associates commented that mentoring is more difficult for women to come by than men. Relationships among women at the firm were described as competitive and, according to one associate, "the women partners do not mentor other women."

The single partner respondent disagreed with some of the associates' views, remarking that women do enjoy equal partnership prospects and that the criteria for advancement are "excellent work product, skill, talent, relationships, reputation." She did concur with the view that "mentors are essential" and with the fact that attrition is "due in large part to hours [and] schedules that aren't family-friendly."

Firm leadership is "still predominantly male."

Attitudes and atmosphere: Casual social interactions at the firm are said to be comfortable. "The social interactions between women and women are congenial and respectful (with a few exceptions)," according to one associate, and the " 'boys' club' is largely gone," in the words of another. Nonetheless, firm leadership is "still predominantly male."

A senior associate described the firm as "generally *not* a comfortable place for women." She remarked, "Women's concerns [are] not addressed." She added that most women feel that they must postpone having children until after they come up for partnership. A midlevel associate agreed that, in her opinion, there

is "a degree of insensitivity to women's issues and challenges facing women."

One associate recounted the tale of two male partners who "took one of the firm's biggest clients to a strip club, at the client's request." When a female attorney objected, she was reportedly told she was "overreacting."

However, according to the partner, who has been at the firm for more than a decade, during that time the attitude has "changed dramatically for the better."

One associate described Brobeck as "fairly sensitive" for a big firm, with the caveat that "billing 2,000 hours a year does not leave a lot of time for family/personal life."

Balancing work & family/personal life: Sustaining a balance between work and family has reportedly become more difficult in recent years. According to one associate, "Several years ago it seemed the firm was genuinely interested in quality of life issues," yet she believed this is no longer the case. In the past, she wrote, the firm appointed a task force to report on issues of special concern to women, including maternity leave and childcare, but, in her estimation, never developed a "universal approach to these questions" and has now "retreated from the liberalism it seemed to be adopting."

This associate further commented that although most women postpone having children until after making partner, even those who become mothers as young partners may feel they will not be considered "dedicated."

Although the firm "praises men who bring their kids to work on 'bring your child to work day' as if they can manage it all," it does not, in the eyes of this lawyer, recognize women "for doing the same." She added, however, that "if you choose to work less and the firm apparently likes your work—you can swing it."

According to a couple of associates, pressure to put in more hours is on the rise. A midlevel associate commented that associates are "pressured" to bill 2,000 hours per year and that this pressure "has increased over the last few years as the firm is watching its budget more closely than ever (despite record profits last year)."

An associate said, "It is difficult to create a family life" while working at the firm because the work "is very demanding—both in terms of number of hours and stress." She commented that her few friends who have children "usually feel very torn between work and family."

Two respondents expressed a different viewpoint. One associate described Brobeck as "fairly sensitive" for a big firm, with the caveat that "billing 2,000 hours a year does not leave a lot of time for family/personal life." And the partner commented that balancing work and family is "very difficult, but possible." She advised, "Children should always be your priority, so work has to accommodate their needs/schedules."

> *"Rarely do women feel comfortable asking for [part-time] and even if they get it, [they] end up working more than what they've arranged."*

Flexibility of work arrangements: Brobeck is still taking baby steps when it comes to part-time work, according to several lawyers. This year the firm reportedly instituted a 75-percent part-time policy, "which is not supposed to affect partnership," according to one respondent. The program is said to be available to primary caregivers (of children) who have been at the firm for at least two years.

For most associates, although it may exist in theory, part-time work is not perceived as workable in practice. A senior associate believed that only one woman partner and two women associates in the firm's San Francisco office currently work part-time. She added that working part-time, as far as she was concerned, "*does* affect your chances of making partner."

According to another associate, she believes that those opting for part-time schedules will be penalized when it comes to partnership. Yet another associate commented that, in her opinion, "rarely do women feel comfortable asking for [part-time] and even if they get it, [they] end up working more than what they've arranged."

There was some confusion over the availability of part-time options at partnership level. According to one associate, part-time is "more acceptable" once you are a partner. Another associate, in contrast, wrote that she knows of no part-time partners and does "not believe the firm would consider such a policy."

> *"...overwhelming numbers in upper management tend still to be white males."*

Diversity: Respondents gave Brobeck low ratings when it came to diversity. The firm, reported one associate, has one black partner and one black associate in an office of 150-plus attorneys. She added that although diversity and women's issues are "touted as desirable concerns," reality demonstrates "that they are not considered a priority." She suggested that politics and alternative life styles are "always better left at the door."

Another associate observed that she could not "think of a single nonwhite female attorney." She added that one lesbian attorney "who is treated well" will, in her view, "never ascend to a leadership position in the firm." Another associate agreed that the firm "does *not* offer an environment conducive to diversity." Although "the firm is trying to change this culture to be more open to diversity," this attorney believes that "it's going to be a real challenge."

Even the partner respondent commented that political leanings or background do not matter, "but overwhelming numbers in upper management tend still to be white males."

According to the 1997 National Directory of Legal Employers, Brobeck employs two black, seven Hispanic, one American Indian/Alaskan, and two Asian/Pacific Islander attorneys.

> *"Virtually none of the women partners work to promote the opportunities and quality of life for other women—there seems to be an attitude of, 'If I had to struggle to make it, so should you.'"*

Women in leadership positions: Few if any women are perceived to wield power at this firm. According to a partner, "Power follows business," and although women sit on all committees of the firm except for the policy committee, which she described as the "most powerful," women do not really hold true power. She added that this is "not the fault of the firm—it's just the makeup of that committee depends on who has the biggest book of business."

Perceptions of the firm's most senior women are mixed. One associate remarked that the women partners in the firm are "perceived favorably." She added, "They work very hard and have a limited family life (kids in boarding school, etc.)."

Two associates believed that the firm's female partners do little to promote more junior women. According to one of them, the more influential women have no interest in promoting others because doing so would threaten the power they have.

The other associate added that, in her opinion, "virtually none of the women partners work to promote the opportunities and quality of life for other women—there seems to be an attitude of, 'If I had to struggle to make it, so should you.'"

Brobeck, Phleger & Harrison No. of Responses: 6	Strongly agree	Agree	Disagree	Strongly disagree
Women's prospects for advancement at the firm are as strong as men's		1	2	2
I am satisfied with the firm's family and personal leave policies		3	1	1
There are women in positions of power and influence in the firm		4	1	
Women are as likely as men to receive desirable work assignments	1		4	
Women attorneys feel they can discuss family obligations openly		2	1	2
Women are as likely as men to be mentored by senior attorneys		1	1	3
Women attorneys enjoy a high level of job satisfaction		1	2	2
Women in the firm are supportive of their women colleagues		2	2	1
Firm management is receptive to the concerns of women attorneys		3	2	

CHADBOURNE & PARKE LLP

Rating: 65

Chadbourne & Parke LLP
30 Rockefeller Plaza
New York, NY 10112
212-408-5100

No. of Attorneys: 223
No. of Women Attorneys: 67
No. of Partners: 72
No. of Women Partners: 9
No. of Survey Responses Received: 19

Respondent Profile: 2 partners, 16 associates, and 1 counsel responded. Many respondents did not reveal their department; corporate was the only identified practice area.

Summary: Our hats go off to Chadbourne & Parke for taking some steps in the right direction by implementing a formal part-time policy, hiring an external consultant to conduct a firm-wide survey on work issues, and holding diversity seminars, in response, evidently, to its poor showing in the first *Presumed Equal* survey. Nevertheless, respondents perceive that much room for improvement remains. Women's opportunities for advancement at the firm are hampered, in the eyes of many respondents, by inadequate mentoring and the exclusion of women from rain-making and networking opportunities.

Advancement: While the two partners were effusive about prospects for advancement at Chadbourne, 11 of the 16 associates who responded were cautious, at best.

Several associates reported that fairly dramatic changes were made in response to the firm's poor showing in the first edition of *Presumed Equal*. One observed, "In large part because of [the *Presumed Equal*] survey, I think that now is an excellent time to be a female attorney at Chadbourne & Parke. Your survey, while based on the responses of just a small portion of females here, caused the firm to hire an outside consultant...to survey the entire firm on work-related issues...The results showed not that there was a gender problem at

Chadbourne & Parke, but rather that it is a demanding place to work that sometimes interferes with one's personal and family life. The lack of diversity at the firm was also noted as a problem. In response to the [firm-wide] survey, the firm took several concrete steps, including implementing a part-time policy for working parents...and organizing several committees of partners and associates to address issues raised in the [firm-wide] survey."

One partner gushed that advancement prospects are "wonderful—women are as likely as men to advance to partnership. Hard work, intelligence, and dedication are all factors central to the advancement of everyone" at the firm. Another partner wrote, "Talented women who are willing to play the 'big New York law firm game' are as likely to advance to partnership as talented men."

Five associates agreed. One midlevel corporate associate reported, "C & P, like most firms, bases its partnership decisions on economic factors: Does the group have the financial wherewithal to support another partner, and will this associate bring new clients to the firm or make a significant contribution in keeping current clients at the firm?"

Eleven associates perceived their chances in a less favorable light. A corporate associate observed, "I firmly believe that qualified women are not given equal opportunities to advance to partner and are purposefully kept out of networking and marketing." Another associate reported her view that movement is "absolutely not equal" on the road to partnership. She perceived that the firm's "mentoring program is limited to fancy luncheons, not substantive support for midlevel and senior women in outside bar activities and other business development groups. No wonder women never have their own clients at [this firm]." A corporate associate also criticized what she perceived to be the inequitable opportunities for mentoring and assignments, contending that "mentoring—if there is any at all—favors men. Allocation of assignments seems to be improving, but is still subject to substantial 'favoritism.'"

According to a litigation associate, chances for women to move up in that department are, in her estimation, "bleak indeed. We have one woman partner, but she serves as an example of the appalling obstacles women here face." Another litigation associate concurred, characterizing as "ridiculous" the presence of only one woman partner in the litigation department in the New York office.

> **"...while men here are appreciated as members of the team, women are shunted to peripheral roles."**

Attitudes and atmosphere: Most respondents were satisfied with the atmosphere at Chadbourne, with many describing the firm as comfortable, professional, and even politically correct. A partner wrote that in the recent firmwide survey, no gender discrimination was detected. Another partner reported that she has always been comfortable at the firm. One associate reported that the firm recently conducted gender and discrimination sensitivity training for all staff and lawyers. A corporate associate described her relationships with her colleagues as friendly and relaxed.

A junior associate said that while the atmosphere at the firm is very professional, it was her view that some "senior women associates [are] bitter, unhelpful to younger associates, and know they will not make partner." Another associate wrote it was her assessment that "there are still many inappropriate comments toward women that are tolerated."

A litigator framed things differently, observing, "The worst aspect of being a woman in this department is the profound alienation one feels." It's her impression that "it's not sexist jokes that do it (although I have learned some new ones). It's that while men here are appreciated as members of the team, women are shunted to peripheral roles." She further observed, "If you're a woman, it doesn't matter if you happen to have a family, you're presumed to be less serious about your work than the men."

A junior associate reported, "Personal life suffers tremendously."

....

Balancing work & family/personal life: Working hours and client demands are described as onerous, though no different than those at any other New York firm. One lawyer suggested that things are getting worse: "The firm culture is going through a transformation (spearheaded by the corporate finance group, which arrived in 1995) in an attempt to be more 'white shoe.' Hours expectations and salaries are up (the bonus floor has recently been removed)."

A partner described the balance as difficult but possible. She wrote, "If a woman is very organized and diligent and has a supportive mentor, it is possible." A second partner noted, "[There are] plenty of men who are unhappy about the time demands and pressures of large New York firms, but many of them are afraid to speak out about this (not 'manly,' you know)."

A junior associate reported, "Personal life suffers tremendously." Another associate commented that, in her view, while the firm is willing to accept special work arrangements with individuals on a private basis, these offers are frequently turned down by associates "because there is a perception that they will receive a lower caliber of work/lesser status after taking the offer."

"Women who work part-time are still called in on their days off and generally do not get the respect they deserve."

....

Flexibility of work arrangements: As part of the reform process instituted "to address the bad PR from the first edition of *Presumed Equal*," Chadbourne transformed an *ad hoc* part-time system into a formal one. While respondents suggested that actual schedules are still negotiated on a case-by-case basis between individual attorneys and the partners for whom they work, lawyers who have been at the firm for at least three years are permitted to work part-time for up to a year. One associate characterized part-time as involving four long days or five days with hours from 8:30 a.m. to 5 p.m. for 80 percent of the salary.

A couple of respondents with part-time schedules offered favorable reports. One partner said that, prior to the introduction of the new policy, she worked part-time for several years as an associate and that while it worked for her, it was not easy, from her perspective or the firm's, because of client expectations and demands. Another respondent reported that she came to the firm as a staff attorney, a reduced-hours, nonpartnership-track position. She wrote, "Although I had some concerns about the position, I have found that those I work with respect my schedule and treat me as a valuable member of the group."

Several associates said that, the new policy notwithstanding, they believed that significant pitfalls were still associated with part-time. One corporate associate characterized the new policy as "unevenly administered and dependent upon support of the department and partners." Further, she wrote that, in her estimation, there is "no additional compensation if hours exceed the agreed-upon amount—even if that excess is substantial or continues for several months." Several respondents reported that there are no part-time partners. Most agreed that because the policy is so new, it's too soon to tell how taking part-time status will affect partnership chances. One respondent was concerned that "women who work part-time are still called in on their days off and generally do not get the respect they deserve." Another lawyer said that, in her opinion, "only one attorney has been part-time for a year or more, and she does only document review."

A partner stressed that the touchstone of successful part-time arrangements is flexibility on the part of the lawyer. However, a junior associate told of two colleagues who turned down the opportunity to go part-time "after being told they could work three- or four-day weeks, but should hire full-time sitters for their children so they would be available to come in to work if necessary. Both reportedly rejected the offers and left the firm for true part-time work status at other law firms." (A spokesperson for the firm claimed to have no knowledge of any such associates.)

> *"Friends [at the firm] who are African-American have informed me that they still feel uncomfortable here—like the token minority."*

Diversity: A majority of associates perceived that Chadbourne lags behind in the area of diversity. One was concerned that "one or two [minorities] come to work. When they leave, the next one or two get hired." Another respondent attributed this to what she perceived as the firm's efforts to refashion its image

in recent years: "One aspect of the cultural transformation [at the firm] is the end of recruiting at local schools...and a focus on Harvard, Yale, Columbia, and NYU. This strategy tends to have a negative impact on diversity." In the opinion of a corporate associate, "The firm's dedication to supporting a diverse legal work force is pathetic." Another associate dryly commented that, in her opinion, Chadbourne is "willing to underestimate women of all political leanings, personalities, and life styles." A junior associate wrote that the firm seems to be supportive of diversity, but added, "Friends [at the firm] who are African-American have informed me that they still feel uncomfortable here—like the token minority."

A handful of respondents attested to the described firm sensitivity to diversity and the steps taken towards that end. Several respondents' comments agreed with one who perceived that "the firm does recognize [that] it should increase the number of African-American and Hispanic lawyers it employs."

> *A junior lawyer reported that the women partners do not seem willing "to rock the boat."*

Women in leadership positions: The vast majority of respondents clearly perceived that that there are no women who hold real power and influence at the firm. No women sit on the management committee, numerous respondents wrote, nor are there women in other powerful positions. "I do not think there are any women in positions of policy making," suggested one associate. Another associate noted her increasing frustration "with the lack of female role models and mentors for younger associates." While some thought this was likely to change soon, others predicted that it would be a while before real change occurs.

One associate noted that a partner who came in laterally "actively participates in improving quality of life for women associates through mentoring." She described the other women partners as "not inspirational." A midlevel associate said of one woman partner, "[She] has the ear of a powerful partner, thus her vision, ideas, goals are filtered through him...[but] the woman partner can stand on her own and is highly competent." Another junior lawyer reported that the women partners do not seem willing "to rock the boat."

One associate was slightly more upbeat, describing the firm as a "place in transition...depending on how willing or able the firm is to accommodate part-time arrangements without placing an attorney on the permanent 'mommy track.'" If that doesn't happen, she predicted, women will leave for alternative jobs, and power within the firm will not be obtained by women.

Chadbourne & Parke No. of Responses: 19	Strongly agree	Agree	Disagree	Strongly disagree
Women's prospects for advancement at the firm are as strong as men's	5	3	7	4
I am satisfied with the firm's family and personal leave policies	5	8	5	
There are women in positions of power and influence in the firm		4	11	4
Women are as likely as men to receive desirable work assignments	7	6	4	1
Women attorneys feel they can discuss family obligations openly	1	6	10	1
Women are as likely as men to be mentored by senior attorneys	4	4	5	4
Women attorneys enjoy a high level of job satisfaction	1	7	8	2
Women in the firm are supportive of their women colleagues	1	13	4	1
Firm management is receptive to the concerns of women attorneys	3	11	5	

CHOATE, HALL & STEWART

Rating: 7

◀◀◀◀◀

Choate, Hall & Stewart
Exchange Place
Boston, MA 02109
617-248-5000

No. of Attorneys: 165
No. of Women Attorneys: 50
No. of Partners: 69
No. of Women Partners: 11
No. of Survey Responses Received: 20

Respondent Profile: 6 partners and 14 associates responded. Practice areas included corporate and litigation.

Summary: With the possible exception of the firm's grueling hours, Choate, Hall & Stewart is by all accounts a fine place for women lawyers. The firm's atmosphere is discrimination-free, and part-time arrangements are used with some frequency. Moreover, although it's perceived that the chances of anyone making partner may be slim, women who stick it out are just as likely as men to be promoted.

Advancement: Although several associates were of the opinion that few attorneys are making partner at Choate, Hall these days, respondents were in overwhelming agreement that the women who stick it out for partnership consideration are as likely to make it as men. "Right now, very few or no partners are being made," observed one corporate associate. A senior associate concurred that, in her opinion, "[it is] very difficult for *anyone* to make partner."

According to another lawyer, "Provided they are willing to make the same personal sacrifices and devote as much time and effort to the firm as their male counterparts," women will make it as often as men. Nevertheless, despite women's bright prospects, one litigator opined, "the problem is that women are rarely up for partner—attrition seems to take a higher toll on the senior women

associates than on the men—the pressure [with regard to] hours tends to be tougher on women."

Many respondents commented that assignments and reviews are handled in a gender-neutral fashion. A junior corporate associate has found it "pretty easy to get involved with exciting assignments." Those who discussed partnership selection criteria emphasized the importance of mentoring and a high-quality work product, and placed less stress on business generation.

Part-time work is apparently relatively common for women, but some perceived that it may delay advancement. According to a corporate associate's opinion, "Any woman who has a child works part-time for at least some part of her career and this has a negative effect on 'the business.' " A partner seemed to agree, but qualified her answer: "[There is] no question that it is harder to succeed if you choose to work part-time whether you are a man or a woman, [but] in time, it is possible for part-timers to achieve the level of professional distinction that will support your election to partnership."

History may well support this view. Another partner commented that the first two women partners had both spent several of their associate years working part-time. She added that there have subsequently been several women elected to partnership while working part-time, "including one who had never worked on a full-time basis at the firm before election as a partner."

All associates at Choate, Hall are reportedly assigned partner mentors, and women at the firm have "rotating partner/associate lunches and meetings to address particular areas of concern." A senior associate noted that she had received "excellent mentoring and assignments and received very fair reviews."

Choate, Hall has a distinguished history of contributing to the advancement of women in the profession. According to several partners, the firm was the first in Boston to elect a woman partner, in 1971. One partner commented, "[The firm] seeks to neutralize the impact on its women attorneys of the disadvantages [that] women unfortunately face outside the firm." She remarked that any "suggestion that particular assignments should not be given to women would not be tolerated." Another partner who has sat in on many evaluation sessions reported that women enjoy an equal shot at partnership and that they are "given strong praise for their ability to balance family/work duties." One partner, although she agreed

that the firm's policies are designed to support the advancement of women, said that, in her opinion, "[there is still] more that the firm can do to achieve this end—such as better support for communications links to the firm from home."

A number of associates commented on the important role that golf is perceived to play in firm life.

....

Attitudes and atmosphere: Most associates expressed satisfaction with the atmosphere at Choate, Hall, and their sole complaint related to the prominence of golf activities. Most respondents reported not having experienced gender discrimination in any form and that the firm has roughly equal numbers of male and female associates. One midlevel associate described "great camaraderie between associates, regardless of gender." A junior associate commented that some of the "most exciting high-tech/venture work comes from a woman corporate partner."

A number of associates, however, commented on the important role that golf is perceived to play in firm life. "Golf is a big thing here. Some women play, but more men than women are involved," as one associate put it. A midlevel associate reported that despite the firm's efforts to sponsor "other nonsports-oriented informal events," there remains, in her estimation, "an annoying 'golf clique' [that] is very male-dominated."

In direct contrast, a second-year associate commented, "The firm has sponsored more 'women's lunches' since the results of the last *[Presumed Equal]* survey, [and] that is a move in a positive direction." According to a junior associate, "While many of the sporting activities don't get the women's attention, recent associate/partner golf, bowling, and tennis challenges have had equal attendance of men/women. This is not a 'boys' club.' " Another associate agreed that the firm is hospitable to women: "Some of the older male partners are rather self-conscious about the need to treat women attorneys equally, but even they are aware of gender issues."

The women partners who responded did not comment on the impact of sports on the firm's atmosphere and were wholly positive in their comments. One reported that she has "always experienced a high degree of professional regard and acceptance."

One associate reported that women with young kids "come in early, leave early, and work from home at night when necessary."

Balancing work & family/personal life: Choate, Hall is a hard-driving place, and the partners acknowledged that striking a balance given those demands is difficult. Nevertheless, one partner announced that the firm is "committed to attracting and retaining people (both men and women) with healthy, fulfilling family and social relationships, not workaholics with no outside life or family." Allowing lawyers to achieve this balance, however, is "tricky." A corporate partner commented, "It's the nature of the beast to be very demanding of hours," but, she said, "[the firm does] what it can [to assist] by providing access to Work/Family Direction (an employee assistance program with excellent childcare referral resources), by providing various means for people to 'hook in' from home, by being flexible with respect to working hours, by permitting compensatory time off, by insisting that people take vacations, etc."

According to associates, while the balance may be possible, it is no cakewalk. A corporate associate observed, "[It] is difficult for anyone to sustain a personal life. If I have a family event or vacation planned, I can usually shift assignments. However, I can't imagine being able to leave at 6 p.m. each night to pick up children from day care." Another associate reported that the firm is family-oriented, that most attorneys are married and many have children, but said that, in her opinion, apart from providing "some tax benefits for childcare and emergency childcare," the firm does little to make life easier for parents. In direct contrast, one associate reported that women with young kids "come in early, leave early, and work from home at night when necessary."

The burdens ease considerably for those who opt for part-time. One lawyer wrote, "In many ways, it is a relief to be on a 'mommy track.' It means you don't have to spend all your free time marketing." She added, "The firm supports mothers, [and] you can talk openly about taking time out for family activities." Another part-timer agreed: "By working three days a week, I have been able successfully to sustain a satisfying personal/family life."

According to one partner, the firm was the first in Boston to promote a part-timer to partner.

Flexibility of work arrangements:
Women lawyers at Choate, Hall apparently opt for part-time arrangements with some frequency, and many women with young children are reportedly on part-time schedules. Many of the partners noted that most of the women partners at the firm served extended part-time stints at some point in their careers while their children were young.

Part-time arrangements are available for both associates and partners, and one woman partner at the firm is currently on a four-day-per-week schedule, respondents reported. According to one partner, the firm was the first in Boston to promote a part-timer to partner.

A partner reported that part-timers receive compensation adjustments if the time "actually worked exceeds the agreed-to specified percentage." She added that the firm provides associates with a "generous computer allowance" to enable them to acquire home computers, and "the firm's [computer] personnel will travel to the home to set things up and make sure the connections to the firm are fully operational."

According to an associate who is part-time, her arrangement is working, and the firm is "very sensitive to my needs because they don't want me to leave." She added that the firm has generous maternity leave policies, and that most women take six months off.

Among associates who have not taken advantage of part-time opportunities, perceptions of the trade-offs involved were more mixed. A senior associate said that, in her estimation, "*many* women take advantage of excellent policies, but long-term, I think they suffer."

> *"It's a pretty homogenous place, and I don't perceive a serious commitment to change this."*

Diversity: Choate, Hall's partners were effusive about the diversity of personalities at the firm, yet a midlevel associate declared that, in her opinion, "We are not a particularly diverse crowd." A junior associate wrote that the firm is tolerant of difference, but, in her experience, the "attorneys are overwhelmingly white and upper-middle class." (According to the 1997-1998 National Directory of Legal Employers, Choate, Hall has two black, two Hispanic, and one Asian/Pacific Islander attorney.)

A midlevel associate's opinion was even more blunt: "[The] firm is not committed to diversity. They prefer people [who] fit their 'work hard and be eager' mold, but what else can you really expect?" A corporate associate agreed: "It's a pretty homogenous place, and I don't perceive a serious commitment to change this."

A junior associate wrote that, in her estimation, the firm's lawyers include fewer single women than one might expect, but added, "I'd say the political spectrum is covered and personalities definitely run the gamut from social butterflies to workaholics to do-it-all young mothers." The partners echoed this position, with one pointing out that there are attorneys of "all religions, races, and political persuasions," and another stating that "many different and unusual personalities make Choate, Hall an interesting and fun place to work and exchange ideas."

According to one partner, women have held leadership positions "far longer than at most firms..."

Women in leadership positions: Women lawyers have reportedly made major inroads into leadership positions at Choate, Hall. A woman has reportedly held a long-term position on the firm's executive committee, an elected post. The current chair of the firm's hiring committee is a woman, as is the chair of the associate training committee. According to one partner, women have held leadership positions "far longer than at most firms, [and now]

women sit on and chair committees [because] women are truly integrated into the management and administration of the firm, not because of a superficial policy of tokenism, as I fear is the case in some firms." A woman also reportedly sits on this year's compensation committee, which sets the compensation levels for all partners. A partner commented that while Choate, Hall has not yet had a female managing partner, she "expects that will come before long."

Another partner remarked that the most senior women have been "actively interested in promoting the interests of women in the firm and are sensitive on gender issues of all kinds."

Choate, Hall & Stewart No. of Responses: 20	Strongly agree	Agree	Disagree	Strongly disagree
Women's prospects for advancement at the firm are as strong as men's	12	7	1	
I am satisfied with the firm's family and personal leave policies	13	7		
There are women in positions of power and influence in the firm	7	11	2	
Women are as likely as men to receive desirable work assignments	14	6		
Women attorneys feel they can discuss family obligations openly	7	8	3	
Women are as likely as men to be mentored by senior attorneys	11	5	3	
Women attorneys enjoy a high level of job satisfaction	7	10	2	
Women in the firm are supportive of their women colleagues	11	7	1	
Firm management is receptive to the concerns of women attorneys	12	6	1	

CLEARY, GOTTLIEB, STEEN & HAMILTON

Rating: 42

♦♦♦

Cleary, Gottlieb, Steen & Hamilton
One Liberty Plaza
New York, NY 10006
212-225-2000

No. of Attorneys: 288
No. of Women Attorneys: 93
No. of Partners: 71
No. of Women Partners: 7
No. of Survey Responses Received: 33

Respondent Profile: 5 partners, 27 associates, and 1 counsel responded. Practice areas primarily included corporate and litigation. Several respondents did not identify their practice area.

Summary: Cleary, Gottlieb, Steen & Hamilton appears to offer a pleasant work atmosphere for its women attorneys and a hospitable environment for all lawyers. Nevertheless, a majority of respondents didn't believe women's chances for advancement were very good and half were unimpressed with the availability of mentoring, though most thought women were, at the very least, making inroads into upper management.

Advancement: While many respondents seemed to agree that women are underrepresented in the partnership at Cleary, they were split as to why, a disagreement clearly mirrored by their perception of women's chances for advancement. One midlevel litigator characterized the existence of only seven women partners in the New York office as "*very* demoralizing." According to one partner's opinion, "Women have excellent chances of advancement but choose to leave the firm before reaching senior levels." An associate said that, in her opinion, "women demand a more integrated life" and thus reject in larger numbers "the complete absorption of all else that career advancement requires."

Though societal factors took part of the blame for lower rates of advancement at the firm, several respondents perceived that there "are also flaws" with the firm itself. One litigator stated that, in her department, it is "very important [that women project] a 'macho' confidence level. Suggesting that you're not 100 percent dead sure of a position or a proposal is definitely seen as a weakness." A colleague asserted that, in her estimation, "men's work at Cleary is much more appreciated than women's work [and the firm culture], with its emphasis on brash, self-starting, macho lawyering, tends to exult in men who fit that type and to take for granted women who do excellent work but are not as aggressive about it."

A partner—and partners were generally *more* positive about Cleary—wrote that, in her estimation, the firm's "informal and unstructured [atmosphere] makes it more difficult for someone who is quiet and does not take initiative to get good work, get to know partners, find mentors, and so on."

There was clearly dissension on the subject of mentoring, just as there was disagreement that women had no problems receiving plum assignments. One partner wrote that women do "work on the high-profile assignments and have ample opportunity for client development, foreign assignments, etc." A corporate associate disagreed, saying that, in her opinion, "assignments that typically lead to partnership are not given to women with the same frequency as they are given to men." A second corporate associate wrote that "the best projects gravitate to those associates with whom the partners feel most comfortable" and added that she fears "beneficiaries of the system appear to be white men."

Half a dozen respondents commented that mentoring is critical, yet, in their estimation, an effective mentoring program is not in place. A partner conceded that "our mentoring is improving but still has a ways to go."

> ***The atmosphere at the firm was described by respondents as "informal," "progressive," and "open-minded."***

Attitudes and atmosphere: The majority of respondents were upbeat about the environment at Cleary. Overall, the atmosphere at the firm was described by respondents as "informal," "progressive," and "open-minded," and several attorneys stated that the abundance of women in the associate ranks contributes to high comfort levels. One respondent indicated that civility is "highly valued and 'screamers' are few and far between" at the firm.

One partner reported that although the firm is very comfortable at the "lowest levels," in her opinion, it is not so for women partners. She stated that, in her experience, Cleary is not "a place for someone who thrives on positive reinforcement."

A handful of respondents reported what they characterized as sexist attitudes on the part of some of the firm's clients, particularly those from Latin America. One respondent reported instances of women "being ignored and interrupted during meetings by clients," or arriving at a foreign location only to face banter that is condescending to women. A junior associate, however, reported that when she encountered "minor problems with Latin American clients," she found that her colleagues were "very clear that such behavior is not tolerated."

A first-year associate observed that Cleary is "*nothing* like an 'old boys' club'—the firm bends over backwards to ensure that the atmosphere is comfortable for men and women." A senior associate thought Cleary was "far more enlightened than most corporate workplaces in the U.S."

While this was the strongly prevailing view, one associate disagreed, stating that, in her opinion, "male assignment partners often make hostile comments to women about their capabilities in the corporate area."

The firm reportedly has an active Women's Working Group with regular meetings and frequent firm-wide lunches.

Maintaining a satisfying family or personal life is "not possible and those who say otherwise are either in denial or have shockingly low expectations for their home life."

Balancing work & family/personal life: While firm higher-ups are reported to be fairly understanding "on a one-to-one basis" about family responsibilities, at a firm-wide level, those seeking to maintain a personal life are up against difficult odds. One associate noted that, while the firm does not circulate billable totals, "it seems to me that 2,400 to 2,500 billables may be average." According to the opinion of one unmarried senior associate, maintaining a satisfying family or personal life is "not possible and those who say otherwise are either in denial or have shockingly low expectations for their home life."

There is an anxiety that being a mother and a lawyer at the firm seems either to drive these women out or demand a tremendous amount of childcare. "Cleary is no harder on families than any other law firm," in the words of one respondent, but that is not saying much. The firm does, however, offer emergency childcare.

Being an unmarried woman at the firm is no picnic, either. One lawyer described the balance as "hard, especially for single women." One midlevel associate observed that given the hours at the firm, "it can be hard to so much as [find time to] pay one's bills, let alone do anything personally satisfying." A senior associate recalled that during one period of time, she "spent more nights 'crashing' on [her] office floor" than going home. One associate remarked that answering this question made her sad and added that at times, she has "felt that the work in itself was enough for satisfying all my needs," but at other times, she has been "miserable at having to postpone [having] children and many aspects of a personal life."

The ability to balance also apparently varies by department. Hours are reportedly somewhat more predictable in litigation, "but corporate associates are expected to drop everything at any time to come in to work," according to one lawyer, who added that vacations will be canceled if you are "really needed for a deal" and that "you can forget about your weekends."

One associate suggested that part-time "means 9 a.m. to 7 or 8 p.m., rather than 9 a.m. to 11 p.m. or midnight."

Flexibility of work arrangements: Though there was considerable confusion among respondents regarding the availability of part-time work arrangements, many lawyers had gripes about part-time work at Cleary. Several attorneys reported that the firm recently introduced a reduced-hours arrangement, which is available at partnership level to those with primary childcare responsibility, yet others were unaware that part-time options were available to partners. One lawyer reported success with her own alternative arrangement, but added that she must protect her schedule aggressively and suggested that her situation would not be easy to replicate.

Regardless of what they perceive the formal policy to be, respondents generally agreed that part-time arrangements have significant downsides. One associate suggested that part-time "means 9 a.m. to 7 or 8 p.m., rather than 9 a.m. to 11 p.m. or midnight." According to another, part-timers "simply cram the same amount of work into fewer hours and do nothing well." Part-time schedules are perceived as not "viable" for those on partnership track and may preclude choice work assignments. Nevertheless, a partner contended that two of her colleagues "worked on a reduced schedule for a significant period as associates; one made partner with her class and the other asked to be deferred."

Most lawyers acknowledged that the obstacles to part-time work are by no means unique to the firm. According to one senior corporate associate's perception, part-time work in her department is not a realistic option, not as a result of firm policy, "but because of the 24-hour, on-call nature and intensive travel schedule of the work."

Cleary has "recently made serious efforts to hire a more diverse group of associates in terms of race and ethnicity."

Diversity: Cleary received mostly high marks on the diversity front. The firm reportedly has a diversity committee and has held "mandatory diversity training." Cleary has "recently made serious efforts to hire a more diverse group of associates in terms of race and ethnicity," in the words of one lawyer. "And there always seems to be a good-sized group of gay and lesbian attorneys," including some partners, according to an associate. A junior associate reported that the firm has a gay lawyers group that meets regularly, and another lawyer says that the firm extends health insurance to domestic partners of gays and lesbians.

According to another associate, there are plenty of "quirky personalities," and the firm is "very tolerant" of differences. Another lawyer reported that she was "deeply impressed by [the firm's] commitment to the handicapped." A woman who describes herself as a member of a minority group reported that her "views on firm policies, programs, and goals are always encouraged." Nevertheless, one associate said that, in her opinion, the firm is a "comfortable place as long as you don't scratch too deeply."

"Cleary's female partners are very supportive of other women and seem committed, by and large, to the progress of other women at the firm."

Women in leadership positions: Although a strong majority of respondents reported that a handful of women hold influential positions at Cleary, they were divided as to whether this signals women's ascension to the top rung of Cleary's power structure. One partner noted that a woman partner on a reduced schedule is head of the firm's legal personnel committee, "traditionally one of the most important committee positions." But another partner reported, "[There is] no woman on the executive committee, alas." The firm reportedly does have a woman assistant managing attorney. An associate stated, "Cleary's female partners are very supportive of other women and seem committed, by and large, to the progress of other women at the firm."

A couple of respondents were decidedly less sanguine about the sway women hold within the firm. One senior associate reported that, in her opinion, women partners are "definitely *not* in positions of real power vis-à-vis being rainmakers or running the place." According to a junior associate, while there are two "very strong" women partners in the Latin American group, in her estimation, "the older male partners carry much more power at the firm."

Perceptions of the women in power at the firm were all over the map. One senior associate remarked that she believed that senior women were "quite well-perceived not only by their male colleagues and seniors but by women looking up." But this view was not always echoed by younger attorneys. One associate stated, "[The] woman in this firm I consider powerful I also do not trust." Another lawyer opined that the women partners in New York are "viewed as nice hard-working women who do not rock the boat over anything."

A few associates lauded the women partners, with one noting that they, along with counsel, "have worked hard in advancing the role of women in the firm" by raising issues such as equality of assignments and part-time work and by creating the Women's Working Group.

Cleary, Gottlieb, Steen & Hamilton No. of Responses: 33	Strongly agree	Agree	Disagree	Strongly disagree
Women's prospects for advancement at the firm are as strong as men's	4	11	9	6
I am satisfied with the firm's family and personal leave policies	13	17	1	1
There are women in positions of power and influence in the firm	5	18	9	1
Women are as likely as men to receive desirable work assignments	15	14	2	1
Women attorneys feel they can discuss family obligations openly	7	15	8	2
Women are as likely as men to be mentored by senior attorneys	7	10	12	2
Women attorneys enjoy a high level of job satisfaction	4	15	10	2
Women in the firm are supportive of their women colleagues	12	14	3	2
Firm management is receptive to the concerns of women attorneys	10	15	3	1

COVINGTON & BURLING

Rating: 6

↖↖↖↖↖

Covington & Burling
P.O. Box 7566
1201 Pennsylvania Ave. NW
Washington, DC 20044
202-662-6000

No. of Attorneys: 296
No. of Women Attorneys: 93
No. of Partners: 121
No. of Women Partners: 15
No. of Survey Responses Received: 21

Respondent Profile: 5 partners, 15 associates, and 1 counsel responded. Practice areas included primarily litigation, as well as several other departments.

Summary: Covington & Burling, by most accounts a conservative yet collegial workplace, is viewed nearly unanimously as a meritocracy, inspiring confidence in most women lawyers that partnership is theirs for the taking. Although the work is a grind and the pressure intense, part-time options are said to be highly satisfactory, mentoring is a Covington strong suit, and women are very much involved with running the firm, although some associates gave senior women poor marks.

Advancement: With only three dissenting voices, the women at Covington agreed that women's prospects for advancement equal men's. One partner's comments summed up the views of her peers: "Advancement is merit-based. Women who provide exceptional legal services to clients advance to partnership to the same extent that men do." A partner claimed to know "firsthand that the deciding factors are related to job performance and not to gender."

A striking number of associate reviews characterized Covington as a "meritocracy." Most agreed that, although "the standards for advancement are tough, the same factors that apply to men are equally applicable to women." A senior associate observed that those "without children or with at-home spouses seem to do best. Statistically, this is usually men." An associate reported that while assignments are "hit-or-miss," it is possible "to steer your own course if you do not care for a particular area or assignment."

Several associates commented that the firm's women are "supportive of each other and try to provide guidance and a forum for expressing concerns and building relationships." Another lawyer wrote, "[Women at Covington] take care of each other."

Mentoring is also a strong suit at Covington. The firm has reportedly initiated a formal mentoring program, and junior attorneys evidently enjoy a great deal of informal mentoring. Several women raved about their own personal mentors, most of them men, reporting that these senior partners had taken a great interest in their careers and provided a supportive ear and sound advice.

A small minority of respondents had less favorable views about women's advancement at Covington. One associate feared that women are less likely to make partner and that the firm "insists that it is committed to excellence, but defines excellence in a way that favors men (or women with no family responsibilities). [I have] received absolutely no mentorship from anyone...[They] expect women to be good lawyers, but only to play a supporting role, i.e., be in charge of documents, case administration, etc., *not* substance."

Another remarked, "The 'superstars' are still more likely to be men, partly because they are mentored by young male partners." Yet another associate complained that clients' perceptions affect advancement opportunities, in that clients "tend to view male senior associates in leadership positions, which feeds into the partnership evaluation."

Several attorneys lauded the firm's leadership for setting "an appropriate tone."

Attitudes and atmosphere: The atmosphere at Covington is reported to be pleasant and relatively trouble-free for most women. Although the firm is described by some as "conservative," it is also reported to be, in the words of one, a "collegial" environment where there is "no premium placed [on being] a 'tough guy' or macho." A litigator described the firm as having "team spirit." Social interactions between women and men are characterized as "common and comfortable."

Several attorneys lauded the firm's leadership for setting "an appropriate tone," being responsive to the concerns of women attorneys, and making it clear that discrimination and harassment will not be tolerated. Two first-years were effusive in their praise of the firm, with one describing it as a "family," and the other saying that it is a "safe haven from gender discrimination" and that "[as long as my work] lives up to C & B standards, I know I will continue to advance toward partnership."

Although portrayed far more favorably than many firms, Covington is not paradise to all. In a senior associate's opinion, Covington is "the land of dowdy, mannish women. To be successful here, you must give up outside life, attractive appearance, etc. [Those] who project a different, more fashionable appearance and may even have interests outside the firm are perceived to be not serious." And a first-year associate observed that "attorneys and staff are more likely to assume that a woman is a staff member rather than an attorney."

Interactions between old male partners and young women associates could be better, according to one associate, who remarked that, in her estimation, "Senior male partners still are uncomfortable working with young women, taking them seriously, and understanding their often different approach to litigation."

"[Family responsibilities] are viewed as the best excuse for not being able to take on or complete a task."

Balancing work & family/personal life: Most respondents found achieving such a balance possible, though not easy. The hours are sometimes long, and there is a fair amount of pressure, they wrote, but the firm is generally sensitive to their outside responsibilities.

According to one partner, "[Family responsibilities] are viewed as the best excuse for not being able to take on or complete a task." She reported that in more than a decade at the firm, she has not been forced to miss a day of planned leave. In contrast, a junior associate reported that her outside interests and time with her husband "are sometimes compromised because of my junior status here—I'm basically on-call for the partners."

Another attorney characterized the attitude as, "You get your work done and then you go home—whenever and as soon as you can." In one litigation associate's opinion, the firm "definitely [includes a] 'mommy track' [and] holds out one or two women as proof that you can have kids and still make partner, but it's really not realistic."

One part-timer wrote, "[The firm] has made every effort to work with me to allow me to achieve a satisfying family life." She reported that her part-time hours are respected and that the firm has accommodated her need to work at home on occasion. A married associate with children wrote that Covington has been "amazingly supportive of me and my efforts at balancing." When circumstances requiring "extra family attention" have arisen, the partners for whom she has worked have been "uniformly supportive in pitching in to cover for me. I could not have asked for more."

> **The firm is, according to one respondent, "very flexible about crafting part-time schedules."**

Flexibility of work arrangements: Most respondents expressed satisfaction with Covington's attitude toward part-time arrangements.

Several respondents had in the past or were currently taking advantage of the firm's part-time policy, and all reported having favorable experiences. One lawyer reported that she has worked part-time since having her first child: "[I] determined the amount of time that I felt comfortable being away from my child and suggested to the firm that I be allowed to work short days. My proposal was accepted (as is virtually every proposal in which a lawyer works 60 percent time or more) and the firm has respected it."

Although Covington's policy works on a "case-by-case" basis, the firm is, according to one respondent, "very flexible about crafting part-time schedules," and the need for individuals to negotiate their own arrangements does not seem to deter potential part-timers.

A senior associate reported that she chose to go to Covington in part because its part-time policy was, at the time, "by far the best among the top D.C. firms." A partner noted that the availability of part-time arrangements is not restricted to parents and that accommodations have been made to permit "childcare, completion of education, pursuit of artistic interests, or the like. These arrangements are and have been made for men and women, associates, counsel, and partners."

A couple of respondents did not view the part-time policy favorably. One remarked that she is "concerned" that some who go part-time may not be "perceived as partnership material."

The firm is reported to have an active diversity committee that sponsors programs, handles concerns, and promotes diversity efforts.

Diversity: Most lawyers applauded the firm's efforts to achieve and maintain a diverse environment. Several noted that Covington was the first firm in D.C. to offer benefits to the domestic partners of gay and lesbian attorneys. The firm reportedly has "several minority associates and some openly gay associates." According to one respondent, the firm makes a "big effort to hire African-American women." Several associates agreed with one's comments that, "unlike other D.C. firms that have a given political affiliation, C & B is refreshing in its diversity of political and personal leanings." The firm is reported to have an active diversity committee that sponsors programs, handles concerns, and promotes diversity efforts. A partner related that she considers herself "to have a diverse background, personality, and life style," and that the firm has made a number of adjustments to meet her needs. She stated that the firm makes "every effort" to hire persons of unique backgrounds.

An associate who is active in firm recruiting said that Covington takes its obligation to further diversify its staff seriously and, accordingly, contacts campus organizations of minority students, and solicits faculty recommendations of diverse students. The firm then reaches out to ask the recommended students to interview with them.

A couple of associates disagreed. According to one associate's perception, Covington is "officially" devoted to diversity, and "is a very *civil* place, and nothing inappropriate is ever said or done." Another lawyer chided the firm for restricting its recruitment efforts to "Yale and Harvard law grads, as well as U.S. Supreme Court clerks." She predicted that "a broader hiring base could benefit the firm in greater diversity of backgrounds and life experiences."

Women are "very much a part of running the firm."

Women in leadership positions: There is (and reportedly has long been) a woman on the firm's five-person management committee, and there are, in one respondent's opinion, women on "all significant firm committees." Women have in the past served as the firm's hiring partner, managing partner for legal personnel, associates' assignments partner, chair of the firm's business committee, member of the evaluation committee, and have held high positions in the ABA. Women are reportedly "very much a part of running the firm," in the words of one respondent. The woman member of the management committee was described by one associate as an important role model: "She has two children, leaves each day at 5 p.m., litigates, and stresses the importance of balancing work and family. She is highly regarded at our firm." One associate described a relatively young female partner as "the leading 'rainmaker' " in her practice group.

The most senior women were described by an overwhelming majority of respondents as "very supportive and encouraging. They are sensitive to women's issues and take time to mentor associates," as one associate wrote. Two women partners, according to a respondent, were reported to "make an effort to get to know all the new woman associates through informal lunches" and other gatherings.

A minority of respondents were less impressed with the representation of women in positions of power. "Very few women have 'real power' as a part of management or as rainmakers or career makers for associates," in the estimation of one senior associate. A partner wrote,

"[I] would like to see women even better integrated into the organization, particularly at senior levels."

An associate reported that the one experience she had at the firm in which "sex played a role" was when she worked for a woman partner who, in her estimation, "[gave me] less responsibility and recognition for my work than the male partners do." Another associate also perceived that "the women partners here, especially [older ones], seem overtly hostile to younger women who are unwilling to sacrifice *everything* to make partner."

Covington & Burling No. of Responses: 21	Strongly agree	Agree	Disagree	Strongly disagree
Women's prospects for advancement at the firm are as strong as men's	13	5	3	
I am satisfied with the firm's family and personal leave policies	16	3	1	
There are women in positions of power and influence in the firm	13	5	2	1
Women are as likely as men to receive desirable work assignments	14	5	2	
Women attorneys feel they can discuss family obligations openly	10	7	3	
Women are as likely as men to be mentored by senior attorneys	13	5	2	1
Women attorneys enjoy a high level of job satisfaction	7	9	3	1
Women in the firm are supportive of their women colleagues	15	4	1	1
Firm management is receptive to the concerns of women attorneys	13	8		

CRAVATH, SWAINE & MOORE

Rating: 49

◤◤◤

Cravath, Swaine & Moore
Worldwide Plaza
825 Eighth Ave.
New York, NY 10019
212-474-1000

No. of Attorneys: 353
No. of Women Attorneys: 89
No. of Partners: 72
No. of Women Partners: 6
No. of Survey Responses Received: 15

Respondent Profile: 14 associates and 1 senior attorney responded. Practice areas were primarily corporate; several respondents did not identify their practice area.

Summary: Cravath, Swaine & Moore, an exceptionally hard-driving and intense firm, is home to relatively few women and, obviously, a low number of women partners. Nevertheless, a solid majority of respondents believed women have equal prospects for advancement and are as likely as men to receive desirable work assignments. Some perceived motherhood as incompatible with success at the firm, perhaps because respondents deemed part-time arrangements largely impractical.

Advancement: Although most respondents noted that women make up a tiny percentage of the firm's partnership, their opinions were divided as to whether this is a function of women choosing to leave for life style reasons or a dynamic at the firm. One associate's opinion gave credence to the former: Women tend to be underrepresented in entering classes at the firm. (Nevertheless, the firm reported that for the last five years, women have comprised between 25 and 35 percent of incoming classes.)

Another associate perceived that the reasons for women's underrepresentation at Cravath, while complicated, boil down to lack of mentoring and support because of the small number of senior women at the firm. In her opinion, "Cravath is *not* a good place for women. Period. There are so few of us here. We have no mentors, no support network, no partner backers; in short, there is nothing for us here. Male associates, on the other hand, are constantly mentored, supported, backed...Women associates don't have that luxury. We drift." Yet another associate contended that, in her estimation, "[the] concept of meritocracy is a sham. How can it be a meritocracy when there are no women left by the seventh year to compare, by merit, with the men?"

One corporate associate described what she characterized as an "unspoken process by which certain men are singled out for mentoring, shepherding through preferred rotations, and grooming." Questioning whether this process has worked for women, she described one male associate who is slated for partnership: "He has been taken with three other partners on golf trips, routinely travels with the managing partner of the firm, and has essentially been spoon-fed a lot of business from that partner."

Two respondents commented on the firm's unusual assignment system, whereby associates are paired with specific partners on a rotating basis for 12- to 18-month periods, which, in the words of one, "ensures objectivity in allocation of assignments." Another associate disagreed, stating that, in her opinion, "[women] are more than capable of handling the work, but once they reach a certain level, they don't typically get it. Either they are seen as not being there for the long haul because they already have babies, or maybe because they will go off and have them just when they begin to become profitable to the firm."

Numerous respondents, on the other hand, were satisfied with their personal experiences at Cravath and were optimistic about the partnership picture. A junior associate reported that the low numbers are changing, in that two women were made partner last year and one is expected to be promoted this year. One corporate associate reported that she has been assigned "some of the highest-profile work available and [has] been mentored/guided by several very well-respected male partners."

Another junior attorney in the corporate department surmised that women's chances for promotion are as good as men's, but she said, "[It is] important to prove early that you're good, because first impressions seem to count for much. People are labeled 'stars' early on, but the 'stars' are not disproportionately men or women."

> **"In spite of the efforts that [Cravath] has made to make [itself] more gender-friendly, it is still overwhelmingly a male firm."**

Attitudes and atmosphere: Respondents offered mixed views of the atmosphere for women at Cravath. On the positive side, several noted that they had not experienced any gender discrimination at the firm, and that women are treated as equals. One junior associate wrote, "You are left alone to do your job, to be a good lawyer. You don't have to worry about clothes, politics, gender, mentoring, etc." According to another associate, life at Cravath is "fun because the women who are here are typically strong-willed and not 'shrinking violet' types."

Several commented that, notwithstanding the scarcity of women at the firm, they believed that women do not feel excluded. A senior attorney wrote that Cravath is "far more gender-discrimination-free" than most other New York firms because "work is king, and men's and women's contributions are given equal weight." A litigator noted that she feels at home at the firm: "Of course, there will always be a few jerks anywhere. But on the few occasions when an attitude has offended me, I have felt free to express that." A corporate attorney agreed that there are "some male associates who are chauvinists, but that behavior is not at all encouraged or tolerated."

Several associates were considerably more critical of the tone set at the firm. In the opinion of one junior associate, "In spite of the efforts that this firm has made to make Cravath more gender-friendly, it is still overwhelmingly a male firm, both in terms of numbers and culture."

Another associate perceived that Cravath has difficulty both attracting and retaining women associates: "Cravath is such a lonely place for a woman—why would she want to stay? There is a real 'boys' club' atmosphere here." Another associate reported that, in her opinion, women must be "better than men" to get attention and even that "won't get you very far, unless, perhaps, you also play a mean game of golf." She said that, in her estimation, women are used to show how "progressive this stodgy old place is, but are never given any true access to power." In her estimation, "[Women] are never encouraged to go out and network or pal around with clients as some male associates are, [but rather are] trotted out during interview season to show that there may be few of us, but we're wonderful and happy to work here."

> *Maintaining a personal life requires a willingness to "fight for it and compromise some of your work for it."*

Balancing work & family/personal life: By all accounts, Cravath is an intense place, with long hours and demanding partners. Several associates observed that one can never make plans in advance and that, according to one respondent, "everything is subject to cancellation at the very last moment (and this happens more often than not)."

Because associates work for individual partners for extended periods, their ability to carve space for a personal life reportedly depends heavily on the attitude and flexibility of the partner to whom they are assigned. A corporate attorney stated that most are "sensitive if you say you have a family commitment (though you probably wouldn't want to bring it up too often)." Another corporate attorney said she has worked for partners "who have rich lives outside the firm and thus respect this desire in others, [as well as partners] with very little regard for the value of one's time outside the firm." In her experience, she said, the latter have been in the minority. Yet another corporate attorney reported that she has not found it difficult to work activities or engagements in, adding, "It might take some juggling and I might have to come back to the office or take work home, but we're certainly not chained to our desks."

Quite a few respondents agreed that maintaining a personal life requires, as one associate put it, a willingness to "fight for it and compromise some of your work for it." Another associate stated that, in her estimation, "[to complete work] perfectly (or near perfectly), I would have to be here many more hours than my marriage can afford."

Another associate contended that, in her opinion, the "mommy track" is "alive and well here at Cravath," which she believes means if you "become a 'mommy' [you won't] become a partner." One associate did note that colleagues reach out to help one another, and "overworked attorneys consistently say 'I'll take care of that' in order to free someone else up for a specific event."

Several associates expressed gratitude for the firm's on-site emergency childcare center. One noted that the center is available to provide full-time childcare for periods of up to three months.

> *Several corporate associates commented that part-time schedules are incompatible with the pace and nature of the work they do.*

Flexibility of work arrangements: Most respondents did not seem to regard part-time arrangements as practical. A litigator described part-time as not "an often-offered option," but reported that some senior associates do take advantage of it. "It works well for them and the work they get is still good," she remarked, but going part-time, in her opinion, "takes you out of partnership contention." One associate suggested that part-time typically entails three or four days per week, "but hours for those days are not limited." Another corporate attorney said that, in her estimation, part-time is feasible in the tax and trusts departments only, but that the firm is "receptive to proposals and definitely gets credit for trying." Another respondent commented that although, in her mind, there are limits to the type of work part-timers may do, several associates on reduced schedules "seem quite happy with their arrangements." According to a litigator, there are currently two women in her department who recently had children and have returned on a part-time basis and are still on partnership track. Despite this example, she surprisingly contended, "The chances of making partner under these circumstances are slim because of the inability to undertake partnership responsibility on a part-time status."

Several corporate associates commented that part-time schedules are incompatible with the pace and nature of the work they do. One respondent wrote, "My clients call up for crazy things at all times, new deals come in, and you have to travel on an instant." In the opinion of a junior associate, "Part-time is not an option at any level! The partnership track here is very set—up and out!"

> *"No one cares what you do on your own time."*

Diversity: Most associates wrote that because the environment at Cravath retains a single-minded focus on work to the exclusion of all else, personalities, backgrounds, and political leanings are largely irrelevant. One corporate attorney remarked, "It truly is a firm where the work comes first and foremost. Thus, one doesn't find incessant 'bonding' activities or focus groups." One associate wrote, "No one cares what you do on your own time." A litigator reported that the firm has "at least two openly gay partners, openly gay associates, outspoken Clinton, Dole, and even Perot supporters."

An associate observed that, in her opinion, Cravath "never discusses diversity. The most diverse this place gets is to recognize that if you're Jewish, you might be out on Yom Kippur." She added that, in her estimation, because the "standard attitude is still one of a WASP male [and people] fit fairly well into a mold, [those who] don't typically leave after they've paid off enough of their loans." Another associate reported that partners are "supportive of the homosexual associates—a few years ago one female associate married her female life partner. It was very open, many partners attended and [they] continue to be supportive of her."

Two associates maintained that Cravath's indifference to personalities and attitudes has not, in their opinions, contributed much to ethnic and racial diversity. One asserted that there are no minority women partners and "very few minority men, too." Another said that, in her opinion, diversity "does not exist here at Cravath—check your NALP form." (We did—there is one African-American partner and six other African-American attorneys. There are also five Hispanic and 14 Asian/Pacific Islander attorneys.)

Most associates reported that the firm's women partners are well-respected for their abilities.

Women in leadership positions: With only six women partners out of 72—and two of them having been promoted very recently—respondents not surprisingly reported that women do not hold significant power within Cravath. In one lawyer's opinion, no women hold any of "the few figurehead positions that exist."

Yet women partners received pretty high marks. One associate praised a woman tax partner as "wonderful, in that she focuses on and supports women's issues," by holding occasional dinners, and "helps get firm money to sponsor tables at things like the annual breakfast for the New York Women's Agenda." A senior attorney wrote that all of the women partners are "concerned about the future advancement possibilities for women at the firm and are valuable mentors."

Most associates reported that the firm's women partners are well-respected for their abilities. However, in one respondent's opinion, "These women were

promoted in order for Cravath to remedy the perception that it is a 'man's' firm and not because of their merit." Another associate vehemently disagreed, writing that no one perceives the women partners as tokens.

Cravath, Swaine & Moore No. of Responses: 15	Strongly agree	Agree	Disagree	Strongly disagree
Women's prospects for advancement at the firm are as strong as men's	4	7	2	2
I am satisfied with the firm's family and personal leave policies	5	7	1	
There are women in positions of power and influence in the firm	1	5	5	3
Women are as likely as men to receive desirable work assignments	8	4	2	
Women attorneys feel they can discuss family obligations openly	2	6	4	3
Women are as likely as men to be mentored by senior attorneys	3	6	3	3
Women attorneys enjoy a high level of job satisfaction	1	5	4	2
Women in the firm are supportive of their women colleagues	4	8	3	
Firm management is receptive to the concerns of women attorneys	3	8	1	1

CROWELL & MORING LLP

Rating: 29

◄◄◄

Crowell & Moring LLP
1001 Pennsylvania Ave. NW
Washington, DC 20004
202-624-2500

No. of Attorneys: 209
No. of Women Attorneys: 66
No. of Partners: 79
No. of Women Partners: 10
No. of Survey Responses Received: 14

Respondent Profile: 5 partners, 7 associates, and 2 counsel responded. Practice areas included government contracts, health care, environmental, and litigation.

Summary: Crowell & Moring, a relaxed and young firm, is guided by a spirit that values time outside the office and supports lawyers who are trying to balance work and family. Despite this attitude, the firm is reportedly still coming to grips with part-time work, and going part-time is perceived by some to hurt one's chances for advancement. Crowell is said to be unwaveringly committed to diversifying its work force.

Advancement: A substantial majority believed women's prospects are excellent, though several described obstacles they perceived might still make it difficult for some women to reach their potential.

In one associate's opinion, "The partnership prospects for both men and women are not as good as they once were—the firm is simply making fewer partners [in part] because it's a very 'young' firm, and they can't make too many partners without becoming top-heavy."

Most respondents gave Crowell high marks on mentoring and distribution of assignments, and attributed any shortcomings to external factors, such as women's life-style choices or natural mentoring relationships that spring up among men. One counsel remarked, "In terms of allocation of 'choice' assignments and review criteria, women are on par with men." And one partner confirmed, the firm is "gender-neutral in terms of advancement/partnership opportunities. The reality, however, is that a lot more men than women have made the life-style compromises necessary to move into partnership consideration over the years."

Advancement criteria, another partner reported, include "mentoring (either male or female), lots of smarts, drive and determination, and to some degree, luck of the draw in group and assignment staffing."

Several respondents, however, perceived that friendships and mentoring relationships tend to occur more frequently along gender lines. One respondent suggested that this is a product of "natural tendencies to be more comfortable (and less concerned about possible perception problems) around those of the same sex."

A couple of junior associates expressed satisfaction with the quality of their own mentoring. According to one, mentoring at Crowell comes in "three forms—an assigned mentor who is an associate, unofficial mentors, and professional development advisers." She noted that her male professional development adviser "has been wonderful—encouraging me to switch practice groups, talk to folks about work I'm interested in, etc."

Another said that she had had "some great assignments and experiences," and been given "mentoring-type feedback" from numerous attorneys.

One senior associate's opinion was decidedly more negative: "Women are not as likely to advance" within the firm. To change this perception, in her opinion, there would "need to be a change in the male partners' attitudes towards women."

The firm and its partners are relatively young, and thus "accustomed to women professionals."

Attitudes and atmosphere: Most respondents described Crowell as a relaxed firm where lawyers value having a life outside the office. Gender discrimination is unheard of, and a first-year associate said, "The firm leadership would not tolerate it if any were pointed out." According to a junior associate, "Everyone seems very relaxed and friendly," and there is "a comfortable level of social interaction, e.g., going for ice cream in the afternoon spontaneously with a group of mixed—male/female—associates." The firm and its partners are relatively young, and thus "accustomed to women

professionals," as one put it. Recent classes of associates have included large numbers of women, and, according to several partners, they have created a positive and supportive environment for one another.

A partner observed that, in her experience, Crowell is as comfortable "as any traditionally male-dominated, hardcharging workplace could be. The attorneys are not discriminators; I've had more issues, over the years, with clients."

One partner acknowledged that, in her estimation, "assignments to women are not always the 'plum cases'" in some practice groups. And in the opinion of an associate, "[There are] individuals here who don't respect women or make this a comfortable work environment, [but] we probably have fewer 'bad apples' here than most other firms."

The emphasis is on "your work, not whether you're seen late at night or on weekends."

Balancing work & family/personal life: The firm's partners appear to be a mixed bag when it comes to sensitivity to family and other outside responsibilities. One partner concluded that it is "difficult for anyone" to juggle their personal life with the demands of the firm, and that this is "a universal problem driven in part by the nature of the work," and by what she described as "inflexible, outmoded attitudes." An unmarried junior litigation associate reported that the firm's working hours are "pretty reasonable" and that "face time" is not required. According to another associate, "Attorneys can and do occasionally telecommute. Many male lawyers have 'no weekend' policies for themselves that make it easier for women to assert their needs for family time without raising eyebrows." Yet another noted, the emphasis is on "your work, not whether you're seen late at night or on weekends."

Achieving a balance is perceived to be substantially more difficult for those with kids. One senior attorney said that she "rarely mentions family commitments as a reason for being unable to make a firm commitment. I try to downplay that role." An associate reported that the firm "appears to bend over backwards to accommodate" those with family obligations, but another associate maintained that, in her opinion, partners "often do not respect the pressure put on women to keep a sane and productive professional life while on-call to be a good parent."

One respondent, who is also a mother, gave Crowell high marks for the flexibility it has offered her. She reported, "As long as I work a 60-percent-type schedule, I believe I am 'off' the partnership track, but this suits me fine and seems equitable as well." She concluded that she has been practicing "long enough [and] know[s] enough women at other firms" to say that Crowell is probably the best in this arena.

Part-time is "getting pretty commonplace and widely used, particularly by attorneys who are mothers."

Flexibility of work arrangements: Crowell is, according to one partner, "struggling" with issues surrounding part-time work, although part-time is "getting pretty commonplace and widely used, particularly by attorneys who are mothers." Several attorneys reported that the firm has recently introduced a formal part-time policy, which one partner described as "fair, if not overly generous." She added that this new policy "will permit associates to routinely opt for part-time status." One partner stated that, in her opinion, the policy does not apply to partners.

A respondent who is on a part-time schedule had nothing but praise for her arrangement: "[My] (largely male) colleagues could not be more supportive... They are unfailingly supportive and flexible about my schedule (and I try to be flexible in return)."

By some accounts, however, part-time is perceived to be the "kiss of death" from an advancement perspective, even for those who work part-time for a year or two before returning to a full schedule. A partner stated that, in her estimation, "no part-time attorneys have joined the partnership ranks." One associate with children remarked that while the firm gives what she called "lip service" to part-time and other alternatives, she believes she has been discouraged from taking advantage of such arrangements "because it is perceived as a lack of commitment." In the opinion of a partner, part-time arrangements are "viewed as a necessary evil and hold back career progression significantly." A junior associate, reflecting this belief, cynically remarked that part-time seems to be perceived as a "temporary measure to facilitate retention, rather than a profitable option for the firm."

A midlevel associate expressed her concern that the firm "frowns" on part-time work. Another associate suggested, "Part-time associates miss out on some of the more challenging assignments because of a perception that they can't be counted on to come through in a pinch."

Crowell reportedly has one part-time partner who is the mother of an infant, but most respondents perceived that the firm is generally unreceptive to part-time at partnership level. In one associate's estimation, the firm is "floundering on how to handle the issue [and] clearly does not want part-time partners." One partner commented that although part-time is, in her experience, "not officially available" to partners, "the reality is that partners have more autonomy and flexibility to arrange their schedules to accommodate alternative demands." Another partner stated that, in her opinion, the firm's failure to relax the "rule requiring partners to be full-time [is due] mostly to financial realities."

The firm does a decent job of trying to make a diverse group of lawyers feel at home.

Diversity: Most respondents concluded that the firm does a decent job of trying to make a diverse group of lawyers feel at home. One senior associate wrote, "[The firm] makes extraordinary efforts to recruit attorneys from diverse backgrounds—not only people of color and different ethnic and religious backgrounds, but also people with differing sexual orientation."

Inroads into the partnership are being made, according to one partner, who reported that there are two African-American female partners and one Hispanic female counsel at the firm. She added that Crowell has committees that work to "assure support for and exposure of all women attorneys to leaders in

the firm." The women partners are also said to focus, as a group, on supporting individuals and influencing the firm to address diversity concerns. One respondent, who described herself as a minority, remarked that Crowell "has taken a firm commitment on diversity issues. It [isn't] looking for cookie-cutter attorneys."

An associate noted that the firm is "not a politically driven place." Another associate described Crowell as "a lot more liberal than many other big firms." One attorney maintained that, in her opinion, "if there are any aspects of the 'politically correct' agenda that one does not subscribe to, one would not necessarily feel free to express that here." One partner noted that the firm has had openly gay attorneys, "including lesbians who seem to feel comfortable about bringing partners to events."

One partner reported that Crowell was the first D.C. firm with more than 200 lawyers to have a woman as management committee chair.

Women in leadership positions: A few select senior women do apparently hold positions of real power at Crowell, and most notably, the firm recently had a woman partner heading up its management committee. One partner reported that Crowell was the first D.C. firm with more than 200 lawyers to have a woman as management committee chair. According to an associate, this woman was a lateral partner who joined the firm from a high-level government position. This partner recently "rotated off" the committee and, according to the associate, "it remains to be seen whether this

---

was an isolated incident, or the beginning of a trend."

There are several other women who hold high posts at Crowell, including heads of the recruiting and the diversity committees. These women are apparently "key players in attracting and retaining strong women lawyers."

Respondents gave mixed reviews to the level of interest shown by the firm's women partners in the well-being of female associates. One partner wrote that the women partners meet monthly to discuss issues of shared concern, and

another described her fellow women partners as "effective and tireless advocates for all women in the firm."

In one attorney's estimation, "Perhaps as a result of being so busy, the female partners do not seem to go out of their way to encourage and mentor younger women and, in fact, often seem unapproachable/distant." A colleague also perceived that several of the partners "do not really make themselves notice[able]— i.e., hide behind office doors and do little to encourage female associates."

Crowell & Moring No. of Responses: 14	Strongly agree	Agree	Disagree	Strongly disagree
Women's prospects for advancement at the firm are as strong as men's	3	8	1	2
I am satisfied with the firm's family and personal leave policies	3	11		
There are women in positions of power and influence in the firm	4	10		
Women are as likely as men to receive desirable work assignments	8	4	1	
Women attorneys feel they can discuss family obligations openly	3	5	6	
Women are as likely as men to be mentored by senior attorneys	5	4	3	1
Women attorneys enjoy a high level of job satisfaction		8	4	
Women in the firm are supportive of their women colleagues	9	5		
Firm management is receptive to the concerns of women attorneys	1	9	2	1

DAVIS POLK & WARDWELL

Rating: 37

◤ ◤ ◤

Davis Polk & Wardwell
450 Lexington Ave.
New York, NY 10017
212-450-4000

No. of Attorneys: 427
No. of Women Attorneys: 186
No. of Partners: 113
No. of Women Partners: 17
No. of Survey Responses Received: 7

Respondent Profile: 3 partners, 3 associates, and 1 counsel responded. Practice areas included litigation, corporate, tax, and mergers and acquisitions.

Summary: Davis, Polk, described by one partner as a white-shoe firm without a "boys' club" atmosphere, provides women with relatively favorable opportunities for promotion and fosters a collegial atmosphere. Respondents were noticeably split about the influence of the firm's top women lawyers and whether balancing work and family life was doable or difficult. The firm's part-time policy, lauded by partners, is considered fairly liberal for a large New York firm, although not all associates perceived it as practical.

Advancement: Davis, Polk & Wardwell reportedly has an impressive record for promoting women. While all three partners were optimistic, two of the three associates were not.

According to one partner, women are just as likely to advance "if they stay the seven- to eight-year course," although many "self-select out of the process." The firm, she reported, has promoted 36 attorneys to partner during the past four years, 12 of whom are women. This year, the firm reportedly elected four new women partners out of a total of 11. She added that a recent *American Lawyer* survey ranked the firm fifth out of the 249 largest firms in the country for its overall percentage of women attorneys (38 percent), which was "the highest ranking for any major New York law firm by a considerable margin."

A corporate partner wrote that prospects for women at the firm are excellent, "aided by our part-time program, which permits women to stay at the firm while raising children and then, upon return to full-time, they may be promoted."

In one partner's opinion, women can succeed "so long as they are willing and able to devote the same level of effort and show the same level of commitment as men." Nevertheless, it is "harder for women to find mentors than it is for men," in her view, although she noted that a mentor relationship is not essential for advancement if women have "broad support from the partners in their practice area." She also contended that despite the evenhandedness with which attorneys are evaluated, she believed that the review "criteria and the overall value system of the firm continues to be one that is typically associated with male characteristics (toughness, strength, commitment to work and the firm, lack of emotionalism, etc.)." Although the firm is "gradually coming to accept that there might be more than one way to achieve a desired result," she predicted this transformation would be a slow process.

Some associates suggested that advancement prospects vary dramatically depending upon practice area. "Women in the litigation department do not advance to partner," one senior litigator averred. (A spokesperson for Davis, Polk confirmed that they have made two women litigation partners in the past five years, one in 1994, the other in 1997.) An associate asserted that, in her estimation, "women senior associates are not treated as colleagues by the partners, whereas men senior associates are." Another said that women are at a disadvantage because she perceived they "are not given the better assignments, particularly at the junior level." She further stated that, in her opinion, "women who want a shot at becoming partners should wait to have children until after they are up for partner."

Respondents from the corporate department reported a much higher likelihood of advancement. One lawyer dryly viewed the factors central to advancement as "working 24 hours a day, never mentioning any personal obstacles that might interfere with working 24 hours a day, being very smart, and being politically astute." In the tax department, prospects for women "are equal (or even perhaps marginally better) than men, provided they are willing to work as hard (no part-time or reduced hours)," according to a senior associate.

> *"From top to bottom, everyone believes and knows that women are equally capable."*

Attitudes and atmosphere: The firm is described as a very comfortable environment for women. According to a partner, "This is an old white-shoe firm, but I never felt that there was an old 'boys' club.' " Another partner agreed: "I have never felt excluded or uncomfortable. From top to bottom, everyone believes and knows that women are equally capable." According to a corporate partner, the firm is particularly comfortable for women associates. She reported that gender "discrimination or harassment are not problems."

According to associates, the firm is generally comfortable for most women, although it is perceived that certain groups of women can have a rough time. One lawyer commented that "there doesn't seem to be a 'boys' club'; assignments are 'sex blind'; everyone is overburdened." The only difficulty arises, she speculated, "when you are pregnant, because it restricts your ability to work 24 hours per day and travel." Also, upon return from maternity leave, women seem to be punished by being given huge amounts of work that often involve distant travel."

> *There is the perception of "a distorted sense of pride among some with regard to how little they let family distract them."*

Balancing work & family/personal life: Respondents concluded that this is difficult but doable, provided you need little sleep and can bring your analytical skills to bear on complicated scheduling problems. Billables reportedly average 2,000 hours, and the firm offers backup childcare to lawyers and staff.

One lawyer described the experience of a partner who decided to rearrange her workday while still working full-time after her first child was born. She came in at 8 a.m. instead of 9.30 a.m. and left at 6 p.m., unless it was critical to stay. This attorney reported she has maintained the schedule ever since, including the year she was up for partnership. She took five-month maternity leaves with each of her two children and was promoted to partner after returning from her second maternity leave.

A litigation associate commented that it is almost impossible for women attorneys to have a meaningful family life and observed that the husband of the one woman litigation partner who has children does not work outside the home. A corporate attorney said, "[The] good news is that there are a lot of working 'mommies' at the firm, and more and more of them gradually are advancing to partnership. Moreover, the 'moms' generally are mutually supportive of each other."

On the downside, in her opinion, "The firm is not particularly sensitive to family responsibilities," as suggested by lawyers who "will speak supportively but then hold it against a lawyer if *he* or *she* seems too devoted to family or unable to keep family from interfering with work." There is the perception of "a distorted sense of pride among some with regard to how little they let family distract them."

"[Some partners] become annoyed, for example, when associates who work only three days a week are not in the office when the partner is looking for them."

Flexibility of work arrangements: Part-time is reportedly available at the associate but not the partner level. For associates, part-time options are said to be viable and legitimate and, according to a partner, a few men have gone part-time, although "not for child-rearing reasons."

One partner characterized compensation as equitable, but other respondents perceived that, in many departments, part-time status becomes "full-time work for part-time pay." According to a partner, the only restrictions on the type of available work arrangements "are those imposed by the need to satisfy client demands (e.g. in transactional work one can't disappear for days off in the middle of a negotiation)." Part-timers are perceived by most to be "off track" for partnership until they return to full-time schedules but, according to a couple of partners, "some women have made partner after working part-time."

The unavailability of part-time options at partnership level was described as "unfortunate" by one partner, and an associate commented that, in her estimation, the policy has led to the existence of "a group of women senior attorneys who will never make partner."

Notwithstanding the fact that the firm's part-time policy is relatively liberal for a major New York firm, some associates viewed Davis, Polk's part-time options as unworkable. One respondent observed that "such arrangements are available in theory but only at a very senior level. In practice, part-time associates are expected to work many more hours than they are scheduled to." She added that despite the firm's general accommodation of part-time schedules, it was her fear that some partners are often not very sensitive to this and "become annoyed, for example, when associates who work only three days a week are not in the office when the partner is looking for them."

Another associate said it was her opinion that part-time status can "result in less desirable assignments depending on the area of practice and the willingness of the person to be flexible in terms of when she/he works (i.e., mergers and acquisitions deals sometimes require very late nights)."

According to a partner, the firm makes a "significant effort" to recruit minorities and diversity is "never discouraged."

Diversity: In the eyes of several respondents, the firm means well when it comes to diversity, but one associate wrote that, in her opinion, there is "not a supportive environment." According to a partner, the firm makes a "significant effort" to recruit minorities and diversity is "never discouraged." Another partner commented that what attracted her to the firm as a law student "is what still attracts me today—the people. We have a broad range of personalities, backgrounds, outside interests and life styles, both male and female." She added that the firm has formed a Personal Relations Committee to address "any issues that may arise relating to our work environment and getting along as a work family."

"To the extent women partners are on committees, they are 'women's' committees like training and personnel relations."

Women in leadership positions: Respondents perceive that women at Davis, Polk have not yet attained what they consider positions of genuine power. Women partners take part in firm committees but "are not in the real leadership positions," as one partner put it. Another partner commented that 17 women partners "is still too few, but a formidable number." An associate wrote that in her estimation, "To the extent women partners are on committees, they are 'women's' committees like training and personnel relations." Another associate believes that the problem lies in the fact that women partners tend to be younger than their male counterparts, and that women have less time to take on added responsibilities. She characterized the problem as "structural—this is a full-time commitment (and I mean *full-time*) and this is very difficult to reconcile with raising a family."

According to an associate, the influential women in the firm, though respected, "if they have children, have generally worked full-time and expect everyone else to do the same. Part-time opportunities were often not available when they were associates, and they feel no need to accommodate others."

Davis, Polk & Wardwell No. of Responses: 7	Strongly agree	Agree	Disagree	Strongly disagree
Women's prospects for advancement at the firm are as strong as men's	3	1	1	1
I am satisfied with the firm's family and personal leave policies	3	1	2	1
There are women in positions of power and influence in the firm	1	3	3	
Women are as likely as men to receive desirable work assignments	5	1	1	
Women attorneys feel they can discuss family obligations openly	2	1	3	1
Women are as likely as men to be mentored by senior attorneys	2	2	1	1
Women attorneys enjoy a high level of job satisfaction	2	3	1	
Women in the firm are supportive of their women colleagues	3	3	1	
Firm management is receptive to the concerns of women attorneys	3	1	3	

DAVIS WRIGHT TREMAINE

Rating: 9

Davis Wright Tremaine
2600 Century Square
1501 Fourth Ave.
Seattle, WA 98101
206-622-3150

No. of Attorneys: 131
No. of Women Attorneys: 43
No. of Partners: 79
No. of Women Partners: 15
No. of Survey Responses Received: 5

Respondent Profile: 2 partners and 3 associates responded. Practice areas included litigation, health care, and corporate.

Summary: Our handful of respondents were almost uniformly positive. They reported that the partnership doors of Davis Wright are open to women lawyers who demonstrate excellent legal skills and the potential to drum up clients. The firm also offers women a supportive and tolerant environment and a free-market assignment system that, by one account, works to the benefit of women associates by enabling them to dodge those partners who are work-obsessed. As for part-time, Davis Wright seems to have come a long way, although clients are said to be a stumbling block.

Advancement: Respondents are unanimous that women are as likely to advance as men, providing they have the right stuff, including client development potential.

According to one partner, what matters at Davis Wright is "excellence as a lawyer and either development of new clients or demonstration of a propensity to develop new clients (or new matters from existing clients)."

Another partner commented that a lawyer's dedication alone is not enough, and that client development potential depends in large measure on having mentors who provide counseling about practice development, training, and "sources of work that build solid, profitable practices."

One associate disagreed with the majority view that Davis Wright is a meritocracy, observing that women succeed *despite*, rather than because of, the opportunities provided by the firm. She also expressed her concern that "we have closet misogynists in our midst, but I have yet to see this kill the advancement of a skilled, dedicated woman lawyer."

According to a senior associate, although women who "submit their names for partnership consideration" are as likely to advance as men, in her estimation, "more women than men withdraw their names from consideration and continue on as senior associates." Attrition occurs, in part, because Seattle lawyers are sheltered from the pressures facing women attorneys in larger, more traditional legal markets and may have escape hatches that are more appealing than those available in New York or Chicago.

According to one partner, attrition occurs "where individuals (be they men or women) make personal life choices regarding the amount of time and energy they wish to devote to practicing law and the availability of positions in hours which may be perceived as offering better opportunities (and stock options, such as Microsoft)."

In the opinion of a senior associate, although many women leave to spend more time with their families, "just as many leave because they are not willing or interested in dealing with the ego-laden, hypercompetitive performance-driven political world of a private law firm."

According to one partner, Davis Wright isn't a perfect firm, but it is "one of the most comfortable that I have encountered or heard about."

....

Attitudes and atmosphere: Davis Wright rated highly as a work environment for women, and firm management is given a great deal of the credit. The leadership evidently recognizes that having more women rainmakers will benefit everyone and has taken active steps to bring this about. According to one partner, Davis Wright isn't a perfect firm, but it is "one of the most comfortable that I have encountered or heard about."

Firm leadership, she continued, is *very* supportive of women and, indeed, includes quite a few women. The firm reportedly sponsored a development retreat for female attorneys and is said to be supportive of equality.

A senior litigation associate commented that, although she works in a predominantly male department, she has had no problems she would characterize as gender-related. She reported that support and mentoring are good, and that the firm makes a conscious effort to attract more women to join, as evidenced by the fact that last year's summer associate class consisted of eight women and one man. She added that there is a "sizable group of women who meet from time to time, firm-wide, to brainstorm about women as rainmakers."

According to another associate, with women in top posts both within the firm and as clients, the firm is as comfortable for female attorneys as for males. The women at Davis Wright, she added, are "well aware of how well men are able to network among themselves, and the firm has sponsored activities for the women to focus on developing their own networking abilities."

Another associate agreed with the positive sentiments, writing that her male colleagues treat her as an individual and that she has "heard no inappropriate comments or seen any inappropriate behavior." Her sole complaint, she said, was that the firm "occasionally values a person's billable worth over his [or her] value as a mentor and teacher."

The only exception to women's warm feelings for the firm related to the occasional social event. According to an associate, "Many of the firm events are sports-related." A partner agreed, speculating that although firm social activities are designed to appeal to all, "because of the interest in golf by many male partners, associates interested in golf may have a social advantage. More male associates seem interested in that sport."

> **Many senior partners "encourage their associates not to live only for their careers."**

Balancing work & family/personal life: Four of the five respondents commented almost identically, noting that, although the firm is sensitive to family responsibilities, clients—"the ultimate arbiters of success in a private practice," as one partner described them—are not. The respondents added that balancing is no tougher for women than for men, "except when it comes to childcare." Inevitably, it is "a struggle for all lawyers" and "sometimes you have to make hard choices," in the words of one partner.

One associate offered more telling details, commenting that, in her estimation, there are "inconsiderate louts" at Davis Wright, but that associates can "discover who they are and walk away from them." She reported that the firm offers associates "supreme flexibility," insofar as they are not assigned to particular departments and can seek work wherever they want.

Many senior partners, she added, understand the importance of family and "encourage their associates not to live only for their careers." Such partners find associate assistance easier to come by, and the less enlightened are left "combing the halls for help."

Another associate said that, in her experience, sensitivity "varies so much from practice group to practice group." While philosophically the firm supports life-style choices, the billables requirement of 1,800 and the pressure to produce high-quality work quickly can take their toll. She added, however, that many attorneys simply hit, rather than

surpass, the 1,800 target "without negative results."

> **The firm reportedly permits part-time for either gender for any reason. One associate reported, "Many have gone part-time merely for a slower-paced life style."**

Flexibility of work arrangements: According to one respondent, the firm has "come a *long* way" with respect to part-time options. There are reportedly a large number of both male and female part-time attorneys, including a few working at partnership level. One respondent nevertheless claimed that, in her experience, no part-time associates have applied for partnership, and she believed "there is doubt about whether the criteria would appropriately be adjusted."

The majority had a far more positive outlook. One part-time attorney wrote that she was "encouraged to continue to work toward partnership, even as a part-timer." And a partner commented that the firm's attitude is quite flexible, and that there appears to be no stigma attached to part-time status.

The firm reportedly permits part-time for either gender for any reason, although most part-timers are mothers. One associate reported, "Many have gone part-time merely for a slower-paced life style."

Part-time has been used at the partnership level, though not widely. One respondent wrote that it was her impression that partners who take advantage of part-time generally shift, by choice, from equity to contract status. One partner, who said she had worked part-time for a year as a partner, admitted that the arrangement "presents challenges, not from the perspective of the firm's attitude but, simply, from the perspective that managing large client accounts is difficult to do on a part-time basis." A senior associate said she was concerned because of her perception that "part-timers take a larger than appropriate pay cut."

The firm has only a few minority attorneys.

Diversity: Davis, Wright has apparently not succeeded in creating a diverse work force, despite many attempts. The firm has only a few minority attorneys.

One associate commented that she would "blame societal forces before I blamed the firm" for the lack of diversity. Another associate agreed that the absence of male or female people of color at the attorney level is "not a deliberate act by the firm. There are simply fewer and fewer candidates spread among all the large firms." Recruitment, she concluded, "needs to occur at the law school level." According to one partner, although the firm has "a recognition of the need for diversity," it was her perception that they had "no plan to obtain greater diversity."

As far as politics are concerned, the firm has a "pretty high commitment" to diversity and "the two leading political parties are both well-represented," according to an associate.

"Real power is epitomized by substantial client responsibility. Only a few women begin to reach the levels of the most powerful male lawyers."

Women in leadership positions: Although nearly half of the firm's executive committee, which governs the firm's 12 offices, consists of women, and women chair several key departments, this does not equal true power, in the estimation of one partner. She commented that women sit in high managerial posts, but, in her opinion, "real power is epitomized by substantial client responsibility. Only a few women begin to reach the levels of the most powerful male lawyers."

According to associates, the firm's more influential women vary with respect to their interest in more junior women attorneys. One associate reported that some women partners do promote opportunities for female associates, "but gender issues are not a real problem for young women lawyers."

Another associate commented that she perceived the senior women "rightly or wrongly, as somewhat cold," and as not having done much to change the firm. She speculated, "It is due to the battles they have fought to get here that they are not as nurturing as I would wish." She commented, however, that by contrast, the younger women in the firm "though strong and competent, also feel free to mentor and be themselves."

Davis Wright Tremaine No. of Responses: 5	Strongly agree	Agree	Disagree	Strongly disagree
Women's prospects for advancement at the firm are as strong as men's	2	3		
I am satisfied with the firm's family and personal leave policies	2	3		
There are women in positions of power and influence in the firm	4	1		
Women are as likely as men to receive desirable work assignments	2	2	1	
Women attorneys feel they can discuss family obligations openly	1	2	2	
Women are as likely as men to be mentored by senior attorneys	2	1	1	
Women attorneys enjoy a high level of job satisfaction		5		
Women in the firm are supportive of their women colleagues	4	1		
Firm management is receptive to the concerns of women attorneys	3	2		

DEBEVOISE & PLIMPTON

Rating: 26

Debevoise & Plimpton
875 Third Ave.
New York, NY 10022
212-909-6000

No. of Attorneys: 312
No. of Women Attorneys: 104
No. of Partners: 80
No. of Women Partners: 7
No. of Survey Responses Received: 16

Respondent Profile: 2 partners and 14 associates responded. Practice areas included corporate and litigation; a substantial number of respondents did not identify their practice areas.

Summary: Debevoise & Plimpton, a comfortable and liberal firm according to respondents, distinguishes itself by providing a formal mentoring program and a viable part-time policy. Both partners and most associates were uniformly positive. Nevertheless, it's perceived that women associates leave in droves at the senior level, resulting in only a handful of influential women partners.

Advancement: "There is a noticeable dearth of women in the senior and even midlevel associate ranks—and, obviously, among the partners," as one associate observed. A new associate wrote, in her estimation, "The utter lack of women in the partnership ranks makes career advancement for women seem dismal."

For those who stay, opportunities are reported by the vast majority (both partners and 10 of 14 associates) to be equal. One partner described central factors for partnership as "talent, ability to bring in business, dedication, and practice area." The firm has a formal mentoring system that several respondents applauded. It is aimed to facilitate "a more nurturing and personal relationship between partners and associates," as one described it. One partner wrote that she had a mentor from her first year on and still does. She further commented,

"Reviews, discussions of career development, and work assignments are handled in a gender-neutral manner."

Four associates disagreed. One associate said that, in her estimation, "more men are 'groomed' for partnership than women." A litigator observed that women in her department do not make partner, because women either leave or become counsel. A litigation associate reported that she knew of few experienced attorneys "who do not have one or two mentors." One corporate associate, however, complained that she felt there is no "consistent mentoring of women."

According to a partner, the firm's leadership "sets a strong egalitarian standard and has been an important speaker for the advancement of women and others at the firm."

Attitudes and atmosphere: Most characterized Debevoise as a very genteel firm, populated by generally sensitive men, with no traces of gender discrimination. The atmosphere is hospitable in most respects, according to one litigator who reported that "no skirts or jackets required, no confusion of attorneys with support staff, no harassment or sexism." A midlevel litigator reported that the partners "openly discuss and try to foster a nurturing environment for women." Another reported that she has never felt that women are "excluded from either social or business opportunities." According to a partner, the firm's leadership "sets a strong egalitarian standard and has been an important speaker for the advancement of women and others at the firm."

The atmosphere is by no means perfect to all. One partner wrote that there remain "a couple of dinosaurs who tell dirty jokes." In one litigator's opinion, men seem better able than women "to master D & P's passive-aggressive management style (i.e., giving unclear orders, then criticizing others' failure to follow them)." A junior associate commented that at team meetings, she has witnessed "inappropriate remarks delivered to women by male senior associates." Although she admitted that these remarks were delivered behind a "veil of humor," she perceived the humor to be "feigned and the remarks hostile." Another associate observed that some partners are "wonderful people for women to work with," yet others are "just not comfortable with women attorneys and make this clear through remarks and behavior."

> *One respondent wrote that she had "never dealt with nonsense like 'face time'" and that many people work from home for a variety of reasons.*

Balancing work & family/personal life: Maintaining a personal life while working at Debevoise is seemingly easier than at many other large New York firms. Although the hours are long, most respondents reported that they were able to strike some balance, and that the firm shows respect for family commitments. An associate noted that although the corporate and litigation departments are "notorious" for demanding long hours, the tax area offers "far more predictable work and less laborious projects." One respondent wrote that she had "never dealt with nonsense like 'face time'" and that many people work from home for a variety of reasons.

One junior associate recounted an occasion in which the firm flew the husband of an associate, who was on a long-term, out-of-town assignment, to see her on weekends when she could not return home. Another corporate lawyer wrote that the firm takes a pro-family approach and provides emergency childcare.

One lawyer tried to explain how she viewed the balance: "I think you need to view your child as a demanding and important client or else you can always come up with reasons that you need to work on your days off. Sometimes, the only way to stay home is to just do it, as if your 'client-child' had a multimillion dollar deal closing that day." She finds the firm "exceptionally sensitive" to family responsibilities.

Some respondents, however, were less optimistic about the ability to maintain a satisfying balance, particularly those lawyers who are single and childless. Several lawyers commented that the personal lives of single people are more easily imposed upon, and that they "don't really have what's considered a good reason for saying 'no' to work." A corporate associate perceived that the firm's "rhetoric about how the partnership wants people to have the ability to spend time with their spouses and children...can make people without [spouses or children] start to wonder whether their reasons are considered equal." The result is that, in her opinion, work at the firm can have "a devastating effect on your personal life" if you are single.

"It helps if when you are introduced as part-time, the partner reminds the client and opposing counsel of your schedule and covers for you when necessary."

Flexibility of work arrangements: The majority of respondents rated the firm's part-time policy favorably, but noted that it may be practical only in certain practice areas. Part-timers must be careful to police their arrangements, according to one associate, because, in her experience, "unless you are quite firm about your hours (and have the support of a partner who can back you up on this), people will continue to dump more work on you than anyone could ever handle on a part-time basis."

One partner reported that several women partners at the firm work part-time, as do "approximately 20 associates (including one man)." She added that the part-time plan has some very good features including "comp pay or time if hours exceed a certain percentage over the firm average for the prior six months, and advancement to partner even though part-time." She concluded that the program, for her, "has been superb; for others, they have continued to work too much."

Several respondents remarked on the feasibility of part-time within specific practice groups. One corporate associate observed that, in her opinion, no women had been "entirely successful in accommodating the demands of a transactional practice within the part-time program." A partner disagreed, reporting that the firm's three women part-time partners are all mergers and acquisitions lawyers, which she sees as "evidence that it's possible to have a very exciting career and fulfilling family life."

One corporate associate observed, "It helps if when you are introduced as part-time, the partner reminds the client and opposing counsel of your schedule and covers for you when necessary." Another corporate associate stated, however, that as far as she knew, "partners seem unwilling to 'confess' to a client that a woman lawyer on the team is a part-timer."

Several respondents commented that part-time is not seen as an impediment to partnership. One senior associate remarked, however, that she would "have faith in the part-time program when [more] men take advantage of it." One associate wrote that, in her assessment, there are partners who view part-timers as "less serious" than other associates, and "think that any woman could become pregnant (and therefore unavailable for work) at any time, without warning—

and therefore treat women generally as being less committed than men."

Finally, one partner commented on the availability and use of maternity and paternity leave. The firm offers at least 10 weeks paid disability leave, and two weeks paid parenting leave is available for both men and women.

"If you're from a minority background but went to the right schools and live in the same neighborhoods as the white male partners, you'll do fine..."

Diversity: Respondents perceived that there are few minorities in the more senior ranks at Debevoise, and that the women partners are "not a diverse group." One midlevel attorney wrote that the same is true in the associate ranks, and that "if you're from a minority background but went to the right schools and live in the same neighborhoods as the white male partners, you'll do fine. Other minority women might feel less comfortable." Another associate observed that the firm is "fairly white, though it's not happy about that fact, I think."

Respondents were divided as to the status of gay and lesbian attorneys in the firm. One associate wrote that "no one is openly gay or bisexual," whereas others wrote that there are several openly gay attorneys and that gay lawyers have brought their partners to social events. Two respondents noted that while gay men seem very welcome, they perceived, "it is not clear that the same is true for lesbians." Yet one respondent who identified herself as a lesbian commented that she has "never felt a moment of discomfort" at the firm, which is

"markedly different from my experience at another firm."

One associate wrote, "Political correctness is the mode of communication." She added, "It's not just that same-sex domestic partners [have been] covered by the firm's health benefits for several years, but that people would be absolutely *shocked* if that weren't the case." Nevertheless, one partner said that the firm is "pretty liberal politically, but it's mostly apolitical."

There are a handful of powerful women at Debevoise & Plimpton, and at least one, a part-time partner, is reported to wield real clout.

Women in leadership positions: There are a handful of powerful women at Debevoise & Plimpton, and at least one, a part-time partner, is reported to wield real clout. One associate described her as a "powerhouse lawyer and rainmaker" and declared she was "certainly perceived as one of the most powerful partners here, regardless of sex."

Several other respondents reported that there are three or four powerful women partners at Debevoise. Apparently, no women currently sit on its management committee, although there are reportedly women on most other committees. One litigation associate noted that, in her view, "firm governance is kept such a mystery, I don't know who's on the 'power' committees."

Reviews were mixed on the attitude of senior women partners toward their female underlings. Respondents reported that some take their mentoring seriously, but others are reported to be uninterested in mentoring "or even identifying with women associates at all." One associate noted that some partners "had a hard time as associates and seem to think all women following in their footsteps should have an equally difficult road." One corporate associate wrote that the junior attorneys in the firm perceive the women partners as "having made extraordinary personal sacrifices for a goal (partnership) that just doesn't seem worth it."

Debevoise & Plimpton No. of Responses: 16	Strongly agree	Agree	Disagree	Strongly disagree
Women's prospects for advancement at the firm are as strong as men's	5	7	4	
I am satisfied with the firm's family and personal leave policies	8	4	2	1
There are women in positions of power and influence in the firm	4	11		
Women are as likely as men to receive desirable work assignments	7	7	2	
Women attorneys feel they can discuss family obligations openly	1	8	3	
Women are as likely as men to be mentored by senior attorneys	7	4	4	
Women attorneys enjoy a high level of job satisfaction	1	7	4	2
Women in the firm are supportive of their women colleagues	3	12	1	
Firm management is receptive to the concerns of women attorneys	5	8	1	

DECHERT PRICE & RHOADS

Rating: 4

🪓🪓🪓🪓🪓

Dechert Price & Rhoads
4000 Bell Atlantic Tower
1717 Arch St.
Philadelphia, PA 19103
215-994-4000

No. of Attorneys: 236
No. of Women Attorneys: 58
No. of Partners: 84
No. of Women Partners: 11
No. of Survey Responses Received: 10

Respondent Profile: 3 partners and 7 associates responded. Practice areas included litigation and mergers and acquisitions.

Summary: Prospective women litigators should rush their resumes to Dechert, Price & Rhoads, which boasts a litigation department with numerous women partners, an inclusive and supportive environment, and women clients to boot. Regrettably, the firm has apparently yet to replicate these excellent conditions in its mergers and acquisitions department, in which senior women are scarce and part-time arrangements are described as unworkable.

Advancement: Respondents were unanimously positive in their assessment of women's chances for advancement at Dechert, though they also agreed it is a grueling trek.

Several respondents commented that women can advance in step with men, "if they have the same traits as those men who are successful here," as one respondent put it. This demands, as an associate put it, "a willingness to be completely devoted to work at the expense of family and, for women in particular, putting off having children until after partnership." A partner commented, "Women are as likely as men to advance to partnership—if they want to stick around long enough."

The partnership track is reportedly eight years long, and there is a concern that many women are unable or unwilling to put family life on hold for the duration. Those who are "good enough to be on partnership track," according to an associate, "tend to get loaded up with so much work, they have no time for personal life." Many women find it too demanding and not worth the sacrifices involved.

Those who choose to take time off, work part-time, or limit their full-time hours in order to spend time with their children may weaken their prospects for partnership. As a result, an associate observed, "there is a fairly high level of attrition after the fifth year." Most women who leave the firm are said to become corporate counsels where they work substantially lighter hours. Those who go the distance "tend to be very ambitious and hard-working."

All respondents expressed satisfaction with the quality of the assignments they have received, and most associates said they were easily able to forge relationships with partners at the firm.

One litigation associate reported that women associates receive "the same mentoring opportunities as their male counterparts and are as likely to receive good assignments." Review criteria, she further noted, are "always fair."

A midlevel litigator agreed that she has "experienced nothing to make me believe that my partnership prospects are diminished because I am a woman." A senior associate commented that she has "a great mentor who has helped me develop tremendously as a lawyer" and that the assignments she receives "are as challenging if not more so than those the men in the group receive."

Factors central to advancement, according to a partner, are "excellence of lawyering skills, people skills, and potential for growth." A midlevel litigation associate observed that advancement hinges on work quality, hours, ability to bring in and retain clients, and relationships with peers.

> **Assignments "are as challenging if not more so than those the men in the group receive."**

Attitudes and atmosphere: Because of the numbers of women partners and women in leadership positions in the litigation department, the firm as a whole is described as a comfortable place for women by many of the respondents, though not unanimously. An associate reported, "There are a number of women in firm leadership roles (both official and unofficial) and, as a result, I think the atmosphere is very comfortable." She added that many of the firm's clients are women. Several respondents reported that they had never experienced any gender discrimination whatsoever.

Despite what one associate described as "some inhibition on both sides," a few partners "make efforts to be friendly to the women (including them in lunch groups, etc.) [and] working interactions are generally very good—egalitarian." A litigation associate reported that she has been treated "with courtesy and respect by male partners, and as an equal by male associates." Another litigator remarked that she is "asked quite often to participate in social activities with senior attorneys and clients, whether they are men or women."

Because the prominent women at the firm are heavily concentrated in the litigation department, not everyone believes that their influence necessarily pervades the entire firm. A respondent from the corporate department commented that she believes there are "groups of men who have formed a 'boys' club.'" Despite some respondents' assertions to the contrary, Dechert confirmed that the business team in the Philadelphia office includes three women (with an additional five in other offices).

> **Dechert is "tops in reasonableness of hours."**

Balancing work & family/personal life: Most respondents rated the firm more accommodating than most. An associate who has children reported that she has succeeded in maintaining a "manageable work life," working most days from 9 to 6, leaving evenings and weekends for her family. A midlevel litigator wrote that despite long hours and work pressure, she has never had to give up "an important day or weekend or other piece of time for firm business." She added that she occasionally works from home and "both male and female attorneys take advantage of this flexibility as needed."

Another associate opined that sustaining a balance is doable and that the firm is "tops in reasonableness of hours." A litigator without children noted that she has time for a personal life and that the "work is demanding and the hours are long, but not unreasonable." The firm also reportedly offers subsidized emergency childcare assistance.

Though family obligations are respected, Dechert, Price & Rhoads continues to stress the importance of hours, according to respondents. A senior associate commented, "People don't make it only on merit/talent—hours do count." She added that the firm's management is "very bottom-line conscious." Another associate commented, "Both men and women work equally hard so we're all equally exhausted by end of the week."

The pressures are reportedly most acute in the corporate group. A corporate associate expressed concern that "a woman who has a child [might be] devalued as a lawyer here unless she proves herself by sacrificing family for work."

Yet partners described the firm as a wonderful place for women attorneys to enjoy both family and career. One partner with a child reported that men leave "openly to go to their children's plays [and] softball games, too."

Another partner opined that although free time is in short supply,

"Dechert is as sensitive as any big law firm to these issues."

"No one—associate or partner—who has requested part-time has been refused."

Flexibility of work arrangements: Part-time options are alive and well at the firm, and most respondents said they were pleased by the firm's alternative work arrangements. Attorneys can work at 60- to 90-percent schedules. An associate said that a colleague worked part-time after having a child and frequently worked from home when her child was ill. She asserted that this was "totally acceptable to both the partners for whom [my friend] worked and [her] clients who knew they could call [her] at home." She now works full-time, but has "the flexibility to change to part-time and can work at home when necessary (assuming [she's] not in the middle of a trial)."

A litigation associate reported that she works three days a week and that partners have been "very supportive." According to a partner, "No one—associate or partner—who has requested part-time has been refused." She added that at any given time, seven to 19 lawyers may be working part-time.

Part-time, according to several associates, seems to work for people in every practice group except mergers and acquisitions. A respondent agreed, characterizing the party line on part-time as, "It is acceptable, but it takes you off partnership track." She perceived the view of part-time as "an accommodation to a 'formerly' valuable employee with the hope and expectation that the employee will return to complete dedication to the firm and become valuable again."

Part-time is apparently available at partnership level, although several respondents perceived that associates cannot make partner while working part-time. One partner reportedly has successfully worked part-time for more than two years and continued to be the partner in charge of many interesting, challenging litigation representations.

The conclusion seems to be that although part-time does not necessarily impede partnership, some associates believe it can cause considerable delay.

> *"If I were a woman of color, I probably would not feel extraordinarily comfortable here because there are very few women of color here."*

Diversity: The firm is reportedly very open to attorneys with diverse personalities and political leanings but has few minority lawyers. According to a partner, "There is no Dechert 'type' " and the firm has handled some "politically controversial litigation cases *pro bono*—e.g., opposing pro-lifers blockading abortion clinics with full tolerance by the firm." An associate observed that the firm "tries to develop people as attorneys based on their own personalities—rather than trying to change personalities. The attorneys with whom I work have helped me develop in a way that takes advantage of my personality (I am quiet and reserved—I have learned how to put this to my advantage)."

Another associate remarked that there are "people who work on high-profile women's legal issues, people who ride motorcycles to work, people who own farms."

Nevertheless, not all respondents expressed satisfaction with the firm's level of diversity. One associate suggested, "If I were a woman of color, I probably would not feel extraordinarily comfortable here because there are very few women of color here." She added that, although she is unaware of racism at the firm, in her estimation, "we probably could do a better job recruiting people of color to work here." The firm lacks a "critical mass" of minority attorneys necessary to draw others, she noted.

Another associate agreed that the firm is "not a particularly diverse place" and that although Dechert attorneys would not "do anything to make someone uncomfortable," nonetheless, "the lack of people with diverse backgrounds and beliefs seems to keep us from attracting diversity to begin with."

> *Some women have worked to establish part-time options, emergency day care, and a relaxed dress code.*

Women in leadership positions: Respondents cited several examples of prominent women at Dechert: Women sit on the firm's policy committee, a woman chairs the hiring committee, and women are co-chairs of several practice groups. In addition, some women have apparently played key roles in promoting opportunities and quality of life for other women, such as working to establish part-time options, emergency day care, and a relaxed dress code.

One partner observed that several women have acted "in a very significant, aggressive way" to make the firm more hospitable to women.

The women at the top are also generally respected. The hiring partner, according to one associate, "plays an invaluable role in helping women develop as lawyers."

Another associate reported that there is "one female partner with real power, and she is very supportive of other women," but added, "I wish there were more."

The one dissenter expressed a less hopeful view: "The most powerful woman here is a single woman with no children who is completely dedicated to work. There is little to no mentoring or role models."

Dechert, Price & Rhoads No. of Responses: 10	Strongly agree	Agree	Disagree	Strongly disagree
Women's prospects for advancement at the firm are as strong as men's	7	3		
I am satisfied with the firm's family and personal leave policies	7	2	1	
There are women in positions of power and influence in the firm	7	2	1	
Women are as likely as men to receive desirable work assignments	8	2		
Women attorneys feel they can discuss family obligations openly	3	6	1	
Women are as likely as men to be mentored by senior attorneys	6	2	1	
Women attorneys enjoy a high level of job satisfaction	4	6		
Women in the firm are supportive of their women colleagues	6	3	1	
Firm management is receptive to the concerns of women attorneys	1	9		

DEWEY BALLANTINE

Rating: 58

Dewey Ballantine
1301 Avenue of the Americas
New York, NY 10019
212-259-8000

No. of Attorneys: 287
No. of Women Attorneys: 97
No. of Partners: 84
No. of Women Partners: 10
No. of Survey Responses Received: 15

Respondent Profile: 1 partner and 14 associates responded. Practice areas included corporate, litigation, environmental, tax, and trusts and estates.

Summary: Dewey Ballantine generally offers women a pleasant work environment and supports diversity among its lawyers, but being a mother and working in the associate ranks at the firm is perceived by some to be an uphill battle (unless one joins the trusts and estates or environmental group, where hours are reportedly more reasonable). Even if opportunities to advance are gender-neutral, as reported by several associates, some were concerned the free-market mentoring system may leave women adrift.

Advancement: Respondents were somewhat divided on whether women enjoy prospects for advancement equal to those of men, though a distinct majority answered positively. The sole partner who responded wrote, "Women are as likely to make partner as men. In fact, this year more women made partner than men." Several other respondents also commented that women have advanced at Dewey Ballantine in recent years, and that chances are as good for women as for men, assuming that the individual is willing to make personal sacrifices. Many expressed a fear that having children poses a serious obstacle to progressing at Dewey Ballantine.

A minority of women, however, viewed women's partnership chances as poor. According to one senior associate's opinion, "Women are definitely less likely to advance to partnership. [Dewey Ballantine] is still very male-dominated. The few women partners at the firm do not mentor other women and don't seem to care to help other women." A midlevel associate predicted, "Women are less likely to stay long-term because there appears to be little opportunity at the top."

Several women reported difficulties finding mentors at Dewey Ballantine. One associate observed, "I don't know whether there is simply no mentoring here or whether it's just women who don't get mentored—but, personally, I have not received any mentoring." A corporate attorney said that although the picture is improving for women, in her perception, "the inability of some male partners to be able to view women as 'one of the boys' and the double standard regarding behavior—men get angry, women panic or get hysterical—still exists."

Opportunities for advancement are worse in litigation, in the estimation of one associate: "The partners in litigation pick 'pets'—these happen to be people with whom they have the most in common. Since most partners are men, most 'pets' are men." Noting that it is possible for women to form close connections with male partners, another associate, nevertheless, pointed out that "the two senior-most female litigators just left."

The trusts and estates department appears to be a different kettle of fish. A junior associate wrote that women there are mentored and are likely to advance.

> *One associate suggested that "paternalistic/sexist attitudes" sometimes come from older partners, "but more typically from clients."*

Attitudes and atmosphere: Most respondents were pleased with the atmosphere, with one junior associate characterizing the firm as "gender-friendly." A corporate associate wrote that the firm is "comfortable for all who do their job. We operate as a group, not individuals." Associates in the environmental, tax, and trusts and estates departments indicated that they were extremely comfortable, which they attributed to the substantial number of women attorneys in their respective practice areas.

Five respondents reported problems, however. One said that although the firm is probably as comfortable as any in New York, it remains a "boys' club." Another remarked that differential treatment, in her estimation, is subtle in that people

"simply judge men's and women's behavior differently, both in terms of reactions to job situations...as well as failing to acknowledge that women may relate to clients differently but not necessarily less effectively than men." One senior attorney wrote that, in her opinion, there is "still a fair amount of [poor treatment] that makes it uncomfortable at DB for women."

According to one associate, "There is a 'boys' network' here." She suggested that "paternalistic/sexist attitudes" sometimes come from older partners, "but more typically from clients." Another associate's opinion was more pointed: "What affects women the most...is the 'boys' club,' " including "the golf-playing, cigar-smoking, strip-joint-going bonding among males, men [reacting to] a strong woman they find threatening to their manhood..."

> *"The expectation is that associates should give everything to the firm, particularly if they have any interest in partnership."*

Balancing work & family/personal life: Although the one partner respondent maintained that the firm is "generally quite sensitive to your outside life," most associates disagreed. One commented that finding a balance is "very difficult. The hours and pressure make it almost unbearable." Another reported that most associates bill 2,000 hours per year. Several associates indicated that one's ability to sustain an outside life varies tremendously by practice group, with the environmental and trusts and estates departments being much more flexible and supportive than others in the firm. One lawyer reported that by avoiding the corporate and litigation departments, she works 9 a.m. to 8 p.m. on a "regular day," has dinner with her husband, and does not come into the office most weekends. Further, she added, when she had to take days off because of family illness, there was support.

According to one midlevel associate, striking a balance is impossible and "the expectation is that associates should give everything to the firm, particularly if they have any interest in partnership." A respondent who works part-time said things are marginally better for her, but, "I get calls in the evening, on weekends, and on my day home for which I am not paid. No one at DB knows, or believes, I am part-time. Working hours are long (10- to 12-hour days) and I am still under a lot of pressure to get through my workload."

A married junior associate observed, "Women seem afraid to make it visible that family life is a concern for them," and added that, in her opinion, the problem is "really a combination of the firm not being true to its apparent sensitivity and women not wanting to risk the consequences, real or imagined, of being open about their needs."

One corporate lawyer was relatively positive, stating that "at least the people I work with are cognizant of the fact that we all have responsibilities outside the firm."

"If your ultimate goal is not partnership," working part-time "is a very attractive option."

Flexibility of work arrangements: Part-time arrangements are available for associates at Dewey Ballantine,

although some perceived that their use is not encouraged. According to the one partner who responded, although part-time and flextime are available, "as the associate ranks near 50/50 (men to women), if every woman were to take advantage of these arrangements, the firm would grind to a halt on Friday." She added, "The firm has been so accommodating to part-time that at times in some departments it has become difficult for those not on part-time to cover for all the part-time lawyers."

One associate who is on a part-time schedule wrote that her arrangement has worked out well, that she has time with her family, and that her work "has not suffered." Another part-timer's experience was less positive—she observed that while working part-time she was "definitely treated like a second-class citizen by the partners and not taken as seriously." Part-time, in her estimation, "automatically takes you off partnership track. I have billed more hours than some of my full-time colleagues, only to have to plead for fair compensation."

A senior associate expressed her concern that going part-time means that one "cannot be placed on major matters" and thus, "prospects for advancement become very limited." She added, however, "If your ultimate goal is not partnership," working part-time "is a very attractive option." A midlevel associate agreed that, in her opinion, although a part-time policy exists, "in practice it is discouraged, and the women who use it generally end up leaving."

Several associates reported that Dewey Ballantine provides emergency childcare services on the weekends.

> **"DB is okay, not particularly supportive...but definitely it is a place where one can have her own beliefs, life style, etc."**

Diversity: Most respondents gave high marks to the firm's commitment to diversity. A first-year associate wrote that her entering class "was very diverse, with two openly gay men, two Asian associates, an African-American associate and an Indian associate." Another associate wrote that there are "many minorities" at the associate level.

According to a corporate associate, "DB is okay, not particularly supportive... but definitely it is a place where one can have her own beliefs, life style, etc." According to a senior associate, the firm hires women of diverse political, religious and ethnic backgrounds. A minority respondent wrote that her "color or culture was not an issue."

According to an associate in a smaller department, "It is difficult to encourage diversity in a conservative/commercial/corporate law firm, which tends to attract a certain type of person." Still, she concluded, Dewey Ballantine is "on the whole a pretty tolerant place (within certain bounds)."

> **"The women who are partners... have no real power. They tend to be male-like, dress-wise and personality-wise. They don't foster any mentoring for women at DB."**

Women in leadership positions: Most respondents perceived that women do not hold the reins at Dewey Ballantine. According to one associate, "There are women who are respected because they are truly brilliant (and probably smarter than many male partners), but I would not say they are powerful. Power at a big firm comes from a strong client base, and most women partners just do not have that." The partner respondent observed that although there are no women on the firm's management committee, most members of the committee have practiced law for more than 25 years. She explained: "There simply has not been an abundance of women in the practice of law until quite recently. 'Real power' generally comes after years of practicing."

One lawyer noted that although more women have been promoted to partnership recently, in her estimation, none are "visibly powerful."

In the opinion of a senior associate, "The women who are partners...have no *real* power. They tend to be male-like, dress-wise and personality-wise. They don't foster any mentoring for women at DB." A corporate associate disagreed, saying that "several of the more senior women of the firm head departments and are widely respected."

The firm's women partners got mixed reviews with respect to their willingness to lend a hand to younger lawyers. According to a midlevel associate's viewpoint, the women partners do not take an active interest in mentoring women associates or assisting them with career issues: "It seems most women here—at all levels—try to pretend there's no difference for women in matters of day-to-day work, career planning, business-social functions, and family life concerns. The atmosphere is not conducive to seeking women mentors for these types of issues."

Another associate recounted, "As one partner put it, 'I made the choice (between work and family) and so must you.' The perception is that women of the 1990s have it too easy and expect too much without the struggle/fight."

A dissenter from the corporate department wrote that women partners are "supportive of those women more junior to them in terms of providing advice and guidance."

Dewey Ballantine No. of Responses: 15	Strongly agree	Agree	Disagree	Strongly disagree
Women's prospects for advancement at the firm are as strong as men's	3	5	3	1
I am satisfied with the firm's family and personal leave policies	3	4	5	2
There are women in positions of power and influence in the firm	3	4	3	4
Women are as likely as men to receive desirable work assignments	6	7		1
Women attorneys feel they can discuss family obligations openly	1	6	6	2
Women are as likely as men to be mentored by senior attorneys	4	5	2	3
Women attorneys enjoy a high level of job satisfaction	3	4	5	2
Women in the firm are supportive of their women colleagues	4	7	2	1
Firm management is receptive to the concerns of women attorneys	3	5	4	2

DICKSTEIN SHAPIRO MORIN & OSHINSKY .

Rating: 56

**Dickstein Shapiro Morin
& Oshinsky**

2101 L St. NW
Washington, DC 20037
202-785-9700

No. of Attorneys: 219
No. of Women Attorneys: 55
No. of Partners: 92
No. of Women Partners: 10
No. of Survey Responses Received: 24

Respondent Profile: 7 partners, 15 associates, and 2 counsel responded. Practice areas included litigation and subdepartments of litigation, though many respondents did not identify their practice area.

Summary: Dickstein seems to be a firm in transition, with some old-school aspects and some attempts at serious reform. To its credit, the firm has recently adopted a very progressive part-time policy and a job-sharing arrangement. On the downside, respondents fear that politics infects partnership decisions, to the perceived detriment of women candidates, and a large majority (including four of six partners) suggested that senior women had little power or influence.

Advancement: With one claiming that advancement is "extremely rare" for attorneys of either gender, a relatively large majority of respondents believe that women's chances for advancement are poorer than those of men. A partner stated that, in her opinion, "[in] any close case, women lose" and in "decisions about women, the relative importance of the criterion where she is weakest increases." Many associates perceived that the availability of partnership slots at Dickstein hinges on the vibrancy of the practice area and its prospects for growth, hours, rainmaking potential, and on having tight connections with influential partners.

Showing an optimism shared by a few junior associates, one first-year associate wrote that Dickstein sponsors "a wonderful mentoring program" and that she has found her colleagues "extremely accessible and easy to communicate with." Her assignments, she wrote, "have been as diversified and as challenging as I would want," and review criteria are unbiased.

A litigator declared that, in her opinion, "Two women who were widely acclaimed to be superior lawyers were passed over for advancement, while arguably less-qualified men (who happened to be supported by political heavy hitters) were promoted."

Another associate echoed these sentiments, reporting that one year two men and a woman were up for partner at the firm. The woman who was up for partner "had very positive reviews for her entire career, [a] significant amount of business, demonstrated potential for more rainmaking capabilities," and had billed hours commensurate to the two male candidates. By her account, the two men made partner and the woman did not. In this respondent's opinion, "None of the explanations can alter the undeniable fact that, for *whatever* reason, male candidates who are up continue to be more likely to make it than female candidates who are up."

It is "a rougher road" for women for a variety of reasons, respondents maintained. For one thing, there is a concern that "male partners tend to mentor males rather than females," although one senior associate had observed some "encouraging exceptions" to this trend. An associate wrote that, in her opinion, "attractive women are more likely to be mentored than unattractive women." A partner commented, "Business generation is a big part of advancement, and women tend to generate less business at our firm," but she remarked that she thought men and women fared similarly in terms of mentoring, allocation of assignments, review criteria, and reasons for attrition.

Several associates said that the firm has opened its eyes and established a gender and quality of life committee and that progress is predicted.

Attitudes and atmosphere: More so than most other firms, Dickstein is divided into sections, each of which is perceived to have its own norms and tone. Some are reported to be very comfortable for women, others not so. Overall, the firm is said to have given a great deal of attention to addressing problems faced by women during the past year.

One associate wrote that, in her estimation, as a result of the first *Presumed Equal* survey, "in which Dickstein did rather poorly, [some] significant changes have occurred here." The firm leadership, "with encouragement from the women partners, who in turn, were approached by several women associates," reportedly conducted a firm-wide survey on gender and quality-of-life issues. As a result, a series of recommendations were made, and Dickstein is seeking to improve in various areas, including the provision of emergency day care. In this associate's opinion, the survey also brought to light "that pressure [to achieve] high billable hours contributed to significant dissatisfaction among most attorneys" and that attorneys on an alternative schedule were "considered less respected." She claimed that, as a result, the firm has modified its part-time policy.

Although everyone agrees that women's comfort levels vary by department, there was disagreement about which sections are most and least hospitable. An associate wrote that, although her section is "dominated by males," she has "always felt that this firm was a very comfortable place to work." Yet her colleague wrote, "I would not recommend the IP section to the classmate who stole my 2L paper." A junior corporate associate said that her section is "generally supportive and friendly." But she added that, although one can succeed without being a white male who plays golf and smokes cigars, in her opinion, "it does make life easier if you have these attributes." A senior associate characterized the male leadership in her section as setting an example "based on a very stereotypical macho culture that emphasizes extraordinarily high billable hours and forbids any sign of weakness."

A litigator said that the firm is comfortable for those who are "confident, outgoing, and have a sense of humor. Mild-mannered, shy, demure men or women do not fare as well here."

A partner wrote that while her (unnamed) section is "great," the firm's men seem to be "more comfortable with one another overall" and that, in her opinion, the firm's leadership is "definitely from the 'good old boys' club.'"

Another partner thinks Dickstein is a great place to work, despite what she characterized as "some jerks," and that any "manifestations or incidents of [poor treatment of women] are a product of a few individuals, not the firm culture."

"You must buck a lot of peer pressure as well as management's expectations to succeed" at balancing work and personal life.

Balancing work & family/personal life: The firm's traditional emphasis on billable hours takes a heavy toll on attorneys' personal lives, although some say that with the advent of a new part-time policy and other innovations, change is in the works. "The predominate atmosphere remains, however, that billable hours matter most, at least for younger associates—and this is especially true in certain sections," according to one associate. She recounted that in her section, associates are told their billable budget once a month and that "the pressure to stay at or above the budget is overwhelming."

Another associate remarked, "You must buck *a lot* of peer pressure as well as management's expectations to succeed" at balancing work and personal life. In contrast, a partner commented that the firm is as sensitive as any to family responsibilities, and that it is common for men as well as women to request that meetings be pushed back to enable lawyers to take their children to day care or tend to other family obligations. According to an associate, the firm is wonderful in responding to family and personal crises and shows great understanding and support.

As one associate put it, Dickstein "is no longer an 'up-or-out' firm."

Flexibility of work arrangements: The firm has a very new, very progressive part-time policy, and respondents ranged from wildly enthusiastic to cautiously optimistic about how well it will work. According to some, the policy is "one of the most advanced ever seen," and was even described as "amazing" by one respondent. Under the policy, one can be made a partner with as little as a 50-percent load of hours, "although the track will be longer depending on the length of the arrangement," in the belief of one respondent. The policy also includes the creation of a position for an "advisor" whose role is "to help make all such arrangements successful and to open a dialogue if anyone is experiencing a problem." The plan also includes emergency day care.

In addition, the firm has introduced job-sharing arrangements. One senior associate explained that the firm has two part-time options: "part-time on track" and "part-time off track." In her opinion, the former entails a reduced schedule and salary, but the lawyer's schedule must remain flexible, "so that if the firm needs you, you are expected to be available." Those who opt to go off track are not expected to have the same flexibility, "a *great* option for those who choose it."

A litigator commented that she hoped the new policy would "overcome the past stigma associated with part-time attorneys." An associate, however, wrote, "Personally, I'm skeptical—it smacks more of P.R. than substance." One lawyer wrote, "[I have] always been treated fairly and my flexibility needs have always been addressed."

A partner reported that Dickstein has two part-time partners, and that one became partner with her class after working an 80-percent schedule for most of her time with the firm. Her arrangement has always worked well and "been respected" by the firm. As one associate put it, Dickstein "is no longer an 'up-or-out' firm" and "this is a great benefit to those associates, male and female, who want to maintain a challenging legal career, but do not want to sacrifice all (or even most) of their life to the career."

"The firm's efforts to achieve racial diversity have not been successful enough yet."

Diversity: Most respondents indicated that Dickstein has made an attempt to recruit minority lawyers, but according to one partner, "The firm's efforts to achieve racial diversity have not been successful enough yet." In an associate's opinion, "Two black female [associates] and one black contract attorney along with approximately six other minority

women (male minorities are low, too) is too small of a number for any firm anywhere, [but] particularly in D.C." She added that the firm "does recruit heavily," but wishes that the numbers were higher. One associate wrote, "Huh? Check our statistics. We have few attorneys, male or female, with 'diverse backgrounds.'" (According to the 1997-1998 National Directory of Legal Employers, Dickstein has five African-American, three Hispanic, one American Indian/Alaskan, and six Asian/Pacific Islander attorneys.)

The firm is reported to be "liberal" and heavily Democratic "with a few closet Republicans and even fewer open Republicans." One associate noted that, in her opinion, the firm likes women who are "good sports and not too feminist."

"Rainmaking ability equals power, and there are no real women rainmakers."

Women in leadership positions: An overwhelming majority of respondents (including four of the six partners) perceived that women are not powerful leaders at Dickstein, at least partly because, in their opinion, power comes with the ability to generate business, something women at the firm sorely lack. As one put it, "Rainmaking ability equals power, and there are no real women rainmakers." Although two women will reportedly be assigned to sit on the firm's executive committee, the woman who already occupies a seat was viewed by one associate as a "token," and there are evidently no women on the compensation committee.

A senior associate wrote, in her opinion, "When a real decision has to be made, the women either don't have enough political capital or are not willing to expend the political capital necessary to actively create the opportunities." One associate contended that, in her opinion, the women partners have been "relatively passive and have not actively promoted opportunities and quality of life for other women attorneys— *until* last year's survey portrayed the firm in such a negative light." In her estimation, "Once the (overwhelmingly male) partnership became concerned about the bad PR, they blessed efforts of the women partners to address some of the concerns raised."

Dickstein, Shapiro, Morin & Oshinsky No. of Responses: 24	Strongly agree	Agree	Disagree	Strongly disagree
Women's prospects for advancement at the firm are as strong as men's	5	4	13	
I am satisfied with the firm's family and personal leave policies	8	14		
There are women in positions of power and influence in the firm		6	13	3
Women are as likely as men to receive desirable work assignments	5	13	3	
Women attorneys feel they can discuss family obligations openly	5	7	9	1
Women are as likely as men to be mentored by senior attorneys	3	4	7	8
Women attorneys enjoy a high level of job satisfaction	1	10	9	2
Women in the firm are supportive of their women colleagues	4	13	5	
Firm management is receptive to the concerns of women attorneys	7	13	2	

DUANE, MORRIS & HECKSCHER

Rating: 17

◄◄◄◄

Duane, Morris & Heckscher
4200 One Liberty Place
Philadelphia, PA 19103
215-979-1000

No. of Attorneys: 153
No. of Women Attorneys: 38
No. of Partners: 69
No. of Women Partners: 14
No. of Survey Responses Received: 10

Respondent Profile: 4 partners and 6 associates responded. Practice areas included litigation and the reorganization and finance group.

Summary: Although partners were almost uniformly positive, associates were divided about Duane's atmosphere, family and personal leave policies, and the support they receive from senior women. Although Duane insists that its lawyers take adequate personal time, associates did not perceive its part-time options as practical, not surprising since partners expressed a lukewarm attitude toward part-time work. Respondents were virtually unanimous in their belief that women's prospects for advancement are positive.

Advancement: All four partners who responded maintained that women enjoy bright prospects for advancement, as did six of the seven associates.

According to a litigation partner, although women may find it slightly more difficult to attain partnership, Duane treats women fairly, and women receive challenging assignments, equal opportunities for mentoring, and "are judged rigorously on the same criteria."

Another partner described key factors for advancement as "quality of work, keeping existing clients happy/satisfied, enhancing business, involvement in firm activities, and other factors."

And a third partner wrote that the firm "rewards results, diligence, intelligence, and loyalty."

Although a large majority of associates appeared to agree, some added caveats. According to a litigation associate, "Women who don't mind playing by the men's rules have equal advancement opportunities [as] men. However, many women don't want to—and shouldn't have to."

One senior associate observed that women can advance apace with men only "if they have no children or choose to allow others to raise them," while they work "full + time." She claimed that, in her estimation, the firm "needs to make changes...because many women are *leaving*" Duane.

Another associate predicted that despite the firm's relatively large percentage of women partners, as women opt to go part-time to raise children, "this number will drastically decline" because, in her experience, part-time work, "no matter for how many years, disqualifies you from partnership track."

"Issues such as dress and all-male clubs went away in the 70s and haven't been an issue in the 90s."

Attitudes and atmosphere: Here again, partners' and associates' observations sometimes contradicted each other. Partners asserted that the firm is bias-free, and associates reported a less-than-supportive environment. According to a partner, because women have been at the firm for 25 years, "issues such as dress and all-male clubs went away in the 70s and haven't been an issue in the 90s." She characterized the firm's tone as "fair and unbiased in all possible areas."

Another partner agreed, hailing the firm as a great place to work and asserted that she has never experienced gender discrimination. Another partner commented that despite "lots of golf," the firm has "been amenable to financing nonsport client entertainment" such as trips to museums and the orchestra. And a litigation partner wrote, "During my years as an associate, partners, on several occasions, went out of their way to convince a few clients who were skeptical of 'female attorneys' to have one handle the matters."

Some associates were less effusive. One reported that, in her perception, the head of a major department "is [opposed to] women developing 'women's niche' business, which, in my opinion, is the wave of the future." According to a midlevel associate, although social and professional interactions between men and women are positive, there were "a few Neanderthals." But she stressed

that Duane "doesn't tolerate...gender discrimination."

One junior associate expressed a greater level of comfort, commenting that it was one of the factors that drew her to the firm. She characterized her male colleagues as friendly and the men in the litigation department as fairly sensitive.

"[Although the firm is] a pretty good place to try and balance work and family, it would be nice if 'face time' counted less than it does!"

Balancing work & family/personal life: Although Duane refreshingly insists that its lawyers take adequate personal time, some associates perceived that the firm could do more to help working parents. Although a partner without children remarked that she found our question "offensive" on the grounds that family concerns affect men *and* women and the firm is sensitive to these issues. Duane, she declared, "provides extensive support to each individual who requests it."

An associate said that sustaining a personal life is difficult "because of billing concerns, marketing, and the endless details," and maintained that, in her opinion, attorneys who work part-time go off partnership track.

Another associate said that, in her estimation, the biggest impediment to sustaining work and family life is "the lack of support from the female partners" who, along with the firm as a whole, fail to "realize that there are certain family pressures put on working women that those male attorneys in the corner offices with the stay-at-home [wives] don't have." She predicted that, unless changes are implemented, the firm will continue to lose women associates to in-house positions. She also reported that although the firm is "a pretty good place to try and balance work and family, it would be nice if 'face time' counted less than it does!" On the upside, she applauded Duane for providing the computer software necessary to enable people to work at home.

A senior associate declared that one of the firm's best attributes is that the "hierarchy insists on its lawyers taking adequate personal time." A junior associate noted approvingly that she has never "felt pressured to work weekends or extended hours—although I have done so at times, in order to complete assignments in a timely manner."

Several partners offered advice on how to cope with competing pressures that are extraordinary in magnitude. One noted that she has "always taken work home and recommend others do the same so they can leave the office regularly by 6 p.m." Another partner commented that she has found "the least stressful, although most expensive, way to manage an unpredictable work schedule and childcare is to have full-time childcare coverage (i.e., 12 hours a day) even though my child is in school. By eliminating or minimizing the stress, both work and personal time are more enjoyable."

One associate chided the women partners for not supporting the associates in making part-time arrangements easier to attain.

Flexibility of work arrangements: Part-time arrangements at Duane reportedly can be negotiated on a case-by-case basis. Many associates voiced dissatisfaction with their perception of part-time options. One respondent explained that, in her experience, those seeking part-time schedules are at the mercy of the partners for whom they work. As a result, "many women cannot predict whether they will be able to take advantage of a part-time schedule." This associate chided the women partners for not supporting the associates in making part-time arrangements easier to attain. Part-time, she added, has worked well in one department, "and hopefully other departments will look to that example and see that if approached in the right way, part-time schedules can be beneficial to the lawyer and the firm."

According to another associate, part-time options are available in every department except corporate. A spokesperson for Duane confirmed there are currently no part-timers in the corporate department, although there may have been in the past. Other associates perceived that those who go part-time are removed from partnership track, and, as one stated, "Incredibly, the firm gives *no* credit to part-time women for partnership." (The firm stated that there is no effect on partnership if a full-timer takes maternity leave and returns to full-time work, although returning part-time may affect partnership, depending on the attorney's seniority.) According to a junior associate, part-timers are "considered just as important and integral to the firm as full-time associates are."

The partner respondents expressed a lukewarm attitude toward part-time work. One commented that, in her experience, "because of the reality that part-time is less time, partnership is postponed." She added that part-time arrangements are difficult to monitor to keep everyone happy and there is a "great risk of the part-time lawyer feeling exploited." Another partner agreed that because "a client's needs and time deadlines are paramount, it can be difficult to manage part-time work arrangements." According to another partner, the absence of a firm part-time policy is, in her estimation, "purposeful," in that the firm wants to maintain flexibility.

There were some differences of opinion on whether partners may go part-time. According to several associates, there are no part-time partners at the firm. Yet, according to several partners, women in the partnership have in the past opted for part-time.

"The more traditionally feminine women are thought of more highly, which is unfair."

Diversity: Although responses to this question were skimpy, most respondents concluded that Duane is moving to increase diversity. According to a partner, "there is no cookie-cutter mold here" and the firm "prides itself in its attempt to hire from as many diverse backgrounds as possible." An associate agreed that the firm "genuinely wants people of different political leanings, ethnic backgrounds, and personalities," but commented that, in her opinion, "the more traditionally feminine women are thought of more highly, which is unfair." Another associate commented that although most women are treated equally irrespective of background or politics, there are "always going to be some partners who don't appreciate or approve of a feminist or liberal point of view."

According to one associate's opinion, "No one openly lives a diverse life style."

As far as race is concerned, another associate wrote that, in her estimation, the firm "tries, but cultural diversity at all large Philadelphia firms is just not terrific."

"As for mentoring and helping out female associates, well, the female partners seem to disappear into the background on those issues."

Women in leadership positions: Most departments include prominent, well-respected women partners, although some respondents maintained that women have yet to penetrate what they perceived to be the most elite corridors of power. As one partner explained, the firm is "managed by an executive committee and partners' board," and there are no women on the five-person executive committee. Women do take part in other committees and hold positions such as hiring chair, but again, as one associate claimed, the center of power is all male and, in her opinion, is unlikely to change any time soon.

One partner remarked that one of the "wonderful aspects of our firm is that we have almost four 'generations' of women: the early pioneers from the 70s; those who came in the early 80s and expanded on the achievements of the first women; those who came in the later 80s; and now those of the 90s. Each group has continued to assist those that follow and has moved the issues forward to the benefit of all."

The more influential women received mixed marks on their willingness to aid those beneath them in the ranks. According to one associate, "Women do promote women here, as do many of the senior men." A junior associate contended that some of the women partners have endeavored to get to know and offer support to women associates in the form of good assignments and advice. Another associate noted, "As for mentoring and helping out female associates, well, the female partners seem to disappear into the background on those issues." Yet another commented that although the women partners are well-received, she believed the firm "still has a ways to go in embracing women's different viewpoints and perspectives."

Duane, Morris & Heckscher No. of Responses: 10	Strongly agree	Agree	Disagree	Strongly disagree
Women's prospects for advancement at the firm are as strong as men's	4	5	1	
I am satisfied with the firm's family and personal leave policies	5		4	
There are women in positions of power and influence in the firm	4	4	1	
Women are as likely as men to receive desirable work assignments	8	1	1	
Women attorneys feel they can discuss family obligations openly	2	6	1	
Women are as likely as men to be mentored by senior attorneys	4	5	1	
Women attorneys enjoy a high level of job satisfaction	3	5	2	
Women in the firm are supportive of their women colleagues	4	3	2	1
Firm management is receptive to the concerns of women attorneys	4	3	2	

FAEGRE & BENSON LLP

Rating: 48

🔨🔨🔨

Faegre & Benson LLP
2200 Norwest Center
90 South 7th St.
Minneapolis, MN 55402
612-336-3000

No. of Attorneys: 220
No. of Women Attorneys: 52
No. of Partners: 134
No. of Women Partners: 19
No. of Survey Responses Received: 11

Respondent Profile: 5 partners and 6 associates responded. Respondents who identified their practice areas work in the intellectual property, litigation, and labor/employment departments.

Summary: The atmosphere at Faegre & Benson is "okay," though not "perfect," with some respondents attributing their discomfort to the low numbers of women. The higher a respondent's status, the more likely she felt Faegre offered equal opportunities for advancement. The firm's part-time policy is reported to be a work in progress.

Advancement: Partners and associates had distinctly different impressions of advancement opportunities at Faegre— four of the five partners were positive while associates were split down the middle.

During their first few years of practice, men and women progress equally, according to one associate. However, she wrote, "As attorneys become more senior and intangible criteria play a greater role in such prospects, women are disadvantaged." She also observed that women are less likely "to find good mentors within the firm or to be perceived as attorneys who will ultimately generate business." Another associate perceived that women are "less likely to be involved in the 'old boys' network,' which often leaves them out of marketing opportunities.

One partner wrote that single women and women without children "have every opportunity to advance to partnership that men do." Married women with children, she added, may be in the same position if they "do not take substantial leave, work part-time, or have a lot of childcare issues." This partner faulted women partners and senior associates for failing to "do a good job of mentoring" and added that her own mentors were men.

An employment law associate agreed that women are as likely to advance as men "as long as they do not decide to work part-time to raise children." She further noted that she has developed mentoring relationships "with more than one senior attorney, including two women," and that in her experience, assignments are allocated without regard to gender. Another associate commented that her experience has been "for women to be given more supportive roles (writing) and less up-front roles (trials)."

On a positive note, respondents report that women's advancement is apparently the focus of attention. According to a partner, the firm is now trying "various ways to improve retention," including "a formal mentoring program, marketing for and by women lawyers, and increased sensitivity to family-friendly policies." The results of these initiatives, she noted, "won't be apparent for several years." Another partner reported that the firm "is working to improve promotion." Nonetheless, she predicted that because "women are not in positions of power and there is not a critical mass of women in almost any group," instituting change may be difficult.

Virtually all respondents contended that women leave the firm in larger numbers than men, and attributed this primarily to family demands. An associate suggested that many women "appear to self-select themselves out of the process by taking in-house positions or otherwise leaving to do something different." One partner wrote that, in her opinion, "Historic pattern shows the firm needs to address retention of women."

The firm's management "wants to be sensitive and responsive, but some are completely clueless and others who really do understand the issues don't really know how to address them..."

Attitudes and atmosphere: The atmosphere is reportedly "okay," but not "perfect." Several respondents observed that they find the firm to be a hospitable place to work; others noted that because women are outnumbered, the environment can be unpleasant. According to

one partner's view, "There are still bastions of 'the boys' club' in the context of those who golf together, lunch together, drink together, but it isn't bad [enough] as to be uncomfortable." Although there are "certainly men here [who] live in the dark ages, they are fewer and fewer." Another partner sees "a need for 'sensitivity' training for male lawyers—young and old."

As to the firm's management, one partner observed that it "wants to be sensitive and responsive, but some are completely clueless and others who really do understand the issues don't really know how to address them. The issues are tough, they have to do with the very nature of large firm practice and women's values, which may be very different from men's—or at least from the men who are in power."

One associate commented that any discomfort stems from the low numbers of women. She described a recent experience in which a firm secretary assumed that she, too, was a secretary. "I had phoned someone to look for a fax without identifying myself. The woman at the fax center asked what attorney I was working for and was flustered when I said I was the attorney."

Another partner commented that the firm's atmosphere, though not without room for improvement, is comfortable and collegial, with an emphasis on "professionalism and mutual respect." According to a labor lawyer, her practice group contains roughly equal numbers of men and women. She wrote, "[It is] only when I attend larger, firm-wide functions that I notice I am a minority, and then it's only the visual impact of all the suits and ties, not the way I'm treated." One partner said that she has had "very positive experiences" and has "many close male and female friends in the firm."

> *"The firm is an okay place to work. It's a job—sometimes great, fulfilling, interesting—sometimes not great, unsatisfying, and boring..."*

Balancing work & family/personal life: Although Faegre reportedly does not demand singular devotion to the firm, maintaining a satisfying balance is by no means easy. One partner summed it up: "The firm is an okay place to work. It's a job—sometimes great, fulfilling, interesting—sometimes not great, unsatisfying, and boring. But the firm doesn't require crazy hours or that people live only for the firm." Another partner wrote, "People in the Midwest value quality of life," and the firm, although demanding, has "reasonable, realistic expectations."

According to another partner, being a "top-notch woman lawyer with family in large-firm, private practice" is very tough, and added, "the individual lawyer must want it to work *very much* or it definitely won't happen." Another partner commented that although she has generally struck a satisfying balance, "there are times when work pressures and family guilt are still high."

Most associates agreed that sustaining the balance is difficult for all attorneys, and especially for women, because they bear most household and child-rearing responsibilities. One partner reported that when she joined the firm, "Men and women did not talk about their children. Now it is completely acceptable and makes work/family balancing easier."

> *Faegre has made "great strides in allowing flexible and part-time work."*

Flexibility of work arrangements: The firm's part-time policy is reported to be a work in progress. One partner proclaimed "great improvement" in the past 10 years "from no policy on childcare or maternity leaves to current policies of defined part-time (with no limit) and childcare leaves for men and women." She noted that there are part-time partners on an "official basis" and concluded, "[As] more people try out these policies, it will become more the norm." Another partner agreed that Faegre has made "great strides in allowing flexible and part-time work."

Another associate believed it would be difficult, if not impossible, for a woman to take significant leave or a part-time stint and get back on track for partnership purposes. She observed that the problem is not easy to solve, but is "among the most significant obstacles to women's success in the firm." Another associate commented that although a part-time policy is available for associates, in her view, "there is a negative perception toward those who take part in it."

In the past, part-time options have been exercised by associates, reportedly with varying degrees of satisfaction. Several respondents, including a partner, wrote that part-time has generally been considered to jeopardize—at the very least—an attorney's prospects for ever making partner.

> *Although the firm is "trying to welcome diversity, attitudes of individuals are slow to change."*

Diversity: Many respondents either left this question blank or stated briefly that the firm has a "commitment" to diversity, but "a ways to go," in the words of one. One associate who elaborated said that the firm is "generally open to different political leanings and personalities," but that there is "such a small diverse population in terms of race and 'life style' (sexuality)," that it is difficult to assess the firm's attitude on these issues. She added that there is "a good amount of goodwill about these issues among partners." Nevertheless, this respondent concluded that her "appreciation of this perceived goodwill has lessened over time.... The problems are not that subtle. The longer these issues are confined to an internal, bureaucratic process, the more I see that process as a form of denial."

A partner noted that although the firm is "trying to welcome diversity, attitudes of individuals are slow to change." Another partner commented that the small number of women at the firm contributes to Faegre's approach toward its women lawyers: "Until there are more women generally in the firm, other lawyers won't see just how diverse 'we women' are."

Faegre is "a traditional place, [and] traditionally the leadership [has] been senior men. The change is gradual—too gradual for some."

Women in leadership positions: Although there are some respected women partners, the firm's all-male, six-member management committee apparently "perpetuates itself," in the eyes of one respondent. Because so many women leave the firm, one associated contended, "there is an extremely small pool of women who might be contenders for a management committee position."

Women do apparently serve on the legal personnel committee and one heads the summer associate program, although one associate did not perceive these partners as "truly powerful."

A partner disagreed, remarking that the presence of women on the recruiting and marketing committees has helped to make "women's issues" more visible.

One woman partner proclaimed the absence of any women managers "inexcusable." According to another partner, Faegre is "a traditional place, [and] traditionally the leadership [has] been senior men. The change is gradual—too gradual for some." She added that in a partnership, unlike a corporation, "you cannot impose new leadership from the top. Rather it evolves by consensus as relationships are created and developed."

An associate commented that the "women partners have not traditionally been very forceful in focusing on women's issues." Another remarked, "[The firm] lacks strong female leadership and has few attractive role models for women. Senior women have not promoted opportunities of young women in the firm in any meaningful way."

Another associate disagreed, noting that despite the absence of women on the management committee, "there are a few senior women who are both very well-respected by their male peers and also attentive to advancing women."

Faegre & Benson No. of Responses: 11	Strongly agree	Agree	Disagree	Strongly disagree
Women's prospects for advancement at the firm are as strong as men's	2	5	4	
I am satisfied with the firm's family and personal leave policies	4	3	4	
There are women in positions of power and influence in the firm		4	5	2
Women are as likely as men to receive desirable work assignments	5	5	1	
Women attorneys feel they can discuss family obligations openly	2	5	3	
Women are as likely as men to be mentored by senior attorneys	2	4	3	2
Women attorneys enjoy a high level of job satisfaction	1	3	4	1
Women in the firm are supportive of their women colleagues	3	6	1	1
Firm management is receptive to the concerns of women attorneys	3	6	1	

FOLEY, HOAG & ELIOT LLP

Rating: 3

🔨🔨🔨🔨🔨

Foley, Hoag & Eliot LLP
One Post Office Square
Boston, MA 022109
617-832-1000

No. of Attorneys: 166
No. of Women Attorneys: 48
No. of Partners: 79
No. of Women Partners: 14
No. of Survey Responses Received: 7

Respondent Profile: 3 partners and 4 associates responded. Practice areas included litigation and business.

Summary: Our handful of respondents uniformly portrayed Foley, Hoag as a highly satisfactory firm for women. Although there is an anxiety that attrition among women associates continues to plague women's advancement on the whole, the firm offers women an unusually sensitive and supportive work environment, as well as a viable part-time policy for those seeking partnership. Despite these accomplishments, however, respondents reported that diversity is lacking.

Advancement: All respondents agreed that the high attrition rate among women associates results in fewer women coming up for partnership, but those women who stay at the firm are reportedly afforded equitable treatment. Thus, despite the absence of bias in advancement decisions, women's patterns of promotion still do not match men's.

A partner concurred that although the prospects for advancement for men and women are "very close," advancement is "not the same—largely due to different rates of attrition. Women are more likely to leave due to time conflicts with family demands." An associate agreed that attrition is a problem, but that when "women advance to partnership level here, they are made partner." Consequently, the firm has "a relatively high percentage of women partners," but "a relatively low percentage of women associates."

Another associate said that some of the reasons women leave the firm, "include deciding to stay home with children, opting for more predictable hours by working as in-house counsel or in the government, or following a spouse to a new city." She added, "The underlying issue is that fewer women than men actually want to be partner, so they jump at opportunities to leave."

For the few who have stuck it out in recent years, advancement opportunities have reportedly been favorable. According to one associate, three of the last five partners promoted were women, and recently the firm promoted a woman with two small children who was working part-time, as well as another woman with a small child who was on a full-time schedule.

Several respondents reported that assignments and reviews are meted out impartially, although one associate noted that with regard to mentoring relationships, she sensed that "very few such relationships exist for female associates." One partner remarked that the firm is "still a firm that rewards professional excellence. Rainmaking is not a prerequisite for partnership, although it is—as I believe it should be—a requirement for advancement to the top echelon of compensation." She advised that women seem to do best "when they develop expertise in emerging legal areas where they can establish a level of independence."

> *"I assumed that my perceptions would change as soon as the 'honeymoon' was over, [but I soon] realized that this is really the way it is. The work atmosphere is very pleasant. I sense no gender discrimination."*

Attitudes and atmosphere: Respondents had no complaints about the atmosphere at Foley, Hoag, which was universally described as "very comfortable." According to a partner, the firm "works hard at maintaining an environment free of overt or subtle gender discrimination," and associates agreed that these efforts have paid off. The firm is said to have "gone through a yearlong self-examination and put a process in place to foster awareness and sensitivity," according to one respondent.

An associate commented that the firm now has "excellent policies (leave, part-time, sexual harassment) and follows them." A self-described "outspoken feminist," this associate reported that her "ideas about policy have been given a respectful hearing and, in most cases, have been implemented."

According to another associate, her colleagues at the firm are "collegial, noncompetitive, open, and helpful." Male and female attorneys, she observed, "interact easily, without any tension or obvious gender-based assumptions." Another associate characterized the firm as "exceptionally comfortable." She recalled that when she first joined the firm as a lateral, "I assumed that my perceptions would change as soon as the 'honeymoon' was over, [but I soon] realized that this is really the way it is. The work atmosphere is very pleasant. I sense no gender discrimination."

> *"Some partners at FHE actually do leave at 5 p.m. every single day, and this example makes it easier for associates to try to leave at a decent hour, but first the work has to get done."*

Balancing work & family/personal life: Respondents gave Foley, Hoag credit for trying to ease the burdens on working parents, although all agreed that there is no easy solution to the dilemma of balancing the demands of firm life with family needs. As one partner put it, "It is difficult to sustain or even achieve the ideal family life—this firm has not found the cure for this problem."

Another commented that it is difficult for both male and female associates "to feel that they are giving both job and family enough time and attention" because the way the firm operates "demands almost instant responsiveness to clients."

As one associate put it, while the firm is "pretty good" as compared to other Boston firms, being both a litigator and a mother has meant that she has "sacrificed months of sleep." The firm reportedly has a lower range of required billable hours than other firms in the city. But respondents reported that associates still work more than they would like.

One associate wrote that, in her estimation, most attorneys "cannot leave work in order to be home for dinner by 6 p.m., and this wears people down and makes family life hard." Women, she added, "especially feel burdened by the length of the day because many of us are trying not just to get home for dinner but to cook dinner. When you have a hungry 4-year-old desperate for dinner every night, it starts to seem impossible."

Respondents indicated that the firm does what it can to accommodate those shouldering competing sets of demands. According to one associate, "Some partners at FHE actually do leave at 5 p.m. every single day, and this example makes it easier for associates to try to leave at a decent hour, but first the work has to get done."

Fellow attorneys are also said to be willing to pitch in for one another when problems crop up. A partner commented that she personally has "had to reschedule, ask for substitutes, etc., because of children's illnesses and everyone has been very helpful." The firm reportedly also offers a "fantastic" backup childcare arrangement and, according to one respondent, unlike most firms, Foley, Hoag does not require attorneys to make a co-payment in order to take advantage of the service.

> *"The presumption is that anyone with a child under a year old can work four days a week, and anyone with older children can apply for part-time status."*

Flexibility of work arrangements: Foley, Hoag received high marks for its part-time policy, which was recently revamped. According to a partner, the firm "has become much more flexible in accommodating alternative work arrangements, both for men and women." Under the current arrangement, according to an associate, "the presumption is that anyone with a child under a year old can work four days a week, and anyone with older children can apply for part-time status."

The firm is also said to be generous when it comes to parental leave. One partner reported that the firm "has added a four-week paid parenting leave for men and women (birth and adoptive). This is in addition to the eight weeks paid to women. Also, men and women may take a total of one year [unpaid] parenting leave."

Several respondents reported that men have taken advantage of both the parental leave and the reduced-hours policies, and that part-time arrangements are available at partnership level. One respondent who has taken advantage of the part-time policy described the firm's approach as "very good" and reported that after the birth of her child, "I worked half-time briefly (every afternoon) and then gradually returned to full-time."

Although one associate predicted that going part-time for more than a year "will almost certainly affect the timing, if not the prospect, of partnership," part-timers can and do advance at the firm. A partner reported that one woman in the litigation department was made partner on time after taking two six-month leaves after the births of two children and working an 80-percent schedule for about 18 months. As a partner, she reportedly remains on a reduced-hours schedule.

Another woman who has taken a three-month leave is "on track for partnership consideration this coming fall," according to a respondent. A partner commented, "Both women and men have made partner after extended parenting leaves."

Part-time is reportedly easier to implement in some departments than others. One associate observed, "It is always hard to make part-time hours actually work for litigators, because trials, briefs, and other work develop suddenly."

The firm, in one associate's view, "says the 'right things,' but one look around belies diversity."

Diversity: Racial minorities might find Foley, Hoag a lonely outpost. In the view of one associate, the firm "says the 'right things,' but one look around belies diversity." She added that although it is committed to diversity "in theory," in practice, "*virtually all* of the attorneys are white."

Minority hiring is "tough," according to an associate, and the firm has apparently been unable to get "a critical mass." According to some respondents, however, the firm's poor record in terms of diversity is not for want of effort. A partner commented that the firm would like to be more diverse and is "working toward that goal."

Nevertheless, respondents reported "a number of openly lesbian and gay associates and partners" and said that the firm offers benefits to same-sex partners.

One respondent commented that when women partners are invited to attend monthly women associates' lunches, "they willingly come and offer useful advice, information, and support."

Women in leadership positions: Several women have apparently achieved positions of real power at Foley, Hoag. The woman who sits on the elected five-person executive committee was described by a partner as "powerful and effective" and reportedly provided an "outstanding" contribution to the firm in building a practice area from the ground up.

Another reported that, although "most of the big rainmakers are men," two women serve on the firm's distribution committee "that determines partner compensation and reviews partner performance."

The firm also had a woman partner at the helm of its litigation department until she was appointed to the federal appellate bench, and women have chaired several other smaller practice groups including trusts and estates, real estate, and environmental, as well as the firm's hiring committee.

The influential women here are said to be well-respected by associates. One respondent commented that when women partners are invited to attend monthly women associates' lunches, "they willingly come and offer useful advice, information, and support." A dissenting partner remarked, however, that although "this is changing," in her experience, the "most senior women partners rarely mentor women associates."

Foley, Hoag & Eliot No. of Responses: 7	Strongly agree	Agree	Disagree	Strongly disagree
Women's prospects for advancement at the firm are as strong as men's	5	2		
I am satisfied with the firm's family and personal leave policies	5	2		
There are women in positions of power and influence in the firm	5	2		
Women are as likely as men to receive desirable work assignments	6	1		
Women attorneys feel they can discuss family obligations openly	4	3		
Women are as likely as men to be mentored by senior attorneys	3	1	2	
Women attorneys enjoy a high level of job satisfaction		6		
Women in the firm are supportive of their women colleagues	3	3	1	
Firm management is receptive to the concerns of women attorneys	3	4		

FRIED, FRANK, HARRIS, SHRIVER & JACOBSON

Rating: 67

**Fried, Frank, Harris, Shriver
& Jacobson**
One New York Plaza
New York, NY 10004
212-859-8000

No. of Attorneys: 305
No. of Women Attorneys: 102
No. of Partners: 82
No. of Women Partners: 13
No. of Survey Responses Received: 14

Respondent Profile: 4 partners and 10 associates responded. Practice areas included litigation, corporate, and mergers and acquisitions.

Summary: Despite rave reviews on the diversity front and its predominantly hospitable work environment, many respondents were concerned that striking a balance between work and family is difficult. Success is said to be excessively linked to hours, and some associates feel seriously neglected by the firm's women partners.

Advancement: Most respondents perceived that women make partner relatively infrequently at Fried, Frank, although few could explain why. In one senior associate's words, "There's no way that women are as likely to advance as men; the numbers belie any claim to the contrary." She added that, in her opinion, "the women who ultimately make partner have worked longer and harder than men at the same level."

One litigator concluded that families are the culprit, and that to succeed, in her opinion, "one has to be a man." Another associate agreed: "Men are in a better position than women to accommodate the firm; the expectation of the firm is that you are readily available at any time, until any time of the day, weekdays or weekends."

A corporate associate feared there was a pronounced double standard in the way men and women are evaluated, and claimed that the few women who stay long enough to be considered for partnership are less likely to become partner than their male peers.

[In her estimation,] central factors for advancement are long hours, good relationships with peers and partners, and postponing a family. Nevertheless, she noted, for men, "hard work alone and intelligence seem to be enough." Finally, she observed, spending time with family instead of attending firm social functions is seen "as a lack of interest in the firm."

Inadequate mentoring may explain the paucity of women in the partnership ranks, according to several respondents. One corporate lawyer concluded that, in her opinion, female partners "do not seem committed to mentoring female associates." Even a corporate associate who reported that women are not treated differently overall, and that assignments are allocated without any bias, agreed that it is much easier for a man to find a mentor. One litigator believed that lack of mentoring is "not just a woman's problem, it is a firm-wide problem." One associate did point out that there has been an effort to promote woman-to-woman mentoring during the past year.

According to the firm's women partners, women are at no disadvantage "if they choose to stay the requisite time and demonstrate the required performance level." One partner noted, however, that, in her experience, "More and more women generally are less willing to make the sacrifices necessary to advance."

> **"Fried, Frank is a firm where women have been welcomed— not just tolerated, but affirmatively welcomed—in all departments for decades."**

Attitudes and atmosphere: Most respondents reported that the atmosphere at the firm is comfortable. One partner wrote, "Fried, Frank is a firm where women have been welcomed—not just tolerated, but affirmatively welcomed— in all departments for decades. Few of its peer firms can make that statement."

The firm reportedly includes equal numbers of men and women at the junior-associate level, and several respondents commented that assignments are handed out in a gender-neutral way. According to several associates, woman-to-woman networking is strong. One associate reported that a working mothers' group has recently been created and meets once a month on the firm's tab— to discuss issues and make proposals. Another associate noted that some events are scheduled that are open to women lawyers only.

One litigator wrote that most of her male peers are sensitive to gender-bias issues, but that, in her opinion, the older men are sometimes not as sensitive. A junior associate observed, however, "While there are a number of 'old school' stalwarts, the atmosphere is such that women have no problem *immediately* calling *anyone* on inappropriate behavior."

A junior associate observed that although women at the firm are as outspoken as men, some male partners tend to bond more with male associates. A midlevel associate commented that she has never felt discriminated against or uncomfortable because of her gender, but that the "boys' club" atmosphere, "although not pronounced or encouraged, still seems to thrive in a certain sense."

According to two associates, the worst thing about the atmosphere at the firm is the long hours expected. One associate perceived Fried, Frank as "very workaholic" and wrote that billing 300-hour months is considered "proof of competence and loyalty."

> **"A need to go to the gym is accommodated but a need for daily contact with kids is not."**

Balancing work & family/personal life: It is not easy to juggle much in addition to one's responsibilities as a Fried, Frank associate. In one associate's opinion, the firm "considers families 'excess baggage.' " A litigator wrote that she feels such pressure that even when her schedule is light, she's always waiting for a new fire to put out. According to one working mother, although the number of junior associates with children is on the rise, the firm, in her estimation, is "not sensitive to family issues at all." Another associate agreed, saying she believes that "women leave the firm at a much higher rate than men, and that women, especially mothers, find it an inhospitable place to work."

For some unmarried women with limited outside responsibilities, combining the workload with a personal life is said to be manageable, although others feel they must pick up the slack for working parents. A junior associate observed, "Married people, especially with children, are less exploited than single people." Another associate seemed to have the opposite impression. She observed, "A need to go to the gym is accommodated but a need for daily contact with kids is not." According to another associate, "A man is respected even while asking for time off for his season tickets...but few women would feel comfortable asking for time off for family."

One corporate associate reported that a few departments seem to accommodate mothers on an informal basis. According to a junior associate, although the firm "makes a real effort to accommodate women who have small children," overall, there are no strict guidelines.

The partners gave the firm more credit for supporting lawyers with outside obligations and contended that juggling does become easier as one becomes more senior and gains more control over scheduling. One partner described the firm as "quite sensitive—but within the narrow limits of the demands of the job."

She added that although partners have more room to maneuver, "given the demands of clients and the work itself, it is not easy to accomplish a very satisfactory balance." The firm reportedly offers an off-site, partially subsidized emergency childcare center.

Those who do work part-time are perceived to be off partnership track and are "not taken seriously."

Flexibility of work arrangements: Although some respondents characterized part-time arrangements as "unusual," the firm confirmed that there are currently nine part-time associates and that it is in the process of drafting a written policy.

One partner stated that part-time arrangements are considered legitimate and viable options by the firm. A couple of associates reported that the firm convened a part-time committee to explore alternative working arrangements, but they estimated this group had met only a few times and had not made any proposals in two years, a situation the firm is now obviously addressing.

Nevertheless, according to a litigator, there is a perception that those who do work part-time are off partnership track and are "not taken seriously." Although there are currently no part-time partners, there was at least one in the past.

The firm reportedly has a diversity committee and sponsors "a lot of events solely for people of color."

Diversity: Most respondents were enthusiastic about Fried, Frank's efforts on this front. As one associate put it, "Basically, nobody here cares who you are or where you're from or what you do outside the walls of your office. All the firm really cares about is that you do your work, and that you do it well."

Despite some reported trouble recruiting and keeping diverse attorneys, Fried, Frank is said to do better than most of its peers on this front. The firm reportedly has a diversity committee and sponsors "a lot of events solely for people of color," in the words of one respondent. In addition, the firm sponsors a Mexican-American Legal Defense Fund fellowship program.

There are reportedly several openly gay attorneys at the firm, and Fried, Frank's attorneys are involved in an array of *pro bono* projects. The firm is also said to recognize that its attorneys have interests and needs that go beyond the law. One associate reported that Fried, Frank has a choral group, invites speakers from different political parties, and is generally supportive of religious needs. One partner traced the firm's record on diversity back to the 1970s when its first African-American female partner was named.

A single associate dissented from the prevailing view, stating it was her opinion that "the few diverse attorneys that remain at the firm find it particularly insensitive to minority needs."

> *"Until women become substantial rainmakers, they will not have real power."*

Women in leadership positions: Although several women partners reportedly wield genuine power at Fried, Frank, they nevertheless received a hearty round of criticism from their junior colleagues. Most respondents agreed that several women in the partnership are quite influential, but as one associate put it, "until women become substantial rainmakers, they will not have real power," although she noted that this was also the case at other firms with which she was familiar. One partner disagreed, noting that some of the firm's women partners *are* "major rainmakers."

One associate commented that women partners are perceived in extreme ways—as either "terrific, great, the best," or as "horrible, nasty, a nightmare."

According to virtually all associates, although their presence is consoling, the women partners at the firm have "not taken particular interest in helping out the more junior women in the firm." The consensus seemed to be, in the words of a midlevel associate, that the women partners had "given up a lot to get where they are now," and, as a result, "their attitude is 'I had to give up a lot—you do it, too.' " The female partners are, in one litigator's estimation, "men in women's clothes."

Several associates noted that women partners are perceived as more difficult to work for than many of the men in the firm. Yet one partner reported that the women partners "occasionally meet to discuss issues related to the quality of life of women attorneys and are supportive of the women associates."

Fried, Frank, Harris, Shriver & Jacobson No. of Responses: 14	Strongly agree	Agree	Disagree	Strongly disagree
Women's prospects for advancement at the firm are as strong as men's	3	3	6	
I am satisfied with the firm's family and personal leave policies	3	2	5	2
There are women in positions of power and influence in the firm	3	6	3	1
Women are as likely as men to receive desirable work assignments	5	6	1	1
Women attorneys feel they can discuss family obligations openly	2	2	4	4
Women are as likely as men to be mentored by senior attorneys	3	1	6	2
Women attorneys enjoy a high level of job satisfaction	2	2	5	4
Women in the firm are supportive of their women colleagues	3	5	2	3
Firm management is receptive to the concerns of women attorneys	3	2	2	4

FULBRIGHT & JAWORSKI LLP

Rating: 69

Fulbright & Jaworski LLP
1301 McKinney St.
Suite 5100
Houston, TX 77010-3095
713-651-5151

No. of Attorneys: 271
No. of Women Attorneys: 76
No. of Partners: 140
No. of Women Partners: 17
No. of Survey Responses Received: 7

Respondent Profile: 2 partners and 5 associates responded. Practice areas included litigation, tax, and environmental.

Summary: Our handful of respondents was almost evenly split about opportunities to advance at Fulbright (both partners were positive, three of five associates were negative), but seemed unanimous that part-time or other flexible work arrangements were not workable in practice. Diversity? Depends on whom you ask.

Advancement: According to a bare majority of respondents (both partners and two of the five associates), women are as likely as men to advance at Fulbright, though even those with positive views sometimes went out of their way to qualify them.

Women attorneys, a litigator opined, "are still viewed as either single or 'mommy track.'" They are nudged toward "the 'sensitive' administrative jobs around the firm," in this associate's opinion, rather than the high-profile assignments that lead toward promotion. A tax associate also observed that "women often get passed over for the better assignments, [and thus must] fight harder to advance" than men.

A midlevel associate said it was her belief that "it is much more difficult for women at this firm to advance to partner." In part, she observed, the blame lies with women partners who are often "less willing to mentor female associates to assist them in the advancement of their careers." And a partner agreed that, in her estimation, mentoring is "usually done by other male partners." Two of the five associates maintained that women are as likely as men to advance, assuming there are no major work/family conflicts.

In "the last year, the attrition rate among female associates has been quite high," in the opinion of one lawyer. Many women who have stayed have waited to have families until after they "have made partner," according to a junior associate's observation.

A partner advised that those seeking to advance "must take on—and insist on receiving—challenging assignments." In addition, she wrote, "now more than ever, one must demonstrate business development skills *visibly*."

> *"If there is a 50-year-old male partner near a file, the assumption will be that he brought that work in, whether he is the billing partner or not."*

Attitudes and atmosphere: A partner reported that the firm is generally comfortable, although, in her estimation, it varies from section to section depending upon the number of women in the practice area and "the age of the attorneys." According to another partner's opinion, although the firm offers good opportunities for "smart women," there "will always be a 'boys' club' as long as there are boys—it's a fact of life."

One partner perceived what she termed the "unwritten disbelief that women can generate business. If there is a 50-year-old male partner near a file, the assumption will be that he brought that work in, whether he is the billing partner or not." According to an associate's perception, although she feels the firm has "done an excellent job of raising 'subtle discrimination' awareness," the problem remains that, in her opinion, "some dogs can't learn new tricks."

Another associate believed that the city's premier country club, "where [some] partners are members," does not permit women to play golf on certain afternoons. "This creates a problem with client development activities," she remarked, "because women are excluded from the group."

> *Although one is expected to bill at least eight hours per day, "it is up to the individual when and how those hours are completed, within reasonable limitations."*

Balancing work & family/personal life: Although the firm is reportedly flexible about when billable hours are put in, the billable pressures are nevertheless intense. According to a midlevel associate, the billable requirement here is 1,900 hours per year, yet she believed "the unwritten rule is that this is the *floor* and you should be at least 25 percent above this figure." Because, in this lawyer's view, the firm gives "no clear direction" on this issue, "everyone bills as much as they can—to the detriment of their personal lives." She added that she would "not even consider having children while here." A junior associate agreed, commenting that she works "too hard to have a personal life."

According to another junior associate, although one is expected to bill at least eight hours per day, "it is up to the individual when and how those hours are completed, within reasonable limitations." Another partner commented that the firm's sensitivity to outside demands depends on the practice group, but that there are no face-time requirements.

> *"Choices need to be made on what is more important. If a woman chooses to have a family and not work full-time—great— but you can't expect to proceed on the same track as others."*

Flexibility of work arrangements: Although part-time is available to associates, some feared that opting for this schedule apparently takes one permanently off partnership track and, thus, part-time is perceived as "not an option" by all associates who responded.

One partner applauded what she perceived to be the current policy (or lack thereof), declaring that part-time was not really viable and, moreover, that she "does not frankly think it should be in a large firm where everyone is expected to produce and progress." In her view, "Choices need to be made on what is more important. If a woman chooses to have a family and not work full-time—great—but you can't expect to proceed on the same track as others."

According to an associate, because the firm, in her opinion, has yet to recognize part-time and alternative work arrangements and, in fact, "does not even encourage work at home via computer," it ends up spending "an enormous amount of money and time training people who then leave because of the firm's inflexibility." According to another associate, the firm offers three months of paid maternity leave and an additional nine months of unpaid leave, although, it was her believe that "few women take more than six months."

> *"Gay? Not something one would advertise. Diverse life styles—probably not. We are a large traditional firm, although not very stuffy."*

Diversity: Responses were split. One associate opined, "Fulbright should receive high marks in this category," and a litigator agreed. Two other associates, however, expressed the opposite view. One wrote that, in her estimation, the firm is "not very diverse" and that "if they are trying to achieve some sort of diversity, they are not succeeding." According to another associate, everyone "looks a certain lawyer-like way." She added that she does not think "we have much diversity at large firms in the South."

Partners offered equally mixed accounts. According to one, the answer to whether Fulbright is diverse is indeed "yes and no." She recounted that, because of the leadership of Leon Jaworski, it was the first Houston firm "*years ago* to have a Jewish partner or an African-American partner." Nowadays, she observed, although very accepting of different life styles and personalities, the firm, "like most organizations controlled by men in their 50s" is, in her opinion, led by persons who "are somewhat threatened by advocates of women's rights."

According to another partner, the firm includes women who are black, Hispanic, and Asian. She continued, "Gay? Not something one would advertise. Diverse life styles—probably not. We are a large traditional firm, although not very stuffy."

> *Women associates gave their higher-ups low ratings when it came to mentoring or showing an interest in women rising through the ranks.*

Women in leadership positions: "Absolutely not," stated the one partner, dissenting from the overwhelming majority view, adding that this "is my major complaint about the firm." She reported that, in her estimation, there has "never been a woman on the firm's appointive executive committee or on the appointive partner's committee, the only committees with real power at the firm." In one associate's opinion, "Basically, the firm is composed of white males and has often been characterized (appropriately) as a 'good old boys' club.' " One associate, however, was of the view that although very few women have any real control, there are several who "make the firm mega-bucks" and are members of committees.

Women associates gave their higher-ups low ratings when it came to mentoring or showing an interest in women rising through the ranks. One associate observed that "many of them have actually made it more difficult because of their 'I paid my dues' mentality. F & J could improve greatly if this situation was resolved."

Another associate agreed, commenting with respect to the more influential women that "I haven't noticed any of them promoting other women in the firm." A partner remarked that although women partners refer work to one another, they "don't necessarily have the time to spend a lot of time mentoring others."

Fulbright & Jaworski No. of Responses: 7	Strongly agree	Agree	Disagree	Strongly disagree
Women's prospects for advancement at the firm are as strong as men's		4	2	1
I am satisfied with the firm's family and personal leave policies		5	1	
There are women in positions of power and influence in the firm		6		1
Women are as likely as men to receive desirable work assignments	2	3	1	1
Women attorneys feel they can discuss family obligations openly		1	6	
Women are as likely as men to be mentored by senior attorneys	2	3	2	
Women attorneys enjoy a high level of job satisfaction		3	2	1
Women in the firm are supportive of their women colleagues		4		3
Firm management is receptive to the concerns of women attorneys		1	5	1

GOODWIN, PROCTER & HOAR

Rating: 32

◣◣◣

Goodwin, Procter & Hoar
Exchange Place
Boston, MA 02109
617-570-1000

No. of Attorneys: 312
No. of Women Attorneys: 100
No. of Partners: 119
No. of Women Partners: 19
No. of Survey Responses Received: 15

Respondent Profile: 2 partners and 13 associates responded. Practice areas included corporate, litigation, and labor and employment.

Summary: Goodwin, Procter is evidently a fantastic place to be a woman partner—both of those who responded to our survey strongly agreed with every positive statement in our chart. Associates were not always so positive. The atmosphere was characterized as "work hard/play hard," pressures and billables are high, though part-time is reportedly viable throughout most of the firm.

Advancement: While both partners agreed that if women can put in the hours and stick it out for seven years, they have a fair chance at advancement in most departments, associates were split right down the middle—and those in the litigation group characterized prospects as bleak.

One partner declared, "Because the firm is so busy, the women are getting fabulous opportunities to stretch and experience new things." For those who do stay on, women mentors within the department are *"great."* The other partner noted that woman-to-woman mentoring opportunities exist, yet said, "It is also possible to learn a lot from the styles male mentors use, and because of the numbers, there are simply more styles to learn from if you look to male mentors as well as female."

Several respondents suggested that men who have wives with less demanding careers are at a huge advantage. "Review criteria are the same for men and women, but favor the married man with a stay-at-home spouse," in one associate's opinion. The pressure on those seeking partnership, she observed, "is so intense that those most likely to succeed are men with wives who can organize/run their lives and accept the upheaval and long absences required." Another associate maintained that, in her estimation, there are *"few* two-wage earner families among senior associates/partners where both husband and wife have high-pressure [jobs]."

According to a midlevel associate's perception, "There has never been a way to make partner other than to do good work (lots of it) and ultimately demonstrate that you are adding value to the bottom line (generally by bringing in business)." Women, she contended, "just haven't been willing to give up other parts of their life to make that happen."

Women litigators are less satisfied, with one saying that litigation, in her opinion, "lags behind in the advancement of women into the partnership ranks," and that the department "is sorely lacking in female role models." The paucity of women litigation partners, is, in one associate's estimation, "pathetic for the largest law firm in Boston."

Respondents were somewhat divided on the issues of mentoring and assignments. Although a junior associate perceived equitable treatment on these fronts, a more senior associate disagreed, maintaining that, in her opinion, "the fundamental problem is that men do the larger, public company transactions, which are higher visibility, more billable hours, and often with the big rainmaking partners." According to a midlevel associate, while assignments are handed out equitably, in her opinion, women lawyers tend to be assigned to clients with women CEOs or general counsels.

According to one litigator, the firm is introducing measures to redress what she characterized as the inequities in the litigation department, "including establishing a gender committee composed of individuals with clout, and taking steps to improve formal and informal mentoring relationships."

The firm has "a very individualistic style—each to [his or her] own."

Attitudes and atmosphere: Goodwin, Procter apparently has a "rough and tumble, work hard/play hard" atmosphere. According to a partner, the firm's ethos is "very independent [and] initiative is rewarded," creating an environment where anyone with the right traits can thrive.

About half of the respondents described Goodwin, Procter as a very comfortable milieu for women. According to a midlevel associate, the firm has "a very individualistic style—each to [his or her] own." An associate observed that the firm has "no fake stuffiness," although another clearly disagreed, claiming that she finds Goodwin, Procter to be "a very stuffy, unfun place for anyone to work, male or female."

According to one associate, "[The firm] seems to take pains to ensure a nondiscriminatory workplace," and despite the presence of insensitive individuals, sexual harassment and discriminatory treatment "are nonexistent." One associate, however, said that, in her opinion, the firm's management is "receptive to the easy issues, like family leave, but not the hard ones, like promotion." A partner commented that the firm's leadership is "very inclusive" and that women are "highly respected and valued members of the team." Although all attorneys are treated equally, one associate said that, in her opinion, "the secretaries, almost all of whom are women, are treated quite poorly."

Several respondents reported that they interact comfortably with male colleagues. One associate reported strong friendships between male and female associates, and a corporate associate commented that Friday happy hours sponsored by her department attract wide attendance by lawyers of both genders.

According to a midlevel associate, despite a "healthy" environment for women on a day-to-day basis, "the 'boys' club' attitude still lurks below the surface." One associate quipped, "Some of the more senior partners still appear amused that young women are practicing law."

We received one unique response to this question. According to a corporate associate's opinion, "There is definitely a 'boys' club,'" although membership therein by no means guarantees advancement. She added that some "'members of the club' who are popular golf and drinking buddies" have nonetheless received criticism of their work. As a result, membership "may help, but it's never going to make you partner here." This respondent concluded that although she may not be included in nighttime activities, it has "never caused my work to be less respected."

Respondents lauded Goodwin, Procter for its emergency on-site day care and other efforts they've made to substantiate their support of working parents.

Balancing work & family/personal life: Although pressure and billables are reportedly high, respondents lauded Goodwin, Procter for its emergency on-site day care and other efforts they've made to substantiate their support of working parents. As one associate put it, "[The firm is] generally sensitive and supportive of family responsibilities, but at the end of the day your billables have got to be in and you've got to be available for your clients/colleagues." As we've seen with many other firms, a double standard is perceived to exist in terms of

taking time to parent. An associate remarked that everyone, including very junior lawyers, thinks it is "great" when a man leaves the office at 6 p.m. everyday to have dinner with his family but, in her opinion, when "a woman does that, she's [perceived as] not dedicated to her job."

The strains of life at Goodwin, Procter were characterized as particularly intense in the corporate department, "which is why many women eventually leave and go in-house or to small firms," in the opinion of one associate. Another associate commented, "We are all scratching our heads to figure out how to give clients the service they expect from a big-firm corporate department on a part-time/alternative basis." A corporate partner, however, asserted, "[The firm] gives everyone a wide berth" to determine one's own pace.

Litigators feared that the part-time arrangements now underway will have little, if any, effect on their department.

Flexibility of work arrangements: Part-time is viable throughout most of the firm, although advancement opportunities for part-timers remain uncertain.

Although mindful of the incompatibility of fast-paced transactional work with part-time schedules, corporate respondents generally contended that the firm does what it can to make part-time tenable, although one associate observed that Goodwin, Procter "is still working out the kinks regarding whether part-time really is part-time, rather than full-time with less pay." Alternatively, some women apparently opt for less transactional corporate work, such as banking and licensing. Part-timers can "cut their own deals" as long as their department "signs off—which always happens," according to another partner.

Partnership prospects for part-timers at the firm are unclear. According to several respondents, part-timers have been promoted to the income partnership level. According to a corporate associate, however, "it's too soon to tell how it will flesh out in equity partnership decisions and continuing success at the partnership level for these women."

Litigators feared that the part-time arrangements now underway will have little, if any, effect on their department. According to a midlevel litigation associate's assessment, going part-time will probably doom an attorney's career. Two other litigators were also of the opinion that in their department, a decision to work part-time is "effectively a decision not to pursue partnership, [and] does not seem to work." Only one litigator is part-time, and she is perceived to be "off track." According to a litigator, "[Far too many of] the other women have left, many for other firms in which they have found mothering and lawyering more compatible."

Goodwin, Procter is committed to diversity in theory, but has not fully achieved it in practice.

Diversity: Goodwin, Procter is committed to diversity in theory, but has not fully achieved it in practice, according to many respondents. The firm "emphasizes that it understands everyone is different and in a different situation," and exerts no overt pressure for "conformity with anything except a high level of quality legal work," as one associate

put it. A new associate characterized the firm as "stuffy and WASPy, not diverse." Another associate observed that there are "very few women of color," and no "out" lesbians. (According to the 1997-1998 National Directory of Legal Employers, there are 10 African-American and 12 Asian/Pacific Islander attorneys at the firm.) One associate commented, "The women who fit in are the ones who make it and, historically, that hasn't included much diversity." She added that, in her opinion, the firm's leadership is "aware that this is going to have to change, but (to their credit, I think) still places the greatest emphasis on quality legal work."

There is a woman in the corporate department whom many believe may become the firm's first female managing partner.

Women in leadership positions: Several women reportedly hold powerful positions at Goodwin, Procter—including a woman in the corporate department whom many believe may become the firm's first female managing partner. While the corporate department reportedly has several "power houses—including women with children," as well as some younger women partners who show great promise, litigation is perceived to be a desert when it comes to women's leadership. One litigator commented that while the department has a gender committee of its own, in her opinion, "the majority of the women on it have fallen into the trap that one has to be 'like the boys' to succeed. It doesn't have to be that way."

Nevertheless, a partner noted that "the women in positions of power and leadership have helped to ensure that, for example, maternity leave has no effect on advancement or compensation."

According to some associates, while well-meaning, the women partners leave something to be desired as trailblazers. One commented, "The only women with power have gotten that way without any balance in their life. They have modeled themselves after men." Another associate complained, "While they are

successful, strong women, none has had to struggle with the burden (in part, financial) of balancing work and family, or if they have, they have chosen to sacrifice their family to too great an extent (at least in my opinion)."

The litigation department reportedly has efforts underway to remedy the perceived dearth of mentors. There are also less formal efforts underway, such as women-only lunches and dinners, "and other types of supportiveness," according to one litigator.

Goodwin, Procter & Hoar No. of Responses: 15	Strongly agree	Agree	Disagree	Strongly disagree
Women's prospects for advancement at the firm are as strong as men's	3	5	5	1
I am satisfied with the firm's family and personal leave policies	7	6		
There are women in positions of power and influence in the firm	6	5	1	2
Women are as likely as men to receive desirable work assignments	7	5	3	
Women attorneys feel they can discuss family obligations openly	4	4	5	1
Women are as likely as men to be mentored by senior attorneys	9		6	
Women attorneys enjoy a high level of job satisfaction	2	6	5	1
Women in the firm are supportive of their women colleagues	5	5	3	1
Firm management is receptive to the concerns of women attorneys	5	6	3	

HALE and DORR LLP

Rating: 13

◄◄◄◄

Hale and Dorr LLP
60 State St.
Boston, MA 02109
617-526-6000

No. of Attorneys: 250
No. of Women Attorneys: 62
No. of Partners: 146
No. of Women Partners: 26
No. of Survey Responses Received: 26

Respondent Profile: 15 partners, 10 associates, and 1 counsel responded. Practice areas included litigation and corporate. About half of the respondents did not indicate their practice area.

Summary: The conscious and long-standing efforts by Hale and Dorr's management to ensure that women lawyers receive the mentoring, training, and support they need to thrive at the firm have been largely successful, although many lawyers perceived that retaining women lawyers continues to be a problem. On the downside, the firm's widely acknowledged "eat what you kill" ambiance may be off-putting to some women, and the firm's part-time arrangements, while highly satisfactory for partners, received negative reviews from some associates.

Advancement: A majority of respondents (12 of 15 partners, the counsel, and six of 10 associates) declared that women enjoy equal prospects for advancement at Hale and Dorr, although a few perceived that women seem to advance more slowly and appear less likely to ascend to senior partnership status. One partner reported that a decade ago, the firm's managing partner (a man) convened a women's issues committee on the grounds that women made up approximately half of graduating law school classes and that the firm had an obligation to ensure that it was attracting and retaining women "in order to continue to practice at the highest level". The committee worked to heighten sensitivity to issues including mentoring, staffing, and promotion of women.

According to most, the firm's efforts have paid off, and women enjoy good opportunities to work on choice assignments. A senior partner who is involved in "the elevation process" confirms that Hale and Dorr is "dedicated to advancing women." The firm reportedly offers mentoring and training programs designed to give associates "the opportunity to develop the skills and support network to succeed." Another lawyer asserted that women are evaluated fairly, and "male partners enthusiastically support and mentor women lawyers."

Despite the support they receive from the firm, women associates and junior partners are perceived to leave the firm in large numbers. One partner commented that the firm has had the "bittersweet" experience of watching clients hire away several top women lawyers. To its credit, the attrition of women attorneys is reportedly a matter of serious concern to Hale and Dorr's management, which has responded by turning "an eye [toward] advancing the position of women," according to a junior associate.

Some respondents suggested that women are *less* likely than men to receive the mentoring and backing they need to advance. According to one partner's assessment, male senior partners "pass along [clients to] male protégés, [which] happens less often with women." Another associate feared that "women only make partner the second time around." Advancement to senior partnership level is perceived as difficult for everyone—and especially hard for women—because women "are not perceived to be able to devote the time to large cases (in litigation) or deals (in corporate)," due to the competing demands of work and home. Advancing to junior partner level is apparently considerably easier, with one corporate associate reporting that everyone eligible for elevation during the past four years has made it.

> *The managing partner is described as "one of the most vocal proponents of advancement of women in law."*

Attitudes and atmosphere: The firm's management, led by a managing partner who is described as "one of the most vocal proponents of advancement of women in law," has shown a genuine commitment to ensuring that women find the firm hospitable, and these efforts have born fruit in the eyes of respondents.

Women are present in large numbers and appear to be well-integrated into the firm at all levels. Most respondents said that they were unaware of any instances of gender discrimination, and that sexism of any kind would "be considered shocking," in the words of one respondent. The firm's atmosphere was described by a partner as "dynamic, stimulating, and supportive."

The firm culture is apparently very "hard-working" and has a reputation for preferring "aggressive personalities," in one partner's opinion. According to some, Hale and Dorr is proud of its mantra that "you eat what you kill," meaning that business production determines monetary reward. One partner quipped that the system creates "an atmosphere akin to having lunch with the Donner party (and trying to stay off the menu)."

According to a partner, although Hale and Dorr offers an interesting practice with prestigious clients and good compensation, "these virtues create its defects—the personalities gathered together to promote this undertaking tend to the brusque and monochromatic." According to one associate's opinion, "[When the results of the *Presumed Equal* survey were published in 1995], and the firm did so poorly, the atmosphere was like a 'witch hunt' for weeks, with partners quizzing associates as to whether they filled out the survey."

Respondents seemed to agree with one lawyer who said, "solidarity and support is encouraged among the women associates and partners" and reported that the firm sponsored a women's leadership seminar involving a full day outward bound program open to all women associates and partners.

Hale and Dorr lawyers "sometimes work very long hours by Boston standards and even, in some cases, by New York standards."

Balancing work & family/personal life: Hale and Dorr has apparently been very busy of late, and although the firm has reportedly taken steps to ease the burden, some perceived that its "up-or-out approach" may be a factor in many women with families leaving the firm. One partner commented that Hale and Dorr lawyers "sometimes work very long hours by Boston standards and even, in some cases, by New York standards."

The firm is described as receptive to outside obligations, but certain partners are considered less sympathetic. Although the firm is "a good place to be [for women who] can be creative at balancing," in the words of one partner, some feared that parents who are not prepared to work full-time at full throttle, or who lack both full-time household help and a flexible spouse, tend to leave.

Recognizing the "high costs associated with attrition," the firm has sought to ease the burden on associates by hiring laterals and providing on-site emergency day care and a fitness center.

Although billables are high (2,500 per year), a partner maintained that there is "no pressure [to bill hours] simply for the sake of billing hours." In an associate's view, however, "The unwritten rule is significantly higher than the stated policy." A partner noted that the best associates will always have high billables because "the partners want to work with them."

Hale and Door has a generous home computer policy and pays for and installs computers, printers, copiers, and faxes in the homes of attorneys who want them.

Flexibility of work arrangements: Associates and partners differed markedly in their perceptions of working part-time at Hale and Dorr. Although partners tended to view part-time arrangements as widely used and well-accepted throughout most of the firm, the opinion of many associates was that part-time schedules have not been successful at Hale and Dorr.

According to most partners, Hale and Door offers "excellent formal policies," including a reduced-hours policy under which attorneys may drop down to 60 percent of hours, as well as a flex-time policy, under which lawyers can work from home. Attorneys reportedly become eligible for part-time arrangements after two years at the firm. Hale and Door has a generous home computer policy and pays for and installs computers, printers, copiers, and faxes in the homes of attorneys who want them. The firm reportedly offers three months of paid parental leave to men and women, as well an additional nine months of unpaid leave, and one respondent reported that paternity leaves of up to two months have been taken.

Several partners observed that although part-time stints and extended maternity leaves may slow down an associate's progress to partnership, they do not pose a barrier to advancement. One partner wrote, "[The firm is] now making stronger-than-ever efforts to make sure the policies really work" and that individualized arrangements are available in addition to the formal options.

Not everyone agreed—not even every partner. A partner concluded that part-time, though encouraged and promoted, "does not work," in her estimation, as "the nature of litigation is such that you need to be available almost literally all the time." Several partners noted that some types of work simply do not lend themselves to part-time availability, suggesting that part-timers should expect to get less interesting assignments. For example, in the opinion of one respondent, corporate attorneys who go part-time would likely have to shift from time-sensitive transactional work to more routine securities law compliance work.

Most associates sided with the skeptics on the issue of part-time arrangements, perceiving that the firm's partners and clients often demonstrate a lack of receptivity to such arrangements.

Noting that the trend in the legal workplace generally is "to move away from the up-or-out formula," one associate suggested that Hale and Door is not a "trend-setter in this area or with family-friendly policies."

remarked that there are openly gay and lesbian attorneys, as well as gay partners. Political leanings are said to run the gamut. According to respondents, there is a broad range of personalities at the firm. In the words of one associate, "Stronger [personalities] work best." Evidently, because of the lack of social mingling among attorneys, lawyers can and do keep their private lives "pretty private."

Despite the low number of minority lawyers at Hale and Dorr (according to the 1997-1998 National Directory of Legal Employers, six African-American, one Hispanic and four Asian/Pacific Islander attorneys), the firm is said to be dedicated to improving minority recruitment. The firm participates in the Boston Law Firm Group, a consortium dedicated to promoting minority attorneys and has made efforts to "understand the dynamics of minority retention," according to one respondent. One minority respondent remarked that partners have been supportive of her development and have demonstrated receptivity to working with women and minorities on issues of concern.

> *Despite the low number of minority lawyers at Hale and Dorr, the firm is said to be dedicated to improving minority recruitment.*

> *The more powerful women in the firm are well-respected both within the firm and in the broader legal community.*

Diversity: While Hale and Dorr places little pressure on its attorneys to conform, and the firm is making efforts to diversify, there remains "a startling lack of diversity among attorneys," as well as very few people of color in leadership positions in the firm, according to respondents. However, several lawyers

Women in leadership positions: According to respondents, a woman serves as the vice chair of the firm's executive committee, a woman chairs the hiring committee, and three women serve as vice chairs of departments. Nevertheless, some respondents suggested that women have not yet climbed to the top tier of firm leadership, as evidenced by the fact that Hale and Dorr has no women department heads. One woman partner is "wholly devoted to training," although a partner commented that, in her opinion, she "seems to not be supported firm-wide." Several of the women partners are active on the firm's women's issues committee, which hosts dinners and social events and plays a role in developing and implementing family-friendly policies and in ensuring mentoring for female associates.

Most respondents declared that the more powerful women in the firm are well-respected both within the firm and in the broader legal community and are viewed by many respondents as strongly supportive of women lower down in the ranks. One partner described her female colleagues as an "incredibly energetic and inspirational group" that is "very active in promoting women's issues and mentoring young women."

A minority of respondents were less enthusiastic about the firm's women partners. One lawyer observed that the senior women "display a good deal of ambivalence towards other women at the firm, in some cases demonstrating an unwillingness to create an atmosphere better than the one under which they labored as junior lawyers." An associate commented that, in her estimation, the top women seem "so worried about protecting their own internal lines of business that they do not speak up or help younger women associates." And another associate remarked that what would be "refreshing is for the women who are respected here to do some informal mentoring and really take an interest in women associates' careers—that might start a new cycle for younger women to follow."

Hale and Dorr No. of Responses: 26	Strongly agree	Agree	Disagree	Strongly disagree
Women's prospects for advancement at the firm are as strong as men's	13	6	5	2
I am satisfied with the firm's family and personal leave policies	18	6	1	1
There are women in positions of power and influence in the firm	11	8	6	1
Women are as likely as men to receive desirable work assignments	17	5	2	1
Women attorneys feel they can discuss family obligations openly	8	8	7	1
Women are as likely as men to be mentored by senior attorneys	13	5	3	4
Women attorneys enjoy a high level of job satisfaction	6	14	2	1
Women in the firm are supportive of their women colleagues	17	5	2	1
Firm management is receptive to the concerns of women attorneys	18	5	1	1

HELLER EHRMAN WHITE & McAULIFFE

Rating: 15

◄◄◄◄

**Heller Ehrman White
& McAuliffe**
333 Bush St.
San Francisco, CA 94104
415-772-6000

No. of **Attorneys:** 168
No. of **Women Attorneys:** 50
No. of **Partners:** 67
No. of **Women Partners:** 14
No. of **Survey Responses Received:** 23

Respondent Profile: 9 partners, 13 associates, and 1 counsel responded. Practice areas included litigation, corporate, and real estate, although many respondents did not identify their practice areas.

Summary: Most respondents were effusive—Heller, Ehrman is a great place for women, they proclaimed, with two calling it "an oasis" and a "dream." Yet most associates thought the firm's part-time options, if utilized, might dampen their potential for advancement. Partners firmly disagreed. Efforts have clearly been made to recruit minorities—not necessarily successfully—but the firm is said to treat lesbian attorneys warmly. It reportedly has an eclectic though decidedly liberal culture, and the women in leadership positions received near unanimous praise.

Advancement: The partners were unanimous in reporting that advancement operates equally for women and men. Although most associates agreed with them, a minority contended that women face unique barriers.

Partners were overwhelmingly upbeat about all factors contributing to women's prospects for advancement. One partner observed that women associates are "assigned to important cases and develop strong relationships with important firm clients—which helps them advance." Another opined, "[Partners] took an active role in making sure I worked with the right people and got placed on appropriate committees etc., for proper exposure." A couple of partners emphasized the good prospects for women in the firm's litigation department. One

observed that some of the "top business-getters" in that department "have done a great job of integrating senior women associates and junior women partners into their practices."

One partner had a different perspective, writing that it is "harder for women to be taken seriously at every level—associate, partner. The guys still get slightly better mentoring, assignments. Strong women lawyers are still apt to be labeled aggressive. But the picture is changing."

Several junior associates reported having received good mentoring, with one noting that she had received "a great deal of responsibility, as well as latitude in approaching problems" during her first year at the firm. One litigator reported that opportunities are equal and remarked that women who "actively seek a specialty and a mentor seem to fare better."

Virtually all those who had observed parity in the firm's willingness to advance associates perceived that women remain under-represented in the partnership due to their higher attrition rate.

Those who thought women did not enjoy equal opportunities for advancement described the problem in a variety of ways. One litigator wrote that, in her opinion, women "tend to do more than their share of administrative tasks (hiring, etc.) to the detriment of their careers." A first-year associate feared, "Mentoring for women at this firm is very poor. It still feels like an 'old boys' network' in terms of who you work with and the amount of responsibility you're given to develop your skills." A colleague agreed that, in her estimation, men "are given better assignments and better clients, [as well as] more encouragement and mentoring, and, when they speak, others (from staff to partners) listen more deferentially."

A senior associate noted that many men at the firm are "pleased to mentor women and have successfully sponsored many women who have become partners."

"The firm lives on a daily basis its progressive reputation."

....

Attitudes and atmosphere: Most respondents described the firm as a great place for women. Respondents cited no overt manifestations of gender discrimination, and men and women are said to build solid working relationships and friendships. In the opinion of one

respondent, "The firm lives on a daily basis its progressive reputation." Two partners remarked that, compared to other companies and law firms where they have worked, the firm is an oasis. As one put it, "This firm is a dream." The firm is reported to be highly intolerant of bias in any form. One partner noted that she has received support when confronted with such bias by clients and opposing counsel.

Most associates and partners were enthusiastic about the firm's atmosphere. One junior associate reported feeling entirely comfortable traveling on business with men from the firm. She added that the firm holds biweekly Friday happy hours and that men and women "often go out together afterward." Another associate described the firm as "a wonderful place for women," notwithstanding her perception of "subtle [differences] in terms of work assignments and advancement."

Three women voiced criticisms of the firm's atmosphere. One wrote, "As sad as it sounds, it is a bit of a 'little boys' club.'" In her estimation, "several male partners are very sexist." A corporate associate wrote that the firm is comfortable only if one accepts "the realities" of advancement. A senior associate perceived that many male partners do not seem comfortable working with senior women, "and the women are always concerned that bringing a senior man onto the team will mean the man will try to take over."

"[The firm] pays a lot of lip service to being family-friendly, but billable hours are still the bottom line."

....

Balancing work & family/personal life: Most attorneys agreed that Heller, Ehrman is on par, though not superior, to comparable firms in San Francisco on this front. The balance is tough for everyone, but the firm is described as fairly sensitive. One partner observed, "We all juggle frantically." Another partner reported that levels of receptivity to outside obligations depend upon the department, partners, and clients for which one works.

Associates gave more mixed reviews. Several associates noted that the firm places tremendous emphasis on billables. One corporate associate opined that the firm "pays a lot of lip service to being family-friendly, but billable hours are still the bottom line." In contrast, one junior associate observed that most lawyers do strike a balance between professional and personal life and that parents can "place their families above their work without fear of censure." This associate added that she had noticed parents, for example, "rearranging meeting schedules to accommodate a child's sports event." One associate remarked that, in her estimation, however, "Very few women with children stay very long" and that, as far as she was concerned, "a woman who has children while she is an associate will not become a partner in San Francisco."

"The prevailing view is that the 'marginal' hours—weekends, evenings—are the most grueling and the real sign of commitment. Part-timers do not suffer enough and therefore do not deserve equal treatment."

Flexibility of work arrangements: Attorneys are permitted to go part-time for up to one year after the birth of a child, according to one partner, yet most associates agreed that although part-time is theoretically available, they feared that adopting such a schedule might adversely affect their prospects for advancement.

Despite this perception, several partners reported that they had taken advantage of this option and that their colleagues were respectful of their reduced schedules. One partner wrote that she had "committed a high number of hours, although less than the full-time expectation" and that the firm "does not discount my compensation and has been quite fair." Another partner noted that although part-time "inevitably slows down one's professional development," it is "not a barrier to advancement."

Most associate respondents commented they do not see part-time options in quite the same light. "Such arrangements are not perceived favorably for those women associates who wish to advance to partnership," noted one junior associate. A midlevel corporate associate wrote, "[Part-time] is only acceptable as a short-term strategy." One associate suggested that no one has made partner after going part-time "in at least a decade." Another associate claimed that not a single woman at the firm "has had a child and *then* made partner."

Although one part-timer wrote that she has received fantastic support, another reported that she "definitely" feels "like a 'second class citizen.'" One senior associate feared that "the prevailing view is that the 'marginal' hours— weekends, evenings—are the most grueling and the real sign of commitment.

Part-timers do not suffer enough and therefore do not deserve equal treatment."

> **"[The] only group that would not find a comfortable home here are political conservatives."**

Diversity: Respondents uniformly agreed that the firm does a poor job of attracting and retaining women of color, although the environment is extremely hospitable for lesbians. The firm makes efforts to recruit minority lawyers, but the payoff has been minimal, according to respondents. A partner commented that, in her estimation, while Heller "talks diversity, it does not practice diversity. The white male lawyer is still the preferred candidate."

An associate said that women from racial minority groups, "who are very, very few—are very isolated." She added that, in her opinion, problems of general concern to women attorneys appear to be "greatly multiplied if you are a woman of color."

The firm is said to treat lesbian attorneys warmly. One partner wrote that she is an "out" lesbian and has received a great deal of support from her colleagues. A lesbian associate noted that her male mentor has "gone out of his way to make clients I regularly deal with sensitive and comfortable with my personal life. The firm always, as a matter of course, includes my partner in events, etc."

The firm is described as uniformly politically liberal. An associate remarked that although some might criticize the firm "for being 'too' liberal, it is the type of environment where people feel free to speak their minds and act on their beliefs." One partner strongly disagreed.

She wrote that the "only group that would not find a comfortable home here are political conservatives."

In terms of personalities, the firm reportedly has "a famously eclectic culture," in the words of one partner, and is full of people with varied interests and backgrounds.

> **"Our 'glass ceiling' is lying in pieces on the floor."**

Women in leadership positions: Respondents indicated that women hold many leadership positions here. Women are reported to serve as managing partners of the firm's Los Angeles and Palo Alto offices, and a woman serves as one of the two managing partners in the San Francisco office. In San Francisco, a woman reportedly co-chairs the litigation department, and women manage the labor department and several other smaller departments. The firm's partnership evaluation committee is chaired by a woman, and a woman is co-chair of the hiring committee. Women also reportedly sit on the firm's compensation committee and policy committee. According to a partner, "About 90 percent of these women in leadership positions have children." In another partner's view, "Our 'glass ceiling' is lying in pieces on the floor."

Still, in the eyes of a small minority, there are very few women who wield true influence. "The real movers and shakers in the firm are all white males," asserted one associate. Several associates made comments to the effect that women still do not have "the ultimate power positions." There are reportedly few women rainmakers.

The women at the top are, for the most part, described by associates as "well-respected" and "committed in various ways to promoting opportunities for women." One associate wrote that these women are "wonderful advocates for younger female associates," and another commented that they are "perceived as role models, not only for women attorneys, but for attorneys generally."

A minority of associates were more critical of the senior women at the firm.

One litigator wrote that, in her opinion, no women involved in firm management "have gone out of their way to advance other women." Another remarked that women still do not appear to have firm-wide power positions and that "some women associates would argue that this might be a good thing because a few of our women partners are perceived as being likely to hold women back."

Heller Ehrman White & McAuliffe No. of Responses: 23	Strongly agree	Agree	Disagree	Strongly disagree
Women's prospects for advancement at the firm are as strong as men's	10	7	5	
I am satisfied with the firm's family and personal leave policies	9	11	2	
There are women in positions of power and influence in the firm	11	11	1	
Women are as likely as men to receive desirable work assignments	16	2	3	2
Women attorneys feel they can discuss family obligations openly	10	7	4	
Women are as likely as men to be mentored by senior attorneys	11	8	1	2
Women attorneys enjoy a high level of job satisfaction	4	12	4	2
Women in the firm are supportive of their women colleagues	12	6	3	
Firm management is receptive to the concerns of women attorneys	10	10	1	

HOGAN & HARTSON LLP

Rating: 12

🔨🔨🔨🔨

Hogan & Hartson LLP
Columbia Square
555 Thirteenth St. NW
Washington, DC 20004
202-637-5600

No. of Attorneys: 468
No. of Women Attorneys: 158
No. of Partners: 228
No. of Women Partners: 44
No. of Survey Responses Received: 28

Respondent Profile: 10 partners, 17 associates, and 1 counsel responded. Practice areas included health, international trade, education, litigation, energy, and corporate.

Summary: Hogan & Hartson, egalitarian and relaxed, offers women lawyers an exceptionally supportive working environment in its health care practice area. Other groups, in contrast, appear more typical of large firms. Although booming business places stress on lawyers, the firm's widely used part-time policy eases the burden of balancing work and home life. A memo from the executive committee even stressed the importance of reasonable work hours and vacation time.

Advancement: Hogan & Hartson was described by most respondents as a thoroughly egalitarian firm with a long and strong tradition of women partners, although a group of senior associates thought the firm was overrated as a place for women to make their careers.

Nearly all of the partners were highly optimistic about women's prospects. One commented, "Now that women sit on all committees of the firm and have advanced to positions of power within the firm," junior women are just as likely to advance. A partner in the health care group echoed this observation: "In some areas of practice, women are beginning to outnumber men, including as superstars." According to a partner who has been involved in the firm's partnership selection process in recent years, "All are judged on an individual basis."

Some associates shared this bright view of women's prospects within the firm. Several associates reported that women are as likely as men to receive choice assignments. A health care associate observed, "Women are not given preferential treatment," but noted that she has "not seen discrimination against women, ever."

According to some respondents, however, the picture painted by some of the firm's women partners is incomplete. According to a dissenting partner, while women have constituted a large percentage of those most recently promoted, she believes that "in general, women do not make partner at the same rate as men." She observed that women are "more heavily concentrated at the counsel and special partner level" (a sentiment echoed by a regulatory associate), and that the criteria for promotion at Hogan appear to be getting stiffer, "with emphasis on billable hours and originations." She further asserted that women, and particularly women with families, often have a difficult time meeting the stricter standards.

Several associates agreed that while prospects for partnership are equal for those women who "*stay here* and stay *full-time,*" as one put it, there is a belief that women are far more likely than men to leave the firm or opt for alternative arrangements that can delay or impede advancement.

> **Certain practice areas are dominated by women and are said to offer a uniquely hospitable environment.**

Attitudes and atmosphere: Most respondents spoke favorably about the atmosphere at Hogan, although several noted that men's tendency to bond over social and sports activities sometimes leaves out women. Certain practice areas, including the health care group and other regulatory practices, are dominated by women and are said to offer a uniquely hospitable environment.

The health care practice group is reportedly more than half female, and most of the women partners have families. An associate in this department wrote that she has many good role models and mentors and has not experienced any gender discrimination. A health care partner reported that she has "always felt nurtured and included here, both on a professional and personal level." A health care associate said that the firm is "a *great* place to work."

Outside of the regulatory practice groups, some respondents were less than enthused about Hogan's atmosphere. According to an associate, certain groups and attorneys are "perceived as making women uncomfortable." A litigation partner observed that while the comfort level is "quite good" and that men and women share friendships, mentoring, and collegial relationships, there are, in her estimation, " 'boy cliques' even among younger partners." Another associate asserted that, in her opinion, "it is much more difficult in general for women, [because] there is less respect, a less clear path, and few role models." A corporate attorney commented that it appears as if "female attorneys are used to get the work done, but are not incorporated into the 'team' and made to feel integral to the firm."

In contrast, an international trade partner commented that the firm is "extremely comfortable" for women and that even subtle gender discrimination is not tolerated. A litigation associate reported that the women associates' "rapport and support of each other is excellent" and that the women themselves "are some of the best things about the firm and a big reason I came."

The one problem cited by many respondents involves " 'male jock' events," including Saturday morning basketball and golf. Although some sporting activities, including softball and volleyball teams, are co-ed, others include only men.

> **"The ethic here—even if not always fulfilled in practice—is to respect and value personal/family life."**

Balancing work & family/personal life: Although traditionally one of the most family-friendly firms in D.C., Hogan has become extremely busy of late, placing its lawyers under heavy pressure. There is also reportedly considerable variation in the sensitivity of different practice groups in the firm, with the regulatory practice groups and the litigation department said to be the most amenable to attorneys balancing work with family.

"H & H has a lot of work these days and not enough attorneys," as one associate put it. Another respondent agreed: "The firm is really busy and people have been working *long* hours lately." Although the firm's billable hours requirement is 1,800 per year, a number deemed by most to be bearable, and "intended to allow all lawyers to have a life," most lawyers seem to exceed this requirement.

On a positive note, a midlevel associate reported that, in response to the fact that business is "booming" and associates are working so hard, "the executive committee sent around a memo describing how they are trying to eliminate the problem and how vacations and reasonable work hours are important and should be the norm."

Under these conditions, women attorneys "place a lot of pressure on themselves to 'do it all'—so they assume full case loads, even though they have kids," according to one associate. This approach, in turn, "creates an inordinate amount of stress on women at times, e.g., when trial begins in a week and you have a child in the hospital." Hogan does attempt to assist women who find themselves in a bind, for example by "adding people to a case to take over some work when family obligations arise."

She added, "There are many women in the firm, all of whom are willing to lend assistance and understanding when problems arise." Another associate commented, "The ethic here—even if not always fulfilled in practice—is to respect and value personal/family life."

Several partners commented that shouldering dual sets of burdens can be harder for partners than for associates. A litigation partner remarked, "The truth is that the sheer responsibility of being a partner—not just financial pressure, but client pressure—has us all, male and female, under stress."

Being a parent at Hogan reportedly bears no stigma. According to one partner, "As more of our male partners have to balance family and work because they have wives who work outside the home, the sensitivity to discrimination has been enhanced, and the atmosphere of the firm has also been enhanced." Many of the attorneys have young children, and, according to a health care associate, men and women alike "express family priorities, and many partners leave at a particular time several days a week to attend to childcare responsibilities." An associate commented that baby showers are held for all expectant parents, male and female.

. Hogan & Hartson reportedly provides an emergency childcare center that earned high marks from most respondents. An associate reported that newborns can remain at the center for one month after a parent returns from family leave to "ease the transition and facilitate breast feeding," a unique accommodation among the firms surveyed. According to another associate, the firm also has "a great network of maternity clothes and baby equipment loans," contributing to an atmosphere that is "sensitive and welcoming to family and personal needs."

> *While Hogan is "one of the best firms [for part-time], it's hard to be part-time and taken seriously (anywhere) unless you're a star."*

Flexibility of work arrangements: Part-time options are available and widely used (even by some men), but many respondents believe that taking advantage of them entails stepping off partnership track, possibly permanently. It is perceived that part-timers can advance to counsel status and, according to some respondents, may come up for partner once they return to full-time schedules.

Two partners commented that they had taken advantage of the firm's part-time policies and were pleased by the results. One partner said she was recruited by the firm to become counsel on a part-time basis and that she was promoted to partner while working an 80-percent schedule. She noted, however, that while Hogan is "one of the best firms [for part-time], it's hard to be part-time and taken seriously (anywhere) unless you're a star." And another partner said that her experience with part-time was great and that the firm was entirely receptive to her request to work a two-thirds schedule for two years following the birth of a child. And when she billed at a 90-percent schedule, the firm's management "recognized my situation and, with no prompting on my part, compensated me for the time I spent."

The firm reportedly has no formal part-time policy and, according to one

associate, it is her opinion that "many in leadership here advocate this case-by-case policy as beneficial to 'good' women." Those seeking part-time schedules must negotiate individually with their practice groups, and are likely to encounter widely differing results depending on their practice area and the partners for whom they work. Part-time is reported to be most doable in the regulatory practice areas and least so in the corporate and litigation groups.

A health care associate commented that virtually all part-timers seem to work at least 80-percent schedules, and that although part-time schedules are accepted for valued members of a group, she "can't say they're encouraged or mentioned as options." A senior associate stated that some attorneys may believe that part-timers "are put on the 'mommy track' [and] women with tight schedules or who take days off for sick kids or school events are similarly categorized as less serious and less committed to partnership."

According to another associate, the firm has "the best family leave policy that I have seen at any company or law firm." Hogan, she reported, allows the "primary caregiver" to take three paid months off and to "tack on" vacation time.

> *While the firm is described as somewhat left-leaning, it is said to be home to both genuine liberals and staunch conservatives.*

Diversity: While Hogan is accepting of diversity, many respondents commented that the firm could do a better job of promoting it. Several respondents commented that the firm's management embraces diversity and that the firm is "laid back and accepting of all types."

While the recruitment and retention of minorities is "taken seriously by firm management," according to one partner, what many partners do not seem to consider is that it may take "extra effort to find and mentor associates who were not 'to the manor born.'" She added that those who are aware of the need for extra efforts "spend a lot of time making it happen." Another lawyer commented that Hogan has a large *pro bono* practice "that involves much work on behalf of minority and female groups." Nevertheless, one attorney suggested, "Traditional values are expected and nontraditional American appearances are not easily accepted."

On the political front, as a Washington firm, Hogan tries "hard to avoid being identified with either political party or point of view," according to a partner. While the firm is described as somewhat left-leaning, it is said to be home to both genuine liberals and staunch conservatives.

> *The senior women in the firm are "very much a part of making the firm more 'female-friendly' than most."*

Women in leadership positions: All but one respondent agreed that several women do wield power at Hogan. A woman partner was recently reelected to a second term on the firm's five-person executive committee, and women serve as chairs of five of the 15 committees and as practice directors in the regulatory departments.

Most respondents wrote that the more senior women in the firm are well-respected and are "very much a part of making the firm more 'female-friendly' than most," in the words of one. An associate remarked that several women partners "are known to champion the causes of women," and another commented that "the management committee member is terrific [and has] done a lot to make the firm a better place for men and women alike."

As is true virtually everywhere, Hogan's leadership remains male-dominated, partly because the female partners are just beginning to penetrate the more senior ranks of the partnership. Nevertheless, the influential women at the firm, according to one partner, "feel an obligation to help others up the ladder." Another stressed that women partners are "numerous and collegial and bond well."

Hogan & Hartson No. of Responses: 28	Strongly agree	Agree	Disagree	Strongly disagree
Women's prospects for advancement at the firm are as strong as men's	12	11	2	1
I am satisfied with the firm's family and personal leave policies	12	11	1	
There are women in positions of power and influence in the firm	13	12	1	
Women are as likely as men to receive desirable work assignments	15	8	2	
Women attorneys feel they can discuss family obligations openly	8	9	3	1
Women are as likely as men to be mentored by senior attorneys	12	4	6	1
Women attorneys enjoy a high level of job satisfaction	8	11	4	1
Women in the firm are supportive of their women colleagues	15	5	2	1
Firm management is receptive to the concerns of women attorneys	7	13	3	

HOWREY & SIMON

Rating: 43

🔨🔨🔨

Howrey & Simon
1299 Pennsylvania Ave. NW
Washington, DC 20004
202-783-0800

No. of Attorneys: 246
No. of Women Attorneys: 58
No. of Partners: 100
No. of Women Partners: 15
No. of Survey Responses Received: 12

Respondent Profile: 6 partners and 6 associates responded. Practice areas included litigation and antitrust.

Summary: The experiences of women lawyers at Howrey & Simon vary depending upon whom you talk to. Partners unanimously proclaimed that women lawyers' prospects for advancement are highly favorable, that the firm's atmosphere is bias-free, and that management supports those seeking to sustain a life outside of the firm. Half of the associates were more negative about women's potential to advance, and some criticized the firm's sponsorship of social events that exclude women. Both camps agreed, however, that Howrey & Simon is moving in a positive direction with regard to flexible and alternative work arrangements.

Advancement: Associates and partners didn't always agree about women's potential for advancement at Howrey. One midlevel associate wrote that, in her opinion, it is more difficult for women to advance at Howrey & Simon than men, because "this firm is very much an 'old boys' club.' The male partners and male associates go out drinking after work, and play golf together on the weekends. And there is *no* attempt that I see on the part of the women partners to help the women along."

Another midlevel associate perceived Howrey & Simon as "still somewhat chauvinist—but tries not to be." She added that the women partners are now talking about mentoring—although, in her assessment, nothing has happened yet.

Two of five associates viewed women's chances as equal to men, provided "they continue on to the point where they are considered for advancement." They observed that far fewer women than men last that long.

The partners, in contrast, were unanimous in concluding that women at Howrey enjoy equal prospects for advancement. Several noted that mentoring is vital to success, although one partner suggested that "women have not received the mentoring they need, and have too often been inadvertently excluded," although it was her opinion that this is changing.

One partner commented that she has experienced "no inequity in assignment allocation or review criteria." Another partner concurred and wrote,

"Women are at least as likely as men to be selected for partnership, although, due to attrition, the pool of women candidates at partnership time is too small."

> *"[I have] been subjected to some very chauvinistic and inappropriate comments that almost prompted me to leave last year."*

Attitudes and atmosphere: The dissonance between partners and associates was evident in their descriptions of Howrey's atmosphere. The main concern, according to a handful of respondents, lies in the firm's sponsorship of social events that appear to exclude women. According to one midlevel associate, she perceived that "the firm has something of a 'boys' club' atmosphere" and it was her impression that, "at times male partners let male associates get away with irresponsible behavior more easily."

Another associate wrote that, in her experience, "[I have] been subjected to some very chauvinistic and inappropriate comments that almost prompted me to leave last year."

Most women emphasized Howrey's recent improvement in this area. One claimed that "women are included as equals in all firm-sponsored events, including a 10K running team." According to one partner, the firm is "an increasingly comfortable place for women due to growing numbers of women in the partnership and the associate ranks." She reported that Howrey has an excellent sexual harassment policy, and that it has been supportive of an initiative to showcase the women partners. Another partner remarked that the women partners at the firm have sought "to increase the variety of firm functions to ensure that no unintentional male-dominated events take place, or at the very least, to make sure that they are balanced by other, more female-dominated events."

According to one partner, social interactions at Howrey & Simon are "professional, appropriate, but not stilted." She added that the firm's leadership is "committed to fostering a tone of equality and advancement for women [and] also sees important benefits that its female partners and associates bring to...the firm." One associate concurred, reporting that the firm's atmosphere is comfortable, that her work is respected, and that the "tone set by firm leadership is favorable to women in the firm."

> *Howrey's clients "pay high hourly wages [and] expect virtually unconditional commitment."*

Balancing work & family/personal life: Several respondents commented that the practice at Howrey entails considerable travel, which imposes a heavy burden on women with children, although many reported flexibility in managing their workload. Although one associate remarked that the firm's partners are sensitive to family responsibilities, another was anxious that "if you really put time into your family—you'll never make partner." One partner described striking a balance as "a constant battle," despite the firm's efforts "to accommodate competing personal issues and to recognize the need for people to have well-rounded personal lives." She commented that Howrey's clients "pay high hourly wages [and] expect virtually unconditional commitment."

A litigation partner noted that Howrey's technological support permits lawyers to work seamlessly at home. An associate agreed that this is a trend, and said that the firm is making an effort to make working from home a more viable option.

A partner reported that her clients and the partners with whom she works are flexible, knowing that the work will get done in a timely fashion even if she spends a morning chaperoning her child's field trip. One partner wrote that "if the work doesn't demand it, there is no expectation of 'face time,' such as on weekends or late nights."

Advancement to partnership for part-time associates is possible, according to the partners, but several perceived that it may be delayed.

Flexibility of work arrangements: Part-time options are available, and attorneys are reportedly beginning to experiment with telecommuting options. Although one associate believed that part-time arrangements are not available for associates, most partners reported that they are. One commented that the firm is "far more open than other firms about this issue." Several partners reported that five women partners and six women associates work part-time. Advancement to partnership for part-time associates is possible, according to the partners, but several perceived that it may be delayed.

According to one partner, part-time status has been "successful for some individuals." The factors influencing success, according to a litigation partner, include: "the level at which part-time status begins and whether the person has been able to establish credibility

before going part-time; the amount of flexibility in the part-time schedule, including travel; and the type of work performed (litigation with court imposed deadlines vs. counseling)."

"[The firm] doesn't necessarily demonstrate, at least outwardly, much of a commitment to diversity."

Diversity: Many respondents chose not to comment on diversity at Howrey, or provided very general remarks. One associate expressed her concern that the firm is not very diverse, and another said that, in her opinion, "[the firm] doesn't necessarily demonstrate, at least outwardly, much of a commitment to diversity." One partner clearly disagreed, "[There is] tremendous diversity among life styles, political leanings, and personalities among the women in my firm." Another partner reported that she had "not heard any complaints in this regard or been aware of any issues involving diversity at the firm." She added, "Several of our partners are openly gay...We have partners of all races, religions, and political leanings." Yet, inexplicably, it was another partner's opinion that Howrey's commitment to gender diversity is "not as strong as it should be for women of color and practically nonexistent for gays and lesbians."

One partner said women partners are on the ascent and "are attempting to pay attention to the needs of women."

Women in leadership positions: The three most senior women partners in the firm were reportedly recently appointed as the first women to join the firm's policy committee.

According to several partners, at least two of the three women on the policy committee have played a major role in promoting opportunities for women at the firm and supporting flexible work arrangements for women with families. Nevertheless, one partner suggested, "The power in the firm is overwhelmingly male. Although many of these men are relatively enlightened, they still think like men, and many fail to appreciate what women [lawyers] are going through." She added, however, that women partners are on the ascent and "are attempting to pay attention to the needs of women."

Howrey & Simon No. of Responses: 12	Strongly agree	Agree	Disagree	Strongly disagree
Women's prospects for advancement at the firm are as strong as men's	2	6	2	1
I am satisfied with the firm's family and personal leave policies	4	6	1	
There are women in positions of power and influence in the firm	4	7	1	
Women are as likely as men to receive desirable work assignments	2	7	2	
Women attorneys feel they can discuss family obligations openly	2	5	4	
Women are as likely as men to be mentored by senior attorneys	2	5	2	3
Women attorneys enjoy a high level of job satisfaction	2	5	4	
Women in the firm are supportive of their women colleagues	1	9	1	
Firm management is receptive to the concerns of women attorneys	3	4	3	

HUGHES HUBBARD & REED LLP

Rating: 41

◣◣◣

Hughes Hubbard & Reed LLP
One Battery Park Plaza
New York, NY 10004
212-837-6000

No. of Attorneys: 151
No. of Women Attorneys: 49
No. of Partners: 53
No. of Women Partners: 12
No. of Survey Responses Received: 10

Respondent Profile: 1 partner, 8 associates, and 1 counsel responded. Practice areas included litigation, corporate, and mergers and acquisitions.

Summary: With a distinguished history of promoting women, Hughes Hubbard & Reed is one firm in which women's full integration into firm life fosters a high level of comfort for women lawyers, although women with children may still perceive it as a rough road. It received virtually unanimous high marks for diversity, and almost all respondents agreed that a handful of women partners are truly influential.

Advancement: Although Hughes Hubbard has received accolades for its strong record of promoting women, the road to partnership is not without sacrifice. According to a partner, "Since 1969 or so, when Amalya Kearse became the first woman partner of color at a major law firm, and a litigator at that, our firm has had a history of sensitivity to women and advancement of women." She added that the firm recently won an award from the National Organization for Women for "the highest number of women partners per major New York law firm." This partner concluded that women's advancement history is excellent and that women "are an enormous resource at the firm."

Several junior associates agreed with this assessment. A first-year litigator remarked, "It seems like women have as much opportunity as men for advancement to partnership." A colleague described the firm as "very forward-thinking where women are concerned." A junior corporate associate observed that because the firm has so many women associates and partners, it was not necessary to ask during interviews: "What is it like being a woman at [Hughes Hubbard]?" She added that the firm's banking department has twice as many women as men.

A minority of senior associates painted a different picture, focusing on the difficulty of rearing children while moving up the partnership ladder. According to one respondent's perception, "Although our firm received an award for the percentage of female partners, the number is still low. The atmosphere is not conducive to family life." A litigator wrote, "Women are as likely to succeed as men if they are willing to forego time with their kids." According to this respondent, "The attitude among the female partners is, 'I put in the hours and never saw my family—you can do it, too.'"

A senior associate described the advancement issue as "a tricky question," asserting that, in her experience, "the women who made partner made huge sacrifices (i.e., bringing up their children) or aren't married at all." Although women do enjoy equal chances at partnership, she added, "once children come into the picture, it becomes more difficult."

> **According to a first-year associate, the firm "tries to be a comfortable place for women to work."**

Attitudes and atmosphere: Most respondents described the firm as very comfortable, largely because of the high numbers of women at all levels. According to most respondents, women are not made to feel excluded. A midlevel associate reported that summer and entering classes include at least 50 percent women. She added that, in her estimation, only one of the firm's teams has a reputation as a "boys' club," adding that the members of this predominantly male team go to the gym together, go out drinking together, but "it does not carry over to the rest of the firm."

According to a first-year associate, the firm "tries to be a comfortable place for women to work." She added that men are "definitely open about women working and achieving success, [but] the problem is, the legal arena in general is male-oriented."

Three respondents were less enthusiastic about the firm's atmosphere. One reported that, in her opinion, mentoring of women is "very weak, especially at the critical passage to midlevel associate." According to another's perception, the way you are treated "depends on who you work for." In her opinion, some partners "don't see you at all except for your work, others prefer short-skirted women." Women, she added, "play into these games to get ahead, so both are to blame." In short, this associate clearly believed that "future and physical allure are closely linked" at the firm.

Another associate claimed that during last year's holiday party, two women sat on the lap of a partner "while he 'jokingly' wrote promises of raises and vacations on napkins"—conduct the associate thought "reinforces the treatment of women as sex objects and makes it hard to believe that we are taken seriously by top firm management."

> **The unpredictability of work schedules makes it virtually impossible to have a social life, leading one respondent to conclude, "[It is] almost easier to be married before you get here so that at least there's someone at home when you are there."**

Balancing work & family/personal life: Several respondents reported that, in their experience, few, if any, women associates with children work full-time at Hughes Hubbard because "life in a big firm is just that—your life." According to a partner, although the firm is "sensitive to these issues, the clients have real time sensitivities that make the balancing difficult." A corporate associate agreed that "the firm is understanding of the existence of a life outside of the firm, but it still is a large New York law firm."

According to an associate, the hours at Hughes Hubbard are "better than elsewhere in the city" but still "bad." She noted that for junior associates, the unpredictability of work schedules makes it virtually impossible to have a social life, leading her to conclude that it is "almost easier to be married before you get here so that at least there's someone at home when you are there." Another unmarried associate commented that there is "inter-firm dating and even an upcoming marriage!" She added that the hours in corporate are "either overwhelming or tolerable, depending on the stage and type of transaction."

Another respondent agreed that partners and associates "with enough hours to survive can't have a home life," although all this changes for women "with their own business." A senior associate commented that it is very difficult for any attorney to sustain balance, because "12-hour days are not conducive to seeing one's loved ones." She added that even without children, this is a struggle and that "the only way to really balance it is to work part-time or at home for a while."

> *Senior men are perceived to be "indifferent" to the firm's part-time policy, and "women at the top do not support it."*

Flexibility of work arrangements: Part-time is available on a limited, case-by-case basis at Hughes Hubbard. One partner remarked that she and others have adjusted their work schedules to fit their "home schedules," although she did not clarify whether this was a formal arrangement.

Most associates expressed skepticism about the practicality of part-time. According to a litigator, several women in the department are currently on maternity leave and may seek part-time arrangements thereafter. Another litigator noted two women with part-time schedules and indicated that the firm "was not reluctant to give them these arrangements." She added, in her opinion, "I don't know if they really have the opportunity to advance to partner—I doubt it."

Another litigator commented that, in her opinion, part-time arrangements are "not highly looked upon but definitely available." A more senior litigator reported that part-time work becomes more viable as one grows more senior. Prospects for part-timers are no better in the corporate department because of the nature of the work, according to one associate. She further noted that although trusts and estates and non-transactional corporate lawyers can and do work part-time, there are, in her estimation, "no further opportunities within those departments."

According to an associate, the firm's attempts with part-time have "not worked." It was her perception that senior men are "indifferent" to the firm's part-time policy, and that "women at the top do not support it."

> *"Relatively speaking, HH & R is attracted to people of diverse backgrounds, culturally, ethnically, and socially."*

Diversity: Hughes Hubbard received strikingly favorable marks on diversity. One respondent declared that it has an "excellent record of tolerance" and is "supportive for women in general and for women of diverse ethnic backgrounds, as well." The firm reportedly works hard to recruit and keep women of diverse ethnic origins and according to one respondent, appears to be "very supportive of various religions and religious practices."

According to another associate, "Relatively speaking, HH & R is attracted to people of diverse backgrounds, culturally, ethnically, and socially." A junior associate agreed that the firm's attorneys "are not the cookie-cutter lawyers one typically sees, but are eccentric, offbeat, and very diverse." She added that the firm has "been trying for years to increase its minority hiring."

Another associate commented that the firm has left—and right—leaning attorneys and that it "might be hard to be openly gay and a partner, but who knows?"

> *"[Women are] among our most successful and highly compensated partners and have been for some time."*

Women in leadership positions: Most agreed that a handful of women at Hughes Hubbard are truly influential. Women reportedly serve on the firm's executive, personnel, and compensation committees, and lead several practice areas. According to a partner, women are "among our most successful and highly compensated partners and have been for some time."

One associate reported that she has "heard talk that when the current chairperson steps down, a certain female partner will succeed him." According to an associate, one of the firm's five biggest rainmakers is a woman.

Associates commented favorably on the role that senior women play within the firm. One remarked that they are "very open to comments and suggestions from other women." Another associate agreed, "There is a lot of respect and admiration for these women," and although some are more supportive than others, "generally the women partners and associates are supportive."

According to one respondent, the female partners "do try to help—inviting us to seminars, etc." She noted, however, that it is "the behind-the-scenes sort of issues that are harder to deal with." A litigator complained that she believed the strong women partners at the firm "don't give *any* talks to the women lawyers as to how to balance personal life with career" and "only talk about business opportunities for women."

One associate commented that a few of the senior women "are perceived very well," but that there are "also some women partners who are perceived poorly and who illustrate the stereotypical difficult woman in power."

Hughes Hubbard & Reed No. of Responses: 10	Strongly agree	Agree	Disagree	Strongly disagree
Women's prospects for advancement at the firm are as strong as men's	2	4	3	1
I am satisfied with the firm's family and personal leave policies	4	4	1	1
There are women in positions of power and influence in the firm	6	3	1	
Women are as likely as men to receive desirable work assignments	4	5		1
Women attorneys feel they can discuss family obligations openly	2	3	5	
Women are as likely as men to be mentored by senior attorneys	2	4	3	1
Women attorneys enjoy a high level of job satisfaction	1	5	2	
Women in the firm are supportive of their women colleagues	1	6	1	
Firm management is receptive to the concerns of women attorneys	1	5	3	

HUNTON & WILLIAMS

Rating: 51

Hunton & Williams
Riverfront Plaza
East Tower
951 E. Byrd St.
Richmond, VA 23219
804-788-8200

No. of Attorneys: 211
No. of Women Attorneys: 54
No. of Partners: 88
No. of Women Partners: 8
No. of Survey Responses Received: 6
Respondent Profile: 3 partners and 3 associates responded. Practice areas included litigation, corporate, and securities. We also received two surveys each from the New York, Washington, D.C., and Atlanta offices, and one from the Raleigh, N.C., office. Some of these comments were included in the text, though *not* in the chart.

Summary: Several women reportedly hold positions of power at Hunton & Williams, and most respondents believed that they were helping to move the firm in a positive direction. But going part-time is feared by some to be a dead end, and the substantial billable requirements and perceived lack of mentoring may hinder women seeking to climb the partnership ladder. In addition, although the firm fosters a supportive atmosphere for most women, a minority complained of exclusion from the perceived "boys' club."

Advancement: The road to partnership at Hunton & Williams seems to look shorter and smoother in hindsight, as reflected by the disparate responses between partners and associates. According to a litigation partner, the firm is "committed to the advancement of women," and women and men have an equal shot at partnership. She added that adequate mentoring is assured by "the direct responsibility that each partner has for the associates on that partner's team." A partner colleague agreed that the firm "exhibits great equality in elevating women to the partnership."

Another partner wrote that women "are actually given more opportunities because mentoring and allocation of assignments receives more attention from management where women and minorities are concerned."

One partner had a different perspective, writing that, in her opinion, women are "not as likely to advance as men because they have a more difficult time finding mentoring relationships."

Most associates perceived more stumbling blocks on the way to promotion, especially inadequate mentoring and meeting the substantial billable requirements that may be difficult to achieve if one is a primary caregiver. According to one's perception, associates advance by "billing at least 2,000 hours each year, every year, and by bringing in business. Either of these reasons can alone be sufficient if the numbers are good enough—well over 2,000 hours or $500,000 annual business, for example."

She added that, in her opinion, the time commitment required for partnership is more than most women with children can handle and "beyond what men who play an active role in their family life can handle."

Another associate claimed, "I have not yet seen a woman have both a family and a strong part-time practice. This is, of course, disappointing."

A corporate associate noted that, in her opinion, women were somewhat less likely to make partner because of self-selection and the tendency of some to "fall through the cracks" as far as mentoring is concerned. One associate, who reported that she had received "outstanding reviews," nevertheless perceived that women are less likely to advance as "mentoring is critical and there are not many opportunities for women to bond professionally with their male supervisors."

In the opinion of one partner, "Women need to be attractive to be taken seriously while men have more latitude in their appearance."

Attitudes and atmosphere: Respondents gave the firm's environment mixed reviews, with some expressing concern about lack of mentoring and exclusion from the "boys' club," and others reporting that the firm is quite supportive of women. A litigation partner described Hunton & Williams as "an *excellent* place for women, because of the firm's leadership." Another partner agreed that the firm's leadership is supportive of strong, talented women, asserting that she had experienced no gender discrimination.

But according to one partner, the corporate department has so few women "that it is difficult for women to find a peer group to help override the dominant male atmosphere. Golf and talk of sports govern many discussions and social gatherings." She also contended that, in her opinion, "women need to be attractive to be taken seriously while men have more latitude in their appearance."

Associates were equally divided on the atmosphere for women at the firm. One senior associate suggested, "There still remains a 'boys' club' tone on terms that are dominated by men."

One midlevel associate stated that, in her opinion, women enjoy less respect than men in the firm, and that even if they have mentors, these mentors may not always back them up. She sensed that junior attorneys "perceive this lack of support and get away with not doing work" for a woman that would regularly be done for other male attorneys. In her experience, "Staff sense the lack of support and openly complain about women attorneys or, worse, refuse to do their work....[I] cannot express how demoralizing it is to work in this environment. The only reason I stay is because I think I may be strong enough to make it and, perhaps, help other women."

Two associates were decidedly more positive. One wrote that the firm is "a good place for an ambitious, hardworking, smart woman to work. Most men here are modern and do not exhibit discriminatory behavior." A litigator remarked that the firm is "accepting of women attorneys and recognizes us for our skills [and] abilities."

> **"[Partners] talk as if there is sensitivity to time off for family, but if there is work to be done—and there always is—family is forgotten."**

Balancing work & family/personal life: One respondent reported that the firm requires of associates 2,000 hours a year in billables and 400 hours a year in nonbillables, including 40 hours of *pro bono*. Respondents diverged widely with respect to how this plays out in practice. An associate commented that despite the long hours, the firm is sensitive to family life, especially crises. One partner commented, "Given the demands of the practice, women need to make a choice as to firm versus family. Even with a 9 a.m. to 6 p.m. job, women, in my judgment, have elected to have someone else raise their children."

Another partner agreed that it is "difficult to sustain a family life for both male and female lawyers, but more difficult for women with children." Nevertheless, a junior litigation associate commented that she has had "no difficulty sustaining a personal life." She noted that she averages a 60-hour work week, "which leaves me enough time to work out daily and attend social gatherings."

A midlevel associate, however, maintained that she has no family life. In her opinion, partners "talk as if there is sensitivity to time off for family, but if there is work to be done—and there always is—family is forgotten." She added that although Little League and soccer practice are "acceptable reasons for leaving work," in her opinion, reasons "associated with mothering—childcare/illness, etc., are not."

> **"[Part-time is] viewed negatively, and part-time associates have a very difficult, if not impossible, time making partner."**

Flexibility of work arrangements: Part-time options do exist at Hunton & Williams, although skepticism about the practicality of such arrangements persists. According to one partner's opinion, there is "some thought that a lawyer ceases to develop work skills once [she has] gone part-time." Another partner noted that the availability of part-time possibilities is, in her estimation, contingent upon the individual's performance being satisfactory and the lawyer's willingness "to be flexible enough to meet client needs."

According to the perception of some associates, part-time is not a viable choice for those seeking to remain on partnership track. One associate remarked that, in her opinion, part-time is "viewed negatively, and part-time associates have a very difficult, if not impossible, time making partner."

> **"[The firm is] seemingly less tolerant with women who have 'difficult' personalities."**

Diversity: The few respondents who addressed the diversity issue on the survey indicated that Hunton & Williams is accepting of attorneys with diverse backgrounds. One partner reported that the firm has a "strong commitment to diversity." According to another partner, although the firm is "very comfortable with diversity of backgrounds, politics, and life styles," it is, in her opinion, less so with respect to personalities, and "seemingly less tolerant with women who have 'difficult' personalities." She added that the firm's attorneys hail from all parts of the country, are active in both political parties, and vary in sexual orientation.

"Women do not speak with one voice as to what the firm should do about quality of life, 'mommy track,' advancement, etc."

Women in leadership positions: Several women apparently hold positions of power at Hunton & Williams—women reportedly sit on the firm's executive, partnership admissions, associate, and other high-profile committees. According to one partner, however, one of these women is, in her characterization, "a token," but other women at the firm *are* concerned about women's issues and *do* play significant roles in firm management.

Another partner commented that Hunton & Williams' women partners meet every two years to formulate an agenda for the future. One associate praised the senior women for having attempted to provide support and mentoring to other women, though she suggested that most "think mentoring should come within your practice area and be gender-neutral."

A partner observed that the firm's most senior women are well-respected, and that "one needs to wonder whether they would lose respect if they focused more on quality of life issues." She surmised that the most serious problem faced by women at the firm is that "they are not of like minds. Some elected not to have children, some had children raised by others, and other women have focused more on their children at the expense of their advancement. Given this, women do not speak with one voice as to what the firm should do about quality of life, 'mommy track,' advancement, etc."

According to another partner, the perception of the most powerful women in the firm depends on your vantage point: "Senior women tend to view them with hostility or indifference, junior partners and associates are more supportive." She added that, given the "significant changes in policies and practices affecting women in the past few years, these women clearly have made a difference."

Despite the generally positive comments about senior women, one respondent reported that she believes she is "very much alone and feels no support whatsoever from any of the women around me—partners or associates."

Hunton & Williams No. of Responses: 6	Strongly agree	Agree	Disagree	Strongly disagree
Women's prospects for advancement at the firm are as strong as men's	2	2	1	1
I am satisfied with the firm's family and personal leave policies	1	4		1
There are women in positions of power and influence in the firm	1	4	1	
Women are as likely as men to receive desirable work assignments	2	3	1	
Women attorneys feel they can discuss family obligations openly	1	2	2	1
Women are as likely as men to be mentored by senior attorneys	2	2		2
Women attorneys enjoy a high level of job satisfaction	1	2	1	1
Women in the firm are supportive of their women colleagues	1	3	1	1
Firm management is receptive to the concerns of women attorneys	2	3		1

IRELL & MANELLA LLP

Rating: 34

Irell & Manella LLP
1800 Avenue of the Stars
Suite 900
Los Angeles, CA 90067
310-277-1010

No. of Attorneys: 160
No. of Women Attorneys: 37
No. of Partners: 79
No. of Women Partners: 10
No. of Survey Responses Received: 9

Respondent Profile: 1 partner and 8 associates responded. Practice areas included litigation, bankruptcy, employment law, and others.

Summary: Despite the firm's predominately liberal and relaxed atmosphere, respondents feared that Irell's grueling demands upon its attorneys and the paucity of women role models lead to widespread female flight during the mid- and senior-associate years. But those who stay are rewarded with equal opportunities for advancement and, if they choose, the ability to work under the firm's equitable part-time arrangements.

Advancement: Respondents perceived that Irell's hard-driving pace drives women out of the firm in large numbers, yet those who stick it out have an equal shot at partnership. One litigator feared that "[there is] an alarming trend of female associates leaving Irell & Manella at the mid- and senior-associate levels."

In the opinion of one litigator, the reasons for greater female attrition are the same as with any firm of this size: "It is a grueling life, and women are not willing to pay the price." According to a midlevel associate, the expectations placed on an associate being considered for partner are high, and both men and women "face the same difficulties in trying to reach the point of partnership consideration—spotty feedback and uneven mentoring."

An associate observed that part of the reason the firm "has a hard time attracting and keeping women is that it *has* very few women." She says, "There seems to be no rational explanation for that other than Irell's sometime reputation of being a bad place for women, which is undeserved."

Most respondents, taking into account that very few women stick it out for partnership review, concluded that those who do receive a fair shake. One associate commented that Irell & Manella "offers an environment that [is] significantly better than other firms of its caliber in terms of development and advancement." Several respondents commented that women's likelihood of receiving good assignments, fair reviews, and mentoring are equal to men's. One associate noted that despite her perception that men have enjoyed greater success reaching partnership in the past few years, "there is no evidence that this is attributable to any design or intention." She continued, "To the contrary, the firm has made a concerted effort to determine why fewer women have stayed until they reach senior associate levels."

A litigator reported, however, that although women are just as likely to receive quality work, mentoring for all associates is, in her estimation, "rather poor, and worse for women [because] there are so few women partners (especially in litigation)." Another lawyer feared, "[The firm] tolerates certain negative characteristics in male associates more readily than it does in female attorneys."

> *"Senior male partners seem unclear about how to praise or mentor female associates, other than to treat us as they would a daughter, which isn't always appropriate."*

Attitudes and atmosphere: The atmosphere is described as casual and liberal. The one partner said that the firm is "liberal politically and dedicated to advancement of women and minorities, making it a comfortable environment for women to express their issues and concerns." An associate agreed that people at the firm don't stand on ceremony or tradition. A senior associate remarked that the firm is always seeking to eliminate any manifestations of gender preference.

One litigation associate perceived the firm as "very masculine and aggressive, which makes some people uncomfortable." An associate believed, "Male associates

receive more and better mentoring... Senior male partners seem unclear about how to praise or mentor female associates, other than to treat us as they would a daughter, which isn't always appropriate."

A junior attorney in a smaller department has had a better experience. She wrote, "I get a fair amount of praise for doing a good job. I also get criticism in a constructive way. It is not sugarcoated, nor overdone or rude."

> *"Pressure is intense, and attorneys are expected to work seven days a week, no questions asked..."*

Balancing work & family/personal life: The hours and demands at Irell sound fairly brutal, placing life outside of the firm out of reach for some. In one litigator's experience, "Pressure is intense, and attorneys are expected to work seven days a week, no questions asked. Hours are scrutinized on a monthly basis—if they are not at least 200 every month, regardless of whether they were 400 the month before, the attorney is called to the carpet."

Another litigator agreed that "time pressure (as well as pressure from clients and colleagues) makes it extremely difficult to either establish or sustain a fulfilling personal life. Evenings and weekends without work are extremely rare."

In the opinion of one midlevel associate, "Family responsibilities are respected more than any other excuse for not being able to work," but she added, all the attorneys "end up sacrificing family commitments, especially associates." A midlevel associate perceived Irell as "a typical big firm—not very sensitive (for men or women)."

The partner commented, "[This] profession and motherhood are like oil and water. Both professional and family demands [and] commitments are unpredictable and naturally conflict."

An associate with children described the firm as a whole as family-friendly, although she had observed that several very powerful partners do not support part-time options. She added, "Fortunately, they've been shouted down when they've tried to limit flexibility."

An associate described the firm's part-time system as "one of the only fair part-time policies in L.A."

Flexibility of work arrangements: Associates generally praised Irell for its attitude toward part-time work. Many reported that the firm recently promoted to partner a woman who has worked on a part-time basis since she joined the firm as a first-year associate.

One associate described the firm as extremely flexible about part-time work, and another described its part-time system as "one of the only fair part-time policies in L.A." According to another associate, part-time arrangements are "both viable and common here, both for women and men."

Although the firm has promoted a part-timer to partnership, most associates agreed that this was the exception, not the rule. "Successes like that are rare (the first one yet)," observed one litigator, who feared that "to go part-time is to put yourself permanently out to pasture." Part-timers are "deferred for partnership for an unknown length of time," in the opinion of one midlevel associate.

"[Irell's] emphasis is so strongly on merit that it simply doesn't matter what your gender, race, or background is."

Diversity: Respondents emphasized that the firm's recruiting efforts are entirely merit-based and color-blind. A litigator wrote, "There is a commitment to hire the best and the brightest, without regard to race, gender, religion, etc." Another associate agreed: "Irell is not strong in showing a commitment to encouraging diversity, but it's emphasis is so strongly on merit that it simply doesn't matter what your gender, race, or background is."

The firm is also reportedly a supportive environment for gays. The partner commented that the firm is "accommodating for gay associates and partners," and an associate remarked, "[Irell & Manella] was founded upon values that embrace diversity and is a leader in that regard."

According to a junior associate's perception, "[Irell] recognizes it needs to recruit and retain women and has set up a committee" to address this issue.

The partner predicted, "Women are moving up through the ranks and will be in positions of genuine power eventually..."

Women in leadership positions: A female partner apparently serves on the five-attorney management committee, women serve on the hiring committee, and two women head practice groups, although respondents disagreed as to whether they believed this represented real power for women at Irell.

The partner predicted, "Women are moving up through the ranks and will be in positions of genuine power eventually. At present, most senior/powerful women are 10 to 20 years younger than most senior/powerful men and haven't therefore hit the uppermost ranks of power at the firm."

One associate perceived that the firm "has had a hard time retaining its powerful women; they seem to leave to pursue other opportunities—some with the sense that the power they enjoyed was illusory."

Although partners reported that the senior women had played a role in advancing junior women and women's issues, associates believe that there is room for improvement. One associate was concerned that "[the senior women] are more comfortable assisting more junior women attorneys; more senior women associates are at times viewed as potential threats to their (seemingly) precarious positions of power."

An associate perceived that the paucity of women in the partnership "may make it more difficult for female associates to find a mentor or feel comfortable with the senior partners." She observed, however, "The firm is aware of this and is making efforts to determine what it can do to end up with more women in more senior positions."

Irell & Manella No. of Responses: 9	Strongly agree	Agree	Disagree	Strongly disagree
Women's prospects for advancement at the firm are as strong as men's	2	4	3	
I am satisfied with the firm's family and personal leave policies	5	4		
There are women in positions of power and influence in the firm	1	5	2	1
Women are as likely as men to receive desirable work assignments	4	4	1	
Women attorneys feel they can discuss family obligations openly	1	6	1	1
Women are as likely as men to be mentored by senior attorneys	3	1	4	1
Women attorneys enjoy a high level of job satisfaction		6	2	
Women in the firm are supportive of their women colleagues	4	4	1	
Firm management is receptive to the concerns of women attorneys	3	4	1	

JENNER & BLOCK

Rating: 44

Jenner & Block
One IBM Plaza
Suite 3800
Chicago, IL 60611
312-222-9350

No. of Attorneys: 359
No. of Women Attorneys: 93
No. of Partners: 189
No. of Women Partners: 34
No. of Survey Responses Received: 20

Respondent Profile: 7 partners and 13 associates responded. Practice areas included litigation, commercial law, and labor and employment.

Summary: Jenner & Block provides a relatively welcoming work environment for its women lawyers, but the firm's reputation for progressiveness may be overstated, according to many respondents. Several women expressed their concern about the number of women recently leaving Jenner. In addition, the perception is that it is implementing its newly created part-time, nonequity partnership tier too slowly, a source of discontent in some quarters. Partners were generally more positive than associates—in some cases the two groups' opinions were dramatically opposed.

Advancement: Responses were split on the question of advancement at Jenner & Block, with some attorneys maintaining that women have an equal shot provided they put in the hours, and others contending that women are at a pronounced disadvantage. Several respondents maintained that what happens to women who are actually considered for partnership may be less significant than their concern about women leaving the firm. One associate expressed her fear that, "The number of women at both partner and associate levels has declined in the last year or so. Women depart for various reasons, but there appears to be a failure to recognize these departures as an issue at all."

A couple of associates surmised that double standards and child-rearing place women at a distinct disadvantage. One associate opined: "If women are willing to put the firm first, they can go far." But in her opinion, "women must sacrifice more than men and be more flexible in their time commitments [because] the expectation is always there that they are not as dedicated." Another associate commented, "Decisions to have children during the associate years [may] result in the receipt of lower quality assignments and career derailment."

Respondents who were optimistic about women's prospects for advancement described the firm's assignment and review processes as gender-neutral. One junior associate commented that women's opportunities at the firm are good, but "key to that process is mentoring and an ability to get along well with the most powerful partners, most if not all of whom are men." A first-year associate wrote that women are as likely as men to advance: "As long as you *work hard* and strive to achieve, you will be made partner. In fact, my guess is that they are eager to make women partners, because we don't have a lot of them."

At the partnership level, all but one respondent thought women enjoyed favorable advancement opportunities. A partner stated that women associates receive the same type of experiences and assignments as men and added, "[I] was mentored by both women and men, and I mentor both women and men." Another partner described the firm as "an excellent place for women," partly because of the presence of women on the executive committee and in other firm leadership posts.

One partner had a harsher perception: "If women can stand the generally unsupportive environment and the isolation long enough, they can make partner." She claimed that women are not given equal opportunities "in terms of litigation experience or client development." Women, she believes, "are accepted in a support role, but not as professionals capable of first-chair responsibility, [and they are] consistently viewed as not assertive enough and are never effectively mentored."

"Having women in top positions makes a tremendous difference in creating and maintaining a comfortable atmosphere for women."

....

Attitudes and atmosphere: Most respondents were upbeat about the atmosphere at Jenner, describing it as a "comfortable, down-to-earth place to work." One partner characterized the firm

as "an extremely diverse culture which accommodates highly individualistic attorneys," as well as having "a long history of hiring and retaining female attorneys." Another partner reported that the firm is not home to a "boys' club" and that "those types of attitudes are not tolerated by men or women in the firm."

According to one associate, although "the comfort level varies by practice area [and] many groups are dominated by men who socialize primarily with other men," there is a relatively strong network of women who "occasionally meet as a group to discuss issues such as marketing." A midlevel associate agreed: "Having women in top positions makes a tremendous difference in creating and maintaining a comfortable atmosphere for women."

Most associates reported having experienced little social exclusion at the firm. One new lawyer said she has been invited to "skybox sporting events with clients" and has "been encouraged to do other things (e.g., theater tickets) as well." In short, Jenner is "very comfortable" for everyone and "being a woman simply is not an issue here," in the words of a senior associate.

Several respondents disagreed with this rosy view, reporting more negative experiences. One lawyer described the firm as "mostly a 'boys' club'—when I got engaged, all I heard was, 'Oh, there's another woman gone.'" An associate feared that women are "seen as the brief writers or the organizers, but not the trial attorneys." Another respondent agreed that the number of women partners contributes to an atmosphere that is less than ideal. In her view, the firm is "a moderately uncomfortable place for women to work, largely because there are not very many successful women partners to use as role models." A litigator remarked that while Jenner is "comfortable to a point," women are "held to a different standard." In sum, she believed, "It's a very paternalistic atmosphere."

One partner agreed with these sentiments, observing that none of the men in her department, "from the most senior to the most junior, socialize with female attorneys" nor do they "invite women to lunch or to any other social functions." She added that, in her estimation, "[the] ideal lawyer is a tall, aggressive, *male* lawyer, and women [may feel they need] to downplay their 'feminine' traits."

Another associate commented that problems women experience "mostly stem from certain men's discomfort in working with women," but that this "can be overcome with patience." Overall, she concluded, "men and women are treated as equals."

One associate was concerned that "[the firm] doesn't care at all about family responsibilities, from what I can see."

Balancing work & family/personal life: For those seeking to balance work at the firm with outside responsibilities, Jenner is hardly a supportive environment, according to the opinions of a majority of respondents. Several associates suggested that the firm shows little sensitivity to outside demands and that its attitude is that women should hire others to raise their families. One associate was concerned that "[the firm] doesn't care at all about family responsibilities, from what I can see." A

midlevel associate said that in her opinion, "Almost every woman associate who has had a child before becoming partner has left the firm." She added, "[The] attitude of the firm heavy-weights [is that they] all worked like dogs and expect those who want to advance will do the same."

A litigator described the firm's view as "an uncaring, profit-is-the-only-motive attitude, especially toward associates..."

The solution to some associates appears to be postponing children until after one makes partner, as the balance seems to become more feasible at that level. A partner noted, "[The] overwhelming majority of our female partners have children and have sustained a satisfying personal and professional life." Another partner (with children) said that, in her view, the firm is "sensitive to family needs of all of its attorneys, male and female." Yet another partner with children noted that despite the difficulties, plenty of women and men do strike a balance. "Without adequate childcare," she added, "the situation would be unworkable." One partner noted that in certain departments, some "highly valued women can maintain family lives by working more from home." For the rest, however, " 'face time' is extremely important."

The newly proposed part-time partnership system received mixed reviews from associates.

Flexibility of work arrangements: Jenner has had part-time options at the associate level for about a decade and has recently announced the creation of a part-time, nonequity partnership tier, according to one partner. To date, however, "without part-time partners, it is difficult to say that part-time work is a 'legitimate and viable' option." One associate agreed that while "the idea of part-time work is accepted at Jenner," the reality, in her opinion, "i.e., being unavailable to service clients," is not. Another associate described the firm as "behind the times in this area."

The newly proposed part-time partnership system received mixed reviews from associates. According to one respondent, the proposal is positive and the firm has decided to give part-time a chance. According to a litigator, although management has "approved the 'concept,' it is taking months to work out details and make our part-time associate women partners."

Several respondents commented that part-time associates get a raw deal. According to the fears of one litigator, those on reduced schedules "end up working as many hours [with] less pay." Another litigator commented that, in her experience, quality of assignments for part-timers is poor, so that alternative arrangements are seen as viable options only for new mothers, and only for a short term.

A partner was concerned that part-timers "are often excluded from cases without being consulted, on the assumption they would not put in the time required." One associate remarked that, in her estimation, "The primary reason why women leave this firm is because it is not conducive to a rich family life. The demands of the job—primarily on our time—are too high." Part-time, she added, "definitely takes you off the partnership track."

According to the firm's partners, Jenner includes numerous lawyers working part-time and, in the words of one partner, "generally, those arrangements have worked when the part-timer is flexible" in terms of working a certain number of hours annually as opposed to a certain number of days per week. One partner commented that the firm's maternity leave policies are generous, adding, "I took a five-month leave with my first child and no one batted an eye."

> *One associate said, "I'm never afraid to say what I mean or be who I am."*

Diversity: The firm is said to be strong as far as diversity of political perspectives and sexual orientation is concerned, but reportedly lags behind in terms of racial diversity. There are "few women attorneys who are not white," in the words of an associate.

With regard to politics, the firm reportedly "loves iconoclasts." Jenner is described as "a liberal place [where] conservatives are accepted." The firm is said to include a strong lesbian/gay contingent that is accepted without question. In addition, associates and partners alike bring their same-sex partners to firm functions, according to an associate. Most respondents thought the firm was receptive to a wide range of personalities and viewpoints. One associate said, "I'm never afraid to say what I mean or be who I am."

> *"[The women partners] try to help promote women when they believe it's appropriate, but I believe they are without the power to force certain changes to occur."*

Women in leadership positions: While several women sit on the firm's executive committee, most respondents perceive that the decision-making power lies with a small group of men who sit on the all-male operations committee. Women serve at the helm of one of the firm's five litigation "clusters," as a co-chair of the labor and employment group, and as the chair of the recruitment committee. As a partner put it, "Of the few who really control the firm, none is a woman." According to another partner, this is because "very few women have a sufficient client base to give them any real power."

Most women were relatively positive about the role senior female partners play in promoting younger associates. A first-year associate reported that many of the "older women attorneys try to mentor and assist younger associates through monthly 'women attorney' meetings on topics such as how to generate business [or] jury perceptions of women." Another associate wrote that the senior women "try to enhance the quality of life for the women of the firm, but do not take radical stances." Yet another associate believed that the firm's women partners "could do more to help and mentor the younger lawyers coming up behind them." She added, "They try to help promote women when they believe it's appropriate, but I believe they are without the power to force certain changes to occur in the manner that the men, who do have the power, are able to."

The partners thought highly of themselves as mentors and role models. One reported that the firm's senior women "are powerful members of the firm and outstanding mentors and supporters of the female attorneys." Another partner observed that she and her peers "are perceived with respect and spend a great deal of time mentoring other women lawyers in the firm."

One partner, however, issued a strong dissent, writing that, in her opinion, none of the women on the executive committee "have the ability or willingness to champion women's interests." She added that with one notable exception, the women partners do not reach out to other women and "it appears that the best way to secure your position with the male leaders is to give a rubber stamp of approval 'on behalf of the women' to any proposal that could adversely affect women."

Jenner & Block No. of Responses: 20	Strongly agree	Agree	Disagree	Strongly disagree
Women's prospects for advancement at the firm are as strong as men's	7	6	5	2
I am satisfied with the firm's family and personal leave policies	5	4	9	2
There are women in positions of power and influence in the firm	6	7	6	
Women are as likely as men to receive desirable work assignments	12	4	2	1
Women attorneys feel they can discuss family obligations openly	8	5	6	1
Women are as likely as men to be mentored by senior attorneys	9	2	7	2
Women attorneys enjoy a high level of job satisfaction	4	7	8	1
Women in the firm are supportive of their women colleagues	10	6	2	2
Firm management is receptive to the concerns of women attorneys	5	6	7	2

JONES, DAY, REAVIS & POGUE

Rating: 64

Jones, Day, Reavis & Pogue
North Point
901 Lakeside Ave.
Cleveland, OH 44114
216-586-3939

No. of Attorneys: 230
No. of Women Attorneys: 64
No. of Partners: 87
No. of Women Partners: 7
No. of Survey Responses Received: 8

Respondent Profile: 2 partners, 4 associates, and 2 senior attorneys responded. Practice areas included litigation, employee benefits, and securities.

Summary: At Jones, Day, management is reportedly less driven by politics and personality than many other firms, although some claim there is little attention paid to "women's issues." Although no woman is said to wield any significant power, for the women who can stick out the 10-year partnership track, prospects for advancement are equal.

Advancement: Prospects are reportedly equal for women who stick out the 10-year track working full-time and putting in long hours to prove their commitment, but respondents believed that few choose to do so.

According to a partner who is involved in the assignment and review processes, good systems are in place and women are treated fairly. Another partner agreed that women are judged by the same criteria as men, but noted "[the] time commitment required does cause women to opt out more often than men." Thus, "for the few women who stay at the firm and on track," one respondent said, prospects for partnership are commensurate with those of men.

According to a midlevel associate, "*Extremely* low numbers of women" are still around for partnership consideration, with most others having either left

because of, in part, family pressures or to go on the "mommy track." She concluded that, in her estimation, remaining at the firm "[is] an unappealing choice to most women." One respondent expressed her fear that "[the] major drawback to the advancement of women is that there are no part-time partners, so many women feel it is impossible to have family and succeed through traditional channels."

According to an associate, "The firm is still run by men, but they seem to want to allow women to advance as long as the women fit the traditional big-firm mold." A midlevel associate agreed that female associates who work part-time are "at a disadvantage in partnership consideration." Without part-time options, one respondent said, those who are "not willing to give up their entire personal lives" have little choice but to leave the firm.

One senior associate commented that the problems go beyond work and family. She remarked that due to the scarcity of women partners, "there is little mentoring by women." She added that while her assignments are fairly allocated, notwithstanding her senior status, she thought she was "less likely to be called upon to present my work to clients, a few of whom have mistaken me for a secretary." Although, in her opinion, she is kept out of the limelight, her work "always forms the basis [for], or is, what is presented to the client."

> *"[Management] is heavily focused on merit (and is driven less by politics and personality) than in many other firms."*

Attitudes and atmosphere: Although the firm's atmosphere is reported to be professional and businesslike, most respondents differed with one partner's view that this adds up to an "extremely comfortable" environment for women. To one associate, the tone is "one of dignity, but cold." She added that personal considerations, comments, and interests are not welcomed, "nor is simple friendship or collegiality." An associate commented that the firm is comfortable "if you want to fit into the big-firm pattern." She added that there is little social interaction between attorneys "because no one has time for it." One partner said, "[Management] is heavily focused on merit (and is driven less by politics and personality) than in many other firms."

According to one associate, the annual lawyer outing revolves around golf

and is "horribly one-sided." She believes, "All the guys smoke cigars and play poker" and no attempt is made to make women feel comfortable. Another associate remarked that there are some older partners who "view women in the profession as an oddity and do not take us seriously." Moreover, she added, there is "a macho culture" that discourages taking any time off, weekends included, for vacation or illness.

One litigator was especially concerned that "any type of task force oriented toward perceived 'women's issues' is belittled and viewed as a waste of time by both men and women within the firm." She added that, in her experience, this holds true even when the initiative is related exclusively to business.

One associate believed, "The 'boys' club' is still quite strong" at the firm. She added that men in other practice areas make jokes about her travel schedule, especially when she is required to travel with men.

> *One respondent commented that she could not "see how a woman can stay on track and have a quality family life."*

Balancing work & family/personal life: The work-family balance at the firm's Cleveland office is reportedly no better than in New York or Chicago. Many full-time attorneys are expected to bill between 2,100 and 2,400 hours per year and often travel extensively, making outside commitments difficult to maintain.

One partner commented that the firm "allows great room for individual choice and that will be respected," but associates took a generally dimmer view.

One respondent commented that she could not "see how a woman can stay on track and have a quality family life."

A litigator agreed that she could not "imagine working the hours I work now as a full-time associate and having children." According to another respondent, "*Nothing* is to interfere with client work, so the women are under tremendous pressure to compete with the men, while also having the lion's share of family responsibilities in most cases." Unmarried women, she observed, "survive until they decide they *want* a personal life."

A litigator with children commented that, in her experience, pressure "comes from other women lawyers not in your practice group who have preconceived notions about what is or isn't appropriate for you." She added that her hours are "exorbitant" in view of her area of specialization and that because her children are slightly older, she feels she is "viewed as more expendable than a man with smaller (younger) children and a wife at home."

According to an associate, the level of sensitivity to family responsibilities varies by practice area, and the partners in the employee benefits group are "very supportive and understanding." A litigator expressed her anxiety that using one's personal life "as a basis for any request for relief" may well lead others to question a woman's commitment even though, were a man to make the same request, he would probably be seen as legitimately needed at home.

One partner advised junior lawyers who lack control over their schedules to handle the problem "by setting priorities and having frank conversations with the partners who are assigning work." For partners, she added, long hours are driven by the demands of clients, not the firm, but "again, the demands are high."

Unmarried women "survive until they decide they want a personal life."

Flexibility of work arrangements: Part-time arrangements are reportedly available, although their viability hinges on the practice group. One partner with children was reported to have worked a part-time schedule for several years as an associate, an arrangement that was very successful. Another partner confirmed that going part-time does not foreclose future partnership, although attorneys must return to full-time work if they want to be considered and must remain on full-time status if and when they are promoted.

Most associates said that although part-time may not technically preclude future promotion, as a practical matter, shifting to reduced hours means sacrificing, for all intents and purposes, all chances of advancement, except to senior attorney level.

The availability of part-time is reportedly somewhat select. According to one respondent, for women who are "valued by the firm" and who work in practice areas such as tax, part-time is an option.

One senior attorney was reported to have requested to move off partnership track in her sixth year, and although her hours and compensation are less than for associates, there was "no reduction in the quality of [her] work and no change in how [she] was treated by the partners in [her] group."

According to a litigator, "Many partners complain about part-timers and do not take them seriously, especially in litigation." Another litigator agreed: "It couldn't be any clearer that availing yourself of those options means being taken off the partnership track and not being considered 'committed' to the firm." Another litigator commented that part-time is "usually frowned upon" and that many women who have tried it "[have] sacrificed the partnership track and been relegated to a senior attorney position."

According to one respondent, success at the firm depends heavily on attorneys' willingness to conform.

Diversity: Although the partners profess that Jones, Day has "room for all kinds of people" and provides a "comfortable and supportive environment," other respondents reported experiencing little evidence of this. According to an associate, "The firm has *very few* minorities or women of diverse backgrounds," as well as very few female attorneys who are "involved in anything besides work." Another lawyer wrote, "These issues are *never* discussed." To another respondent, success depends heavily on attorneys' willingness to conform to the "status quo" in politics, dress—whatever. She added that if one has different views, "they are best kept private," although this sweeping opinion did not seem to be shared by most respondents.

According to one respondent, the firm is committed to diversity "but does not alter its standing," meaning that those from diverse backgrounds are welcome "if they fit the big-firm mold."

Women with true power are reportedly nonexistent and what influence women have is "transient and marginal."

Women in leadership positions: Our respondents were hard-pressed to identify any woman at Jones, Day whom they perceived to be a heavy hitter. Women with true power are reportedly nonexistent and what influence women have is "transient and marginal," in the words of one lawyer. A partner reported that very few if any women partners are of the age and experience level of the men who "wield 'real' power."

One partner stated that the firm's senior women are "supportive of junior women," but most junior women disagreed. A midlevel associate observed that she does "not look at any woman partner here as someone I admire as a role model." She further noted that all of her mentoring "has come from men who don't understand family or home pressures because they have wives who do not work." She added that several of the female partners in the firm have "reputations for being especially hard on young women." Another respondent commented that those women who have "a modicum of power do *nothing* to promote quality-of-life issues for women in the firm," and characterized mentoring as virtually nonexistent. A senior associate agreed that although the women partners are "well-thought of," they have not played significant roles in promoting opportunities for other women.

One associate reported that the women partners "recently figured out that they need to do more mentoring and be more supportive of junior attorneys" and that this prompted them to start a professional development program for women at the firm. She added that although it is not perfect, this effort represents a sincere attempt to meet younger women's needs, and is beginning to receive support from the firm at large.

Jones, Day, Reavis & Pogue No. of Responses: 8	Strongly agree	Agree	Disagree	Strongly disagree
Women's prospects for advancement at the firm are as strong as men's	2	2	1	2
I am satisfied with the firm's family and personal leave policies	4	2		1
There are women in positions of power and influence in the firm		3	3	2
Women are as likely as men to receive desirable work assignments	3	4		
Women attorneys feel they can discuss family obligations openly		1	4	2
Women are as likely as men to be mentored by senior attorneys	3	1	2	2
Women attorneys enjoy a high level of job satisfaction		3	2	1
Women in the firm are supportive of their women colleagues	1	5	2	
Firm management is receptive to the concerns of women attorneys		3	3	1

KATTEN MUCHIN & ZAVIS

Rating: 38

◄◄◄

Katten Muchin & Zavis
525 West Monroe St.
Suite 1600
Chicago, IL 60661
312-902-5200

No. of Attorneys: 303
No. of Women Attorneys: 90
No. of Partners: 149
No. of Women Partners: 30
No. of Survey Responses Received: 19

Respondent Profile: 8 partners and 11 associates responded. Practice areas included corporate, litigation, employment, health care, and finance.

Summary: Associates at Katten were generally more positive than its partners, three of whom cited perceived problems with the firm's two-tiered partnership structure, while others were critical of an atmosphere they considered unpleasant for women. On the bright side, Katten's flexibility in offering part-time, flextime, and telecommuting arrangements drew high praise from most attorneys.

Advancement: Although an overwhelming majority of associates thought women's advancement prospects roughly equaled men's, three of Katten's partners offered the caveat that women's "equal prospects," in their estimation, are largely limited to the income partner status, a position they characterized as offering significantly less power and remuneration than capital partnership. As one partner suggested, "In reality, there is little difference" between income partner status and "the status of senior associate."

One respondent wrote that, in her opinion, "Men get clients handed down to them; women do not." Another partner remarked, "[The] rules seem to change constantly." According to this partner's assessment, management "will tell you it's all about business, and then promote a male income partner with no business."

Then, she added, "when strong, aggressive women seem to be doing well, people start saying they are 'too aggressive.'"

Another partner reported a "degree of comfort in having women in the role of practice-development tool for capital partners (i.e., business services)," but, in her view, "[there is] little interest in freeing them from such roles to develop their own practices." Several partners agreed with that perception. As one observed, "Business that is serviced and even developed by women is usually characterized as obtained by a male colleague."

Five of the eight responding partners were more optimistic concerning women's advancement prospects. One asserted, "Women who are career-minded can do very well at our firm." She added that a "women's forum has been established to further the mentoring process, and senior women are very conscious of this issue." Another partner commented that recently several women have advanced to capital partners, "as there are more women with experience and requisite seniority."

In contrast to most of the other firms surveyed, an overwhelming majority of women associates expressed greater optimism about women's prospects for advancement than did the partners. A midlevel corporate associate raved that women are "as likely as men to advance to partnership—the firm made 18 partners in February 1997, 12 of whom were women." She described the firm as a meritocracy, but admitted that equal treatment extended "at least as far as progression to a first-tier partner is concerned." A senior litigation associate wrote, "Women are as likely as men to advance to partnership and have opportunity for mentoring relationships and other 'enablers' on that path."

A partner characterized the firm as having a "macho atmosphere including yelling, bad language, and chewing out in public" and a "paternalistic attitude" toward women.

....

Attitudes and atmosphere: Respondents were sharply divided on the atmosphere at the firm, with more partners than associates taking a critical stance. A partner characterized the firm as having a "macho atmosphere including yelling, bad language, and chewing out in public" and a "paternalistic attitude" toward women. She also reported that, in her estimation, "Dissent is considered trouble-making." In sum, in her characterization, "this place is

[uncomfortable] for women after junior associate level."

But even at the junior level, associates may find the atmosphere unwelcoming. One junior associate wrote that, in her opinion, "Lewd and unprofessional sex-based humor and metaphor is quite common."

One partner commented that while the firm is generally comfortable, in her estimation, "some male partners were more comfortable with my playing a supportive role, doing the work that made them look good."

A partner summarized what she believed to be the firm's attitude: "We have a women's forum, mandatory sessions on sexual harassment and diversity issues, and a good procedure for registering complaints."

Several women gave the firm's atmosphere high marks. An associate commented that the firm is "a more open and comfortable place to work than most large firms," and another characterized the firm as "no more male-dominated than any large workplace." An associate reported, "Men and women interact socially a great deal, and there is a strong sense of camaraderie between genders."

One midlevel associate was positively effusive about the milieu at Katten. She wrote, "In one word—empowering. The firm is a comfortable, relaxed environment, although the firm has an 'entrepreneurial energy' to it that keeps it exciting."

A senior associate commented that most of the female partners have children and "seem content with the balance."

....

Balancing work & family/personal life: The demands on younger associates at the firm are reportedly onerous, although the hours tend to ease up as one progresses up the ladder. Minimum billable hours at the associate level are reported to be 2,000; at the income partner level, this drops to 1,920.

Most respondents reported that, as demonstrated by its flexibility with respect to scheduling and telecommuting, Katten is receptive to its attorneys' family demands. "People don't care when you do your work, as long as you get it done," commented one partner, who added that the firm's attorneys enjoy more flexibility than at most other firms. An associate agreed: "It is probably as good here as it gets in a law firm."

One partner reported that she is encouraged by the rising number of women who are "returning after maternity leave to well-respected positions at the firm," and observed, "they seem happy." A senior associate commented that most of the female partners have children and "seem content with the balance."

There were several dissenters who thought the firm and its individual partners could do more to accommodate persons juggling work and family demands. One associate characterized the working hours as "ridiculous" and noted that she "stayed...until midnight, 4 a.m., all night. For what?" One associate remarked, "I doubt some partners will ever get it or realize that while they were working, their wife's job of raising their children was also 'more than full-time.' " A married partner opined, "What personal life? Between the work, daily commute, and out-of-town travel, I hardly have time to keep up with the laundry! This place is cut throat."

Although the hours and pressure are reported to be toughest in the corporate department, the health care practice group apparently offers substantially more flexibility.

An attorney said that the firm's flexibility gives her "an extremely good attitude about work in general."

Flexibility of work arrangements: Most respondents lauded the firm for its flexibility in offering part-time, flextime, and telecommuting arrangements for attorneys seeking to balance work with outside obligations. Part-time arrangements reportedly "work on a case-by-case basis," and women have taken advantage of part-time scheduling.

Respondents provided conflicting accounts of advancement opportunities for part-timers, with some attorneys reporting that the firm has promoted lawyers to income partner while they were part-time, and others suggesting that part-timers "may no longer be on partnership track."

In addition, the firm has also reportedly granted attorneys flextime arrangements, whereby lawyers can opt for meeting the 2,000-hours-minimum billables requirement and "establish their own informal flex schedules."

Only a handful of attorneys were critical of the firm's alternative work arrangements. A partner feared that, in her estimation, women who go part-time "are seen as loafers and appear more likely to be terminated." A lawyer reported that a woman in her department has taken advantage of an alternative work arrangement, "which has been to the distinct disadvantage" of her colleagues.

Several attorneys said that the firm provides excellent emergency day care across the street.

"The firm has spent a lot of money on diversity training," but, a partner asserted, "it is for the public image."

Diversity: Although a few respondents observed a genuine commitment on the part of the firm to the promotion of diversity, others commented that, in their opinion, the firm's efforts in this regard are motivated solely by self-interest, rather than by a sincere commitment to making the firm hospitable to lawyers from different backgrounds.

According to one partner's perception, "The firm has spent a lot of money on diversity training, [but] it is for the public image." She added that there are "few if any black attorneys, women are mainly in junior positions, and there are no openly gay attorneys."

Another partner agreed, characterizing the firm's approach to diversity and "sensitivity to harassment" as window dressing. With the exception of some men and women "sincerely committed to change," she observed, "I have little reason to believe the real leaders care beyond building a case against future law suits."

A third partner commented that although Katten does sponsor "mandatory firm-wide seminars on diversity and tolerance," she perceived that "the firm is motivated more out of...fear of legal repercussions (i.e., lawsuits) for a failure to honor people's 'right to be different'

than any underlying belief that it is, in fact, the proper approach."

Some associates gave more credence to the firm's efforts to diversify. A junior associate suggested, "Policy-wise the firm is supportive of diversity, though this is not reflected as much as it should be in the population of attorneys." A senior associate described the firm as "more than tolerant of diverse backgrounds."

One senior woman is "a wonderful person who has tried to improve the status of women, but she has 'battle fatigue' from being shouted down by management."

Women in leadership positions: Women serve on the executive and compensation committees and as department heads, according to respondents. One associate remarked, "[The] real estate department in particular has two very successful and powerful women partners. [The] corporate department has lacked influential women partners, but is making progress lately." As one partner claimed, however, none of these women are, in her opinion, "among the two to three partners perceived as running the firm."

Most respondents described these colleagues as highly respected, but views were mixed as to whether those holding senior posts are truly powerful, and on the role these attorneys have played in assisting their juniors. According to an associate, "The female firm leadership is both very much in force and very committed to assisting younger women in the firm." A corporate associate commented that she finds the women partners to be "not only supportive but interested in my career." Another said she viewed one of the most senior women as "a wonderful person who has tried to improve the status of women, but she has 'battle fatigue' from being shouted down by management."

Other respondents, both partners and associates, criticized the most senior women for failing to take an interest in the careers of their younger colleagues. According to one partner, the senior women "tend to be older women who have worked their way up in a male-dominated arena and thus have become somewhat 'one of them.' They generally tend to be not in touch with the younger women and, in particular, those with families." In her opinion, she added, "If anything, they tend to be tougher on younger women than the men."

Another partner commented that there is "perhaps one woman in a real leadership role; however, she is (and is perceived to be) 'one of the boys.'"

Many respondents lauded the creation by the firm's women partners of a women's forum, described as "a loose organization of women that has internal meetings and mentoring, as well as external business-development presentations for clients and friends of the firm." According to an associate, the forum "has grown to a city-wide group of female professionals that gathers periodically to discuss women balancing careers and family and dealing with other real-life issues."

Katten Muchin & Zavis No. of Responses: 19	Strongly agree	Agree	Disagree	Strongly disagree
Women's prospects for advancement at the firm are as strong as men's	5	10	1	4
I am satisfied with the firm's family and personal leave policies	9	6	3	
There are women in positions of power and influence in the firm	5	8	1	4
Women are as likely as men to receive desirable work assignments	11	6	2	
Women attorneys feel they can discuss family obligations openly	5	9	4	1
Women are as likely as men to be mentored by senior attorneys	7	3	4	4
Women attorneys enjoy a high level of job satisfaction	3	13	1	2
Women in the firm are supportive of their women colleagues	9	6	4	
Firm management is receptive to the concerns of women attorneys	3	10	1	4

KAYE, SCHOLER, FIERMAN, HAYS & HANDLER LLP

Rating: 68

Kaye, Scholer, Fierman, Hays & Handler LLP
425 Park Ave.
New York NY 10022
212-836-8000

No. of Attorneys: 259
No. of Women Attorneys: 72
No. of Partners: 87
No. of Women Partners: 13
No. of Survey Responses Received: 7

Respondent Profile: 7 associates responded.

Summary: Although Kaye, Scholer's partnership ranks include a sizable number of women, these numbers may be deceiving—women's potential for advancement is lackluster, according to a slight majority of respondents. Compared to its New York peers, the firm's average billables are relatively modest, enabling its junior lawyers to sustain a life outside of the firm. Finally, the firm's flextime policy, viewed with suspicion by our handful of respondents, could use some shoring up, as could women's power within the firm.

Advancement: A slim majority of respondents reported that despite the relatively sizable proportion of women partners at the firm, prospects are not bright for women coming up through the ranks. An associate commented that although there are "a lot of female partners" for a New York City firm, they are concentrated in the corporate department, with just two in the litigation department. Moreover, the numbers can be misleading in that one respondent asserted she knew of no woman who was made partner in the past five years. An associate said that although she is impressed with the number of female partners at the firm, it means little for her own chances, as "most were lateral hires who were already partners at smaller firms."

Business generation is reportedly critical to advancement prospects at the firm, but generating business is linked to a variety of forces that can operate against women. In one associate's assessment, "The likelihood of partnership is bleak for men and women. The focus is on business and clients, and a woman would be just as likely to make partner as a male if she were to have business."

Although respondents were virtually unanimous that women are as likely as men to receive desirable work assignments, the dissenting associate said, in her opinion, "To advance within the firm, it is essential to perform while on high-profile assignments, to be mentored by a powerful partner and to be perceived as a potential rainmaker." In her estimation, women have difficulty getting good assignments once they become pregnant. Thereafter, there is a perception that "a vicious cycle develops and the attorneys who staffed the 'better assignments' continue to be assigned to them due to their experience."

Another associate agreed that family can put a damper on women's prospects: "Women have to make family choices that similarly situated males do not have to make, such as timing of having children."

According to one associate, however, "Women leave the firm because they want to stay at home, not because they don't enjoy working here."

Opinions about women litigators' prospects at the firm varied widely. One junior associate commented that she has been highly satisfied with her experience at the firm and that she has received good assignments, "tremendous support, advice, opportunity, mentoring by most of the senior associates and partners with whom I have worked (all of whom are men)."

She concluded that the firm functions as "a meritocracy. The harder you work and the better your work product—the more responsibility and respect you get—*regardless of gender.*"

According to another litigator, however, there is a fear that women "are not as likely to advance—they are still considered 'foreigners.' Although, as with foreigners, they are treated with a sense of deliberate or conscious acknowledgment of their womanhood, they are not a member of the fraternity. As outsiders, they are always looking in through an opening—the size of which is determined by the particular partner."

"...the midlevel female associates work harder than the males in their classes."

Attitudes and atmosphere: Although they agree that Kaye, Scholer is still male-dominated, most respondents find it comfortable on a daily basis, but they never lose sight of the fact that men are in the majority.

Comfort levels reportedly vary considerably by department. According to a bankruptcy associate, she perceived that "the attitude in my group is evidenced by the fact that virtually all the partners (all male), counsel (all male), and associates have spouses who play 'traditional roles.'" She reported that there is "a bit of a 'boys' club' atmosphere and periodically the doors are open to women."

Another associate commented that in departments with female partners and equal numbers of male and female associates, gender discrimination is not a problem.

A litigator contended that women are given work as challenging as that assigned to men, and, "if anything, sometimes we are unfairly given *more* work than our counterparts." Another litigator agreed that, in her estimation, "the midlevel female associates work harder than the males in their classes."

Within the firm at large, relations between the genders are generally collegial. One lawyer reported that men and women socialize, but noted that "tables in the cafeteria often split along gender lines." A litigation associate commented that "social interaction is integrated, although a group of women associates go out for drinks once a week (no men), but they could come if they wanted." Another litigator believed that the "litigation male associates do often socially act like a 'boys' club,' which is quite annoying."

A junior-level litigator reported, "Most of the female litigation associates tend to eat lunch at their desks." One junior described the firm as "very family-oriented" and further noted that "they are/seem to be understanding of women who have children." In terms of work assignments she is "expected to meet the same standards (not higher) that are set for males." She described the firm as not very social, although "many women and men are friends."

> **"As far as big New York City firms go, our hours are relatively sane and allow for some personal life."**

Balancing work & family/personal life: Junior associates concluded that expectations at the firm are reasonable, but more senior attorneys disagreed. According to a first-year associate, "As far as big New York City firms go, our hours are relatively sane and allow for *some* personal life." She added that although some partners have families, most associates are single "so it is hard to tell whether hours are adjusted for family obligations or just as a privilege of partnership."

Another junior associate noted that in the litigation department, two young female associates have children and the other women associates are "all watching eagerly" to see how it works out. She added that, to her knowledge, there have been two or three successful attorney mothers in the corporate department but suggested that "this says little for a firm with more than 200 lawyers."

Another junior associate noted that billables are around 1,900 to 2,000 hours and that the firm is "generally sensitive to family responsibilities, but everyone knows they are running a business and you can't get in the way of that." A first-year litigation associate commented that no "face time" is required in her department and that "generally speaking the working hours aren't bad, but certain practice groups and partners do work associates, regardless of gender, extremely hard."

Two senior associates who responded were significantly more negative. One commented that life at the firm is "a miserable existence for either gender, but women can get out because it is still socially acceptable to raise family in lieu of working." Another commented that the "fact that [many] women self-select out of the firm says it all, I think."

Finally, the firm reportedly offers emergency backup childcare and sponsors a program for "Take Your Daughter to Work Day."

> **Part-time is "not *viable in the long term if one is seeking security and advancement.*"**

Flexibility of work arrangements: Part-time arrangements are said to exist, but they are reportedly not for the faint of heart. According to one associate's opinion, part-time is "*not* viable in the long term if one is seeking security and advancement." She added that although she knows of several women on flextime, "personally I would worry."

Going part-time is said to significantly reduce partnership prospects. A bankruptcy attorney commented that in her department, there is "a view that attorneys must be here full-time to properly service clients and a part-time lawyer will not be staffed on certain types (i.e., career-advancing) of assignments."

Another respondent remarked that although part-time schedules exist, "I am not sure how viable they are—part-timers seem to put in as much work, just in less days." According to one associate, the flextime policy is "being reevaluated by a committee of litigation associates and partners because, while on paper it appears adequate, in practice it's underutilized (attrition) or may be unrealistic." She commented that the firm "really wants to retain women associates and has realized that it loses a lot of investment in training and skill when a good women lawyer leaves because balancing becomes too hard or impossible."

"It could and would be even better if we had more minority female attorneys in the office."

Diversity: According to several associates, the firm is committed to diversity. One respondent noted, "Life style and personality can conflict with the conformity of a corporate law firm. Kaye, Scholer is particularly tolerant and accepting." Another opined, "It...would be even better if we had more minority female attorneys in the office."

One associate wrote that this year's entering class "is more diverse with respect to ethnicity and the schools attended." Another said that the firm "wants quality people who are capable of doing good work without regard to background. In that sense it is comfortable. Are they supportive? I'm not sure they would go out of their way."

"When people talk about the movers and shakers at the firm, they are basically talking about half a dozen older male partners."

Women in leadership positions: Respondents were in accord that women do not wield true power at the firm. The most influential woman most respondents could point to is a co-chair of the recruitment committee. According to an associate, "When people talk about the movers and shakers at the firm, they are basically talking about a half a dozen older male partners." In the opinion of another respondent, "Women do not have the deep client base of male partners in positions of power."

Several associates chided the firm's women partners for playing "little if any role in promoting opportunities for women," in the words of one. One associate reported that some female partners are "perceived to be very tough and cold in general ('bitchy')," although she attributed this to the need "to be strong to compete in a male world." She added that although incoming associates do get advisers, these are not assigned along gender lines and there is "no formal partner-associate mentoring system."

A litigator commented that the department's two female partners "could be more active in the area of women's issues. In all fairness, one has become much more active recently, and it is very important for her to be so if there are to be any changes."

Kaye, Scholer, Fierman, Hayes & Handler No. of Responses: 7	Strongly agree	Agree	Disagree	Strongly disagree
Women's prospects for advancement at the firm are as strong as men's	2	1	3	1
I am satisfied with the firm's family and personal leave policies	2	3	1	
There are women in positions of power and influence in the firm		1	3	3
Women are as likely as men to receive desirable work assignments	2	4	1	
Women attorneys feel they can discuss family obligations openly		2	3	1
Women are as likely as men to be mentored by senior attorneys	1	2	3	1
Women attorneys enjoy a high level of job satisfaction	2	2	2	1
Women in the firm are supportive of their women colleagues	2	4		1
Firm management is receptive to the concerns of women attorneys		3	2	2

KING & SPALDING

Rating: 61

King & Spalding
191 Peachtree St.
Atlanta, GA 30303
404-572-4600

No. of Attorneys: 253
No. of Women Attorneys: 66
No. of Partners: 105
No. of Women Partners: 10
No. of Survey Responses Received: 10

Respondent Profile: 2 partners, 7 associates, and 1 counsel responded. Practice areas included corporate, litigation, and employment. Most respondents did not identify their practice area.

Summary: The two partners who responded were overwhelmingly positive, while associates were often split about many aspects of life at King & Spalding, the firm that ranked Number 1 in our previous survey. Midlevel associates, often in startling contrast to their seniors and juniors, appear to be downright miserable, and their comments reflected it.

Advancement: Although the partners and two of the first-year associates painted a relatively bright picture of advancement for women, the more senior associates had a different view. One partner reported that opportunities are the same for men and women, that mentoring opportunities abound, and that she perceives "no difference in allocation of assignments or review." The other partner concurred that, in her opinion, women are not at a disadvantage because of gender.

Even the first-year associates who were relatively positive did not paint the horizon as quite cloudless. One commented that, as far as she could tell, there is no distinction between men and women, but "the bottom line is hours must be billed," adding that it was her impression that if women devote a significant amount of time to family,

thereby billing fewer hours, "it could affect advancement." Another first-year associate wrote that the prospects for advancement are excellent, but agreed that the number of hours associates must bill might create a career/family conflict.

According to the opinions of more senior associates, equal treatment does not continue as women become more senior. One litigator observed that it is "extremely hard for women to advance." In her opinion, "Partners are more likely to pick male associates as their favorite[s], to give them better work assignments, and more opportunities early on." She further suggested, "The women are stuck researching while the men are sent out to take depositions, to hearings, etc."

Another associate said that, in her estimation, "Most of the senior women leave before they àre up for partnership, when they realize that no matter how hard they work or how well they do, they won't get credit for it and won't be made partners." According to another respondent's perception, "Women are not as likely to advance to partnership in traditionally male-dominated practice areas—such as litigation and corporate—unless women show extraordinary dedication or talent, or just get lucky." Another associate contended that, in her opinion, women were less likely to advance to equity partners than men, "especially in the litigation and bond areas." She characterized the corporate team as a bit more progressive, which, in her opinion, may be due to the increasing number of women who are becoming clients.

> *"...most midlevel associates at King & Spalding are frustrated and miserable, whether they are men or women."*

Attitudes and atmosphere: Respondents were sharply divided about the atmosphere at King & Spalding. According to one partner, the firm exhibits no manifestations of gender discrimination, and she added that she lunches with men as often as women. A corporate associate said that King & Spalding is comfortable "because the leadership goes to great pains to make it so." An employment law associate remarked that the firm is comfortable, although, in her experience, "women still have to work harder to prove themselves."

Three other respondents took an entirely different view. One wrote that the firm is definitely a "boys' club." She reported that women attorneys attempted to organize luncheon programs for themselves as a group, but that "the firm refuses to pay for the luncheons." (A spokesperson for the firm denied any knowledge of this.) "The men balk at such programs and criticize them. They want to be able to have 'men's programs.' Well, every day is men's day here at the firm. The firm does nothing to address women's concerns. We have to do that ourselves."

Another associate said, "As you can read in [the last] *American Lawyer* midlevel-associate survey, most midlevel associates at King & Spalding are frustrated and miserable, whether they are men or women."

In another respondent's opinion, "The firm is not a comfortable place for anyone to work, men or women...It is a very old, traditional silk-stocking type firm that demands a great deal of its people." As for the tone of the firm, she wrote, "There is a friendly surface social interaction between men and women, [but] there is almost no social interaction outside the firm between firm people, except in a very formal way...The tone set by firm leadership is high society—snobbism."

> *"The firm's management is obsessed with squeezing more and more hours and money out of associates..."*

Balancing work & family/personal life: Respondents had few positive comments about the firm's role in enabling lawyers to maintain a life outside the firm. In one lawyer's opinion, "The firm's management is obsessed with squeezing more and more hours and money out of associates, and sees families and outside interests as obstacles." Although one first-year associate reported, "Some partners [set a] good example of fulfilling family responsibilities," another remarked that, even on a team known for being more sensitive and understanding, the mentality, in her experience, is that work comes first: "You can schedule a vacation, dinner, etc., but if work comes up—you'll be pressed to make it."

According to another associate's opinion, "Children are a huge impediment to making partner—unless you have a full-time nanny who is at your disposal on short notice." One respondent suggested that the demands are just as difficult for the unmarried women at the firm. According to one associate's cynical opinion, King & Spalding encourages having a family and children, "but primarily for the reason that [the firm] likes to get its people into financial situations that require them to covet their jobs."

Both partners were much more positive about this question (as they were with every question), with one asserting that many women "appear to be doing a very good job at this difficult task."

One associate believed, "9 to 6 is part-time."

Flexibility of work arrangements: Part-time arrangements are perceived to be impractical at King & Spalding, even by the otherwise positive partners, one of whom admitted that, in her opinion, the firm is "struggling with creating viable part-time options." One associate reported "[The firm] has sought to use at least one woman (who had left the firm to take care of her baby) on a part-time, work-at-home basis." In the opinion of another associate, "There are no part-time positions available (that I've heard of) either at the associate or partner

level." She added that, in her estimation, it is "very unlikely that this sort of arrangement would be accepted by the firm." Another associate believed, "9 to 6 is part-time."

A partner stated that, in her opinion, it is "probably impossible" to make partner while working part-time. Another respondent said that, in her estimation, when some part-time deals are struck, "they are so disadvantageous that the people to whom they are made available soon [grow] weary of the arrangement."

The firm stated that there is no written part-time policy. There is one part-time attorney in the Atlanta office and three others firm-wide.

"[The firm is] not given to supporting diversity of any sort."

Diversity: Responses to this question were divided. One associate described the firm as conservative, though open to diversity. Another sensed, "A liberal, outspoken woman would not fare well here, but the same could be said of a man with the same traits." In one respondent's view, the evidence that the firm is somewhat diversified lies in the fact that King & Spalding has hired younger women and older women who went back to law school after raising a family. She characterized King & Spalding as a firm that "likes conservative dress and speech [and favors] upper-middle income and society types in Atlanta."

One associate expressed her opinion bluntly, describing the firm as "a bad place for women lawyers (and nonwhite lawyers and Jewish lawyers)." Another respondent also asserted that, in her opinion, King & Spalding is "not given to supporting diversity of any sort."

One first-year associate was equally forthright in her opposing view: "[King & Spalding] demonstrates a strong commitment to diversity—in hiring practices and in community involvement."

So few women hold influential positions, "it is difficult to develop mentor relationships with them."

Women in leadership positions: Partners and associates again disagreed about the perceived status of senior women, and, not surprisingly, those women received mixed reviews as to whether they play a role in assisting junior lawyers. One otherwise positive partner said that, in her opinion, the women in leadership positions "have not always focused on support for other women," though she contended that this is improving as more and more women are admitted into the partnership. An associate claimed that while most senior women do try to counsel the women associates, "the common suggestion is [that they should] find a mentor— something many of us cannot do given the makeup of our work groups." Another associate concurred that, in her opinion, so few women hold influential positions, "it is difficult to develop mentor relationships with them." Nevertheless, one litigator asserted that the powerful women are "very supportive," but that the firm is so large that "it's hard to have access to them."

One junior associate, however, gave the senior women high marks. A first-year associate commented that the firm's "handful of high-powered women partners" have taken a "leading role in persuading the firm to make a stronger commitment to issues concerning women attorneys and women clients."

Miscellaneous: King & Spalding was ranked number one in the 1995 edition of *Presumed Equal,* based on responses to questions contained in a chart similar to the one below. One associate wrote that, in her opinion, "Your survey last time ended up giving a misleading picture of King & Spalding. Most of us at the firm were shocked when King & Spalding got rated the best firm in the country for women."

King & Spalding No. of Responses: 10	Strongly agree	Agree	Disagree	Strongly disagree
Women's prospects for advancement at the firm are as strong as men's	3	2	2	3
I am satisfied with the firm's family and personal leave policies	2	6	2	
There are women in positions of power and influence in the firm	2	4	4	
Women are as likely as men to receive desirable work assignments	3	4	3	
Women attorneys feel they can discuss family obligations openly	2	2	4	1
Women are as likely as men to be mentored by senior attorneys	2	2	3	3
Women attorneys enjoy a high level of job satisfaction	2	3	4	1
Women in the firm are supportive of their women colleagues	3	3	3	
Firm management is receptive to the concerns of women attorneys	1	4	1	3

KIRKLAND & ELLIS

Rating: 59

Kirkland & Ellis
200 East Randolph Dr.
Chicago, IL 60601
312-861-2000

No. of Attorneys: 323
No. of Women Attorneys: 80
No. of Partners: 139
No. of Women Partners: 20
No. of Survey Responses Received: 15

Respondent Profile: 5 partners, 9 associates, and 1 respondent who did not identify her position. Practice areas included primarily litigation or corporate, though several respondents did not identify their practice area.

Summary: Women can advance at Kirkland & Ellis, though some respondents were concerned about women's chances of making it to share partnership. It's a hard-driving firm, not necessarily comfortable for lawyers of either gender. Respondents were divided on whether part-time was practical. And its two top women were characterized as virtually polar opposites.

Advancement: A majority of attorneys were positive about women's chances for advancement, but there was a qualification in many responses. Most respondents perceived that women's chances of making nonequity partner were equivalent to those of men, but that women are substantially less likely to make share partnership at Kirkland. Correspondingly, although women are reportedly "well-represented" at the nonequity level, they are few in number at the very top. (None of the five partners who responded indicated whether they are share or nonshare partners; the survey did not ask this.) One respondent said that, in her estimation, those who do achieve share partnership "exhibit a higher level of skill and dedication than their average male counterparts."

Kirkland is reported to heavily emphasize hours as a criterion for advancement, which, in the opinion of some respondents, may play a role in attrition among lawyers of both sexes. A litigation partner asserted that "women are not as willing as men to put up with the demands of the practice. They simply choose not to. Men are starting to do the same." Nevertheless, she was positive about women's chances, though she wrote, "Women who (foolishly?) choose to make the same sacrifices, do as well [as men do]." A senior associate suggested a different explanation for women's higher attrition rate: "Female egos are not as dependent on prestige and power."

With regard to mentoring and work assignments, one partner wrote that, in her experience, "mentoring and the allocation of the best opportunities are the keys. Both become more skewed against women as they grow more senior in the firm." Another partner commented that women who are very good have an equal chance to advance, although, in her opinion, "mediocre women are weeded out faster than mediocre men." An associate stated that although her practice group is composed entirely of men, she has received "valuable mentoring" from senior attorneys.

The difficulties faced by women are reportedly most acute in Kirkland's venture capital practice, apparently one of the fastest-growing areas of the firm. According to one associate's perception, women can find opportunities in corporate "if they want to specialize in either debt or securities, because most male attorneys are not interested in this work," but not if they prefer venture capital "which is the driving force behind the corporate department (and more and more, the law firm itself)." She characterized the number of women venture capital partners as "abysmal" and, declared that, in her opinion, "women as a rule do not feel welcome or taken seriously as attorneys" in this practice area, mostly because of what she characterized as "old-world stereotyping of women by the socially conservative men whom the department attracts, particularly by some of its most powerful partners." These views were echoed by one corporate associate who commented that, in her estimation, men get "the plum venture capital deals, while many of the women gravitate towards securities work or specialty areas."

Despite these views, most attorneys asserted that the firm's assignment system and emphasis on high-quality work product worked to the benefit of women lawyers. A junior level litigator wrote, "Partners ask associates to work on projects, and associates are free to select whatever projects they wish and to decline any projects they wish. This is terrific because 1) you are not subjected to working for anyone you don't want; and 2) you are not pigeonholed and have an opportunity to 'chart your career.'" She added, "Schmoozing with partners, golf outings, etc., will have no impact on whether an attorney advances...Attorneys tend to be very focused on their work, [which creates] a good atmosphere for women."

> *The firm, according to one, is uncomfortable for women, "but no more so than the world of American business generally."*

Attitudes and atmosphere: Kirkland is described as an extremely hard-driving firm that, in the words of both partners and associates, is not necessarily a comfortable place for either men or women. A partner wrote that, in her opinion, the firm is uncomfortable for women, "but no more so than the world of American business generally." She observed that although "the downside is that the playing field is not even; the upside is that that fact is relatively candidly acknowledged."

While a corporate attorney declared that the firm's atmosphere is "pleasant and professional," she also said she was aware of "a few disturbing incidents where attorneys and clients went to strip clubs for 'closing celebrations' (at the clients' request)." Another associate contended the firm would not tolerate gender discrimination or sexual harassment. Yet women, in her opinion, "seem disproportionately to end up in the least desirable secretarial situations (i.e., assigned nonperforming or under-performing secretaries)."

An associate noted that Kirkland & Ellis does not have "an exuberantly friendly atmosphere" and that most associates at the firm are "chiefly focused on their work, not on socializing." According to a senior associate, "The people who thrive here and are happy are self-confident and not afraid to speak their minds." A litigator wrote that although she is now "comfortable" at the firm, during her first few years she worked with a partner who was "overly aggressive and used a lot of profanity" and another who "just plain treated me rudely."

But on a positive concluding note, a partner wrote that although Kirkland & Ellis is a "rather intense place to work," she believed that "no one here cares who your parents are, where you went to school, what clothes you wear, what clubs you join. The key is, will you do good work..."

"You really do have to sublimate all else in your life to the demands of the firm and its clients."

....

Balancing work & family/personal life: Responses were varied on this front. High average billables—2,700 hours per year according to one respondent—and extensive travel appear to frustrate the ability of some respondents to maintain a healthy balance. A partner with children wrote that, in her opinion, maintaining balance is *extremely* difficult," and observed that to succeed at Kirkland & Ellis "you really do have to sublimate all else in your life to the demands of the firm and its clients." An associate who is a mother wrote that, in her estimation, extensive travel has "made it virtually impossible to achieve any sort of satisfying balance." Another partner wrote she has a satisfying family and professional life, "but nothing else in my life for now."

Some respondents were more upbeat, particularly in light of the apparent lack of emphasis on "face time," as well as the *laissez faire* assignment system. One litigation associate noted that many women at the firm "seem to juggle work and family very well—they travel a good bit for work, work on high-profile cases, and do a lot of recruiting but still seem to sustain a good family life and good-natured personalities." A partner wrote, "[I] always have been open about my family's needs and demands and the firm has always put up with it." A senior associate wrote, "Because our firm operates on a 'free market' basis, there are fewer rules about what hours you are supposed to be here, etc."

One partner suggested that women at Kirkland & Ellis "need to start talking about family pressures (e.g., say they're going to the pediatrician instead of making up a meeting). Golf is an acceptable reason to leave at 2 p.m. on a sunny day, and children would be, too, if people acknowledged it."

A partner wrote that going part-time is "viable...although it slows the track."

....

Flexibility of work arrangements: Part-time arrangements are reportedly available at all but the share partnership level, although some respondents believe they are frowned upon by the firm. "Culturally, part-time is still not acceptable," in one associate's opinion. A partner noted that part-time is possible and does not foreclose partnership, but that it is difficult because the firm's clients "tend to be 'all hours' kinds of people." A senior associate disagreed, writing that part-time arrangements are "legitimate, viable options for associates and nonshare partners." When available, part-time arrangements are apparently short-term "i.e., one to two years at most," according to one partner. Kirkland & Ellis reportedly does not "advertise" the availability of flexible arrangements, an associate said.

Respondents were divided as to the impact of part-time stints on associates' advancement. A partner wrote that going part-time is "viable...although it slows the track." In direct contrast, an associate reported that, in her opinion, part-time arrangements are not viable "if a lawyer intends to make it to the top here."

The firm reportedly offers maternity leave, and one partner reported, "Some women here have taken extended leaves when they had children, and still made partner on time." Once again, however, an associate's opinion was distinctly opposite. She thought that requesting family leave "would severely limit partnership opportunities."

Another associate reported that all associates receive laptops that facilitate working from home. A partner confessed that she works at home almost every Wednesday, "unbeknownst to most. Technology makes that possible."

Diversity: "K & E is not a culturally diverse place. Period," in one respondent's opinion, although several others noted that the firm is trying to do better. One senior associate lamented that the firm has difficulty convincing people "that K & E doesn't care if you are Black, white, green, or Martian—as long as your work meets its expectations, which are high."

According to a colleague's perception, however, "I think many partners at the firm would love to have talented minorities work here." Another respondent remarked that, in her opinion, the partners "do not feel significant pressure from firm clients to diversify the partnership. Therefore, there is no meaningful effort to diversify." According to one partner's assessment, "The firm is not comfortable and supportive for women—or for *anyone* who is 'diverse'—or different." But she added, "As long as your work is spectacular and there's enough of it, your diversity is a matter of indifference, generally."

Another associate wrote that personalities are diverse, but life styles are less so: "I know one gay woman, one motorcycle-riding man, two Orthodox Jews, but a lot of married Christian suburbanites." Several associates noted that the firm is home to people of varying political views, although one wrote that the prevailing norm is decidedly Republican.

"The firm is not comfortable and supportive for women—or for anyone who is 'diverse'—or different."

One partner remarked that women are beginning to enter the share partnership in modest numbers, but one partner characterized the pace as "glacial."

Women in leadership positions: There are reportedly two powerful women at Kirkland, one of whom sits on the firm's 15-member management committee, while the other chairs the hiring committee. These two women are clearly perceived as almost polar opposites. An associate wrote that one is "perceived as tough as nails," while the other is "well-liked [and] an excellent" lawyer. Another respondent said that one is a "true role model with a pretty good balance in her life. The other is viewed as too dedicated to the firm and not particularly supportive of women." An associate noted that one of these women is considered "an extraordinary trial attorney—one of these best in the country," and didn't mention the other. A partner wrote of one of the senior women that, in her opinion, "based on the comments of my male partners, it is obvious they perceive her as a token, there because of gender, not merit."

One partner remarked that women are beginning to enter the share partnership in modest numbers, but characterized the pace as "glacial."

The women at the firm generally agree that Kirkland's female partners have played a positive role in creating opportunities for more junior women at the firm.

Kirkland & Ellis No. of Responses: 15	Strongly agree	Agree	Disagree	Strongly disagree
Women's prospects for advancement at the firm are as strong as men's	1	9	2	3
I am satisfied with the firm's family and personal leave policies	1	10	3	1
There are women in positions of power and influence in the firm		9	4	1
Women are as likely as men to receive desirable work assignments	2	9	4	
Women attorneys feel they can discuss family obligations openly		5	7	2
Women are as likely as men to be mentored by senior attorneys	1	8	6	
Women attorneys enjoy a high level of job satisfaction	4	7	3	
Women in the firm are supportive of their women colleagues	5	8	1	
Firm management is receptive to the concerns of women attorneys	1	6	5	2

LATHAM & WATKINS

Rating: 72

Latham & Watkins
633 West Fifth St.
Suite 4000
Los Angeles, CA 90071
213-485-1234

No. of Attorneys: 210
No. of Women Attorneys: 62
No. of Partners: 84
No. of Women Partners: 18
No. of Survey Responses Received: 20

Respondent Profile: 2 partners and 18 associates responded. Practice areas included litigation and corporate.

Summary: That the partnership is open to women willing to devote themselves to billing New York-style hours is the good news for women at Latham & Watkins, according to respondents, though most characterized women's chances for advancement as poorer than men's. Tales of the firm's fraternity-style atmosphere, including male attorneys who reportedly leer at women lawyers and proposition summer associates, struck a particularly low note among firms surveyed. To its credit, the firm is reportedly confronting this issue.

Advancement: Most of the respondents thought that those women who endure the full partnership track and do not have children enjoy prospects for partnership equal to men. Having a family, or opting for other reasons not to devote oneself single-mindedly to work, are reported to preclude virtually all chances of promotion. "As long as women are willing to work the hours and give 110 percent, their chances are generally commensurate with men's," according to one respondent.

Latham was described by another respondent as "fairly typical of big L.A. firms" in that the prospects of advancement for women are, in her estimation, "not equal to those of men in the firm, in part due to the lack of mentoring, in part because of life and family decisions women make more often than men, and in part because of stereotypes that are ingrained in the legal profession and in many of our clients' minds."

Business development is "the overriding factor" in partnership decisions, according to an associate, who contended, "Much of this business development still occurs on the links and in the cigar bars."

A partner said, however, that although business generation is important to partners' prospects of advancing within the partnership, "it's not a big factor in advancement" for associates.

According to several respondents, making partner requires more than simply producing high-quality work. A midlevel litigator contended that the firm puts "heavy pressure" on associates with regard to " 'commitment to the firm'—a catch phrase which essentially translates into enormously high hours."

Another associate added that those who reduce their hours below the required 2,500 to have children "are *not* well-regarded, [and] not thought of as committed."

Although one associate asserted that the firm has both informal and formal mentoring networks, several claimed that the male partners are more likely to develop mentoring relationships with men. One corporate associate complained, "None of the small number of women partners mentor or encourage women associates."

A partner had a considerably different view of women lawyers' potential for advancement, contending that Latham is "as close as a firm can come to a true meritocracy." She said that the firm has endeavored to make partnership decisions "as apolitical as possible" and that partnership recommendations are made by a committee comprised of half partners and half associates, chosen to reflect a diversity of practice areas, offices, gender, ethnicity, and age." She added that prospects for promotion for women are excellent and that 40 percent of the "newest partnership admittees were women."

With regard to equity in assignments, several associates expressed satisfaction, especially since the firm has been busy of late.

A midlevel associate wrote that the firm has an associates committee that assigns work to first- and second-year associates "in an effort to fairly distribute assignments and allow new lawyers to try out practice areas of interest." This committee, she added, also intervenes "if an associate expresses particular work concerns."

"...L & W's reputation as a fraternity or 'boys' club' is well-earned and has been getting worse in the last couple years."

Attitudes and atmosphere: Numerous respondents described the atmosphere at Latham as that of a fraternity. A litigation associate wrote that although she has "a relatively thick skin regarding jokes, flirting, etc.," and therefore does not "usually feel uncomfortable socializing with male peers and partners," she claims to know many women in the office who "feel that L & W's reputation as a fraternity or 'boys' club' is well-earned and has been getting worse in the last couple years."

As one associate described it, the summer program had "devolved into an opportunity for male partners and associates to 'hit on' summer associates." In the opinion of another lawyer, the program was a "meat market." A midlevel associate concluded that the firm "became less comfortable for women" partly because of these episodes, although, to its credit, the firm has reportedly enacted a policy prohibiting dating between attorneys and summer clerks.

A midlevel corporate attorney put it, "If you can't talk sports or play golf, you are much less likely to be invited to the weekend events with clients. It helps if you drink Scotch and smoke cigars, too." She added that although she saw little blatant sexism at the firm, there is plenty of "subtle exclusion from the social interaction...that results in missed opportunities for mentoring and advancement and reduced client contact and development opportunities."

A corporate lawyer reported having "sat through discussions about women's breast shapes by men associates, knowing I was being made to feel extremely uncomfortable." She added that some male attorneys "blatantly stop to leer in the halls at young female associates."

On the other hand, a first-year associate wrote that she has experienced little discomfort except for the "normal men-go-golfing-and-smoking-cigars 'boys' club' stuff." Another associate declared that the firm's social milieu is characterized by "lots of drinking, flirting, etc.," and that there are "lots of intraoffice couples and dating."

A few respondents reported that the firm is trying to deal with these issues. One junior lawyer wrote that although she has heard "many stories of sexist attitudes and behavior in the recent past," she has been "very pleased with the firm's recent attempts to listen to women's concerns and make real changes."

A few respondents contended that if a "club" exists at the firm, it is one that includes women. A corporate associate said that she has found her colleagues friendly and supportive and that the firm's more senior attorneys are "always willing to take the time to explain legal issues to the junior associates."

The two partners who responded find the atmosphere at Latham far more congenial than do their junior colleagues. One wrote that there is "somewhat of a 'club' atmosphere socially but women are completely welcome to participate and there's no loss of opportunities if you do not." The other wrote that the firm

has "bent over backwards to be attuned and sensitive to women's issues. Complaints are taken seriously and fully investigated."

"The recipe for survival requires that Latham comes first, before your personal life, your family, your sleep, and sometimes your health."

Balancing work & family/personal life: The hours are reportedly brutal, with one associate remarking that the firm's average billables are probably the highest of any firm outside New York. Average annual billables are reportedly between 2,250 and 2,500, and many attorneys bill more than 2,500, according to one respondent. A senior associate added, "You are not respected if you work less than 2,200 to 2,300 hours per year, and you definitely can't make partner billing less than that." Leaving before 7 p.m., she added, risks "partners ask[ing] where you're going and mak[ing] comments about 'commitment.'"

A litigator concluded, "[The firm] does nothing to encourage family life," and added that the hours and pressure are "tremendous" and that "if you don't suck it up as a 'team player' at most times, you will be marginalized." Another litigator recounted that at the office, weekends are "no different than weekdays—floors are filled with attorneys and secretaries alike." She added that some partners "won't bat an eye at giving you a project at 6 p.m. to be finished by first thing the next morning."

One corporate associate suggested, "The recipe for survival requires that Latham comes first, before your personal life, your family, your sleep, and sometimes your health." A lone, optimistic first-year associate hoped that "the pendulum is swinging back the other way, though, and the yearly hours are likely to go down."

Although maternity leave is available, there reportedly is concern that actually using it may result in one being involuntarily shunted into the recently created income partnership tier. Several respondents commented on the new tier, or "glorified senior associates," as one lawyer put it, predicting that it may become the "mommy track." Another associate predicted that those who take four- to six-month maternity leaves "run a greater risk of dropping into our second tier of partnership."

Some assessed the creation of a new track as a mixed blessing. One lawyer noted, "There is some concern among the women associates [that] females will tend to be pushed in these positions more than males. In fact, I have heard partners say to me and other women that 'isn't this a great program, you can have a family and still be a partner.' It's a double-edged sword."

A small handful of respondents said that the firm tries to be responsive to the needs of its lawyers and particularly its women. Several applauded the recent introduction of backup childcare assistance, and a partner also remarked that life has been made easier by the creation of a computer network that allows attorneys to work from home "from time to time."

> *"Current top management is not at all supportive of part-time and women generally do not see this as a viable option."*

Flexibility of work arrangements: Part-time exists in principle, but not in practice, most respondents concluded. The firm has a written part-time policy, but in the view of one respondent, "Current top management is *not* at all supportive of part-time, and women generally do not see this as a viable option." An associate agreed, noting that one of the most powerful partners "has openly expressed his dislike of the program." She added that, in her experience, those who have attempted to go part-time have "mostly found it unworkable."

Not surprisingly, there are reportedly "*very few* women in the firm who have chosen to go part-time during the first few years of their children's lives," according to one respondent. She concluded that it was "too early to tell if this will ultimately affect their careers," but several other associates were of the view that a part-time stint would dash one's partnership prospects.

A partner disagreed, reporting that she was aware of "at least one person who subsequently made partner" after going part-time.

No part-time options are available at partnership level, according to several associates, although one partner believed that if asked for, part-time arrangements at partnership level would be handled on a case-by-case basis.

Changes to the part-time policy at the firm may be in the works, however. One respondent wrote that recently, the women associates "held a meeting to discuss drafting a proposal to revamp this policy," and that she understood that management "is receptive to these concerns."

> **"Latham is very homogenous. Diversity has been a focus recently, but it's slow-going."**

Diversity: One associate summed up the views of many respondents on this topic by reporting, "Latham is very homogenous. Diversity has been a focus recently, but it's slow-going." There were some differences of opinion, but most associates agreed that there are few "out" lesbians, few Hispanics, and very few African-American women associates at the firm. The firm has a somewhat larger contingent of Asian-American women, but overall, "it's a very white-male place," as one lawyer put it. One associate observed, however, "There are *many* gay men at the firm who are very open about their sexuality."

Several attorneys agreed that the firm is, in the words of one, "very committed to enriching its hiring base with people from diverse backgrounds." According to another associate, the firm has a "board [that has] made its presence known in recent years by having more training sessions, meetings, etc., and informing partners and associates about its diversity policies, etc."

Despite these efforts, according to an associate, the firm seems "unable to attract or retain a diverse attorney population." Nevertheless, one associate noted that the firm is one of the few with an African-American partner on its executive committee.

In terms of political leanings, the firm is reported to be fairly eclectic. An associate said, "The firm has lawyers and clients who are important in both major political parties."

> **A partner remarked, "We still have a way to go before women are fairly represented in the firm's power structure."**

Women in leadership positions: Although Latham & Watkins' executive committee has recently diversified with the addition of an African-American male, it still includes no women members, several attorneys reported. One associate further noted that there are no women office managing partners or national departmental chairs.

Of the 18 members of the firm's influential associates committee, which makes partnership recommendations and determines bonuses, reportedly only three are women and none of these are partners. As such, according to an associate, "The perception is they are in a poor position to effect much change, although to their credit, they do solicit input from female associates and, I believe, voice those views very strongly." She added that approximately one-third of the committee positions available firm-wide are held by women, and half of these positions deal with "recruiting or equal employment opportunity." A partner remarked that although there are women committee chairs and local department chairs, "we still have a way to go before women are fairly represented in the firm's power structure."

Women did not agree whether the more senior women in the firm reach out to assist their more junior colleagues. Several respondents concurred that the women partners "certainly do not mentor women associates," as one put it. A litigation associate believed that it is almost "as if the senior women came up in a system which was so much less sensitive to gender issues that they're determined to be tougher on women associates than on men." A partner remarked, "Unfortunately, one of the most visible women at the firm [did not] believe in promoting the idea that men and women are different and that some women have different needs to be successful." In the opinion of an associate, one woman partner "who pulls in over one million dollars...[is] not willing to always take a leadership role because she wants to spend more time at home."

Another associate disagreed, reporting that the women partners have organized seminars for the women associates "to address women's issues, teach business development, and promote camaraderie." And a corporate associate wrote, "The support system among women" at the firm allows women to "complain to each other so some relief is available" even though "management has absolutely no ear when it comes to women's concerns and issues."

Latham & Watkins No. of Responses: 20	Strongly agree	Agree	Disagree	Strongly disagree
Women's prospects for advancement at the firm are as strong as men's	3	2	11	4
I am satisfied with the firm's family and personal leave policies	3	4	5	7
There are women in positions of power and influence in the firm	3	3	6	8
Women are as likely as men to receive desirable work assignments	6	6	5	1
Women attorneys feel they can discuss family obligations openly	2	6	7	4
Women are as likely as men to be mentored by senior attorneys	3	2	9	5
Women attorneys enjoy a high level of job satisfaction		5	7	7
Women in the firm are supportive of their women colleagues	4	12	1	1
Firm management is receptive to the concerns of women attorneys	4	4	8	3

MAYER, BROWN & PLATT

Rating: 33

Mayer, Brown & Platt
190 South LaSalle St.
Chicago, IL 60603
312-782-0600

No. of Attorneys: 411
No. of Women Attorneys: 104
No. of Partners: 170
No. of Women Partners: 28
No. of Survey Responses Received: 5

Respondent Profile: 2 partners, 2 associates, and 1 attorney who did not identify her position responded. Practice areas included finance, litigation, and corporate.

Summary: Our handful of respondents portrayed Mayer, Brown as a reasonably comfortable firm for women, in part because of the tone set by the firm's woman managing partner. The firm does not appear disinclined to promote women, but some respondents perceived that the hours and inability to control one's schedule may contribute to women's exodus from the firm before partnership consideration. The firm clearly supports part-time options.

Advancement: In the long term, in one partner's opinion, women may not want what Mayer, Brown—or any other large law firm—has to offer. As she observed, "As I have become older, I am alarmed at the sheer number of women who quit...after they have 'dabbled' in practicing law for a few years." Another partner agreed, commenting that although women "are given the same opportunities as men," they seem to have a greater concern for family issues (and greater financial flexibility) so "they drop out of big firm life more."

At least one partner blamed the women, and not the firm or the profession, for the exodus: "I'm sick of training women who then turn around and leave. And that has nothing to do with firm culture and prospects for advancement."

An associate who observed the same phenomenon gave it a different spin. She perceived that women in the corporate department "are not nearly as likely to advance to partnership as men," because "the number of hours required to succeed" as a corporate/securities attorney and "the inability to control one's schedule are a major stumbling block." In the same associate's perception, the pressure is exacerbated by "how thinly staffed deals are and the speed in which clients today demand deals be done."

According to a midlevel litigator's opinion, women have an "equal chance, however, making partner in part depends on which partners rally for an associate, and it is more likely that a male partner will mentor and rally for a male associate."

> *"The managing partner is a woman with three children, so there is no tolerance of 'boys' club' attitudes."*

Attitudes and atmosphere: According to a partner, "The managing partner is a woman with three children, so there is no tolerance of 'boys' club' attitudes." Another respondent agreed that there is no "anti-woman animus" at the firm and stated that the men are generally decent people who would be shocked to be accused of treating women badly. An associate agreed that the firm is a very comfortable place for women, stating that her colleagues in the litigation department have always treated her as an equal and with respect.

One associate, however, adamantly disagreed. In her opinion, "The 'boys' club' still exists and exists with force. I don't think I'll ever feel as though I fit in or am necessarily wanted." And a partner observed, "[This firm] is an excellent place for women to work, so long as you are content to remain in the background and serve a 'good daughter' role." She added that, in her experience, "while there is no workplace sexism or any sort of 'boys' club' mentality, the women lawyers are invisible."

> *"No one would care if I left early or came in late because of a family matter."*

Balancing work & family/personal life: A litigation associate with children reported that she has always maintained a balance between work and family, and that she seldom, if ever, works weekends. She accomplishes this by billing nine to 11 hours each day during the week, and by making it clear to her colleagues that she has another job at home: mom. "Who can honestly challenge my lack of weekend hours," she wrote, "when I bill over 2,000 hours a year?" A litigation partner with children agreed that it is "possible to have a very rewarding personal/family life at the firm." While the hours are long, she maintained, "no one would care if [I] left early or came in late because of a family matter."

Maintaining the balance is evidently easier in some departments than others. An associate commented that in her practice area, it is almost impossible for "professional and family lives to coexist, [because] family responsibilities are not relevant when it comes to business."

> *"If you want [part-time] to work, it will, but if you whine, avoid responsibility, and expect a free lunch, it won't."*

Flexibility of work arrangements: According to one associate, the firm "institutionalized" part-time arrangements several years ago. She added that a colleague has used it and has been very happy, and that, in her view, the firm supports the arrangement. A partner commented that the firm is very supportive of part-time and other alternative arrangements, although she believes the success of the arrangements rests solely with the degree of professionalism and judgment of each individual lawyer. She concluded, "If you want it to work, it will, but if you whine, avoid responsibility, and expect a free lunch, it won't." According to a corporate associate's perception, while part-time is available, for an attorney in her department "to be taken seriously and allowed to do the high-profile deals, such an alternative is impracticable."

Nevertheless, one partner commented that many partners at the firm have taken part-time status at one time or another.

According to an associate, the firm has few minorities despite active recruitment efforts and a committee to address minority issues.

Diversity: Responses shed little light on the diversity, or lack thereof, at Mayer, Brown. According to an associate, "We seem to be fairly homogenous." She added that, in her opinion, the firm has few minorities despite active recruitment efforts and a committee to address minority issues. One partner suggested that the firm gives "the same lip service to diversity as any other big Chicago firm." Another partner, surprisingly, given the previous comments, said the firm is "very diverse."

"Power relates to ability to bring in clients, and there still is a gap between the number of rainmaking women and men."

Women in leadership positions: Notwithstanding having a female managing partner, who acts as the chief operating officer at the firm, and the fact that women make up a decent percentage of the partnership ranks, respondents wrote that they perceived that the "real power" was not in women's hands.

In a partner's perception, the managing partner is "an appointed seat with no real power." And a litigator said, "Power relates to ability to bring in clients, and there still is a gap between the number of rainmaking women and men." According to another associate's perception, the senior women are "largely ignored."

Mayer, Brown & Platt No. of Responses: 5	Strongly agree	Agree	Disagree	Strongly disagree
Women's prospects for advancement at the firm are as strong as men's	1	2		1
I am satisfied with the firm's family and personal leave policies	2	2		
There are women in positions of power and influence in the firm	1	1	2	
Women are as likely as men to receive desirable work assignments	2		2	
Women attorneys feel they can discuss family obligations openly	1	2	1	
Women are as likely as men to be mentored by senior attorneys		3		
Women attorneys enjoy a high level of job satisfaction		3	1	
Women in the firm are supportive of their women colleagues	1	2	1	
Firm management is receptive to the concerns of women attorneys	2	2		

McDERMOTT, WILL & EMERY

Rating: 70

McDermott, Will & Emery
227 West Monroe St.
Chicago, IL 60606
312-372-2000

No. of Attorneys: 260
No. of Women Attorneys: 88
No. of Partners: 176
No. of Women Partners: 43
No. of Survey Responses Received: 17

Respondent Profile: 9 partners and 8 associates responded. Practice areas included litigation, corporate, health care, and financial services.

Summary: Women are certainly of two minds about McDermott. And perhaps surprisingly, the partners who responded were often more negative than the associates—five of eight, for example, did not view women's opportunities there positively, and seven of nine didn't believe that "there are women of power and influence in the firm." Although once one reaches partnership, balancing career and family seems to become easier. A consensus seemed to agree that there is at least subtle pressure to conform.

Advancement: Although women are reportedly as likely to achieve income partner status as their male peers, a slim majority of respondents maintain that women are less likely to reach capital partner level. And five of eight partners did not view women's opportunities at McDermott positively.

A partner commented, "While I have been promoted and don't have an ax to grind, my observation is that men are much more likely to be promoted than similarly situated women." Another partner summarized her perception of the firm's two-tiered partnership structure: "income partners (glorified associates) and capital partners (equity partners)." She further asserted that, in her view, women are "extremely unlikely to advance to capital partnership."

Respondents attributed women's inability to penetrate capital partnership ranks to the emphasis placed on business generation, and the difficulty women face trying to pull in their own clients.

Several partners cited other factors they felt contributed to women's failure to advance. According to one, "Women are much less likely to be mentored by senior attorneys within the firm and are much less likely to inherit clients or other business." She added that, in her opinion, women associates "serve the role of generating work product in the 'back room,' while men associates are much more likely to be given speaking opportunities and other opportunities for professional advancement."

Several associates suggested that the firm's view concerning work patterns has adverse consequences for women's advancement. As one associate put it, "Once you're on the 'mommy track' it is very difficult to get back on partner track."

A few respondents expressed a different view. One partner commented that the firm places "no institutional barriers to the advancement of women." A litigation associate remarked that there is "no question that women are as likely to advance to partnership as men," and that "gender has nothing to do with it."

> **"If a client expresses any preference for a male attorney, the firm will not back up its women lawyers, but, rather, will accommodate the client's preferences."**

Attitudes and atmosphere: Although several attorneys described the firm as generally comfortable for women, others cited a variety of problems. According to one partner, the firm has "a predominantly masculine overtone" and leadership is "overwhelmingly white, middle-aged, and male." One associate wrote that McDermott remains "a bit of a 'boys' club'—partly because the power in the firm rests with middle-aged men, and the women who have children rarely are in a position of power." One associate reported that she is comfortable overall, but that she felt several older partners have repeatedly made inappropriate comments to her.

There is a perception among associates that women at the firm are "not compensated fairly [and] earn less than men." One associate believed that women tend to have lower billables as a result of outside obligations and, in her view, their bonuses are probably lower

as a result. Another associate reported that when she asked about compensation levels between men and women, management did not satisfactorily address her concerns.

Some women reported that gender issues have an impact on how women are perceived professionally. According to a partner, there is a perception that labor is divided along gender lines with women tending to be "the worker bees" and men having "dominant leadership roles" and more "face time" with clients. Another partner wrote, "Aggressive women are considered 'bitchy' and 'difficult,'" whereas men with those qualities often "command respect." An associate added that, in her estimation, "if a client expresses any preference for a male attorney, the firm will not back up its women lawyers, but, rather, will accommodate the client's preferences."

On the other hand, a partner commented that the firm is "extremely comfortable" and that the "tone set by firm leadership is professional and respectful and this atmosphere is maintained throughout." She added, "The only times I noticed gender at work is on promotion lists and at partner meetings (when there's no line in the women's room during breaks)." Another partner agreed that the firm is "generally" comfortable, but added, the "drag is that there are no women with any real power."

And according to a senior associate, McDermott is "as comfortable for both genders as is possible in today's political environment—the men here are afraid of sexual harassment claims so interaction between the genders is stiff—no jokes or closed doors."

> *"[Department heads] have made it clear that the bottom line is the number of billable hours at the end of the year. There is* no *exception made for...personal reasons such as a sick child."*

Balancing work & family/personal life: Although several thought that McDermott was no less sensitive to family issues than comparable firms, others felt that the intense pressure for hours, revenue, and generation of business puts those with outside commitments in a difficult bind. Associates are reportedly expected to bill around 2,000 hours, plus nonmandatory *pro bono* work.

More than one attorney suggested that the firm's vision of an ideal lawyer (one with a stay-at-home spouse) and the lack of support for family leave for men further discourage women lawyers who are seeking to balance work and family. A midlevel corporate associate noted that department heads "have made it clear that the bottom line is the number of billable hours at the end of the year. There is *no* exception made for...personal reasons such as a sick child."

Most partners seem to fare somewhat better with the balance. A partner with children remarked that so long as clients are accommodated, she has "always felt free to arrange my own schedule to attend school and family events." She added that until recently, "I did not usually announce why I was staying home or was not available for a day—but if I said I was not available, I don't recall ever being asked or required to change my plans."

> *"If you want to advance and be considered a valuable member of the team you will* not *work part-time."*

Flexibility of work arrangements: Part-time arrangements are reportedly available to associates and income partners, yet respondents were divided as to how widely such arrangements are used and as to the level of support part-timers receive. A partner confirmed that many attorneys have taken advantage of part-time options, but remarked that such arrangements "tend to (but not always) interrupt career advancement because they affect experience level." Another partner commented that it is difficult to work out part-time arrangements, but "if you're highly valued, you probably can do it." An associate reported, "although the firm doesn't like to advertise it, its reduced-time policies are pretty liberal and taken advantage of by women in all departments."

Several respondents maintained that McDermott discourages alternative work arrangements through inadequate compensation, disproportionately small bonuses, and by barring part-timers from a shot at equity partnership. In one partner's opinion, "The message is clear: If you want to advance and be considered a valuable member of the team you will *not* work part-time. "

> *An associate wrote that although the firm's lawyers "actually love a diverse group," few of the firm's lawyers are racial minorities."*

Diversity: Respondents expressed widely divergent views of McDermott's approach to diversity. One associate wrote that although the firm's lawyers "actually *love* a diverse group," few of the firm's lawyers are racial minorities. Another said, "The firm is committed to hiring the best attorneys and staff without regard to gender, race, or religious affiliation. If this results in a diverse group, it is purely accidental—to hire *for* diversity is itself discrimination!"

According to a partner, the firm employs "merely a handful of African-American lawyers or other minorities," and she sees little "effort to recruit minorities."

Responses varied on the extent to which the firm encourages conformity. An associate remarked that McDermott "does not support anyone who does not buy into the party line—in other words, conservative, submissive, team player." A partner agreed: "One feels constrained to comport oneself rather conservatively; a loud, brash, or even aggressive female would probably draw criticism."

Another partner commented, "The tone throughout the firm is professional and respectful—deviations from this standard are not tolerated." But another partner disagreed, asserting that there is no need to belong to a particular political party or be a certain personality type. One associate reported that the firm has "been accepting of...friends of mine who are known to be gay."

> **"Many men better promote the issues of women attorneys than other women attorneys."**

Women in leadership positions: Are there women in positions of leadership at the firm? "In a word, no," says one partner, a sentiment shared by seven of the nine partners who responded. (Curiously, five out of eight associates claimed the opposite.) Some respondents lamented that, in their experience, only one woman sits on the 30-person management committee, and no women serve on the compensation committee. An equity partner suggested, "This is one area that needs to come of age at McDermott." On a positive note, one partner commented that there have been "some impressive female lateral partners in the last year or so."

Many respondents—partners and associates—charged that the women partners at the firm have done little to advance the lot of female associates. One partner commented that those at the equity partnership level "are more interested in surviving than they are in helping younger women." And an equity partner observed that in certain respects, "many men better promote the issues of women attorneys than other women attorneys." Another respondent proclaimed that senior partners in the litigation department "show absolutely no interest in helping anyone but themselves—male or female."

Several respondents commented on the lack of camaraderie among women attorneys at the firm. According to one partner, however, "Women are just galvanizing as a group to promote themselves within the firm."

McDermott, Will & Emery No. of Responses: 17	Strongly agree	Agree	Disagree	Strongly disagree
Women's prospects for advancement at the firm are as strong as men's	4	3	3	6
I am satisfied with the firm's family and personal leave policies	5	5	1	5
There are women in positions of power and influence in the firm	1	6	5	5
Women are as likely as men to receive desirable work assignments	8	2	4	2
Women attorneys feel they can discuss family obligations openly	3	4	4	5
Women are as likely as men to be mentored by senior attorneys	5	4	7	1
Women attorneys enjoy a high level of job satisfaction	2	4	4	5
Women in the firm are supportive of their women colleagues	4	5	4	3
Firm management is receptive to the concerns of women attorneys	2	3	4	6

MILBANK, TWEED, HADLEY & McCLOY

Rating: 46

♠ ♠ ♠

Milbank, Tweed, Hadley & McCloy
1 Chase Manhattan Plaza
New York, NY 10005
212-530-5000

No. of Attorneys: 225
No. of Women Attorneys: 57
No. of Partners: 74
No. of Women Partners: 5
No. of Survey Responses Received: 10

Respondent Profile: 10 associates responded. Practice areas included corporate and litigation.

Summary: Although Milbank is populated by a large number of women associates, which sets a comfortable tone for all the firm's women lawyers, a majority of our associate respondents perceived women's opportunities for advancement to be poor. And they were divided about the firm's level of sensitivity to its lawyers' outside obligations and the practicality of its part-time arrangements, although Milbank got high marks for diversity.

Advancement: Although there were a few voices to the contrary, most respondents (six of 10) perceived that women's chances for advancement were poorer than those of their male counterparts. Several respondents, however, remarked that women's advancement is beginning to change for the better. One associate reported that several new female partners have been named, which Milbank confirmed.

A corporate associate noted, "Milbank has changed enormously over the past few years—the balance has shifted." She wrote that in the capital markets department, the male partners rely heavily on women associates who "actually tend to get the better deals, better experience, and better support than male associates." She added that the leader of the practice group had "expressed his intention to support certain female associates in the upcoming partnership decisions." She sensed, nevertheless, that it "takes time to change a firm" that, in her opinion, "once gave women the drudge work and had very traditionalist views of women."

A midlevel corporate associate wrote of a recent trend toward giving women "greater responsibility and more interesting assignments," but also noted that, in her opinion, "mentoring is not available to men or women associates," and that she has not been reviewed since she was a first-year associate.

Some respondents chalked up the discouraging rates of women's advancement to attrition, observing that women tend to leave after their third year or so to "pursue less demanding careers as they grapple with the ordeal of juggling families and careers."

A senior associate wrote that, in her opinion, the low number of women at the top means that there is no one to serve as role models for "associates who aspire to become partners, [and it] fosters an attitude of 'it can't be too terrific a place for a woman to advance—after all, there are few at the top.'"

A small minority of respondents were more positive about women's opportunities for advancement. One corporate lawyer thought women enjoyed advancement prospects equal to men's and that making partner was contingent on ability to "bring in business, be an excellent attorney, or a combination of both." A real estate lawyer wrote that women "who are unfettered by outside burdens or are strong enough and have significant outside support, are roundly supported by the partnership for promotion." Another lawyer wrote that women are treated very well, but it is difficult for her to discern the factors central to advancement "since women are not a large part of the partnership."

> **"[Some partners] have acknowledged that the best associates coming up in the ranks are the women associates."**

Attitudes and atmosphere: Milbank is apparently becoming increasingly female-dominated in the associate ranks with the result that women are beginning to feel more at home. One senior associate stated that some partners "have acknowledged that the best associates coming up in the ranks are the women associates." A project finance attorney wrote that there are "*a lot* of women in my particular group, and we work on cutting-edge transactions in an industry that tends to be male-dominated." A first-year litigator agreed, stating she does not feel isolated, has been given a great deal of responsibility, and is happy with her assignments.

A capital markets associate commented that the firm is "surprisingly open about a variety of matters that are often kept secret by firms—departures, hirings, finances, practice development, bad press, etc." She added that women appear to be more vocal than men in asking questions at practice group lunches.

Another associate in the capital markets group commented that the leadership of the practice changed recently, "bringing with it a more relaxed environment." She could identify "no outward expressions of a 'locker room' mentality," save for, in her opinion, a few midlevel male associates. An associate in the mergers and acquisitions group wrote that although women partners are few and far between, men do serve as mentors, and the assigning partner in her group is "genuinely interested in the development of all associates, whether they are male or female."

> **"When push comes to shove (and it often does) it's you and your family that will pay the price."**

Balancing work & family/personal life: Responses were once again divided on this question, with some respondents characterizing the firm as insensitive toward lawyers' personal lives, and others contending it is better than others in this regard. One unmarried senior associate wrote that sustaining a personal life "is very demanding—keeping this life 'satisfying' is oftentimes simply impossible." She remarked that, in her opinion, the firm is "generally insensitive to family responsibilities—and can be hostile toward them on occasion." Although the firm, in her view, makes "a show" of being supportive, she noted, "When push comes to shove (and it often does) it's you and your family that will pay the price."

Another respondent said that, in her assessment, the firm does not appear to "care much about your personal life or family responsibilities," although it "has outside emergency day care." A corporate attorney reported that, in her experience, most associates work "50 to 60 hours a week and have limited time with family." One midlevel respondent was concerned that while some male partners discuss "how so-and-so will be leaving soon because she is getting married or having children. The same thing is not usually said about men."

A few associates reported that the firm offered the potential to strike a satisfying balance. One senior associate stated that as long as the work is done, "no one really questions hours, etc." She said she has found the firm very supportive of personal issues. One lawyer wrote that partners have "covered" for her to enable her to attend weddings and take vacations. A part-timer wrote that the "nature of a law firm is not, and cannot be, 'sensitive' to family. It is the individual's job to be responsible."

> *"[Part-time is impractical] because the prevalent response is to be resentful of those who are choosing not to give their 110-percent effort to the firm."*

Flexibility of work arrangements: Responses were split, with some observing that part-time is not spoken of, even in jest, and others reporting that many lawyers (men and women) work part-time. One senior associate contended that, in her opinion, "[Part-time is impractical] because the prevalent response is to be resentful of those who are choosing not to give their 110-percent effort to the firm." Part-time is reportedly least workable in the corporate practice area. One corporate attorney noted that part-time is available "based on firm policy," but that, in her estimation, it has never successfully been implemented in the corporate department because "client and partner demands require associates to be available (i.e., in the office) from 9 a.m. to 11 p.m."

An attorney in the capital markets group wrote that while she knew of no part-timers, Milbank "has been extremely understanding to associates with problem pregnancies and death-of-a-spouse issues." There is reportedly a part-time woman of counsel in the mergers and acquisitions department who, according to one respondent, handles her situation well and receives support from the men in the department.

One respondent who works part-time expressed the view that part-time arrangements should not be permitted for everyone at a large firm and emphasized that she never uses her own arrangement as a crutch. She commented that her arrangement entails sacrifice and "only works in a small number of professional positions in a large law firm." She credited the firm with being "as progressive as possible" but opined that "some positions cannot be part-time and younger associates should not be part-time."

> *One lawyer remarked that the firm has "been supportive of me and my interest in recruiting potential minority hiring candidates."*

Diversity: Most respondents gave Milbank high marks regarding its commitment to diversity. A senior associate wrote that this commitment is reflected in hiring practices and that "politics, personalities, and life styles are not criticized, and all appear to be represented here." A corporate attorney reported that there are at least two openly gay male associates in her practice group, and another attorney reported that the firm extends benefits to same-sex partners.

One lawyer remarked that the firm has "been supportive of me and my interest in recruiting potential minority hiring candidates." The firm reportedly has a diversity committee and has taken steps to involve women in recruiting in order to attract female candidates.

> *"The few female partners here could and should do more to foster the growth of women associates."*

Women in leadership positions: Respondents perceived that there are very few women in top positions, and senior attorneys are apparently seen as having done little to promote younger women. A corporate attorney wrote that, in her opinion, not one of the women partners is considered powerful, and that the only woman partner in her practice group "is perceived as difficult to work with." A senior associate reported that there are one or two truly powerful women at the firm and that they are "respected and often called upon to assist the firm in decision-making and client-transaction-representation roles." She observed however, that, in her experience, no woman "has played any role in promoting the opportunities and quality of life of women attorneys." She characterized the firm as "pretty much a dog-eat-dog-place," where women don't have the time or energy to help one another out.

Another attorney wrote that one woman who is a leader at the firm "is not very visible, and, as far as I know, does not focus on promoting the opportunities for women attorneys. She is perceived as aggressive and abrasive." A junior litigator agreed that "the few female partners here could and should do more to foster the growth of women associates." A more junior attorney wrote that women do not hold "typical positions of power—at least with some sort of title," but added that this is beginning to change and, that, in her opinion, there are female partners and associates who are highly respected and exert considerable influence over firm matters.

A corporate attorney noted that there are several senior women associates with a good shot at partnership. A woman in the project finance group reported that the women partners in her group (one with a small child), are "role models for the rest of us."

Milbank, Tweed, Hadley & McCloy No. of Responses: 10	Strongly agree	Agree	Disagree	Strongly disagree
Women's prospects for advancement at the firm are as strong as men's	3	1	5	1
I am satisfied with the firm's family and personal leave policies	3	3	3	1
There are women in positions of power and influence in the firm	1	4	2	3
Women are as likely as men to receive desirable work assignments	6	4		
Women attorneys feel they can discuss family obligations openly	2	5	3	
Women are as likely as men to be mentored by senior attorneys	4	1	5	
Women attorneys enjoy a high level of job satisfaction	2	3	4	
Women in the firm are supportive of their women colleagues	3	5	1	
Firm management is receptive to the concerns of women attorneys	3	1	5	

MINTZ, LEVIN, COHN, FERRIS, GLOVSKY and POPEO, P.C.

Rating: 27

Mintz, Levin, Cohn, Ferris, Glovsky and Popeo, P.C.
One Financial Center
Boston, MA 02111
617-542-6000

No. of Attorneys: 182
No. of Women Attorneys: 57
No. of Partners: 85
No. of Women Partners: 15
No. of Survey Responses Received: 12

Respondent Profile: 5 partners and 7 associates responded. Practice areas included primarily litigation; several respondents did not indicate their practice area.

Summary: While respondents were nearly unanimous that equal opportunities for women exist at Mintz, Levin, several were pointedly pessimistic about anyone's chances of making partner, male or female. The firm is reportedly something of a "boys' club," although one litigator reported that a "girls' club" welcomes those left out of the loop. Achieving a balance between work and family is challenging but doable. Some associates raved about part-time options, but partners cautioned that they may not be without cost.

Advancement: Most associates at Mintz, Levin do not see gender as an obstacle to advancement, although several were pointedly pessimistic about *anyone's* chances of making partner at the firm, female *or* male. One corporate associate reported that although she has received "excellent mentoring," she remains acutely aware that "it is tough for anyone to advance" at the firm. A senior associate confirmed that women have equal chances of making partner, but pointed out that, in her estimation, "that isn't saying much, since partnership will, for most, not be a realistic goal."

The firm's litigators were divided as to women's opportunities in the department. One commented that although she "would like to think I have just as good a chance" of partnership in the litigation department, the small number of women partners in that practice area led her to speculate that women may not be "welcomed in litigation." One litigator disagreed, describing Mintz, Levin as "exceptional in providing equal opportunity for women." She added that the "case in point is that two key section heads are women—one of whom has climbed the ladder while raising a family and working a four-day week. Her position as section head is a tribute to her as well as to the firm and an inspiration for *all* other lawyers at the firm."

Four of the five partners were convinced that the firm's promotion process is fair to women. According to them, review criteria are gender-neutral, and "women are equally likely to be given high-profile cases." Commenting that the

223

factors central to advancement are "commitment to the job—time, attitude, energy and ability to produce good business," a partner noted that "if you are a parent, the trade-offs remain brutal," and that, in her experience, women "leave because of quality-of-life issues."

A handful of respondents observed that any disparity that exists between the advancement rates of men and women is a product of uneven mentoring. One partner remarked that male associates "tend to have mentors and sponsors who are male, some of whom are more powerful," but added that the women partners are attempting to assure that women associates are also mentored.

Respondents contended that the correlation between mentoring and advancement is, in their estimation, more than coincidental. A partner perceived that the "primary criterion for advancement for women" is rainmaking followed by "having a close relationship with our firm's most influential men." Another partner observed that while women "superstars" existed in every class, "men still far outnumber women at [the associate and partner] levels."

mentality, [which] can be quite intimidating." And another partner observed, "Too many male lawyers are rude and boorish," although she made it clear that the firm's management is "committed 100 percent to getting rid of that mind-set."

The firm's "boys' club," in the perception of some respondents, consists of a chummy group of men around whom women can be made to feel uncomfortable. One litigator observed that these men were "threatened by their fellow women litigators. Essentially, these boys simply suffer from immaturity."

Another litigator, who also observed a " 'boys club' atmosphere among certain factions of the firm," added that, in fairness, there is also a "girls' club" atmosphere among other factions.

To one partner, "clubbiness" mattered less than the way in which male/female interactions affect working patterns. She commented that, in her experience, "the social interactions between men and women are okay, [but] the professional interactions could be shored up more."

Another partner proclaimed that Mintz's management "are about as enlightened a group as one could ever, ever hope for."

"For young woman lawyers, there can still exist certain pockets of the 'boys' locker room' mentality, [which] can be quite intimidating."

Attitudes and atmosphere: Mintz, Levin is reportedly something of a "boys' club," although some claimed it's trying to turn itself around. According to one partner's perception, "For young woman lawyers, there can still exist certain pockets of the 'boys' locker room'

"[There is] a lot of pressure especially if you have no family. If you have a family, they understand. With no family, they do not understand."

Balancing work & family/personal life: For unmarried attorneys and mothers alike, achieving a satisfying balance is reportedly challenging but doable. A litigation associate reported that the firm handles mainly complex civil litigation, which demands full-time attention on the part of its lawyers. Thus, she noted, "Even though the firm is very sensitive to family needs/responsibilities, the competitive atmosphere of the legal community makes it very difficult to successfully balance work and family."

Keeping family and career in motion requires "constant juggling," although the firm reportedly "more than does its part" to make it possible. A partner, reflecting on the firm's family-friendly orientation, observed that it is "not considered 'macho' to brag about missing a child's birthday party, for instance—such a statement would rather raise a question of that person's priorities." In the opinion of another partner, men, or at least fathers, are cut more slack than moms: "Men seem to be able to work fewer hours because of children than many of the women do."

According to one associate, because the firm is self-consciously family-friendly, the pinch may be greatest for those who do not have children. She wrote that, in her experience, there is "a lot of pressure especially if you have no family. If you have a family, they understand. With no family, they do not understand." But a partner contended the demands are indiscriminate and "wreak havoc on any person's personal/family life."

> **"[Flexible work arrangements are] legitimate, but you take a cut in salary and are the easiest target for deferral when it comes to partnership decisions."**

Flexibility of work arrangements: Several respondents lauded the firm for its flexibility in fashioning part-time arrangements. One associate described the firm as extremely progressive and in favor of a family, and extremely generous in offering part-time arrangements for mothers." One litigation associate stated, "The bottom line is that if you can propose a work arrangement that is beneficial to both you and the firm—the firm will make every effort to make it work."

Mintz, Levin reportedly has part-time partners and associates, both male and female, but some respondents feared that alternative arrangements were out of the question in certain sections of the firm, because of the nature of the work and the unwillingness of colleagues to be supportive. One senior associate commented that, in her perception, certain departments may be reluctant to give a part-timer significant responsibility on the theory that someone "who isn't 'in the office' five days a week can't be available for clients." She added, "This perception needs rethinking."

Although several of the associates raved about part-time options, partners cautioned that reduced schedules may not be without cost. One partner commented that, in her estimation, it is "*extremely* difficult for any woman to advance here or at any firm when they work part-time. It is done. But at great personal costs, and professional costs." She added that, in her opinion, there are people in the firm whose attitude is "you give it all or you get nothing." An associate concurred, writing that, in her estimation, flexible work arrangements are "legitimate, but you take a cut in salary and are the easiest target for deferral when it comes to partnership decisions." According to a partner, part-time work may be somewhat impractical because of "the nature of a high-profile, big-client/big-firm practice."

For those who are making part-time happen, the potential trade-offs, real or perceived, in terms of image and advancement are evidently worth it. One part-timer commented that sustaining the balance is "refreshingly doable" and another, who described herself as on the "mommy track," noted that she has received "good support" from many colleagues, though, in her opinion, "a few will always be derisive of such arrangements."

The firm reportedly provides on-site emergency childcare.

An associate did not believe that those with "more conservative views would be comfortable expressing them here."

Diversity: Mintz, Levin is said to be a great place if you are gay, but a lonely one if you are a racial minority. Several respondents noted that the firm "includes homosexual attorneys in its family policies," and that it supports gay rights *pro bono* organizations. An associate remarked that she believed the firm has "a sincere commitment without much success," regarding minority recruiting, but, like others in Boston, it must compete "for a handful of top minority candidates."

Although Mintz, Levin elected its first minority partner, an African-American woman, in 1996, one lawyer said that, in her opinion, "while things are woeful for white women, they are even more so for women and men of color."

With regard to political affiliations, one partner reported that many women at the firm "are active politically across the spectrum." In contrast, an associate commented that she regarded the firm as "very politically correct" and that she

did not believe that those with "more conservative views would be comfortable expressing them here."

An associate characterized the few women in power as "savvy and competent, but I don't see many changes that reflect their influence."

Women in leadership positions: Although a large majority believed "women of influence" were clearly in evidence at Mintz, Levin, many respondents thought that women lagged behind men from the standpoint of "real" power. Although one woman reportedly sits on the executive committee, and the firm has a female hiring partner and a woman in charge of the litigation department, according to one partners' perception, "the real 'titans' are still men." She added that, in her opinion, this may be "to some extent a function of age—the most powerful men are in their mid- to late-50s and the highest women are in their mid-40s."

Nevertheless, one associate cited as noteworthy a woman leader who had been "a great trailblazer" with respect to part-time options.

Most associate respondents, however, agreed with the partners that too many of the managerial roles are held by men. An associate characterized the few women in power as "savvy and competent, but I don't see many changes that reflect their influence." One associate commented that when a woman was named to head the litigation section, she sensed that "the other men partners seemed to resent her selection." She added that the women partners "overall, are not supportive of women associates," although she acknowledged that the women partners in the litigation department have started to show some support for associates through a series of group lunches.

Mintz, Levin, Cohn, Ferris, Glovsky and Popeo No. of Responses: 12	Strongly agree	Agree	Disagree	Strongly disagree
Women's prospects for advancement at the firm are as strong as men's	4	7	1	
I am satisfied with the firm's family and personal leave policies	6	5	1	
There are women in positions of power and influence in the firm	3	4	4	
Women are as likely as men to receive desirable work assignments	4	8		
Women attorneys feel they can discuss family obligations openly	3	5	4	
Women are as likely as men to be mentored by senior attorneys	4	4	3	1
Women attorneys enjoy a high level of job satisfaction	2	6	3	
Women in the firm are supportive of their women colleagues	4	5	1	1
Firm management is receptive to the concerns of women attorneys	2	8	1	

MORGAN, LEWIS & BOCKIUS LLP

Rating: 74

Morgan, Lewis & Bockius LLP
2000 One Logan Square
Philadelphia, PA 19103
215-963-5000

No. of Attorneys: 211
No. of Women Attorneys: 53
No. of Partners: 88
No. of Women Partners: 5
No. of Survey Responses Received: 6

Respondent Profile: 6 associates responded.

Summary: Our very small sample of associate respondents did not give Morgan, Lewis high marks. Advancement opportunities are seen to be limited, the milieu is male-dominated, and the hours are grueling. On a positive note, the firm's commitment to diversity was acknowledged by most.

Advancement: Several respondents portrayed Morgan, Lewis as a "man's firm," where, they believe, women either drop out of the race or hit a wall on the road to partnership. Although respondents noted that the allocation of assignments appears gender-neutral, nevertheless, in the opinion of one midlevel associate, the firm "has a reputation in the community...[which] stems from the disproportionate number of male partners." She perceived that there may indeed be "an advantage to being male when it comes down to partnership."

According to another associate, the female associates she has talked with view their partnership chances as "slim to none." She added that as far as she can see, young women, particularly those who are married, "are not viewed as 'partnership material' by the top brass, and it is generally expected that a young pregnant associate will not return to work after having her baby."

Although one associate commented that advancement to partnership "depends on quality of work, ability to bring in new clients, and dedication to the firm," another opined that "hours, hours, hours, clients, [and] golf" are what counts, suggesting that "tall, blond, blue-eyed looks" wouldn't hurt. A litigator commented that women are treated fairly and "get the same opportunities for good assignments and responsibilities commensurate with their abilities," yet, because of the scarcity of women partners, "there are fewer strong mentoring relationships."

Family demands also dampen women's partnership prospects, and one respondent pointed out that many women "ultimately opt out for family values over hectic work schedules because it is a difficult balance." Another associate agreed that most women "drop off the partnership track through attrition due to the desire to have a family (often inconsistent with the partnership track due to the hours required) or to have a life outside the office."

According to one associate, some women who have made partner "have left shortly thereafter." She added that among those who have stayed, the "most successful women partners...behave as male partners and give very little support to other females."

A junior associate reported that the firm is uncomfortable for women, "not because of any sort of harassment but because women are not part of the club."

Attitudes and atmosphere: Two respondents were upbeat about the atmosphere at Morgan, Lewis, but four others reported that the environment is less than ideal. According to a midlevel associate, the firm is *"extremely* comfortable" for women and the "overall tone of firm management is not to make any distinction on a gender basis." A litigator reported that her department boasts a "great atmosphere, very collegial," which she described as the "best part" about the firm.

Another associate, however, wrote that while the firm as a whole is hospitable toward women, the "topic of having children while still an associate" is an uncomfortable one. She added that, in her experience, there is a "bit of a 'boys' club' revolving around golf, tennis, and other activities, which women seem less a part of." The firm's leadership, in her view, is "male-dominated and conservative." A junior associate reported a sense that the firm is uncomfortable for women, "not because of any sort of harassment but because women are not

part of the 'club.' There's a lot of emphasis on male type activities (sports, etc.) outside the office as well."

According to another associate, women at the firm are given challenging work but are "not invited to sports events, outings, beer after hours, etc." Another associate described the firm as *"ultra*-conservative," and said it "epitomizes the notion of the old 'boys' club.'"

"Personal life: Forget it! Nonexistent. Working hours: 24 hours a day (and that's still not enough to satisfy the top brass!). Pressure: A given!"

Balancing work & family/personal life: Work and family are said to be "either-or" propositions at Morgan, Lewis. One midlevel associate described the firm as fast-paced and generating a "tremendous workload," although "that is understood and part of the choice one makes before joining ML & B." She added that the "sophistication of the practice and quality of the client base comes at the price of some personal sacrifice. It's a choice."

A colleague reported that the firm is sensitive to family commitments, yet, she opined, some may fear "it is basically a choice you make—either family first or firm first." Women who do want a family life must "constantly work at it or sacrifice it," according to another. Hours, reported by one associate, average 60 to 80 per week.

Most associates expressed dismay at the firm's failure to help make balance more viable. One quipped: "Personal life: Forget it! Nonexistent. Working hours: 24 hours a day (and that's *still* not enough to satisfy the top brass!).

Pressure: A given!" Another referred to a cartoon posted in one of the lunch rooms with a boss commenting to an employee: "'It's been brought to my attention that you have a life outside of the office." In this respondent's view, the cartoon "says it all."

Another associate said that, in her opinion, "sensitivity of the firm to family responsibilities is not great." She asserted that the firm offers "no leave/accommodation made for those who want to adopt." Nevertheless, it does provide emergency day care.

One associate recounted that one part-time colleague who was "supposed to" work four days a week and was paid to work four days a week, in reality worked more than five days.

Flexibility of work arrangements: In one associate's estimation, "Part-time is not allowed for associates." Although part-time arrangements *are* allowed on a "case-by-case" basis, they are "few and far between" and "not really seen as an option," according to another respondent. She added that those who do go part-time end up working "50-some hour weeks usually."

One associate recounted that one part-time colleague who was "supposed to" work four days a week and was paid to work four days a week, in reality worked more than five days. She further believed that part-time is "usually discouraged, and, if permitted at all, it is only a temporary situation." In her opinion, her section forbids part-time arrangements across the board. In the estimation of one associate, part-time arrangements "rarely succeed, primarily

because of the unbearable workload." Moreover, she added, the partners appear to "frown on such arrangements because of the perceived failure to 'pull your own weight.'"

Although respondents reported that there are a few women currently on part-time status, one associate observed, "It seems the firm is still reluctantly trying this option out." Most female associates who have children, in her experience, "start looking around for other jobs." She said that if she leaves early— "6 p.m."—to relieve her nanny, "it is looked poorly upon—it does not matter that I work at home late at night to catch up. I am losing 'face time.'"

Two associates seemed to favor what they perceived to be the firm's rather restrictive approach to part-time. One litigator commented, "You only get what you put into the firm, so if you are working less, you will probably not make partner, as well as not get the best cases." According to a midlevel associate, choosing to go part-time does not "in any way hamper the quality of assignments and treatment by the firm." She added that a lawyer "working on such an alternative schedule is not partner-tracked. Being a full-time female associate, I believe this practice to be fair."

A spokesperson for the firm disputed many of the negative perceptions about part-time, contending that part-time arrangements are available at *every* level. There is a formal, written "flex-time arrangements" policy for partners, a written policy that lawyers working less than full-time can still be considered for partnership and that, indeed, a part-timer was made a partner two years ago (though the lawyer agreed to go full-time within two years of being made partner).

> *A respondent noted that the firm is "historically extremely conservative."*

Diversity: Morgan, Lewis received relatively high marks from respondents on diversity, although they reported that vestiges of its conservative past persist. One associate confirmed the firm was "pretty good on the diversity front." She reported that the firm includes women of color, women with disabilities, and women of different political leanings and life styles, and that as long as "the attorney meets the firm's high standards, she'll be welcomed and accepted."

According to another associate, although the firm has made an effort to recruit more minorities, its retention rate has "not been very good." One associate blamed what she perceived as a lack of diversity on the hiring pool, commenting that the "people who are drawn to a big firm have a lot in common."

One respondent opined that the firm "makes an effort to inform its lawyers that discrimination or harassment of any kind will not be tolerated," and "goes out of its way to educate employees about its policies on such matters."

One respondent reported that the firm has "lawyers at both ends of the political spectrum." Another said that the firm is "historically extremely conservative," but then commented that it has recently become "somewhat more liberal. Lawyers actually admit to being Democrats now."

> *Although there are "a number of outstanding women partners," management is "dominated by the men of the firm."*

Women in leadership positions: "Trying to think of women in true leadership positions at ML & B is difficult," wrote one respondent. She added that although there are "a number of outstanding women partners," management, in her opinion, is "dominated by the men of the firm." An associate remarked that there is one woman who "has some power but she does nothing to promote the opportunities or quality of life of women attorneys."

One associate said that the firm's more influential women "are well-respected and their opinions are welcomed," and that they do promote opportunities for women. Others disagreed. One respondent noted that the female partners at the firm—"all five of them out of [211] lawyers"—are "not perceived as being helpful in promoting the opportunities of women at the firm." She added that one lawyer has been "instrumental in mobilizing the female associates," but that she is "fighting an uphill battle."

A litigator noted that one of the three female partners in her section has "gone out of her way to promote/improve life of women attorneys and try to mentor as many people as possible." She added, however, that she is "an exceptional individual and needs very little sleep!"

Another associate opined that one woman partner "is clearly marginal—she is hardly ever seen at any events and not invited to very important committees."

Morgan, Lewis & Bockius No. of Responses: 6	Strongly agree	Agree	Disagree	Strongly disagree
Women's prospects for advancement at the firm are as strong as men's		2	1	3
I am satisfied with the firm's family and personal leave policies	1	1	2	2
There are women in positions of power and influence in the firm		2	2	2
Women are as likely as men to receive desirable work assignments	3		1	2
Women attorneys feel they can discuss family obligations openly	1		2	3
Women are as likely as men to be mentored by senior attorneys	2		3	1
Women attorneys enjoy a high level of job satisfaction	2	1	2	1
Women in the firm are supportive of their women colleagues	3	1	1	1
Firm management is receptive to the concerns of women attorneys		1	2	3

MORRISON & FOERSTER LLP

Rating: 28

🔨🔨🔨

Morrison & Foerster LLP
345 California St.
San Francisco, CA 94104
415-677-7665

No. of Attorneys: 210
No. of Women Attorneys: 69
No. of Partners: 70
No. of Women Partners: 13
No. of Survey Responses Received: 5

Respondent Profile: 3 partners and 2 associates responded.

Summary: Our handful of respondents portrayed Morrison & Foerster as a fair workplace for women, although most perceived it to be more daunting if one has children and is a primary caregiver. Chances for advancement are said to be equal for women, juggling work with competing responsibilities is apparently "impossible," and part-time options may look a lot better on paper than in practice. The firm's work environment, however, is welcoming—management is said to have no tolerance for discrimination of any kind.

Advancement: Four of the five respondents agreed that women are as likely to advance at the firm as men, although not necessarily women with children. The other—a partner—was negative about virtually every aspect of the firm.

A partner provided a detailed exegesis of women's problems with advancement. She said that, in her estimation, associates may be criticized for three failings: "Lack of judgment, lack of intelligence, and lack of commitment." She added that although men and women are judged fairly when it comes to judgment and intelligence, women, in her opinion—and especially women with children—"are unfairly judged in the area of commitment." She attributed this to the firm's view that adequate commitment for success is "essentially unlimited commitment."

Therefore, she continued, any "suggestion that other things may or will get in the way of jumping when the client or a senior attorney asks you to jump suggests a commitment problem. Even if you can keep the client happy, you can still be viewed as having a commitment problem."

As to mentoring, this partner wrote that although she had a good male mentor, many men "like to mentor women, but don't like to deal with women who become their peers."

Another partner took a different view, commenting that while women are as likely as men to reach partnership, in her opinion, they are "far less likely to reach the upper tiers of compensation." She observed that there has never been a woman "in the top tier and there have only been two in the second tier."

> *One associate observed that the tone set by management is "definitely a no tolerance for discrimination," and added that "inappropriate behavior or comments are reprimanded."*

Attitudes and atmosphere: Most agreed that MoFo is an excellent place for women, though some respondents perceived that certain problems do lurk. One partner reported that there are "significant numbers of women partners and associates," thereby creating a level of comfort for women. One associate observed that the tone set by management is "definitely a no tolerance for discrimination," and added that "inappropriate behavior or comments are reprimanded." The firm is "better than most," according to this associate.

Despite the absence of discrimination at MoFo, a couple of respondents had complaints. One partner said that, in her opinion, some men are "a little offensive" and others are "a lot." Although the litigation group is home to a large cadre of women, very few women apparently work in the business group and a "boys' club" rules the roost, in one lawyer's opinion.

One associate observed that men "tend to be more competitive and aggressive," which "makes it uncomfortable for some women." The other associate remarked that although she finds the firm "very comfortable," she "might feel differently" if she were balancing work and family, and added that, in her opinion, "the firm has yet to handle the mentoring issue."

On the subject of balancing, one partner reported that despite the encouragement she received from her male colleagues to "take as much time off as possible" when she returned after the birth of her child, she perceived she was "clearly criticized for lacking the commitment of the others who worked all 12 months in a year."

> *A partner observed that, in her estimation, the most successful women at the firm are childless or have grown children.*

Balancing work & family/personal life: Sustaining a satisfying life outside Morrison & Foerster is reported to be impossible for both men and women, a state of affairs possibly comparable to other firms. Like many other firms, the pace seems to be incompatible with the responsibilities of those who are also primary caregivers.

One associate remarked that achieving a balance is difficult for both genders but that women "place a higher importance on it." She added that, in her opinion, lawyers who are dissatisfied with the amount of personal time that MoFo leaves them "end up leaving the firm." Further, lawyers who stay make a sacrifice because "they think it's worth it."

Another lawyer reported that some women manage to take maternity leave and still make partner, but observed, "There are not very many." She noted that, given her experience with other large firms, the balance is "extremely difficult," but "it's easier at Morrison & Foerster than at most comparable firms."

One partner observed that the balance was "extremely difficult" based on "how few women with children work as attorneys here" and how "even fewer successful/senior women with children [are] working as attorneys here." She added that the most successful women at the firm are childless or have grown children and that several women with children have spouses who provide primary care for the children during the week.

> **One part-time partner wrote, "On paper and in concept, this is a decent place for women to work."**

Flexibility of work arrangements: Part-time arrangements, although allowed, are only feasible—and in some cases available—for a select group of lawyers, according to associate respondents. Moreover, going part-time appears to adversely affect one's reputation. Women have reportedly taken advantage of the firm's alternative work arrangements at all levels, according to one partner. Another partner remarked that the firm offers alternative work arrangements but added that "compensation reflects it, as it should."

One part-time partner characterized her own experience with an alternative schedule as positive, but noted that it was not without drawbacks. She wrote, "On paper and in concept, this is a decent place for women to work," given the availability of part-time options. In practice, she sensed that, despite the praise she receives on the quality of her work, leadership skills, and client rapport, she is viewed as "not as committed as my peers." She concluded that her arrangement "works for me—and is tolerated by the firm—only to the extent that I can control my work without adding to others' workload."

The associate respondents took a dimmer view of part-time work at MoFo and suggested that the firm does not go out of its way to promote such arrangements. For the most part, "alternative arrangements don't work out very well," in the opinion of one senior associate. One corporate associate wrote that the firm "does not encourage" part-time work and that such options are "generally only available for those who have already given the firm a major part of their lives" and "are invaluable to the firm in some way." Another associate agreed that "if you're a valued member of the team, [the firm] will help you try to make it work."

> **The firm is "very open to people of all types."**

Diversity: Because of a low response on this topic, a clear picture of the firm's attitude toward diversity did not emerge. Moreover, none of the respondents made any comments about racial diversity. One partner reported that the firm "tries hard to recruit, retain, and support lawyers of diverse ethnicity." Another partner wrote, simply, "not qualified to comment."

The associates reported that the firm is a comfortable environment for all types of lawyers. One noted that, despite the firm's "strong history of supporting liberal causes and Democratic politics," she has "never felt uncomfortable expressing contrary opinions."

Another associate concurred that the firm is "very open to people of all types," and added that "generally just about everyone feels comfortable."

> **"[The] powerful women here are in litigation."**

Women in leadership positions: Are women represented in the firm's upper tiers of power? "Not really," in the words of one partner. Few if any women appear to be major power players at MoFo, according to respondents' perceptions. The firm is run by an executive committee comprised of six people, none of whom are women, according to one partner. She added that the 12-member board of directors does include one woman, but, in the partner's estimation, she has "little power."

The compensation committee also reportedly includes two women (out of a total of 11 positions). But all the heads of the departments are said to be male. One associate reported "very few women at the highest positions in the firm" and added that getting there "seems to be largely related to billings." An associate expressed her view that the top women do not seem to generate the level of respect that the top men inspire; the most "successful" woman at the firm, a rain-maker by one partner's account, is said to be "widely regarded by men and women alike as thoroughly self-absorbed."

Women appear to have taken hold of the reins to a greater extent in litigation than in the firm's business department. One corporate associate noted that, with one exception, the "powerful women here are in litigation." She added that the firm is a "terrific place" for women litigators, who "get hiring jobs, managing office jobs, and key committee assignments." In contrast, in her opinion, the business department "has not had such a great track record over the recent past few years."

A couple of respondents suggested that power and mentoring may not go hand in hand for the firm's most senior women. One associate noted that the senior women do not "particularly try to promote other women, though it has happened in some instances." A partner added that the women in the firm who are "reasonably successful and do seem to care about other women in the firm" seem to "just plug away with not a lot of recognition."

Morrison & Foerster No. of Responses: 5	Strongly agree	Agree	Disagree	Strongly disagree
Women's prospects for advancement at the firm are as strong as men's	1	3	1	
I am satisfied with the firm's family and personal leave policies	2	3		
There are women in positions of power and influence in the firm		3	1	
Women are as likely as men to receive desirable work assignments	2	1	2	
Women attorneys feel they can discuss family obligations openly	1	2	1	1
Women are as likely as men to be mentored by senior attorneys	2	2	1	
Women attorneys enjoy a high level of job satisfaction	1	2	1	
Women in the firm are supportive of their women colleagues	3	2		
Firm management is receptive to the concerns of women attorneys	2	2	1	

PALMER & DODGE LLP

Rating: 14

🔨🔨🔨🔨

Palmer & Dodge LLP
One Beacon St.
Boston, MA 02108
517-573-0100

No. of Attorneys: 167
No. of Women Attorneys: 56
No. of Partners: 71
No. of Women Partners: 9
No. of Survey Responses Received: 14

Respondent Profile: 3 partners, 10 associates, and 1 attorney who did not list her position. Practice areas included litigation, employment, and business law.

Summary: It was a common perception that most women do not stay at Palmer & Dodge long enough to find out what their partnership chances are, but for those who do stick it out on a full-time basis, respondents were nearly unanimous that promotions are within reach. Although some members of the male partnership were characterized as less than sensitive, most women attorneys seem to have managed to avoid them and thus find the firm's atmosphere pleasant and woman-friendly. Expected hours are lower than at many comparable firms, but respondents disagreed about the practicality of its part-time options.

Advancement: All three partners and seven of nine associates were very positive about women's chances for advancement at Palmer, although some feared that women are leaving in droves upon reaching the midlevel and senior-level ranks, with the inevitable result that few are promoted to partnership. One midlevel associate observed that it "seems lately that 90 percent of the associates leaving are women." Where do they go and why? According to one partner, a key factor in being promoted is "business development skills" and women are often "less confident of themselves in those areas and have frequently in the past years made self-limiting decisions to go in-house rather than try to make partner. Many of these women would have made it."

Associates seemed to agree with the comment that "more women than men take themselves out of the running." There was consensus that this is "primarily due to having children," in the view of a midlevel litigator, "but also partly because the big-firm atmosphere is less friendly to women, and there are few women partners." As another respondent put it, women are "better able—financially and emotionally—to accept jobs with less stress, less status and less pay—and see this as a step forward." One respondent suggested that one measure that might help slow the exodus of women is "a more visible commitment to part-time work for associates with young children."

For those who stick it out working full-time, most perceived that partnership is as achievable as it is for men. One respondent said women have as good a chance at advancement as men, "as long as they postpone any part-time options available to them."

Women who do stay but cannot devote themselves exclusively to the firm are unlikely to advance, according to one respondent's perception. A senior associate observed, "Women without children are as likely to advance to partnership—women with children are not as likely to advance due to the competing demands of family on their time."

---

*The firm "is one of the most—if not **the** most—comfortable large law firms in Boston for which a woman may work..."*

Attitudes and atmosphere: Most women expressed very high satisfaction with the atmosphere at Palmer, reporting that they are comfortable at the firm and are aware of no forms of gender discrimination. One senior associate wrote that the firm "is one of the most—if not *the* most—comfortable large law firms in Boston for which a woman may work. The firm leadership is 110-percent committed to a nondiscriminatory environment." One litigator added that she is "doing a bunch of family law cases for *pro bono* work and nobody gives me a hard time."

Another respondent described the firm as friendly, and observed that because there are as many women associates as men, the atmosphere is "less charged by gender." Moreover, because "part-time policies are progressive and

used...it's not unusual to see lots of pregnant women and kids around."

An employment law associate described Palmer & Dodge as "relaxed but business-like," with "absolutely no 'boys' club.' " A partner commented that the firm was one of the first "in the country with a confidential ombudsperson for resolution of workplace issues."

The small minority of dissenters were adamant in their view that Palmer is not a friendly place for women. One associate, who did not identify her practice group, perceived that "women are treated in a disrespectful manner by certain partners and are totally excluded from social interactions with certain partners. Partners in my practice group... flagrantly [criticize] one female associate to another associate. Such behavior is unprofessional and does not foster a good working relationship."

Another associate said that, in her experience, there was "a partner [who] consistently mistreated [some] associates (screamed at them, requested them to perform inappropriate tasks such as personally faxing documents when there's a fax department)." It was the perception of one junior associate that, with certain partners, "it is necessary to take on the persona of a young, slightly helpless (but competent enough) child."

A partner claimed that the firm "does not value people who would happily sacrifice family for firm."

Balancing work & family/personal life: With lower-than-average billable requirements—1,800 hours per year by one account—Palmer attorneys appear to have an easier time than most sustaining a satisfying life outside the firm. The hours are "reasonable," according to one litigator, which she defined as "8 or 9 a.m. to 6 or 7 p.m., occasional nights and weekends." According to a junior associate who is single and putting in many hours, the firm is "busy now but everyone keeps saying that 1,800 to 2,000 hours per year billable is really the norm here. The office is pretty deserted after 7 p.m. and on weekends."

Several respondents described the firm as responsive to family responsibilities, day-care schedules, and sick kids. Nonetheless, P & D remains "a high-pressure, emergency-oriented job that puts a lot of pressure on women with kids." A partner claimed that the firm "does not value people who would happily sacrifice family for firm." A senior associate with children described Palmer as "one of, if not the most family-friendly" firms, remarking that "hours expectations are reasonable and there is little after-hours socializing." She added that the firm provides emergency back-up day care for lawyers and staff.

The schedules of the partners appear a bit cushier. A corporate securities partner reported that her average workday "is 9 a.m. to 5 p.m. or 6 p.m. in the office and one hour at home or on the train commuting. If I work at home, it's after my kids are asleep. P & D has been very helpful—there are lots of great associates to delegate to—and I sense that the firm *wants* it to work."

One junior associate was skeptical about the feasibility of rearing children and lawyering at Palmer. This associate perceived that despite the firm's outward tolerance of family obligations, "While there are some female partners with children, I do not feel that having a child is compatible with advancing to partnership in this firm."

"Women on the 'mommy track' may think of themselves as second-class citizens and may be uncomfortable in that role."

....

Flexibility of work arrangements: Respondents included several part-timers who reported that the firm is generally supportive of part-time work, although opting for alternative schedules is, in some respondents' estimation, not without its drawbacks. One lawyer observed that the firm has "very liberal part-time options available for child-rearing purposes, but taking advantage of those options is viewed...as showing a lack of commitment to the practice of law." As a result, she perceived that "women on the 'mommy track' may think of themselves as second-class citizens and may be uncomfortable in that role." Nonetheless, she concluded that if "the ability to do interesting work on a part-time basis is a goal, then the trade off of lack of advancement may be worthwhile." She further said it was her understanding that those who do not mind stepping permanently off track may stay at the firm "indefinitely without being a partner."

An associate in the employment department observed that part-time options "are both legitimate and viable," although as one becomes more senior, "the pressures from clients, courts, etc., make it increasingly difficult to sustain a reduced schedule, but these 'difficulty' factors are outside the firm. Within the firm, the atmosphere is generally supportive and encouraging."

According to a partner, although the firm is "very receptive to part-time lawyering," most clients are not: "Clients these days expect to be able to reach their lawyer any time of the day or night. Often they want immediate turnaround of documents."

One associate suggested that the firm would lose fewer women if part-time seemed more viable, "but the firm is moving in the right direction—one woman is on a yearlong trial basis, working severely reduced hours with some telecommuting."

> *"We run the gamut from Rush Limbaugh fans up in business law to the much more left-leaning litigation department."*

Diversity: Respondents noted that the firm is diverse in terms of political leanings, but not race.

The firm is "not as racially diverse as it should be," in the opinion of one senior associate. Others commented that the firm has several "out" gay and lesbian attorneys, and that "no one makes a big deal about it." One associate said that the firm is "generally a very liberal environment where women's issues are comfortably discussed." She added that she has worked on "several *pro bono* cases in particular for women involved in domestic violence and family planning rights." In terms of politics, one lawyer said, "We run the gamut from Rush Limbaugh fans up in business law to the much more left-leaning litigation department."

> *One associate reported that the firm "has a special committee devoted to 'gender issues.' "*

Women in leadership positions: Palmer reportedly has a "small handful" of women in powerful positions, including a member of the executive committee, the chair of the business department, and members of other firm committees. According to one partner's perception, however, "that's not 'real power' I'm afraid." She believes, "Real power has nothing to do with firm administration but with the dollar value of a partner's client billings." She added that she was aware of two women partners with billings of more than $1 million, and they "are therefore among the top 20 to 30 partners."

Associates were split as to how the more influential women partners treat their underlings. According to one junior associate, "those women do not bother to meet female associates." A midlevel associate agreed that she and her colleagues "do not perceive women partners as being supportive or promoting younger women." Another associate asserted that the partners "have little interest in helping advance or mentor the women associates in the firm."

A few associates took the opposite view. One wrote that "one of the best things about Palmer is that both [the] male partners and the female partners appear to have taken an interest in advancing women associates." And one associate reported that the firm "has a special committee devoted to 'gender issues.' "

Palmer & Dodge No. of Responses: 14	Strongly agree	Agree	Disagree	Strongly disagree
Women's prospects for advancement at the firm are as strong as men's	6	4		2
I am satisfied with the firm's family and personal leave policies	8	3	1	
There are women in positions of power and influence in the firm	5	5	1	1
Women are as likely as men to receive desirable work assignments	9	3	1	1
Women attorneys feel they can discuss family obligations openly	6	4	1	2
Women are as likely as men to be mentored by senior attorneys	9	2		2
Women attorneys enjoy a high level of job satisfaction	4	5		2
Women in the firm are supportive of their women colleagues	10	2		1
Firm management is receptive to the concerns of women attorneys	6	5		2

PATTERSON, BELKNAP, WEBB & TYLER LLP

Rating: 31

◤◤◤

Patterson, Belknap, Webb & Tyler LLP
1133 Avenue of the Americas
New York, NY 10036
212-336-2000

No. of Attorneys: 135
No. of Women Attorneys: 46
No. of Partners: 42
No. of Women Partners: 7
No. of Survey Responses Received: 7

Respondent Profile: 3 partners, 3 associates, and 1 counsel responded. Practice areas included trusts and estates, litigation, and employment.

Summary: Patterson Belknap offers women some of the sanest hours in New York and an atmosphere that is free of discrimination. Moreover, the firm was until recently headed by a woman managing partner. With that said, women's potential for advancement at the firm still appears discouraging to some. Respondents also report that part-time policies are, for the most part, *ad hoc*, and some male partners remain clueless as to the challenges facing working mothers.

Advancement: Partners and associates were split as to whether advancement is equitable for women at Patterson Belknap. Partners, on the one hand, described the firm as a meritocracy. One remarked, "Prospects of advancement are excellent for talented women." Another agreed that women's opportunities are commensurate to men's, but conceded, "some of the younger women associates may not think so." The third partner wrote that making partner is "tough for everyone," but added, "women have just as good (or bad) an opportunity."

Three of five associate respondents, in contrast, expressed a more pessimistic viewpoint, citing in particular the modest representation of women in the partnership. One employment lawyer reported a "general perception [that] women are not as likely as men to advance to partnership." Two associates expressed the view that the small number of women partners reflects women's relative disadvantage in terms of advancement. One wrote that, in her perception, women are "nowhere near as likely as men to advance."

Associates cited conflicts between work and family life as the primary source of women's attrition and failure to advance. One senior associate reported that during her years at the firm, a number of women had left, in her estimation, because of "the difficulty these women had in balancing their careers with their families." A midlevel associate opined that many women "leave after having their first baby, often because they perceive firm life—the hours required and the expectation that all personal plans and responsibilities can and will be dropped when a partner calls—to be incompatible with family life."

Respondents reported that other obstacles include a perceived reluctance of women partners to mentor their more junior colleagues and reviews that tend to favor men. According to one associate, women partners are "reluctant to make a commitment to mentoring any woman who is not clearly destined for partnership." In her view, this attitude perpetuates the "subtle message" from women partners that "if you do it the way we did it, we'll help you along." The quality of mentoring is also said to vary among departments. Thus, she contended, to "the extent that women of a younger generation have a different approach to pursuing our career paths and goals, we're on our own."

An associate noted that, in her experience, the "criteria used for review are slanted in favor of those without families," including demonstrating a "willingness to cancel vacations and use personal time for business purposes." One partner, however, attributed attrition of women to the "same factors as for men— lack of talent, relocation, [and] different job goals." She did recognize that, "in a few cases," women have left the firm because of "the perception that it is more difficult for women to advance."

One partner, attributed attrition of women to the "same factors as for men—lack of talent, relocation, [and] different job goals."

Attitudes and atmosphere: The firm is, by most accounts, free of gender discrimination. One partner wrote that the firm is a comfortable place, because "there are a lot of us." She added that there is "ample opportunity for conversation about children, childcare problems, etc." Another partner noted that there is a perception among some lawyers that litigation, especially, is a difficult department for women because of "time and travel demands."

Several respondents credited the firm's leadership, including senior female partners, with creating a positive and respectful atmosphere.

Two associates were less positive. One recounted several comments she had heard and observed that the male partners, in her opinion, show little empathy for those balancing work and family. She recalled that one time, when a colleague left to take her child to the doctor, a partner responded, "I have a wife to do that."

Another associate reported that lawyers—both men and women—feel "the need to act as though they are handling family and work obligations effortlessly: It is necessary to 'put on a happy face.'" In the words of one associate, the firm is a "generally" comfortable place for women to work, "particularly if you do not have children."

"Those who work full-time often feel the sacrifices they are making are too great...Most of us wish we could go home earlier to have a normal family dinner."

Balancing work & family/personal life: The firm's hours are said to be quite sane by New York standards, although some respondents didn't think this offered them much relief. The suggested hours are "1,850, rather than the

2,000 to 2,300 hours routinely expected of associates at other New York firms," according to one partner. Some women associates with children reportedly come in early and leave early, and some have spouses who are home in the afternoon so they can come in later or leave later.

Other associates voiced complaints about the firm's level of support for its lawyers' responsibilities outside of the firm. According to one, "Those who work full-time often feel the sacrifices they are making are too great...Most of us wish we could go home earlier to have a normal family dinner."

Another associate reported, "There still are pressures to get the job done at any cost." She observed that the lack of available childcare "furthers the problem." Women are put in a bind, because "[there is not] much understanding in emergencies when childcare arrangements fail," according to another associate's perception. She added that, in her opinion, "mommy track" means that "a lower position will be available for women with children—the track is right out the door." This respondent faulted the firm for failing to understand that "some individuals may wish to be taken off the partnership track in order to achieve more balance in their lives." Although individual partners are said to be sensitive to family responsibilities, she perceived the "majority of partners do not understand the conflicting demands placed on individuals with children."

> *One associate reported that some part-time arrangements have "worked out quite well," including her own.*

Flexibility of work arrangements: Several respondents expressed satisfaction with their own part-time arrangements. Beyond an official policy allowing new mothers to work part-time for three months following a maternity leave, part-time is apparently permitted "on a discretionary basis thereafter," according to an associate. Several associates currently work on part-time schedules that range from two to four days per week, according to a partner.

No partners are currently part-time, although the firm reportedly had one part-time partner. Part-time is reportedly available at the counsel level. One partner reported that the firm is also permitting other alternative work arrangements, including working from home. Part-time options are, by one account, largely unavailable in the litigation department, "with some exceptions."

One associate reported that some part-time arrangements have "worked out quite well," including her own. Although she said she is extremely thankful for her schedule, she reported that it is "very stressful to juggle everything into that time." She added that her colleagues are "very respectful" of her day off and do not "treat it as fair game as a working day." With part-time arrangements, she further noted, the success of such schedules hinges on the woman behaving in a "highly professional and responsible manner" and ensuring that her "schedule inconveniences others as little as possible."

Another associate who is about to go part-time noted that her arrangement was established on an *ad hoc* basis. Going part-time may make partnership "more difficult" unless "significant business" is at stake, in the opinion of the one counsel, who had worked part-time for a period and found the firm "very fair." A partner reported that she worked part-time "for many years," yet it did not hold her back for partnership.

The maternity leave, consisting of 12 weeks paid and 12 weeks unpaid leave, was characterized as "very generous" by one mother.

"[The partnership is] over-whelmingly white and male."

Diversity: Patterson Belknap has succeeded in hiring lawyers of diverse backgrounds, except, perhaps, with regard to racial minorities. The firm has "always been known, accurately, as being accepting of diverse backgrounds and life styles," including attorneys who are "Orthodox, attorneys who are openly gay, and attorneys who come to the firm from less traditional career paths, and others for whom law is a second or third career," as one partner observed. Another partner remarked, "We seem to have just about every political and sexual orientation view." The firm is apparently "very unconcerned with political leaning and life styles." Politically, the firm is said to be "fairly liberal."

Nevertheless, it received some criticism regarding racial minorities. The firm is "not very diverse," in the words of one associate, who added that "recruiting efforts have been made in this regard." In the perception of another associate, the partnership is "overwhelmingly white and male." A partner noted that although the firm is "pretty supportive for women of diverse backgrounds and has gay partners, [it] could do better."

Senior women "could be more supportive to younger women..."

Women in leadership positions: For seven years, Patterson Belknap was headed by a woman managing partner, yet respondents pointed to few other women power players.

No respondents expressed particularly negative views of the firm's senior women, but several urged them to take a greater interest in assisting the junior women. One respondent suggested that the senior women "could be more supportive to younger women," but views this "as an overall problem of the need for women to help women wherever they are." An associate observed that the partnership "seems concerned about the 'gender issue,'" and expressed hope that this concern "will turn into action in the near future."

Patterson Belknap Webb & Tyler No. of Responses: 7	Strongly agree	Agree	Disagree	Strongly disagree
Women's prospects for advancement at the firm are as strong as men's	1	3	1	2
I am satisfied with the firm's family and personal leave policies	2	4	1	
There are women in positions of power and influence in the firm	5	1		1
Women are as likely as men to receive desirable work assignments	5	2		
Women attorneys feel they can discuss family obligations openly		3	2	
Women are as likely as men to be mentored by senior attorneys	2	3	2	
Women attorneys enjoy a high level of job satisfaction	2	1	2	1
Women in the firm are supportive of their women colleagues	2	5		
Firm management is receptive to the concerns of women attorneys	2	3	2	

PAUL, WEISS, RIFKIND, WHARTON & GARRISON

Rating: 77

Paul, Weiss, Rifkind, Wharton & Garrison
1285 Avenue of the Americas
New York, NY 10019
212-373-3000

No. of Attorneys: 295
No. of Women Attorneys: 92
No. of Partners: 84
No. of Women Partners: 8
No. of Survey Responses Received: 22

Respondent Profile: 1 partner, 20 associates, and 1 counsel responded. Practice areas were primarily litigation and corporate, though many respondents did not identify their departments.

Summary: There are some positives to be found at Paul, Weiss—the firm's commitment to diversity is heartfelt and has produced results, and part-time options are perceived to be practical for those willing to go off partnership track. But overall, a large majority of respondents characterized advancement opportunities as essentially nonexistent, observed that women had little power or influence, and were decidedly negative about the overall atmosphere for women at the firm.

Advancement: Respondents were virtually unanimous (the one partner and 15 of 20 associates) in characterizing women's prospects for advancement here as essentially nonexistent.

The problem is perceived to be particularly acute in the litigation department. One senior associate suggested, "It is universally known among female litigation associates that partnership prospects are virtually nil." A midlevel associate reported that there have been only two female litigation partners at the firm "since World War II" and one recently left to become a state court judge. The other, she opined, "was elevated to partnership last year only to avert mutiny."

Another associate reported that the several women who performed the "monumental feat" of advancing at the firm "put all of their energy into making partner and had mentors." In her opinion, "Most of us, however, do not have mentors, do not want to devote all of our energy into making partner, and do not have a commitment-free life."

Respondents report that advancement hinges on strong mentors who are willing to show women "the ropes and allocate key assignments to them," but such mentors are perceived to be in very short supply. In a midlevel associate's estimation, "There is no true women's mentoring program or other programs which serve to promote women."

Several respondents sensed that plum assignments at the firm are more likely to go to men, although a majority thought such distributions were egalitarian. One suggested that women suffer from "an inability to figure out how this firm works politically." She observed that, in her opinion, review of associates' work is "a subjective process and is colored by more than the quality of the work (i.e., ability to take responsibility and to deal successfully with clients), and these more subjective perceptions that partners and senior associates reach are not favorable to women in many cases."

According to one litigator's perception, women "just aren't taken as seriously as men." Another respondent described an unfortunate synergy of factors that, in her opinion, combine to keep women out of partnership ranks: "Women's life choices (often to focus on children over career, as our society demands); assumptions that women are less able to handle big or important matters; an overvaluation of traits often demonstrated by men (such as highly aggressive interaction with others) as being critical to success as a litigator; historical lack of female partners; lack of mentors and mentoring of females; women's lack of confidence in a highly stressful environment; and the failure of male partners to include women in informal socializing."

The most optimistic of the respondents characterized Paul, Weiss as "a pretty good meritocracy," but she still observed, "unfortunately, the crushing workload—for all—leads most promising women to drop out before partnership consideration."

According to a litigator's observations, her department is "extremely masculine," and comments like " 'blow me' [are] not unheard of."

Attitudes and atmosphere: Most respondents were decidedly negative about the atmosphere for women at Paul, Weiss. In one litigator's experience, the partners in her department, with a few exceptions, "appear generally uncomfortable working with women as equals." She added that, in her estimation, "it is routine for the litigation partners to socialize (squash, golf, etc.) with male associates, but unheard of for the partners to socialize with female associates."

An associate believed that "male partners take more of an interest in the men. Male associates go to dinner with partners upon occasion—women do not. Male partners have been known, on one occasion, to take only male associates to a baseball game (opening day at Yankee Stadium)."

According to a litigator's observations, her department is "extremely masculine," and comments like " 'blow me' [are] not unheard of." One department was portrayed by another lawyer as a "boys' club" in which the men "play computer games and office basketball *together* (without asking women). They buy tickets and attend sporting events *together* without asking women. They eat lunch *together* and rarely invite women."

One respondent suggested that the firm "is not for the 'shrinking violet'— you must be assertive, confident, smart, and visible. Many women have a quieter style and do not stand out among the associates." A corporate associate described the firm as fine for those with "strong wits/smart asses—terrible for sensitive types." A midlevel associate stated that, in her opinion, "The most...hostility to female lawyers comes from female members of the support staff." Concrete manifestations of this problem, she wrote, include "secretaries giving lesser priority to the work of female lawyers (even senior female lawyers), support staff employees bothering female lawyers (but not male lawyers) with matters that should be directed to the lawyers' secretaries, receptionists and telephone operators calling female lawyers 'Honey' or 'Dear' instead of 'Ms.'"

On a positive note, one lawyer who came here from another firm commented that, in contrast, women at Paul, Weiss are "viewed as smart and are able to develop as litigators." A senior litigator characterized the firm as "very comfortable" and described the atmosphere as "hyper and gregarious," which "works well for confident, assertive women."

"The pressure and working hours are both so great it is hard to balance anything with work."

Balancing work & family/personal life: The laments here were those typically associated with New York firm life—long, unpredictable hours and highly demanding clients. Striking the balance, in one respondent's opinion, can be "well nigh impossible unless one is willing to go off partner track." According to a midlevel associate, "The pressure and working hours are both so great it is hard to balance *anything* with work."

One respondent observed, "Although plenty of men seem willing to miss their kids' childhoods while trying to make partner," women are, in her estimation, "less willing to make that sacrifice." Respondents were divided about the firm's sensitivity to issues of balance, with some noting that "within the confines of the demands of clients, the firm is generally supportive of family/personal life."

Others perceived that the firm's receptivity to such issues consists of nothing more than "lip service."

"Aside from the fact that women have little chance to advance, the work-family options are quite good."

Flexibility of work arrangements: One litigation associate summed up the general perception of alternative work arrangements: "Aside from the fact that women have little chance to advance, the work-family options are quite good." She explained that parents can work four days a week and take three months' paid maternity leave. The firm also reportedly provides emergency day care.

One litigator reported that some women currently take advantage of the part-time policy, and another asserted that the option "is automatically available for two years and then reviewed on an individual basis." A litigator perceived "a tacit understanding that only women" will take advantage of part-time options and that "any who do will thereafter receive inferior assignments."

The availability of part-time options is apparently a recent development, and opinions varied with respect to their impact upon an attorney's partnership chances. In one respondent's opinion, "Some part-time women report that they are happy and satisfied with the way it is working out. No part-time woman has made partner (but the firm has not had many part-time women for the requisite time period)." Going part-time is perceived to increase the number of years before partnership consideration, but, according to one respondent's experience, Paul, Weiss "won't say what that magic number is."

A corporate lawyer reported that it takes "a strong-willed person to maintain a part-time position as actually part-time." One respondent wrote that, in her experience, "the partners generally shut their ears as soon as you start saying that the work they want won't be done instantly." One attorney said that, in her opinion, the firm's management seems to view part-time as "a great inconvenience to the firm." According to an associate's perception, part-time possibilities "are not advertised within the firm" and are "presumably worked out on an individual basis."

"The firm is very committed to promoting diversity and making everyone feel comfortable."

Diversity: Respondents reported that the firm is committed to diversity and is, to a significant degree, successful. One noted, "The firm is very committed to promoting diversity and making everyone feel comfortable." (And the 1997-1998 National Directory of Legal Employers seems to bear this out—47 out of 295 attorneys are minorities.)

One litigator said that, in her opinion, "Diversity, yes! The firm loves diversity of every kind—political, religious, racial, sexual preference." Another associate recounted that there are "more activities designed for people of diverse cultures in general than women as a group at the firm."

There are said to be openly gay partners here, and the firm has apparently done "a good deal of gay-related *pro bono* work." One respondent, who described herself as a lesbian, reported,

"[Everybody] has been very accepting of me, both personally and professionally." Another associate noted, however, "...feminists definitely are not accepted."

"They call a meeting about once every six months to talk, talk, talk. Solutions seem to be the problem."

Women in leadership positions: Although three associates maintained that there were a small number of powerful women partners, the overwhelming majority of respondents perceived that none have any real influence. The senior women are, with a few exceptions, described as having declined to take the lead in assisting other women. According to one respondent's evaluation, "[There are] really no women in positions of real power. The most senior woman partner has made an effort to promote women and force other partners to consider so-called 'women's issues.' However, she is a newcomer to such causes, and I think her voice is often disregarded by the more insensitive male partners."

A junior litigation associate reported that lawyers are highly critical of the one powerful woman in the firm. According to a corporate associate, the more established women partners made partner in the 60s, 70s, and 80s, and, in her opinion, "delayed having their children until they made partner (with one exception) and basically seem to have a 'we made it in this environment, you can, too' attitude." In a corporate associate's opinion, the women partners in the firm are "second tier/service partners/even 'slackers.' " As for supporting women's issues, she remarked, "Yeah, they call a meeting about once every six months to talk, talk, talk. Solutions seem to be the problem."

Several litigation associates noted that the lone woman partner in their department is also the most junior person on the totem pole. "On the whole," as one associate put it, "this is a male-dominated universe, and women must depend on men to get ahead."

Paul, Weiss, Rifkind, Wharton & Garrison No. of Responses: 22	Strongly agree	Agree	Disagree	Strongly disagree
Women's prospects for advancement at the firm are as strong as men's	1	1	6	10
I am satisfied with the firm's family and personal leave policies	1	6	6	4
There are women in positions of power and influence in the firm	1	2	9	6
Women are as likely as men to receive desirable work assignments	2	8	5	2
Women attorneys feel they can discuss family obligations openly		6	7	5
Women are as likely as men to be mentored by senior attorneys		3	7	7
Women attorneys enjoy a high level of job satisfaction		1	9	8
Women in the firm are supportive of their women colleagues	5	6	5	2
Firm management is receptive to the concerns of women attorneys		6	8	3

PILLSBURY, MADISON & SUTRO LLP

Rating: 50

♠♠♠

Pillsbury, Madison & Sutro LLP
235 Montgomery St.
San Francisco, CA 94104
415-983-1000

No. of Attorneys: 238
No. of Women Attorneys: 81
No. of Partners: 113
No. of Women Partners: 21
No. of Survey Responses Received: 11

Respondent Profile: 4 partners, 6 associates, and 1 counsel responded. Practice areas included litigation, tax, employment, and antitrust.

Summary: It seems to depend on whom you ask about Pillsbury—all four partners were uniformly positive while associates were split on virtually every question. Although some respondents claimed the atmosphere was pleasant, others had reservations. The firm generally received low marks for diversity, high marks for part-time arrangements, and strong praise for its heavy-hitting female partners.

Advancement: Although all four partners viewed women's potential for advancement positively, four of six associates were far more negative. One associate perceived women's prospects as less favorable than men's, attributing this to "the intersection of: 1) women's family obligations, and 2) factors [that] are considered important in making partnership decisions (commitment to the firm, measured by hours)." She described the firm as "very egalitarian with regard to mentoring, doling out assignments, etc."

A partner agreed that, in her estimation, the firm "has lost more women than men in the later associate years," but observed that women who leave "do not cite the firm's attitude or male partners as the reason." According to another partner, the availability of mentoring varies from group to group but is "quite good" in the labor and employment practice area. She suggested that attrition results from "opportunities elsewhere (especially in-house, which is perceived as having a more humane workload); looking at how partners work (generally more than associates) and saying 'no, thanks'; and lack of strong personal connections with co-workers, partners, clients." She and another partner viewed partnership criteria as fair and evenhandedly applied.

According to most associates, however, women are at a disadvantage. One associate portrayed women's prospects at the firm as "marginal," and said that, in her opinion, "mentoring is rare— women partners are too competitive and insecure to assist other women in moving up. I've seen it again and again." A litigation associate wrote that, in her opinion, partnership is "about being backed by strong and powerful partners." She reported that she is fortunate to have had both male and female partners as mentors, but added that, in her estimation, "Most women here have neither—the men mentor straight white male associates and the powerful female partners are few and far between." Another respondent was concerned: "Year after year, more men are promoted than women [because] men are included in business development activities much more than women. On my floor, often there are one or two men working late in the evenings, but several women." In a litigator's opinion, "Women are more likely to become senior counsel than partner, especially those with children who take time to spend with family."

According to one associate, "The key is making yourself known as a friendly, smart (not too smart) team player." According to a tax lawyer, "Women who attack problems and present solutions seem to advance, just as men with these qualities advance."

> **"I don't know that this firm is a comfortable place for anyone to work, but definitely not for women."**

Attitudes and atmosphere: Although most respondents assessed the atmosphere at Pillsbury as comfortable for women, several disagreed. One associate reported that the firm has a "very professional (read nonsocial) atmosphere that does not lend itself to the expression of discriminatory remarks...Of course, political persuasions differ, and some partners have been known to express political opinions which aren't particularly favorable to women."

A litigation associate stated that, her own good experience notwithstanding, the firm has, in her estimation, "very few powerful women." However, in the assessment of a midlevel associate, "The occasional offensive male is viewed as a problem personality by others and frequently harbors other prejudices which tend to isolate him." According to a partner, "The majority of the male partners and associates are gender-aware and try hard to be appropriate."

Yet, according to a midlevel associate, the office as a whole is "refreshingly inclusive." And a junior associate said, "[Pillsbury] strives to be a firm where women feel comfortable [and has been] relatively successful." One partner described the firm as "absolutely comfortable [with] no gender discrimination," while another characterized the firm as "politically correct."

In a junior associate's perception, however, despite the absence of a "boys' club" explicitly operating at the firm, it is "easier for men to bond with and mentor other men, and the *de facto* impact may be the same, although more subtle." Another respondent commented that, in her view, "I don't know that this firm is a comfortable place for anyone to work, but definitely not for women."

A partner reported that the tone of the firm varies considerably by practice group, and that while some departments are very comfortable and have a female majority, and others are average, there is a concern that "a few really are still rather stiff gentlemen's clubs."

> **The implication is, "You should not have a family life."**

Balancing work & family/personal life: Balancing is reportedly quite difficult, and many respondents perceived that a contributing factor is Pillsbury's concern with hours and insensitivity to family obligations. "The firm is not overly concerned about family," in the opinion of one associate. "There is an air of intolerance toward mothers that is not directed towards fathers. For example, a mother leaving early to see a school performance would likely be received with ill grace, while a father leaving to see a softball game would be well-received." A partner wrote, "The firm's view is that everyone is expected to make sacrifices to get the work and get it done."

The two associates who commented on hours perceived that to advance, one must work significantly more than the required minimum, thus, "most junior associates work quite hard." A senior lawyer sensed that those who do not spend 12 to 16 hours per day doing billable hours or business development will not be promoted. The implication is, in her opinion, "You should not have a family life."

One associate reported that the firm is "working on facilitating childcare for attorneys and staff [and] appears quite humane regarding accommodation of family responsibilities. The bottom line, however, is clients must be serviced, and partnership decisions seem to be in large part based on hours."

One lawyer had an entirely different perspective. She wrote: "It is easy to have a family life. I have been married and raised children while at the firm. You have to work hard to do both, but I have enjoyed it."

> ***"If [you are] perceived as 'good,' the firm is willing to work with you."***

Flexibility of work arrangements: Pillsbury has a part-time program that is open to any lawyer in the firm, male or female, partner or associate, according to respondents. Several partners reported that part-time associates have made partner, although one suggested, "The practice demands (i.e., clients, courts, deals) require a lot of flexibility to work intensely from time to time. Without that flexibility, the lawyer cannot have a high level of responsibility." A junior associate perceived that although Pillsbury lawyers take advantage of part-time options and the firm is accommodating, there is a fear that "the nature of the practice often seems to make part-time or other alternative work arrangements unworkable." That is, she explained, part-time turns into 40- to 50-hour weeks.

One associate observed, "If [you are] perceived as 'good,' the firm is willing to work with you." Several associates seemed to agree with the dissenting opinion that, "It's very difficult to do part-time work here. Although in theory it exists, it's the fast track to either oblivion or a smaller paycheck for the same amount of work."

Another respondent said that part-time is allowed, but added that, in her opinion, "It is not a smart career move. You are not considered to be dedicated if you don't work full-time (and then some)." In one associate's estimation, although one can go part-time as a partner, going part-time as an associate will take one off partnership track.

A partner commented that the firm is "reasonably" supportive of diversity, "within the bounds of what we believe is appropriate and professional."

Diversity: Pillsbury received low marks from respondents on its commitment to diversity, especially relative to other San Francisco firms. Several respondents commented that the firm does recruit women and members of minority groups, but according to another respondent's observation, "There is some difficulty keeping them."

According to a partner, notwithstanding the firm's "pretty strong commitment to ethnic diversity," the retention rate is, in her opinion, disappointing. This partner maintained that the firm "definitely is supportive of diverse personalities, politics, and life styles" as long as "you're liked by clients and work hard."

Yet, one respondent who is gay reported that although she has had "a great experience in spite of this," there are, in her estimation, "few people of color, or 'out' gay people, or strong, powerful women here, and it does not feel comfortable."

Another associate assessed the firm as "neither particularly supportive or discouraging of diversity. People of diverse backgrounds coexist here, but not in droves." Another associate wrote that, in her opinion, the firm is "more supportive of racial minorities than gays," and that she has "heard some very homophobic comments."

According to one partner, the firm has "a number of superb attorneys who are women of color."

There are "definitely heavy-hitting female partners" at Pillsbury, Madison & Sutro.

Women in leadership positions: Most respondents agreed that there are "definitely heavy-hitting female partners" at Pillsbury, Madison & Sutro. A woman sits on the executive committee that "really runs the place." Women are also part of the partnership and compensation committees, and two women head up Pillsbury branch offices. According to one partner, two types of power exist at the firm: "election to executive committee...and billing-partner status for large, key clients." Of the latter, she suggested, "Women have been given responsibility for some long-term clients, but have not brought in big new clients."

One partner noted, "[Women at the firm] are paid appropriately, and several are at the top compensation levels. Several of our best rainmakers are women."

According to one associate's divergent perception, although some inroads have been made, women in powerful posts "are definitely in the minority." She noted that while the executive committee has had a woman member for several years, in her estimation, "all other 'powerful' partners are men." Another respondent sensed, "The power is more perceived than real. For instance, we have two women partners who manage individual offices, but this is more an administrative role than a 'power' role. But the firm certainly touts the positions these women hold as an example of how we have women in positions of authority."

The firm's most senior women received positive reviews. One partner, who described herself as having significant management responsibility within the firm," reported that Pillsbury sponsors and supports programs on "networking among women attorneys and similar business development issues." And another characterized the top women as well-regarded: "Most of them are in their late 50s to early 60s and are viewed as extremely smart, well-positioned in the business community, and great diplomats—the prototype at this firm is *not* the angry woman who is meaner than some men and hard to work for."

Pillsbury, Madison & Sutro No. of Responses: 11	Strongly agree	Agree	Disagree	Strongly disagree
Women's prospects for advancement at the firm are as strong as men's	2	3	4	1
I am satisfied with the firm's family and personal leave policies	3	4	3	
There are women in positions of power and influence in the firm	5	6		
Women are as likely as men to receive desirable work assignments	4	4	3	
Women attorneys feel they can discuss family obligations openly	2	5	2	2
Women are as likely as men to be mentored by senior attorneys	3	5	1	2
Women attorneys enjoy a high level of job satisfaction	1	4	4	2
Women in the firm are supportive of their women colleagues	2	7		2
Firm management is receptive to the concerns of women attorneys	1	4	3	1

POWELL, GOLDSTEIN, FRAZER & MURPHY

Rating: 35

Powell, Goldstein, Frazer & Murphy
191 Peachtree St. NE
16th Fl.
Atlanta, GA 30303
404-572-6600

No. of Attorneys: 150
No. of Women Attorneys: 50
No. of Partners: 76
No. of Women Partners: 11
No. of Survey Responses Received: 5

Respondent Profile: 1 partner and 4 associates responded. Practice areas included litigation, real estate, trusts and estates, health care, and corporate.

Summary: Our small survey sample made it difficult to form a clear picture of life at Powell, Goldstein. While the sole partner who responded was uniformly positive, associates sometimes gave different views. A firm that generally ensures evenhanded treatment of women seeking to climb its partnership ladder, Powell, Goldstein's ambiance either is warm and supportive or male-oriented and exclusionary, depending upon whom you talk to. Sustaining a life outside the firm seems particularly difficult for unmarried, childless attorneys, and a majority of respondents gave the firm's part-time options low grades.

Advancement: Although the one partner who responded was pretty positive about virtually everything at Powell, Goldstein, associates were evenly split regarding equal opportunities for women at the firm. The partner observed that women have the same opportunities as men, but, in her experience, "many women choose part-time or counsel positions (more readily than men) for a variety of reasons (life style, family, etc.)."

According to most, the factors central to advancement are, as one associate put it, "the same for everyone (I think)—lots of hours and client development," as well as "excellent work product, team effort, and community service," according to another. According to the partner and two of the four associates, assignments, client development opportunities, and reviews are said to be meted out evenhandedly.

Meeting the partnership criteria, according to a corporate associate, "may be more difficult for women unless they have an amazing husband with a less stressful job [that] allows him to care for kids." As a result, in the opinion of one associate, "most of the talented women choose to leave the firm for non-law-firm jobs."

Another associate observed that there are more women at the income-partner level than at the equity-partner level. One associate from the health care group, however, was adamant that the firm is egalitarian. She wrote: "It's simply a nonissue here. I have never ever perceived or observed any acts by *anyone* that would suggest that advancement for women is less than what is available for the male attorneys here."

> **The corporate department is generally hospitable for women, though one lawyer perceived that "my male counterparts get more guidance, mentoring, etc., than I."**

Attitudes and atmosphere: Responses here ranged from effusively positive to more negative, with some suggestion that the disparities may be a function of the attorneys' departments. On the upside, a health care lawyer characterized the firm as "very comfortable" with "no lines between associates and partners." She added that the firm "invests in attorney training" and that the atmosphere is "conducive to different styles, personalities, backgrounds—everything." Moreover, in her view, no one "feels a need to look like, think like, or act like anyone else," as the firm "encourages independent and creative thought."

A real estate lawyer took a much different view, commenting that, in her opinion, there is "definitely a 'boys' club' atmosphere here." She reported that the men "routinely ask each other to lunch and to play golf, even go shooting together." Worse, she feels women are "rarely asked...to go to client development meetings."

Other respondents expressed more moderate positions on the firm's atmosphere. One respondent, a corporate attorney, wrote that although the firm's management "works hard to set a good tone for women," it is unevenly enforced because she believes "many decisions,

such as extended maternity or alternative hour arrangements, are on a group-by-group basis." The corporate department, she remarked, is generally hospitable for women, though she perceived that "my male counterparts get more guidance, mentoring, etc., than I." With respect to the firm at large, she noted that, based on what she has heard, men "in some other groups do not appear sensitive or open to new ways to handle issues [that] arise from women in the workplace (mostly based on rumors I have heard)."

A trust and estates lawyer reported that the firm is "about as comfortable as it can get," and that the only time she has been put in an uncomfortable position was by a client. A litigation partner commented that the firm has more women than men associates and a growing number of female partners.

> **"If you have children, the firm is more likely to be understanding about hours than if it is a boyfriend or husband or [significant] other."**

Balancing work & family/personal life: Several associates commented that single women seem to face the greatest challenges in this area. They perceived that Powell, Goldstein has little patience for unmarried associates seeking to maintain a semblance of a social life, despite the firm's general sensitivity to family demands. One associate commented that the firm is "pretty accommodating" of family responsibilities but "if you are a single woman, they seem to assume that your life is perfect outside of the firm."

A senior associate, who gets in early, works hard, and leaves early to spend time with her significant other, observed, "If you have children, the firm is more likely to be understanding about hours than if it is a boyfriend or husband or [significant] other."

The partner reported that she had two children as an associate and "took it upon myself to set reasonable hours at work." She added that she frequently "worked alternative hours" in order to spend more time with her children during the day and "never faced any opposition on this."

Although one associate commented that the firm is "more sensitive than many other firms in town to family responsibilities," another respondent remarked that she has recently concluded that "the firm isn't what it says." She suggested that several female associates have been "pressured" to attend an associate retreat although it meant "a weekend away from family." She commented that this "seems outrageous, considering the hours [we] work and the time we spend away from family during the week." Powell, Goldstein, she said, "has more 'face time' than I would like, which I think would interfere with family commitments."

> *"[Going part-time was] the biggest mistake I've made in my legal career. You are treated like a second-class citizen."*

Flexibility of work arrangements: Part-time arrangements are informally available at the partner and associate levels, but their viability and legitimacy seem to be in question, according to several respondents. One midlevel associate observed that there is no formal policy, and arrangements must be negotiated with one's practice group, which, in her estimation, can make things "more difficult."

One part-timer declared that going part-time was "the biggest mistake I've made in my legal career. You are treated like a second-class citizen." An associate said it was her perception that few women associates at the firm have kids, and that many women associates leave once they become mothers. Those seeking part-time status are, in the opinion of this associate, "at the mercy of...partners [who] decide if you get to use the policy. Some get it; most don't."

According to a midlevel associate, the firm is "struggling to work out its position on alternative arrangements." She commented that, in her experience, for a while "women were permitted to go [part-time], but now it seems to be more discouraged." Nevertheless, the firm stated that two partners currently work part-time schedules. One partner noted that her husband stays at home with her children so she didn't have to avail herself of part-time options. One associate described a part-time woman partner as "an extraordinary case" and observed that she has "since left the firm due to familial obligations."

At the associate level, both men and women have reportedly opted for part-time arrangements. An associate noted that in addition to part-time, telecommuting options are available. She added that the of-counsel position is "also wonderful for men and women who are *valued* but may not want the responsibilities of partnership."

> *A senior associate remarked that she does not "believe there are any firms that do a better job addressing diversity issues than PGF & M."*

Diversity: Several respondents wrote about the "diversity training" held by the firm. The partner declared that the firm has "*all* kinds." Powell, Goldstein has evidently made a "considerable investment of time and money in diversity training for *all* attorneys," according to the partner respondent.

A senior associate remarked that she does not "believe there are any firms that do a better job addressing diversity issues than PGF & M." She added that all partners and associates were required to attend the training, which was conducted by a diversity consultant, and that "everyone learned a lot about different perspectives and reactions to similar stimuli." Another associate commented that the firm "made it a point to interview and provide opportunity to a diverse crowd."

> *"There are women partners who are interested in how to best retain good female lawyers who decide to have children."*

Women in leadership positions: According to the partner respondent, it was her perception that no women hold powerful positions at present, although several have in the past. She commented, "Not surprisingly, there is still room for improvement in this area." Nevertheless, this partner is optimistic because, although women currently populate only the junior ranks of the partnership, she predicts that will eventually change.

Associates, again, were evenly divided on this question. According to one, "The firm is constantly trying to strive in this arena." She reported that Powell, Goldstein has had a woman managing partner and a woman on the five- or six-member board of partners. Another associate commented that the more influential partners "play a good role in promoting the status of women," and another reported that "there are women partners who are interested in how to best retain good female lawyers who decide to have children."

In contrast, another lawyer observed that although "some are willing to help young female associates struggling with issues, some say 'you're on your own.' " She added that the female partners are "viewed as 'becoming male,' " a reputation she said is unfair in that "it takes a certain person to be a partner in a large firm and those qualities are generally associated with men." She believed that there "are not many (if any) women who have become partner 'on their terms.' They have conformed to the system."

Powell, Goldstein, Frazer & Murphy No. of Responses: 5	Strongly agree	Agree	Disagree	Strongly disagree
Women's prospects for advancement at the firm are as strong as men's	1	2	2	
I am satisfied with the firm's family and personal leave policies	2	2	1	
There are women in positions of power and influence in the firm	3		2	
Women are as likely as men to receive desirable work assignments	2	1	2	
Women attorneys feel they can discuss family obligations openly	2	2	1	
Women are as likely as men to be mentored by senior attorneys	2	1		2
Women attorneys enjoy a high level of job satisfaction	2	1	2	
Women in the firm are supportive of their women colleagues	3	1	1	
Firm management is receptive to the concerns of women attorneys	1	3		1

PROSKAUER ROSE LLP

Rating: 55

Proskauer Rose LLP
1585 Broadway
New York, NY 10036
212-969-3000

No. of Attorneys: 361
No. of Women Attorneys: 105
No. of Partners: 123
No. of Women Partners: 11
No. of Survey Responses Received: 13

Respondent Profile: 13 associates responded. Practice areas included litigation and employment/labor.

Summary: The firm offers women a generally pleasant workplace and a family-friendly environment, but not favorable opportunities to advance, according to respondents. Although the use of part-time schedules is said to be on the rise, one associate noted that "part-time apparently equals full-time for more ordinary mortals." Finally, Proskauer might improve its reputation among female employees by ridding itself of the unprofessional behavior that is said to be exhibited by some of the firm's male attorneys.

Advancement: Respondents were almost equally divided—a bare majority contended that women's chances of moving up the ranks are good. One litigator wrote that although prospects for associates generally "are not great, for women, they are worse." She noted that it has been "many years" since a "home-grown" woman associate has been promoted.

A labor lawyer reported that women's chances were equal to those of men, but that, in her view, "women who 'take on' male characteristics (e.g., aggressive, harsh) have a better chance of advancement." Another labor lawyer wrote that women in her department are less likely to advance because "they lack mentoring opportunities, they receive less desirable or significant work, and the women partners take little or no interest in mentoring or developing opportunities for women associates to meet other partners, learn important skills, or develop client relationships."

An employment lawyer reported that although women's chances of advancement are decent, "certain partners in the firm feel that women can't be effective litigators." She described one in particular who appears to be "harsher on [women] than on their male counterparts." One midlevel associate contended that there "are noticeably few senior women and so few mentors available."

Several respondents reported that advancement to partnership is highly unusual for both men and women. One junior associate, wrote, "Oh, come on, nobody makes partner! I don't think gender is much of a factor." A litigator asserted that while women's prospects are "dismal," this seems to be because Proskauer is making fewer and fewer partners of either gender. She also commented that office politics "are very important."

A labor lawyer concluded that the main reason women are less likely to be promoted is that "hours worked/billed is a large factor in partnership." She commented, however, that the creation of a new mentor program is a "real positive step." A junior lawyer, however, noted that first-year lawyers have not yet been brought in to the women's mentoring groups.

There is a perception that, as at other New York firms, attrition rates are greater for women than men. One first-year associate observed, "Given the opportunity to leave behind 16-hour days, I think most of us (first-year associates) would escape. Women have the luxury of blaming that departure on babies."

Two litigators disagreed with their colleagues and stated that women have opportunities equal to men. One noted that she has found male partner mentors who take an interest in her advancement and that assignments are allocated in a gender-neutral fashion. A labor lawyer concurred, reporting that she was not aware of any discrimination in assignments and reviews.

> *"[There is] a lot of unprofessional behavior (flirting with secretaries, legal assistants, junior women associates)."*

Attitudes and atmosphere: Most respondents described the firm as generally comfortable, with occasional lapses by individuals into crude forms of sexism.

One senior associate wrote that several years ago, a group of junior women associates in her department "presented a list to the partners of gender bias we had experienced—by superiors, clients, opposing counsel, and even our junior colleagues." In response to that effort, she reported that people "really changed (or, if reminded, will try to change)."

According to one litigator, the firm is a "relatively good place for women," but there is "a lot of unprofessional behavior (flirting with secretaries, legal assistants, junior women associates)." Another midlevel litigator agreed that although gender discrimination does not rear its head often, "there are subtle ways in which a male partner can make a female associate uncomfortable (i.e., dirty jokes, sexual innuendo, and inappropriate glancing)."

A third lawyer from the litigation department confirmed this: "Generally the firm feels comfortable; however, there are still [some] male partners who fall into the category of either 'boys' club'/ macho or slightly condescending/overtly sexual."

> *One litigator noted that although the firm is "kid-friendly," work always comes first. Minimum billable requirements are reportedly strictly enforced.*

Balancing work & family/personal life: Although the firm places a strong emphasis on billables, it is otherwise fairly responsive to attorneys' outside commitments, according to respondents. The firm is described as "more accommodating than others," and "somewhat sensitive to family issues," but, nonetheless, having both a work and a home life is *really* tough."

One litigator noted that while the firm is "kid-friendly," work always comes first. Minimum billable requirements are reportedly strictly enforced, and, in her experience, extra hours yield bigger bonuses.

According to one midlevel litigation associate, however, the hours the firm requires are significantly less than those demanded at other large firms. One corporate associate reported that one of the busiest partners makes time, weekly, to coach his daughter's Little League team. A labor associate, although agreeing that billing 2,100 hours "is okay," noted that this does not count "the large number of hours that you spend writing speeches, helping partners prepare for seminars, etc." She added that the firm's sensitivity "really depends on who you work for."

One junior associate claimed, "There seems to be a 'mommy track' of super senior women associates." She added that the firm is "somewhat sensitive to major family responsibilities, weddings, etc." The firm does reportedly offer emergency child care. One junior associate advised, "If you don't want to stay late every night—don't. They'll take advantage of you if they think they can."

"Part-time apparently equals full-time for more ordinary mortals."

Flexibility of work arrangements: Is part-time available? "Not really," "Sort of," "Maybe," respondents wrote. According to one senior associate, part-time is "legitimate and viable, [but] definitely has an impact on partnership prospects." A colleague agreed: "The firm is supportive, on a selective basis," and added that part-time does "impede a woman's partnership track."

One senior associate believed that the only part-timers at the firm are women and that they are viewed as being "off-track and out of the loop." Another lawyer remarked that part-timers "delay their review by the committee that makes partnership decisions." A litigator asserted that part-time work is "certainly not encouraged."

According to a junior associate's opinion, the firm has "no coherent policy" concerning part-time, and it is available only in certain departments. Still, she noted, "Four-day work weeks (at 80-percent pay) are increasingly common."

In one new associate's estimate, "Part-time apparently equals full-time for more ordinary mortals." A litigator agreed: "If there is work to be done, the label 'part-time' may be a label only, and not reality." Another litigator opined, "The fact that few woman take advantage of these things reflects the incompatibility of working at a high-powered law firm and family life." Another litigator wrote, "Part-time work is not an option...Women must choose either family or career."

Several respondents said it was their understanding that there are no part-time options available at the partnership level, and that there is no sign that this will ever change. More than one associate was under the impression that no part-time arrangements existed at the firm at all.

"[Lesbians] bring their female partners to firm social functions, and such female life-partners are listed (as are husbands) in the directory of firm lawyers."

Diversity: Responses were divided on this question, with several attorneys reporting that the firm is diverse and several others observing that it is fairly homogenous. One respondent wrote that although Proskauer is somewhat keen on diversity, "there is a general understanding that you'll have a better/easier time here if you're Jewish." Another associate had a different perspective, reporting, for example, that lesbians "bring their female partners to firm social functions and such female life-partners are listed (as are husbands) in the directory of firm lawyers."

According to one litigator, "women who are not mainstream are marginalized." She further noted, "There aren't that many women of color here, although a real effort is being made and that may be changing." A junior associate commented that the firm is "as comfortable for women of color as can be expected." Another litigator remarked that the firm employs people of "many political persuasions," while another lawyer remarked that there is "no attention paid, positive or negative, to anyone's political leanings, personalities [or] life styles." She added that although the firm makes an open commitment to supporting the needs of gay associates, it pays "nothing more than lip service" to hiring lawyers of diverse backgrounds.

One attorney who joined the firm after entering law as a second career lauded the firm for welcoming her as well as other second-career lawyers.

One associate noted that women never seem to be put in charge of "anything financial."

Women in leadership positions: There are only 11 women partners (out of 123), and, for the most part, respondents denigrated them as mentors and role models. One lawyer reported "a lack of female leadership, especially since one female special counsel left to go in-house."

According to several respondents, most management positions in the firm are held by men and there has never been a woman on the executive committee, which she perceived was "the only true position of power." One associate noted that women don't seem to be put in charge of "anything financial."

Several women partners, it was reported, seem to have adopted the philosophy that because they advanced the hard way, other women should be forced to do the same. A lawyer characterized one woman partner in her department "by example and treatment of others" as providing no support for the women attorneys. She blamed this less on the lawyer herself than on the fact that "she is so overloaded with cases and professional commitments that she has no time for even conversation, much less mentoring."

Opposing this view, a junior-level labor lawyer noted that there are several partners who "are pretty impressive" and, "in the midst of their hectic lives and careers," have tried to mentor.

One respondent wrote that the women partners in the litigation department are viewed "warily—they are very demanding and tough to work with." A colleague echoed this view: "Many of the senior women partners have the (not uncommon) attitude that today's women attorneys have it easy compared to them, so there is not a strong core of support for upcoming women." She noted that "women at midlevels of power" are more supportive of junior women, "but they are perceived as peripheral and not really in line to succeed to real power."

A midlevel litigator wrote, "Sad to say, I was gleeful when I learned one woman partner was retiring—she seemed fairly hostile to women's concerns." This partner, she estimated, "was part of that 'pioneer' generation of women who believe you have to be a man with a skirt on."

Proskauer Rose No. of Responses: 13	Strongly agree	Agree	Disagree	Strongly disagree
Women's prospects for advancement at the firm are as strong as men's	2	5	6	
I am satisfied with the firm's family and personal leave policies	1	9		2
There are women in positions of power and influence in the firm	2	5	5	
Women are as likely as men to receive desirable work assignments	6	6	1	
Women attorneys feel they can discuss family obligations openly		6	6	1
Women are as likely as men to be mentored by senior attorneys	4	5	3	1
Women attorneys enjoy a high level of job satisfaction	3	2	5	3
Women in the firm are supportive of their women colleagues	2	9	1	1
Firm management is receptive to the concerns of women attorneys		6	4	

ROGERS & WELLS

Rating: 73

Rogers & Wells
200 Park Ave.
New York, NY 10166
212-878-8000

No. of Attorneys: 301
No. of Women Attorneys: 87
No. of Partners: 79
No. of Women Partners: 8
No. of Survey Responses Received: 23

Respondent Profile: 3 partners, 19 associates, and 1 respondent who did not identify her position responded. Practice areas included litigation, corporate, and real estate.

Summary: Rogers & Wells, according to most respondents, is perceived to be a singularly unpleasant place for women to work. Women's prospects for advancement are said to be grim, mentoring was characterized as nonexistent by virtually all respondents, and a fraternity atmosphere is said to pervade firm culture. In short, it is "not tremendously comfortable for women to practice law here," in the opinion of one partner.

Advancement: Respondents were nearly unanimous (two of three partners, 17 of 20 associates) that the prospects for women's advancement at Rogers & Wells are poor, indeed. The few women at the senior level, in one respondent's opinion, "have to prove themselves even more and work much harder than do men to demonstrate their allegiance." Several associates commented on the firm "overlooking highly qualified female partnership candidates," as one junior associate characterized it. In the opinion of a midlevel associate, women who are as qualified as their male counterparts are passed over because of perceptions that "they wouldn't be able to bring in business." A partner had a similar perception: If a woman attorney brings in enough business, "she will be tolerated. [Otherwise,] it will be a long and very difficult, uncomfortable experience here."

Another respondent claimed that, in her opinion, the "prevailing perception" is that "only the protégés of executive committee members or unmarried women have any chance at the brass ring."

An associate characterized the formal assignments process in her department as "barely functional," so it is, in her estimation, "especially important for associates to make contacts that will lead to good work...[This] is sometimes difficult for women." Another lawyer pointed to what she perceived to be a "lack of interesting assignments [and a] preference by those in power for promoting 'their own.' " A litigator also perceived a "lack of quality training and mentoring for all associates," but added that, in her view, the problem is worse for those who "do not fit the 'mold' and are women and/or a minority." A common joke at the firm, one lawyer recalled, is "that the only associates on partnership track are those [who] leave the firm."

According to a partner's concern, the impediments facing women do not end once partnership is achieved. The opportunities, in her opinion, "are weighted toward males, who are much more likely than comparable women to 'inherit' business, to be invited out with clients, to be used on clients' calls, and to be used to generate and maintain client contacts. This translates into dollars," and dollars, she maintained, determine advancement.

Another partner sounded as if she worked at a different firm, writing that women "who have the necessary talents and are prepared to make the commitment [have] excellent prospects for advancement." She added, "Informal mentoring, especially by women partners, is common. Assignments appear to be made fairly, certainly without regard to gender."

A couple of associates commented that they personally had had good luck at the firm. A real estate lawyer observed that in her department, there is no gender bias with respect to assignments or reviews. A litigator wrote, "[I feel] somewhat lucky [because some] men have taken me under their wing to [ensure] I get good work." Another more senior litigator reported that although some may believe women "don't get a fair shot here," when she complained that she was not getting the range of experiences "needed to be a complete litigator," the partner for whom she worked "acted promptly and modified his deposition schedule to provide me with [them]."

"I write briefs while [male peers] go out for drinks with the male partners."

Attitudes and atmosphere: More than one respondent used the word "fraternity" to describe the atmosphere at Rogers & Wells. And although it is trying to change, one associate predicts, "in many cases...you can't teach an old dog new tricks."

A junior associate said, in her opinion, "Vocal, progressive women have difficulty fitting into firm culture," and "most" female attorneys are "not part of the 'in crowd.'" Another associate reported what were, in her opinion, "incidents involving the exclusion of women (summer associates and attorneys alike) from events either sponsored or promoted by members of the firm."

Another litigator said that, in her estimation, women must work harder than their male peers: "I write briefs while they go out for drinks with the male partners." One litigator added that men at the firm "frequently complain that the women are 'bitchy' or hard to work with. I think we are unfairly tagged because there are few women at the senior levels."

Two respondents noted that the firm has held mandatory awareness sessions on issues of sexual harassment with positive results. An associate also noted that the firm is making efforts to respond to women's concerns, but, in her opinion, "can't get rid of" partners who resist these efforts.

A few associates were more positive. A senior associate described the firm as "very comfortable" and said she had found "no gender discrimination at all."

A partner reported that while the firm has somewhat of a " 'frat' atmosphere among the younger associates, [women] are included in the partying if they want." One real estate lawyer commented that in her department, "there is no difference if you're a woman or man."

Associates can easily, and many do, "work around the clock."

Balancing work & family/personal life: Attorneys at Rogers & Wells seem to share the same big-firm laments of lawyers all over New York. Associates can easily, and many do, "work around the clock." A junior associate wrote that during her first year at the firm, it has been "easier to stop making personal commitments than to deal with surprise assignments that cause me to cancel over and over." In a senior associate's opinion, "If a woman has to leave to care for a sick child or attend to a baby-sitting emergency, she is viewed as unreliable or that she is a liability to the firm's success. If a man leaves early to attend to these same emergencies, he is viewed as a caring and devoted dad."

Several respondents said that although the firm does provide emergency childcare assistance, lawyers do not feel comfortable discussing family demands at the office. An associate suggested that a colleague "felt more comfortable telling a partner she was working with that she would be in late because she was waiting for the plumber, rather than tell him she was waiting for her baby sitter." An unmarried lawyer noted that even without family responsibilities, the costs of the Rogers & Wells life style can be enormous. "What personal life?" she lamented.

"At least the women who are married have a husband or family to go home to. I cannot even plan a date [and] sometimes have to work more hours because I do not have a family. How am I supposed to get one?"

Two partners disagreed with these views, with one writing that parental responsibilities are recognized and supported, and the other noting, "By making family a priority, I can work a good balance most of the time."

A senior associate said that, in her opinion, part-time provides only the opportunity to "tread water."

Flexibility of work arrangements: A litigator suggested that, in her opinion, Rogers & Wells maintains a part-time program "because it is a valuable recruiting tool," and the partnership appears to be "far less interested in making it work for the associates."

A senior associate said that, in her opinion, part-time provides only the opportunity to "tread water." In the estimation of another attorney, part-timers reportedly receive "demeaning work assignments (i.e., tasks that are usually reserved for first-year associates)." One part-timer opined that if you don't "say 'no' regularly, you're completely overtaxed. If you do say 'no,' you are penalized with paralegal work and other undesirable assignments."

An associate noted that, in her estimation, other associates "treat part-timers as if they were law clerks, even if the part-timers [have] been practicing many more years than they have." A handful of respondents praised the firm's part-time arrangements. In one partner's view, the part-time program is "excellent." A senior associate reported that the partnership recently asked the part-timers "to prepare a memorandum setting forth issues of concern," adding that, because of this, "commitment to the program appears to be real."

Rogers & Wells has made a genuine effort in recent years to hire minority associates.

Diversity: Most respondents noted that Rogers & Wells has made a genuine effort in recent years to hire minority associates. An associate wrote that although the firm's summer classes have been diversifying, in her opinion, lateral hiring "does not even begin to maintain the levels of minority women" lost through attrition. One associate commented that, in her estimation, the firm is "noticeably nondiverse, which can't be attractive to people of color or homosexuals." She perceived that "[the] white-maleness of the firm can sometimes be overwhelming."

An associate wrote that, in her opinion, "No one talks about the conspicuous lack of diversity. The perception is that management does not care."

Nevertheless, according to the 1997-1998 National Directory of Legal Employers, Rogers & Wells employs 36 minority attorneys, a higher percentage than many of the firms we surveyed.

"[The] firm is committed to giving women powerful slots— there just aren't many to choose from."

Women in leadership positions: A majority of respondents perceived that women hold little power at Rogers & Wells. "There's really only one powerful woman in the firm," in the opinion of one associate, who added, "The rest are hanging on by a thread." One woman sits on the executive committee, but not all respondents were aware of this. Women also reportedly sit on the personnel and employment committees, and a woman partner has been charged with handling discrimination issues. A partner remarked that, in her opinion, "[the] firm is committed to giving women powerful slots—there just aren't many to choose from." Rogers & Wells, according to one litigator, has only one woman who "even approaches consideration as a rainmaker." While the election of a woman to the executive committee is said to have heralded "more of a sensitivity [in] addressing the grievances of female attorneys," some perceive her as "more of a token than a real power," in the words of one.

Numerous associates reported that the few women partners at the firm take their roles as mentors seriously. An associate wrote, "[Several women have] enhanced the quality of life at the firm for me [and] told me how to be a good lawyer, notwithstanding being one step back as a woman." In some disagreement, another associate believed that although the women partners are friendly and approachable, their attitude is, "I made it through, and you can, too."

Rogers & Wells No. of Responses: 23	Strongly agree	Agree	Disagree	Strongly disagree
Women's prospects for advancement at the firm are as strong as men's		4	10	9
I am satisfied with the firm's family and personal leave policies	3	14	3	2
There are women in positions of power and influence in the firm	3	6	9	4
Women are as likely as men to receive desirable work assignments	3	7	10	2
Women attorneys feel they can discuss family obligations openly	2	2	13	3
Women are as likely as men to be mentored by senior attorneys		3	13	6
Women attorneys enjoy a high level of job satisfaction		5	12	4
Women in the firm are supportive of their women colleagues	3	14	3	2
Firm management is receptive to the concerns of women attorneys	1	10	5	4

ROPES & GRAY

Rating: 10

🔨🔨🔨🔨

Ropes & Gray
One International Place
Boston, MA 02110
617-951-7000

No. of Attorneys: 301
No. of Women Attorneys: 88
No. of Partners: 129
No. of Women Partners: 19
No. of Survey Responses Received: 30

Respondent Profile: 9 partners, 20 associates, and 1 counsel responded. Practice areas varied widely, and included tax, corporate, trusts and estates, and litigation.

Summary: Despite its conservative reputation, Ropes & Gray appears to be a comfortable and supportive place for women lawyers. Although making partner at the firm is an uphill battle for all, women reportedly do not face gender-specific barriers. Mentoring and the assignment system also appear to be gender-neutral and received high marks from associates. Partners and associates seemed to radically disagree about the practicality of Ropes' part-time options, and certain vestiges of a "boys' club" are said to persist.

Advancement: There was overwhelming consensus that women enjoy equal prospects for advancement, though many feared they are less likely to stick it out for the full nine-year partnership track. According to one partner, "The corporate and litigation areas, traditionally the most difficult areas for women, have in recent years seen a number of women partners, most with families." A handful of respondents noted that, in response to pressure to diversify the partnership, the firm "goes out of its way to promote women," especially those with children.

This is not to say, however, that partnership at Ropes is there for the asking. "It is extremely difficult to make partner here," one associate believed. Another associate said that the problem of women not advancing "seems to be particularly acute in the litigation department." As is true at many firms, women are underrepresented in the partnership, with most respondents attributing this to the fact that women are more likely to opt out and find the goal not worth the personal sacrifices required to obtain it.

Several respondents praised senior lawyers for providing valuable mentoring and for ensuring the integrity of the firm's assigning process. As a junior associate put it, "Our mentoring prospects are good because R & G works at it (plus most of the women are helpful and caring)." Another echoed this positive view, stating that she has had excellent mentors, been presented with challenging assignments, and found reviews to be fair.

Several respondents reported that choice work assignments are readily available to women who seek them out. According to a partner, the assignment process is "centralized to avoid old-boy favoritism and works well." One litigator, however, recalled several instances in which, in her opinion, women were denied plum assignments.

One partner observed that because the "partnership decisions are not based on a book of business," women have as good a chance as men, even though those with family responsibilities "don't have the opportunity to spend evenings in search of clients."

Ropes & Gray is marked by "civility and mutual respect for colleagues and staff."

Attitudes and atmosphere: The atmosphere at Ropes received high marks. Partners raved about how comfortable the firm is, and associates were only moderately less enthusiastic. According to a partner, Ropes is marked by "civility and mutual respect for colleagues and staff," although another partner characterized it as "not a particularly 'social firm,' so social interactions among lawyers (male or female) are infrequent." According to one partner, the firm "has made it quite clear that discrimination is not tolerated," and believed that any complaint would receive immediate attention.

Several attorneys lauded the creation of a Women's Forum, which, according to one partner, "has been successful in pointing to ways in which women can deal with problems and let down their hair." The Forum, according to one senior associate, "focuses on issues of career development, mentoring issues, alternative work arrangements, negotiating strategies, etc." One partner approvingly noted that its creation was spearheaded by Ropes' male managing partners.

The associates were, for the most part, also positive, reporting that only isolated pockets of "boys' club" ambiance persist. One associate wrote that the men in her department "are quite respectful" and only rarely make "somewhat inappropriate comments."

One corporate lawyer remarked, however, "The most powerful corporate partners are a bit of a 'boys' club,' " although she admitted that some women are part of this club. A tax associate reported, "The only time I get the 'boys' club' feeling is at the annual summer golf outing."

Apparently, the atmosphere for women has improved over time. One senior associate wrote, "Years ago here you sometimes felt out of place in client meetings where you were often the only woman and sports stories and machismo prevailed. That sort of setting is rarer with each passing year as the numbers of women swell."

"...[it is] perfectly acceptable to need to get out of the office for personal/family reasons as long as the work still gets done."

Balancing work & family/personal life: Most lawyers extolled the firm's efforts to assist women attorneys in balancing a very demanding legal practice with a rewarding home life, although several remarked on the firm's failure to create alternative tracks for those wishing to focus on family.

A midlevel associate reported that because "everyone has interests and obligations outside of the office, and everyone is encouraged to engage in outside activities, [it is] perfectly acceptable to need to get out of the office for personal/family reasons as long as the work still gets done." Many respondents lauded the firm's on-site backup day-care center as a "lifesaver."

Although hours in some departments are reportedly terrible and the firm is, by one account, "dreadfully understaffed right now," one partner said that "face time" is unimportant at Ropes. One associate even reported having "had partners stay late to perform tasks most typically performed by young associates to permit the associate to participate in a social engagement."

A few lawyers were not as positive. One associate described the firm, in her estimation, as "nearly oblivious to outside pressures that working mothers must face." A litigator remarked that, to her knowledge, the firm boasts few examples "of people who maintain any semblance of balance." A junior associate agreed that there are no women to look up to and quipped that none of the women partners "know their kids' names." One midlevel associate lamented that the firm does not have a place "for people who are willing to take less money and less prestige (i.e., no partnership) on an alternative track." She added, "For someone like me, the 'mommy track' is not a derogatory term."

> *"It would be impossible to make partner here if you worked part-time for any duration (at least in my department)."*

Flexibility of work arrangements: Part-time work for up to a maximum of two years is reportedly available at Ropes, although partners and associates disagreed about how the policy pans out in practice. The partners reported that many mothers at the firm, including one partner, have done part-time stints. One partner noted that "it is also established policy that availing yourself of these options will not delay partnership." Another said that the firm is "actively engaged in upgrading technology to facilitate working at home."

One part-timer was effusive about her experience: "[Colleagues] have been very conscious of the fact that I may not always be available for early meetings because I must drop my child off at day care. In fact, several meetings have been pushed back to address this concern."

The practice of not delaying part-timers for partnership consideration was lauded by several partners. Nevertheless, an associate observed that the part-time process "seems to fall apart after a year or so for everyone I know who's tried it." A litigator echoed this perception, stating, "It would be impossible to make partner here if you worked part-time for any duration (at least in my department)." A junior associate had also observed variations by department: "Most of the women partners I know (with the exception of those in trusts and estates, tax, and real estate) work crushing hours and appear to have spouses with more 'normal' work hours who take on the greater share of child-rearing responsibilities."

Both partners and associates volunteered that Ropes & Gray offers very generous leave, and an associate said, "Several men [have taken] advantage of paternity leave."

"You can be anything or any-body you want to be here, [as long as] you do good work at an astounding pace under incredible pressure."

Diversity: Most attorneys portrayed Ropes as a relatively conservative firm that is nonetheless open to a wide range of personalities and viewpoints. "You can be anything or anybody you want to be here," according to one associate, as long as "you do good work at an astounding pace under incredible pressure." According to a junior associate, "Very strong women are looked up to and admired." Lawyers at Ropes & Gray are said to keep their private lives private.

One attorney felt herself unqualified to comment on the diversity question, characterizing herself as "a WASP in a WASPy firm in a WASPy city." She did report, however, that the firm is "very Republican/conservative" but that, as a liberal Democrat, she has found that people respect her views.

A litigator described the firm as "*very* white" and reported she did not "know of any openly gay attorneys (or staff, for that matter)." One partner wrote, "[The firm has] had a number of talented Asian women for 10 to 20 years. Black women have recently come in significant numbers."

The firm was reported to have recently adopted a policy of extending health insurance coverage to domestic partners.

"[Ropes & Gray's top women] are working hard now to ensure that women have a supportive experience here."

Women in leadership positions: Respondents reported that Ropes elected its first woman to the firm's policy committee last year, a move seen by one associate as a "big step in the right direction." And a midlevel associate seemed excited about the development: "She is the first woman to hold real power in the firm." Several partners commented that, in the words of one, the new appointment went a long way toward "showing opportunity and support for women at the firm." Women also reportedly head the firm's summer program and the associates committee, which is in charge of associate promotion.

Most associates were positive about the levels of support they have received from senior women at the firm. One corporate associate described its top women as "strong and qualified women who have worked very hard throughout their careers [and] are working hard now to ensure that women have a supportive experience here." A junior associate reported that the firm's more powerful women "are perceived, generally, as wonderful mentors."

Several partners affirmed that management now views having women in leadership positions as "an important factor in the recruitment and retention of talented lawyers." One senior associate reported that in her years at the firm, "the situation has changed drastically for the better."

In the eyes of a small minority of respondents, however, the senior women leave much to be desired. One associate suggested that the women partners "are *very* supportive of women who are willing to try for partner in the traditional mode. However, anyone looking for options is out of luck."

Several other associates agreed, with one stating that she perceives the senior women "as frighteningly driven and committed to work. So I guess this makes me worry that those of us who occasionally do choose life over work will be seen as less committed to the job."

Another agreed that the woman power players "tend to have gotten there the hard way and, despite their good intentions, seem to sometimes have trouble empathizing with younger women."

Dissenting from the views of the vast majority of her colleagues, one respondent was far more blunt and more negative, claiming that most of the women senior associates and partners "have the 'power witch syndrome' and don't like competition from other females. The more females that enter Ropes & Gray, the less 'special' they are."

Ropes & Gray No. of Responses: 30	Strongly agree	Agree	Disagree	Strongly disagree
Women's prospects for advancement at the firm are as strong as men's	13	12	3	2
I am satisfied with the firm's family and personal leave policies	14	9	4	2
There are women in positions of power and influence in the firm	9	16	3	1
Women are as likely as men to receive desirable work assignments	17	11		1
Women attorneys feel they can discuss family obligations openly	10	10	4	4
Women are as likely as men to be mentored by senior attorneys	13	9	6	1
Women attorneys enjoy a high level of job satisfaction	11	13	4	1
Women in the firm are supportive of their women colleagues	19	8	2	1
Firm management is receptive to the concerns of women attorneys	14	10	4	1

RUDNICK & WOLFE

Rating: 24

Rudnick & Wolfe
203 North LaSalle St.
Suite 1800
Chicago, IL 60601
312-368-4000

No. of Attorneys: 205
No. of Women Attorneys: 55
No. of Partners: 120
No. of Women Partners: 15
No. of Survey Responses Received: 16

Respondent Profile: 5 partners and 11 associates responded. Practice areas included litigation, real estate, and health care.

Summary: Possibilities for advancement at Rudnick & Wolfe are favorable for women, although recently increased billable requirements, mounting pressures to attract business, and family needs may drive some women out of the firm. Reportedly as a result of the value that a major client places on diversity, Rudnick & Wolfe is strongly committed to recruiting, training, and developing the careers of women and minority lawyers. A few women have reportedly penetrated the firm's corridors of power, and a woman heads up the firm's 100-lawyer real estate department, though opinion is divided as to how helpful these leaders are to their junior colleagues.

Advancement: Respondents overwhelmingly agreed that women do enjoy equal prospects of advancement and that the strongest forces holding them back are the demands of family life. Women who are willing to put forth the same hours and commitment to the firm as men can move up.

Business generation was cited as a key factor for partnership promotion, but most respondents seemed to think that notwithstanding men's greater likelihood to bring in and receive credit for clients, women do hold their own in this area. One associate noted, however, that women's decisions to leave the firm may sometimes be based on the intense pressure to bring in business.

According to one respondent, women also "self-select out of the most active part of the fray" because they bear disproportionate responsibility in the realm of family life. Respondents reported that reviews at Rudnick are "fair and unrelated to gender."

Several lawyers underscored the importance of mentoring and the backing of powerful partners for advancement. A large majority of respondents agreed that women are both mentored and afforded access to the choice work assignments necessary to attract the attention of senior partners. One associate said she had been staffed on "high profile deals with all women." Despite the additional hurdles to advancement faced by women lawyers, one associate said that they are promoted if "powerful men strongly endorse them."

One associate commented that when she asked several senior male partners to identify the "best associates in the firm (because I was looking for role models)" they "universally" named women.

The lone dissenting partner viewed prospects for women's advancement at the firm as less promising. She noted that, in her opinion, although women advance on an equal basis to contract partnership, they have had difficulty entering the equity partner ranks. In her view, the problem lies in lack of business generation, which, in turn, is a function of women's inability to secure the mentoring they need during their junior years.

> *"Men who are aggressive and forthright are good lawyers, and women who are aggressive and forthright are bitchy, moody, and difficult to work with."*

Attitudes and atmosphere: Most respondents are content with the atmosphere at Rudnick, although a few commented that patterns of entertaining clients tend to exclude women.

Rudnick was described as a social firm where both working relationships and friendships between women and men are strong. According to one partner, the firm is marked by an informal atmosphere where "self-importance is not-so-gently ridiculed." Many women commented that they are unaware of manifestations of gender discrimination at the firm.

Although the firm's leadership was credited with setting a positive tone and

with bringing about an improvement in the atmosphere for women in recent years, when it comes to socializing with clients, women can be left out in the cold. Several attorneys noted that even when they are invited, women may find themselves unable to attend entertainment events because they are scheduled without regard to women's priorities and the demands on their time. One partner said events are often arranged at the last minute, and women attorneys are often unable to attend because of baby-sitting and other obligations. This may put them in the position of their absence being "seen as a lack of commitment when, in fact, it is simply a scheduling conflict."

Activities geared toward women are few and far between. Some men have reportedly nicknamed Rudnick's one annual woman-only event the "Chick Picnic." Women are beginning to launch their own marketing activities with support from the firm.

Although the firm as a whole was described as having "no tolerance for sexism" and a clear majority of respondents thought Rudnick was receptive to their concerns as women, men have been known to call women "dear" and blow them kisses, and the atmosphere of "innuendo" this creates "might seem overtly sexual to some women."

Others faulted the gendered ways in which male colleagues judge women's personalities. According to one partner's opinion, "Men who are aggressive and forthright are good lawyers, and women who are aggressive and forthright are bitchy, moody, and difficult to work with." She added that, in her view, complaints by women are often taken less seriously and that women are often asked to "deal with the male ego."

On the other hand, an associate commented that women who lean too far in the other direction may also suffer the consequences. She believed that women who are "nice and sweet are considered unconfident and meek." One associate remarked that, in her view, the firm seems inclined to nudge women toward roles in the hiring committee and the summer program.

> *One associate remarked, "If a client wants to meet at night but you have carpool or a teacher conference, you are expected to meet the client."*

Balancing work & family/personal life: Even though Rudnick's minimum billable hours requirement is 1,900, the pressure to bill more is felt by attorneys firm-wide, but associates seem to suffer the most. Although some partners were said to be understanding of the competing demands faced by attorneys, others are "not sympathetic." Associates proposed that "it's even difficult to date," in the words of one, and that many cannot imagine having a family while at the firm.

One associate remarked, "If a client wants to meet at night but you have carpool or a teacher conference, you are expected to meet the client." Even attorneys with reduced hours find it difficult to sustain a balance that includes room for their children. Several reported that the firm provides little or no child care assistance.

A few associates clearly viewed the situation differently. One senior litigation associate remarked that working

hours are "reasonable and flexible." Another respondent opined that the firm makes a "real effort" not to relegate women on reduced schedules to the "mommy track."

At the partnership level, the responses were more positive. A couple of partners reported that they can leave as needed to attend to personal matters and that if one's billings and hours are up, there can be a fair amount of flexibility. That said, however, another partner feared that "this begs the question" of whether those who meet the business and billing expectations have anything more than "stress and guilt" left over for their families.

> *Some respondents clearly believed that part-time is only available for "superstars."*

Flexibility of work arrangements: Rudnick attorneys do take advantage of part-time and flextime options, although these arrangements must be negotiated on a case-by-case basis. Efforts to introduce a formal policy concerning alternative work arrangements were reportedly withdrawn by the firm's management, although another initiative to put the policy into writing is supposedly underway. Despite this, most partners were said to be understanding of part-timers' needs and willing to accommodate them.

Respondents reported that the firm permits attorneys to reduce their hours to a minimum of 60 percent for a commensurate reduction in pay. Such arrangements are available at partnership level, although they are perceived to slow advancement for those moving along the partnership track.

Respondents reported that despite the firm's general support for part-time schedules, the firm's clients do not share this view, making such arrangements impractical in certain departments. As a result, part-time schedules are "subtly discouraged" because of the "practical difficulties" associated with them, as one associate put it.

Some respondents clearly believed that part-time is only available for "superstars" and that if you do not bring in business, the partnership is likely to be less receptive to your efforts to negotiate a deal. Nevertheless, according to one partner, the viability of part-time at Rudnick has improved in recent years. Until lately, part-time arrangements were, in her view, "never successful; all women who were part-time were eventually asked to leave for performance reasons."

Although the firm offers maternity leave, one associate reported that the tendency for new mothers is to adopt flextime schedules in which they work full-time hours with some greater control over when the time is put in.

One respondent commented that one of the most positive aspects of the firm is the presence of "so many different personality types."

Diversity: Rudnick is evidently going all out on this front. Owing to input from a major client who has signaled that it values diversity, as well as increased involvement by women and minorities in the firm's hiring process, the firm has recently begun a push to recruit more minority attorneys. In addition to recruitment efforts, one partner

reported that the firm invests in the "training and development" of women and minorities. One partner commented that because of the firm's casual atmosphere, those "outside the white male mainstream" tend to "flourish more easily than in rigidly traditional settings."

As several respondents commented, it is too soon to tell whether these efforts will yield results in terms of actually keeping minorities at Rudnick. For the moment, the firm remains "conservative."

Several respondents took as a bright sign the fact that this year's summer class included six African-Americans, one Chinese law student and one Indian law student in a class of 19. One respondent commented that one of the most positive aspects of the firm is the presence of "so many different personality types," though another said that the firm has a way to go when it comes to "communicating and talking about issues relating to gender and diversity."

"Quality-of-life concerns are generally not addressed or advanced by the senior women."

Women in leadership positions: There is a woman at the helm of the firm's real estate department, which is no small feat given that 100 of 211 attorneys at Rudnick practice real estate law. This partner is also a member of the firm's policy committee, which is apparently its governing board. Other women partners head the firm's health care group, chair the hiring committee, and serve on the "bonus" committee that sets compensation for all but equity partners. Several of these partners were said, by most, to be well-respected, although the single dissenting associate thought their presence in leadership positions was a mere "token." Most respondents seemed to feel that the real power "vis-à-vis finance and policy" remains in male hands.

There was some disagreement as to whether the senior women play a role in mentoring those beneath them. There is an annual women's meeting to discuss issues, and a few associates remarked that they had noticed the top women helping to seek opportunities for others.

In the perception of others, however, the top women are "guys" who either do not have children or have someone else to "run their households," as one associate put it. Some find these women "fairly unsympathetic" to those struggling to balance work, family, and personal lives. A partner believed that "quality-of-life concerns are generally not addressed or advanced by the senior women," although these women are generally supportive of other women in the firm.

Rudnick & Wolfe No. of Responses: 16	Strongly agree	Agree	Disagree	Strongly disagree
Women's prospects for advancement at the firm are as strong as men's	8	5	2	1
I am satisfied with the firm's family and personal leave policies	3	7	5	1
There are women in positions of power and influence in the firm	5	9	2	
Women are as likely as men to receive desirable work assignments	12	2	2	
Women attorneys feel they can discuss family obligations openly	3	7	6	
Women are as likely as men to be mentored by senior attorneys	8	6	1	
Women attorneys enjoy a high level of job satisfaction	4	6	4	2
Women in the firm are supportive of their women colleagues	9	5	1	
Firm management is receptive to the concerns of women attorneys	4	7	5	

SCHNADER HARRISON SEGAL & LEWIS

Rating: 22

Schnader Harrison Segal & Lewis
1600 Market St.
Philadelphia, PA 19103
215-751-2000

No. of Attorneys: 136
No. of Women Attorneys: 46
No. of Partners: 63
No. of Women Partners: 12
No. of Survey Responses Received: 9

Respondent Profile: 3 partners and 6 associates responded. Practice areas included litigation and business.

Summary: Schnader is a firm that is sensitive to its lawyers' lives outside the firm, and is, by most accounts, a pleasant one for women. It fosters a comfortable work environment and reportedly offers lawyers highly satisfactory alternative work arrangements. The women partners are respected and gaining influence. On the downside, the partnership decision-making process is described as extremely political.

Advancement: The road to partnership at Schnader was described by several respondents as a political process that is sometimes perceived to be especially challenging for women. According to one partner, the critical factor appears to be "which partners are supportive of the candidate, and that mostly means men, because they continue to be the power base of the firm (with one or two exceptions)."

An associate asserted that women are as likely to advance if they are able to "perform well and be political just like men." A senior associate believed that women are "probably" as likely to be promoted as men, "but occasionally a woman who's not politically connected may have additional trouble with a perception that she is not as good a litigator because she is a woman." She added that this would probably only happen "in the case of someone who politically doesn't have the pull to get elected. I view politics and good reviews as the most important factors for partnership selection." In contrast, two lawyers who described themselves as relatively new to the firm, reported that they were unaware of any discrepancies between women and men with respect to work assignments or advancement possibilities.

One junior associate observed that the firm has "no real mentoring process" and added that implementing such a system would be helpful. The central factor in achieving partnership, in one lawyer's view, is "taking control of one's career."

Two respondents identified stereotypes by which women litigators are allegedly perceived. A partner asserted that, in her estimation, "Men are more likely to be presumed to have 'stand-up' experience, even when they do not, and women are more likely to be presumed *not* to have 'stand-up' experience even when they do." She continued, "This affects assignments (which lawyers will be accepted on a case) and subjective comments made by partners during the partnership evaluation process. It may be more important for women than men to be perceived as an important assistant to a powerful male partner." She conjectured that the firm's women partners, most of whom are litigators, may encounter a "glass ceiling," in that male partners seem reluctant to share "client-getting credit" with females, and that, to her knowledge, "clients of retiring partners are almost always handed on to males."

According to a midlevel associate, on the other hand, some male associates at the firm "believe that the women associates work far harder and are more committed than the male associates." She concluded, "Aggressive/assertive women are as likely to advance to partnership as aggressive/assertive men." She was less sanguine about the prospect for less forthright women.

> *"There is no pressure for women to be, act, or lawyer like men," and individual styles are "appreciated and encouraged."*

Attitudes and atmosphere: Most respondents applauded the firm for doing all it can to minimize influences that might make women uncomfortable. One associate gave high marks to the firm's environment on the grounds that "there is no pressure for women to be, act, or lawyer like men," and individual styles are "appreciated and encouraged."

According to a junior associate, "For the most part women are happy [here]." She added that there are "many young partners here who seem almost oblivious to the gender of associates." She described the older partners as respectful, and noted that the firm has both male and female leaders.

A more senior associate reported the presence of "a number of women partners who are ready to go to bat on women's issues." Moreover, there are large numbers of women associates who are said to provide support for one another.

A couple of respondents suggested that occasional lapses in behavior are inevitable, but praised Schnader for taking a firm approach. A junior associate commented that, in her opinion, "of course, there are some older male partners who have been with the firm for years who every so often make what could be considered a 'sexist' comment. But by and large, this is the exception to an otherwise very accepting environment" for women.

A senior associate described the firm as possibly "one of the best places" for a woman to work. "There are always going to be sexist lawyers," she continued, "but the firm works hard to blunt their effect on the firm." Another respondent concurred, noting that when she "was the recipient of one very sexist comment," she reported it to the management and it was "immediately and effectively investigated and addressed."

Interestingly, two partners were the ones to voice the strongest criticisms about the firm's atmosphere. One suggested that outside of the office, "there are ways of interacting that involve only male lawyers—such as golf games or squash matches." A litigator said she sensed subtle predispositions on the part of some individuals, "which manifests itself in the nature of assignments (women write briefs, men take depositions) and assumptions about what women want to do (won't travel, etc.)."

"There are always cases and trials where life is difficult, but the firm encourages people to have a life."

Balancing work & family/personal life: According to most respondents, Schnader recognizes and expects that its attorneys will have activities and responsibilities outside the firm, although—as several pointedly noted—the firm does nothing to assist with childcare. Billables at the firm, according to one associate, are 1,900, "plus an additional 400 miscellaneous hours."

A litigator commented that the firm "places a high value on 'quality-of-life' issues" and that both men and women demonstrate an interest in making time for their families. According to one associate, "There are always cases and trials where life is difficult, but the firm encourages people to have a life."

Another associate agreed that the firm is sensitive, adding, "It is difficult to have an arrangement that really works, but Schnader is fairly accommodating." An associate who is also a mother reported that although shouldering dual sets of responsibilities demands "astute juggling and a great deal of energy," she has never been put in a position where she was required to choose work over a family emergency or commitment.

The firm is, according to another associate, a place where "face time" does not matter. A partner agreed that the firm's strength is that it is "institutionally flexible," meaning that if a person gets her work done and done well, "there is no issue about when or where it is done." She added that many attorneys do a substantial amount of work from home.

Concerning the availability of part-time arrangements, part-time partner responded, "Yes! Yes! and Yes!"

Flexibility of work arrangements: Respondents spoke highly of the part-time and flextime arrangements offered at Schnader. Reportedly, both associates and income partners have adopted alternative work arrangements. Several respondents lauded the firm for recently having promoted a part-timer to income partner status. One part-time associate described the firm as "very supportive, as long as we understand that we need to be flexible and delay partnership."

Concerning the availability of part-time arrangements, a part-time partner responded, "Yes! Yes! and Yes!...I can't envision working full-time for many years, if ever."

An associate reported that the firm has been "pioneering" in its approach to alternative work arrangements and that the firm's part-time policies are typically taken advantage of by at least a half-dozen women attorneys. She added that opting for part-time does not threaten attorneys' job security, nor deprive them of the opportunity to work on high-profile matters, serve on firm committees, or supervise more junior lawyers.

A full-time partner described the firm as "very progressive in designing and permitting flexible work schedules for women at all levels." She added that the firm has received significant press coverage regarding its part-time initiatives. An associate noted that the firm's part-time policies were one of the things that greatly attracted her to the firm and reported that there are a number of young women associates who are part-time (three days a week) after recently having children. According to one partner, no female equity partners have had part-time arrangements, but this may be because, to her knowledge, no equity partner has made such a request.

Just one associate thought that part-timers are "mommy-tracked," though another associate asserted, "Theoretically, when you are done being part-time, you are back on track."

One associate made an insightful point about the negative side of working for such an understanding firm: "The only downside to having the firm and its leadership be so understanding about work/family issues is that sometimes partners are the first ones to think of family obligations when assigning tasks on a case, including travel, and paternalistically make decisions for women without asking first and letting the individual lawyer decide for herself the balance she needs to strike."

> **"(Almost) everyone is accepting and tolerant of the beliefs and life styles others choose."**

Diversity: Most respondents reported that the firm has few minority attorneys but does encompass considerable diversity in other respects. One midlevel associate reported that the firm was "founded on a commitment to diversity and takes its history very seriously."

An associate commented that the firm's commitment to diversity is one of the things that attracted her to the firm and that "(almost) everyone is accepting and tolerant of the beliefs and life styles others choose." A partner agreed, while adding a qualification: In her estimation, "We need to do better with minority attorneys."

One partner wrote that the firm demonstrates its commitment to diversity "by encouraging women to participate in a wide variety of political and social events." The firm was described as generally liberal and "very tolerant of different sexual preferences," by one associate. Another associate observed, "We have an openly lesbian woman associate who lives with her partner and their son." The firm is also home to both Democrats and Republicans, as well as personalities that are "as different as lawyers can be."

> **Several women partners were described as highly respected and at least somewhat influential within the firm.**

Women in leadership positions: Women are only starting to rise to positions of power at Schnader, according to some respondents. One woman sits on the firm's six-member executive committee, and several other women partners, including a practice-group chair, were described as highly respected and at least somewhat influential.

Although some questioned how powerful the senior women actually are, several respondents reported that the women partners do try to give the other women in the firm a voice. According to one associate, although women do not have "great prominence in the more senior positions in the firm, they are not noticeably absent either." These women are described as being held in high esteem throughout the firm and as having "a strong sense of self." One partner acknowledged, however, "We could *all* do better with mentoring."

Schnader Harrison Segal & Lewis No. of Responses: 9	Strongly agree	Agree	Disagree	Strongly disagree
Women's prospects for advancement at the firm are as strong as men's		8	1	
I am satisfied with the firm's family and personal leave policies	6	3		
There are women in positions of power and influence in the firm	1	6	1	
Women are as likely as men to receive desirable work assignments	3	3	1	
Women attorneys feel they can discuss family obligations openly	2	4	2	
Women are as likely as men to be mentored by senior attorneys	3	3	3	
Women attorneys enjoy a high level of job satisfaction	2	5		
Women in the firm are supportive of their women colleagues	2	7		
Firm management is receptive to the concerns of women attorneys	2	7		

SCHULTE, ROTH & ZABEL LLP

Rating: 19

🔨🔨🔨🔨

Schulte, Roth & Zabel LLP
900 Third Ave.
New York, NY 10022
212-758-0404

No. of Attorneys: 202
No. of Women Attorneys: 64
No. of Partners: 52
No. of Women Partners: 6
No. of Survey Responses Received: 15

Respondent Profile: 3 partners, 11 associates, and 1 counsel responded. Practice areas included litigation and corporate.

Summary: Schulte, Roth & Zabel, a young and liberal firm by all accounts, distinguishes itself among its New York peers by its level of support for lawyers seeking to balance work and family. Moreover, although attrition reduces the ranks of eligible candidates, women are said to have a fair shot at advancement. One partner remarked that collegiality persists even after associates leave the firm.

Advancement: The women who stick it out at Schulte have as strong a chance of advancing as men, though respondents claim the attrition rate for women here is far higher than for men, which, in their view, results in a significantly lower percentage of women partners.

Several associates lamented, as one put it, "It seems that most of the women who have 'made it' have given up some things to achieve their goals." A litigation associate was concerned that women find it difficult "to appear aggressive and committed enough to make partner unless they are willing to sacrifice family life."

Although advancement may seem to be at the expense of children and an active family life for some women, one partner said a colleague has two children and was formerly a part-time associate and had not expected to be put up for partner, "but the male partners she worked with most closely came to her and asked her okay, then carried the ball." She observed that at Schulte, "you can influence the assignments and people you work with more than young lawyers think." The central factors for advancement are said to include writing and analytical ability, confidence, and the ability to relate to clients and attract business.

Most associates reported that, at their level, assignments are meted out fairly and review criteria are gender-neutral. A junior corporate associate wrote, "Some deals are staffed entirely with women," even when the client is not a woman. She continued that, in her estimation, although women are given significant responsibility, they are "encouraged to be more 'aggressive,'" and she "doubts that male attorneys hear this comment as often."

A second-year associate disagreed, claiming that, in her opinion, "More often than not, men are assigned to the huge document-intensive, long-hour cases. However, I prefer the smaller assignments where I work alone with one partner or senior associate."

According to another associate, the firm "spends a lot of resources to keep associates happy." Initiative and self-sufficiency are key at Schulte, she explained, adding that the mentoring program is "satisfactory, especially if you take charge of your own career and development and don't rely on others to take care of you."

> *Firm leadership is "extremely supportive of women here, and increasing our retention of women after they have families."*

Attitudes and atmosphere: The firm was usually described as a casual and congenial place for men and women. One midlevel associate characterized the overall feeling as "young, liberal, and relaxed." Most respondents reported that they were aware of no manifestations of discrimination and no "boys' club." There are apparently plenty of women in the junior ranks, and most associates reported that they are treated with respect by the partners for whom they work. A partner observed that firm leadership is "extremely supportive of women here, and increasing our retention of women after they have families."

Another partner reported that collegiality persists even after associates leave the firm. She wrote that Schulte makes efforts to place young lawyers in new jobs when they choose to leave and

that "the alumni network is strong and business is referred back and forth on a regular basis." She reported that the discrimination she has experienced has come from adversaries and co-counsel at other firms "who will only return phone calls to the male partner, even if he is not present at the meetings."

On the other hand, one junior associate has "noticed that women in the mid- and upper-level are hypercritical of the few women partners and appear to hold these women to a higher standard than the male partners." She further remarked that there is a perception "many younger male associates appear to believe that the women are partners for political reasons, not because of their ability."

> *Several respondents noted that the firm provides emergency day care both on-site and in attorneys' homes.*

Balancing work & family/personal life: Women at the firm were noticeably more optimistic than those at most other New York firms about the ability to balance work and personal life. Although the hours are long and the pace is intense, most attorneys described Schulte as being more than willing to make adjustments for attorneys with outside obligations.

One partner wrote that "so many of the lawyers at all levels have young children (this is a 'young' firm) that people don't wait to have 'team meetings' at 8 p.m." A corporate associate agreed that many partners "have families and completely understand your family obligations."

Although the demands mount as one becomes more senior and there is "pressure to maintain high billables and sacrifice evenings and weekends to work," as one associate observed, several respondents maintained they had succeeded in sustaining an outside life.

A corporate associate found that "the availability of a part-time schedule is a viable 'way out,' especially since part-time does not exclude advancement to partnership." One associate commented she had "never had even the slightest difficulty taking off, coming in late, or leaving early to take care of personal/family responsibilities." A litigator pointed out that there is an "established 'mommy track' that is not frowned upon."

Several respondents noted that the firm provides emergency day care both on-site and in attorneys' homes. One lawyer wrote that she was permitted to take an "extensive" medical leave with pay when trying to have a family.

A partner observed, "Technology at home has made it possible for many of the lawyers to leave during daylight, coach Little League, etc., and still return messages, finish assignments, etc. This includes partners as well as associates." She added that although there are some at the firm who "choose to spend all their waking hours at work," those who do not are also considered valuable lawyers and given equal opportunities to advance.

> "Especially important is that the respect for my hours is not condescending or otherwise negative. SRZ and I made a deal and each side lives up to it."

Flexibility of work arrangements: Many lauded the firm for promoting to partnership a part-time litigation associate. Part-time is reportedly available at the associate level, and lawyers can choose a percentage of work in return for a percentage of pay, according to a partner.

A partner said one of her colleagues, who was promoted while working part-time, claimed that "there never was any pressure to return to work full-time" and added that after "the initial 'getting used to it' phase," she was given top-notch cases, and didn't feel that her work or status suffered in any way. She noted, however, that flexibility is critical: "When one needs to be out of the office during the day, one does work at night."

One respondent who came to Schulte as a lateral with a part-time deal maintained that her colleagues respect her hours and give her challenging work as well as supervisory responsibility for younger lawyers. "Especially important," she observed, "is that the respect for my hours is not condescending or otherwise negative. SRZ and I made a deal and each side lives up to it."

According to an associate, Schulte "not only has an impressive written alternative work program policy, but it actually honors the policy." She wrote that there are at least eight associates working part-time in all departments, demonstrating that the firm recognizes women's contributions and "is willing to accommodate women's schedules to retain women." One corporate associate noted that part-time is perceived as an "extremely legitimate" option.

A small minority of associates expressed skepticism about part-time options. One expressed the concern that "the firm stresses that nothing is guaranteed and all is open to review." A litigator believed that part-time was rare in her department and that "the onus is on the woman to be flexible in terms of work hours and work days." A corporate associate opined that part-time had not yet been attempted in her department and questioned whether such arrangements would prove compatible with transactional work.

> *Numerous respondents said that Schulte provides a welcoming environment for gay and lesbian attorneys, and that gay lawyers feel comfortable bringing their partners to firm events.*

Diversity: A surprising number of respondents left this question blank. With the exception of one respondent who noted simply that the "associates have many different racial, ethnic, and geographic backgrounds," no one commented on the presence or experience of minority attorneys at the firm.

One associate wrote that, in her opinion, Schulte is diverse "in name only" and that the firm "is largely a Jewish one." She added that "most non-Jews just gradually learn the Yiddish jokes."

Numerous respondents did report that Schulte provides a welcoming environment for gay and lesbian attorneys, that gay lawyers feel comfortable bringing their partners to firm events, and that the firm has actively supported gay fund raisers.

> *"The women attorneys at [the firm] are close and do watch out for each other."*

Women in leadership positions: According to most respondents, there are women in positions of leadership, although there was clearly disagreement.

One partner wrote that the women partners at the firm are relatively junior and do not hold real power. Another described the firm's leadership as male-dominated, but added that she thought this could change.

The firm's senior women were generally viewed as advocates for the firm's junior women. Although one litigation associate remarked that the firm's few women partners do not mentor other women at all, a corporate lawyer asserted that the women in her department "promote the female associates and provide valuable insights." A fellow corporate associate agreed, noting that the more powerful women in the firm "definitely promote the opportunities for women attorneys." A senior associate wrote that notwithstanding their lack of firm-wide influence, "the women attorneys at Schulte are close and do watch out for each other."

A former litigation partner at the firm is now reportedly the partner in charge of professional development for associates. According to several respondents, this partner has the ability to bring important issues to the attention of the firm's male-only executive committee. Yet, according to the concern of one associate, although she is the "only woman close to being in power," she "does nothing to promote women." Another associate wrote, "Many think her role is a farce."

Schulte, Roth & Zabel No. of Responses: 15	Strongly agree	Agree	Disagree	Strongly disagree
Women's prospects for advancement at the firm are as strong as men's	4	7	3	
I am satisfied with the firm's family and personal leave policies	10	3	2	
There are women in positions of power and influence in the firm	2	5	5	1
Women are as likely as men to receive desirable work assignments	9	6		
Women attorneys feel they can discuss family obligations openly	2	9	3	1
Women are as likely as men to be mentored by senior attorneys	7	6	2	
Women attorneys enjoy a high level of job satisfaction	4	6	3	
Women in the firm are supportive of their women colleagues	7	6	2	
Firm management is receptive to the concerns of women attorneys	7	5	2	

SHEARMAN & STERLING

Rating: 66

♠♠

Shearman & Sterling
599 Lexington Ave.
New York, NY 10022
212-848-4000

No. of Attorneys: 416
No. of Women Attorneys: 138
No. of Partners: 105
No. of Women Partners: 14
No. of Survey Responses Received: 31

Respondent Profile: 1 partner, 27 associates, and 3 counsel responded. Practice areas included corporate and mergers and acquisitions, but the majority of respondents did not identify their practice areas.

Summary: Shearman & Sterling has reportedly stepped up its attention to diversity, and a handful of women have made inroads into positions of power, but much room for improvement reportedly remains. Some respondents feared that women who seek advancement will have a better chance if they are childless, and part-time arrangements are perceived to be dead-end, short-term possibilities, at best.

Advancement: Respondents had mixed impressions concerning the likelihood of advancement for women lawyers at Shearman, though a large majority were negative. For those with outside commitments, particularly children, advancement possibilities were seen to be nonexistent, by several associates. One respondent wrote that being a woman "probably does not negatively affect one's chances for partnership," but having a child "changes *everything*! [Once children enter the picture,] all bets are off. No matter how highly the associate had been regarded, once she announces she is pregnant, the associate is no longer considered a serious player and her chances for partnership drop geometrically." A junior associate commented, "[The] 'mommy track' is openly referred to and some women find themselves on it without even being married or with children."

A senior associate remarked that partnership prospects vary by practice group and that although, in her opinion, "mentors are hard to come by," the absence thereof is "fatal."

Her view was shared by a lawyer who is a counsel at the firm who wrote that although assignments and reviews are done fairly, in her experience, mentoring is "almost nonexistent for women." One midlevel corporate associate referred to her experience of "great mentoring, training, and receptiveness to complaints," concluding, "[if] anything, I think I'm over-catered to because I'm a woman." An associate wrote, "Women partners do not mentor women associates. They foster the continuation of the environment in which they function."

A corporate associate opined that men feel more at ease around other men: "They talk to them, joke with them, and get to know them. There are exceptions, but in general, we are not seen as full people." One lawyer said she believed that there is less tolerance for a woman who is difficult to work with than for a man: "A man may be viewed as a tough negotiator, while a woman exhibiting the same personality traits might be viewed as a witch or hormonal." A corporate associate commented that, in her opinion, women "are expected to be feminine (but not too much) and one of the guys at the same time."

A midlevel associate complained that "women receive fewer choice assignments, and the inequity tends to increase with the years." Other respondents stated that women may be held to a higher standard than men in terms of the requisite quality of work necessary for partnership. A midlevel associate said it was her opinion that women who advance are "handed down clients from older partners who no longer wish to work as hard and are close to retirement, while always being subject to the senior partner's supervision, while new male partners are encouraged to develop business on their own and, if handed down a client, are given autonomy...for the particular client relationship."

Several respondents spoke favorably about Shearman with respect to their own experiences and perceptions. One litigator wrote that in her department, women enjoy equal chances of advancement, though "some women have been viewed as making partner because they are women." Another litigator observed that although women are "substantially less likely to advance" than men, they are "probably more likely to advance here than at many other New York firms." An associate wrote, "The key is to seek out the power partners" as mentors.

Although sexual harassment is not tolerated, "the better one looks in a swimsuit, the 'happier' one will be."

Attitudes and atmosphere: Some respondents reported that Shearman is perfectly comfortable for women, but many perceived a demarcation between the sexes, if not outright sexism. One respondent observed that there is "strong propaganda these days" on women's issues, but said she believed it to be "window dressing, mostly. The firm doesn't address the core issue of how to make the system work for women who have different biological, social, and cultural traits than men."

According to a litigation associate, although there are a few partners who are uncomfortable with women, this is the exception rather than the rule.

A corporate lawyer reported that, in her opinion, the women who have come up for partner and seem likely to be promoted "are somewhat gender-neutral." But she expressed her concern that women who are comfortable with being feminine in their dress or their lives in general might become "fair game for the male partners." A midlevel associate agreed that Shearman is "an okay place to be for those women who are willing to pretend they are men."

A couple of lawyers made comments to the effect that "it's much easier to survive here if you are a single woman available to join the 'boys' for drinks than if you have a family and precious little time to discuss the latest Knicks game." One respondent found it ironic that, in her estimation, the firm "represented Shannon Faulkner in the Citadel case, but it won't even listen to its own female partners and associates."

An associate reported "a few incidents of insensitivity here—'boys' night out' with clients, etc.,"—but added that participants were "heavily chastised by both men and women for such transgressions." A midlevel respondent claimed, although sexual harassment is not tolerated, she sensed that "the better one looks in a swimsuit, the 'happier' one will be."

According to one corporate associate, the climate varies by practice group, and "some are very, very unpleasant." A midlevel associate believed that women "are treated more like secretaries or legal assistants."

Two respondents disagreed. A senior associate lamented that in recent years, Shearman has become "quite sensitive to issues of discrimination and harassment." The one partner respondent described "a clear trend in recent years on the part of the firm's management to focus on recruiting, retaining, and promoting female (as well as minority) associates."

One lawyer reported that all-nighters are not uncommon and that she finds it "difficult to have a cat, much less a family."

Balancing work & family/personal life: Maintaining a semblance of balance is all but impossible, given the nature of New York practice, and Shearman is perceived to take few steps to lighten the load. According to one respondent, "The firm only values the 'billable

hour.' We even keep statistics on the number of 'keystrokes' per lawyer and continually compare ourselves to other firms." Another associate perceived that people "have very little sympathy for ongoing personal/family commitments and responsibilities."

Although some maintained that the firm is more receptive to the outside demands faced by parents than to those of unmarried attorneys, mothers by no means appear to have it easy. One mother described the hours as "notoriously bad and unpredictable. I've heard many times that I can take work home and work from there. There is no understanding that parenting *is* work and a woman who is at home with her children is busy and can't just sit on a sofa and read cases or draft an agreement."

Another respondent described her "worst experience," when she had to work until midnight on a Saturday after having communicated to the partner on Friday that her child was running a high fever. "On top of that," she added, "it was a new matter for whom others would've been available."

Single women who wish to have a life outside the firm reportedly may also face difficulties. One lawyer reported that all-nighters are not uncommon and that she finds it "difficult to have a cat, much less a family." Another unmarried respondent recounted that, in her estimation, "you are not expected to acknowledge having the desire to have a personal life. Mentioning that you have concert tickets, a dinner party, or some other activity during a weekday is an invitation for more work."

A few associates were more optimistic in their outlooks. A junior associate observed, "[My hours] make it difficult for me to see my friends and parents, but because I am still very new to my career, I'm not too bothered by it at this point." A senior associate wrote that "sensitivity is dawning in the liberal thinkers" and that the women attorneys show each other "wonderful support."

> *A corporate associate called the assignment of women with children to marketing positions "a damned disheartening habit."*

Flexibility of work arrangements: It is perceived that, though a formal written policy exists, part-time arrangements, may quash one's potential for advancement. Alternative work arrangements "are not really a viable option since once you do part-time, you are off the partnership track and [may] never get back on that track," one associate remarked, a sentiment shared by others. Even the partner respondent acknowledged that although part-time exists, the downside, in her experience, is that part-time associates are often considered to be off track.

Part-time for partners is available only on a case-by-case basis. Part-time is reportedly "frowned upon" by the head of at least one department, according to one respondent. According to another, "They try to pigeonhole you with less challenging work." An associate observed that while the partners seem "happy" with the work done by one part-time associate and mother, "most of the associates qualify any mention of her as 'she's only part-time'—so her status is definitely not exalted." Nevertheless, one part-timer reported satisfaction with her arrangement, noting that it is not a long-term option. She also remarked

that she has received "increasingly more interesting work" and her "schedule has largely been respected."

There was a perception among several respondents that some associates with children who have sought less demanding work schedules have been shunted into nonlegal positions. One corporate associate called the assignment of women with children to these positions "damned disheartening."

When granted, part-time arrangements are reportedly the product of individualized negotiations between attorneys and their superiors. "The firm makes a concerted effort to negotiate each of these arrangements separately and to keep the terms of each confidential," one respondent wrote. A corporate associate reported, "You really have to fight" for part-time arrangements, and she advised, "quitting apparently helps."

One litigator noted that in contrast to the firm's generous term of maternity leave, "the recently instituted paternity leave is only one-week long," reflecting, in her view, "not-so-subtle differences in expectations for men and women." A corporate associate said it was her opinion that taking advantage of maternity leave "curtails one's partnership options."

> *There is a committee of "sincerely concerned partners" seeking to make Shearman a friendlier place.*

Diversity: Shearman has reportedly intensified its commitment to the recruitment of attorneys from diverse backgrounds, although respondents perceived that the firm's efforts have yet to pay off with tangible results. An associate commented that there is a committee of "sincerely concerned partners" seeking to make Shearman a friendlier place. There is a perception that there will soon be an African-American partner.

The firm has instituted mandatory training on sexual harassment and diversity issues, but one corporate associate observed that at the workshop she attended, "some of the more offensive partners sat quietly through it, making occasional 'jokes' to the men beside them mocking the topic then under discussion."

In terms of personalities, political views, and social backgrounds, the firm is reportedly home to all types, although an associate noted that the firm tends to be conservative and that associates who were "too boisterous have not survived." She added that, in her opinion, issues of sexual orientation are "never, never discussed by heterosexuals or homosexuals." Another associate agreed that as "most people look and act pretty much the same," it was doubtful to her that "many alternative life styles would be accepted unless they were very subtle about it."

A strong minority of associates maintained that women wielding true influence are few and far between.

Women in leadership positions: Most respondents agreed that there are a handful of women in leadership spots at Shearman and that at least some of these partners are valuable mentors to their more junior colleagues. One senior associate reported that the women partners meet to discuss "women's issues in the firm and devise action plans to improve things."

A strong minority of associates maintained that women wielding true influence are few and far between, a phenomenon one litigator attributed to "the fact that power comes from billings, and most of the clients who control that are men." There is one woman on the firm's executive committee, although an associate claimed that this woman is "not generally a free thinker—she follows the party line." There are also women who head "various practice groups and offices within the firm," the partner noted.

Another associate was savagely negative in her opinion that the partnership is "rather old, and feels most comfortable with white men or slender single women. Don't be fat, married, a crusader, or a minority if you want to be a partner here."

According to one associate, there are "numerous, extremely well-respected partners at the firm who are women—some make an effort to mentor—others seem to hold a grudge."

Quite a few respondents took a dim view of the support offered by more senior women attorneys. According to one, the women at the top "[have] done precious little to promote quality of life of women because they are the ones who conformed to the rigors of the life style and don't see—or don't want to acknowledge—that things could be different." One lawyer concluded that women "are their own worst enemies, generally, and I think it is true at S & S as well." She added that the women at the top do not understand work-family dilemmas "even when they try." A corporate associate agreed that although some partners lend their backing to junior women, it was her opinion that "there are other female partners who would rather preserve their status as one of a few, [and] see women as a threat and prefer to work with men."

Miscellaneous: According to one respondent, when the first edition of *Presumed Equal* was published, she observed a " 'witch hunt' to find out who had responded."

Shearman & Sterling No. of Responses: 26*	Strongly agree	Agree	Disagree	Strongly disagree
Women's prospects for advancement at the firm are as strong as men's	2	7	10	4
I am satisfied with the firm's family and personal leave policies	3	9	8	5
There are women in positions of power and influence in the firm	4	12	7	1
Women are as likely as men to receive desirable work assignments	8	11	4	1
Women attorneys feel they can discuss family obligations openly	2	5	11	6
Women are as likely as men to be mentored by senior attorneys	4	7	11	3
Women attorneys enjoy a high level of job satisfaction	1	9	12	2
Women in the firm are supportive of their women colleagues	12	8	5	1
Firm management is receptive to the concerns of women attorneys	1	12	7	4

* Five respondents did not return charts at all.

SIDLEY & AUSTIN

Rating: 18

Sidley & Austin
One First National Plaza
Chicago, IL 60603
312-853-7000

No. of Attorneys: 406
No. of Women Attorneys: 111
No. of Partners: 196
No. of Women Partners: 32
No. of Survey Responses Received: 24
Respondent Profile: 10 partners, 13 associates, and 1 counsel responded. We also received 12 surveys from the Washington, D.C., and Los Angeles offices. Comments are included to the extent that they are applicable to issues that are not specific to particular offices. Practice areas included corporate, litigation, health care, real estate, and employee benefits.

Summary: At Sidley & Austin, women's opportunities for advancement are promising overall, with many women deriving substantial support from the large number of women attorneys and partners. Part-time arrangements are said to be legitimate and respected. Nevertheless, remnants of a "boys' club" linger, and women partners, despite their distinguished credentials, are perceived by some to have bumped up against a high glass ceiling.

Advancement: An overwhelming majority of respondents asserted that advancement prospects for women are promising overall, although several partners and associates cautioned that female attorneys may be at a disadvantage in certain key areas. "Talented, aggressive people of either gender succeed," observed one associate. A partner agreed: "[Women are] judged by the same standards as men [and] do not have to fit into a particular mold to be successful." The firm has a large number of "competent, prominent" women partners and has advanced quite a few women in recent years, according to one respondent. A corporate associate remarked that Sidley has taken "great steps to ensure the professional development and advancement of women." These efforts have involved mentoring initiatives, measures to ensure that women receive equally challenging work, and "sessions organized by partners to discuss 'women's issues' and part-time." A partner agreed, writing that the firm offers "excellent opportunities for women" and commenting that she made partner with her class after "working part-time." She added that she received "outstanding work" throughout.

A few partners commented that some obstacles do face women lawyers. According to a litigation partner's opinion, "Women here are less likely to be mentored by powerful men than men," and such mentoring, "which typically results in 'plum' assignments, is key to advancement." According to another partner's opinion, women attorneys "often do not mentor their female (or male) colleagues effectively—partly because outside time commitments (family, etc.)

limit the amount of time women spend in the office." Another partner commented that, in her estimation, while the "formal criteria" for advancement apply equally to men and women, it "takes longer for women to receive client-development opportunities and opportunities to handle major cases."

Two associates sided with those partners who said women were at a disadvantage in terms of promotions. A litigation associate agreed that mentoring is essential and contended that because they find mentors more readily, male associates, in her opinion, "get better work and have the opportunity to display the quality of their work to more people." The other associate remarked that women are less likely to be promoted and perceived that "the percentage of women to men is astonishingly discrepant, [and the] turnover rate is high." A central factor for advancement, in her view, "is toeing the party line."

"There is definitely the 'boys' club.' But we are developing a 'girls' club.' "

....

Attitudes and atmosphere: According to respondents, the large numbers of women at Sidley contribute to women's comfort level, yet remnants of a "boys' club" mentality still linger, making the firm less than ideal for some. Sidley is reportedly not a particularly social firm. At an individual level, however, "it is easy to establish both working relationships and friendships with female and male colleagues," as one lawyer put it. Sidley's management is credited with setting a tone that takes women's issues "very seriously" and supports women's professional development.

Nevertheless, a litigator feared that the men bond in ways that exclude women, "i.e., golf, basketball, other sports, cigars, etc. These relationships naturally spill over into the workplace and [in my opinion] affect the allocation of work." An associate also perceived that because of "male-only sports teams sponsored by the firm and the tendency of the male lawyers to avoid socializing with female lawyers, young male associates have a better opportunity to use social relationships to develop their careers."

In one partner's opinion, "The glass ceiling is high, but it is here." Another partner agreed that while the problem is not "pervasive," in her estimation, some male attorneys seem uncomfortable working with women or "unable to accept advice from female colleagues." Another partner concurred, describing daily interactions between women and men as "smooth," but she said that, in her opinion, "talented and seasoned women litigators [have been] blatantly ignored by some extremely senior firm personnel." Watching men react "as if the women hadn't said a thing," has been, in her words, "quite sobering."

In direct contrast, the firm's management "has a policy of treating everyone equally and giving everyone equal opportunities," according to a partner, who added that gender discrimination "would not be tolerated." An associate commented that she has "never felt—ever—that being a woman was any issue at all." She added that she chose Sidley upon graduating from law school for this reason and that her "initial perceptions were correct." One partner remarked that in the area where she perceived "the 'boy's club' mentality" was most prevalent—the corporate group—

"the firm took steps to encourage positive behavior and to strongly discourage the negative behavior. It appears to be working!" These efforts appear to be less visible at the associate level, as evidenced by one associate's conclusion that "gender is generally not addressed by firm management in any way (either positively or negatively)."

A junior associate commented that Sidley has a strong network of women associates, and that the women partners are accessible, supportive, and "make a real effort to stay in tune with women associates and develop programs especially for us." She suggested, "There is definitely the 'boys' club.' But we are developing a 'girls' club.' "

"Discussions of family activities and responsibilities are encouraged."

Balancing work & family/personal life: Balancing appears to be easier at Sidley than at some comparable firms. Working hours are described as manageable and reasonable, although when client demands kick in, little can be done by even the most sensitive partners to ease the burdens on strapped attorneys.

Litigation appears to be a difficult practice group for those straddling dual sets of obligations. A partner commented, "[It is] hard for any litigator to maintain a satisfying personal life, if by satisfying you include substantial, direct input into your child's mental, moral, and physical upbringing."

According to most respondents, lawyers at Sidley are generally receptive to family obligations. "Discussions of family activities and responsibilities are encouraged," reported one partner, adding

that the firm holds an annual family picnic and that "many attorneys know each other's children." A litigation partner commented, "Of course [family obligations] can be discussed. This is no gulag." But, in her opinion, "If you can't get a brief out due to a childcare breakdown, you are in trouble." Expanded use of home computers, faxes, and modems has helped to make work outside the office possible, and the firm reportedly offers emergency childcare assistance.

Part-time arrangements are reportedly available at all levels of the firm, have been utilized by men, and are not a dead end, career-wise.

Flexibility of work arrangements: Sidley received very high marks for the part-time arrangements it offers. Part-time schedules are "absolutely accepted and supported." One partner commented that she made partner with her class after working part-time for a number of years. She described Sidley as "a great place to work as a part-time lawyer," adding that her compensation is "outstanding" and that she can work "at whatever part-time level I want." Part-time arrangements are reportedly available at all levels of the firm, have been utilized by men, and are not a dead end, career-wise. Sidley's attitude, in the eyes of one partner, is that "people are not fungible," and the firm thus works hard to keep its attorneys. Although part-time "generally slows advancement toward partnership," observed another partner, "it does not preclude it."

The primary difficulty cited in connection with part-time lies in controlling one's hours. Several partners perceived that part-time attorneys do sometimes find themselves working full-time schedules. "The pressure placed on part-time associates by some partners is so great that they either go full-time or work essentially full-time hours but are paid on a part-time basis (always hoping to actually work part-time)," in a partner's opinion. The practicality of part-time also reportedly varies by practice area, with corporate and litigation the most difficult fields in which to limit one's schedule.

Some associates expressed trepidation about taking advantage of part-time options. One suggested, "Don't expect to make partner if you choose this track early in your career." Another associate believed that going part-time "wouldn't be a good idea career-wise [and is] a very bad idea for relative newcomers to the firm."

According to other associates, these fears may be groundless. A junior associate commented that several women colleagues of hers who have had children during their first two years at the firm have reported "no serious adverse effects." A litigation associate reported that a colleague is soon to take her third maternity leave without "any apparent impact on [her] assignments or work." Another attorney noted that she works three days per week and "remains on the partnership track."

> *The firm has committees and task forces dedicated to diversity issues, but "the more difficult task is retention issues and advancement to partnership."*

Diversity: Sidley's showing on the diversity front was fairly typical of many of the firms we surveyed—respondents reported that, despite the firm's commitment to diversity, they perceived that it has had difficulty retaining minority associates. Several respondents, including one lawyer who identified herself as a member of a minority racial group, commented that the firm is "very dedicated to diversity." Yet the firm is, in another associate's opinion, filled with "lots of white upper-middle income people."

An associate noted that the firm has committees and task forces dedicated to diversity issues, but, in her opinion, "the more difficult task is retention issues and advancement to partnership." A partner said that, in her estimation, "very few minority attorneys stay at Sidley very long," and the problem is, "as with women, a failure to mentor someone who is different."

According to the 1997-1998 National Directory of Legal Employers, out of 406 attorneys, 20 are minorities.

In terms of personalities and interests, Sidley is said to be open to most types. An associate commented, "If you are talented enough, you can be as eccentric as you want to be." A midlevel associate commented that the firm would not "look favorably on someone wearing their diversity badge on their sleeve, but things like openly gay lawyers are a nonissue." A partner wrote that political views at the firm span the gamut, "from very liberal to very conservative."

> *One respondent "would like to see more of an effort on the part of female partners to mentor women associates on an informal level."*

Women in leadership positions: According to respondents, no women sit on the firm's management committee, which they characterized as Sidley's upper echelon of power, although two women serve on the executive committee, and the women partners generally appear to be well-respected and supportive of their junior colleagues. One partner wrote that, in her opinion, "The management committee runs the firm. Period." As a partner perceived it, "Since there are no women on the management committee, there are no women in positions of 'real' power." Another partner maintained that only one practice group is headed by a woman.

The women with influence here are widely respected, both within the firm and in the legal community. An associate described these women as "talented lawyers with good political sense."

Most respondents thought Sidley's more senior women were supportive of other female attorneys. An associate commented that the female partners have sponsored group gatherings of women attorneys and "women-only" programs on topics such as rainmaking. The firm has hosted "women in leadership" discussions, bringing together attorneys and women clients. One partner reported that Sidley has been "very supportive of women partners' efforts to develop and expand their practice."

Sidley & Austin No. of Responses: 24	Strongly agree	Agree	Disagree	Strongly disagree
Women's prospects for advancement at the firm are as strong as men's	10	9	3	1
I am satisfied with the firm's family and personal leave policies	12	11	1	
There are women in positions of power and influence in the firm	10	11	2	1
Women are as likely as men to receive desirable work assignments	11	8	3	2
Women attorneys feel they can discuss family obligations openly	7	13	3	1
Women are as likely as men to be mentored by senior attorneys	7	9	6	1
Women attorneys enjoy a high level of job satisfaction	5	16	1	1
Women in the firm are supportive of their women colleagues	14	10		
Firm management is receptive to the concerns of women attorneys	9	12	2	

SIMPSON THACHER & BARTLETT

Rating: 75

Simpson Thacher & Bartlett
425 Lexington Ave.
New York, NY 10017
212-455-2000

No. of Attorneys: 463
No. of Women Attorneys: 129
No. of Partners: 118
No. of Women Partners: 8
No. of Survey Responses Received: 18

Respondent Profile: 2 partners, 14 associates, and 2 counsel responded.

Summary: A majority of respondents were clearly displeased by the pace of women's advancement at Simpson, Thacher, and downright angry because no women are in "meaningful leadership roles." They cited a distinct lack of mentoring opportunities and concluded that many ingredients in the partnership mix were difficult, if not impossible, for women to come by.

Advancement: An overwhelming majority of respondents (including many associates but neither partner) declared that women do not advance at Simpson, Thacher, and most held the firm itself to blame. The pattern of women's advancement in recent years has reportedly been abysmal, and Simpson's women—as well as some men—are apparently not sanguine about this issue.

The firm acknowledged that between 1989 and 1991, 19 partners were made—all men. From 1992 to 1996, six of the 34 who ascended to partnership were women. Although *all* associates are considered for partner after seven to nine years, Simpson, Thacher made seven white men partners in 1995 and eight white men partners in 1996.

Women (and men) at the firm have reportedly not accepted these discouraging patterns quietly, however. One litigator wrote that after the November 1996 partnership announcement, several women associates met to discuss improving their prospects at the firm. She was concerned that the partnership was unresponsive to these efforts. Another respondent wrote that, in her opinion, after the partnership election, "there was an uproar even among male associates." One senior associate had a somewhat more positive spin on the situation, writing that she is encouraged by efforts "[the] firm is making to include more women partners—they've developed a 'task force' and, word has it, are committed to advancing more women."

Many ingredients in the partnership mix are reportedly very difficult for women to come by. Success apparently requires "the mentorship of a strong senior male partner or, less frequently, the support of a small but adamant group of partners," according to one lawyer. She expressed concern that senior men at the firm "do not mentor women" and that groups of partners "do not organize campaigns on behalf of women. Women do not receive high-profile assignments or access to power on a par with men."

Although women tend to be "praised as star worker bees" during their junior years, in a senior attorney's estimation, "things are much worse for women after their fourth year." One attorney said she believed that "[the firm] uses [the] attrition rate as an excuse for its failure to make women partners." Another believed that "notwithstanding the firm's spin," the paltry advancement prospects have "little to nothing to do with family/work issues—even unmarried women with no children who devote themselves to the firm do not advance."

According to a corporate associate, there is a fear that the firm's few women partners "do not 'groom' women associates in the same way that men do." She also raised a concern about disparities in work assignments, writing, "[In my early time at the firm] I was given many crappy research assignments and small projects while my male counterparts were working on transactions in *The Wall Street Journal*."

One associate wrote that when she needs advice on legal issues from more senior colleagues, some are very helpful, but often, in her estimation, her "phone calls go completely unanswered and unreturned. Whereas I've been in a male attorney's office who, when he makes the same call, the phone is immediately answered by the senior attorney." Another respondent agreed that progress for women looks "bleak" and that the problem lies in "old white boys feeling more comfortable with those that look

like them." One corporate associate feared, "There is just a level of camaraderie there that the female can't meet."

These views were not shared by all respondents. Some painted a brighter picture of the firm, claiming that mentoring and assignments are divvied up equally and attributing the glaring gap in partnership prospects to attrition based on "personal choice," as one litigator characterized it.

A partner wrote that attrition is due to family demands and attorneys' desire for less pressure and more predictable life styles—factors that are inducing men as well as women to leave. She maintained that if those who remain are "talented and work hard," the prospects for advancement are the same, regardless of gender.

Another partner wrote that while men are more likely to mentor men, this does not mean women are left out entirely. She added that she had "never perceived a difference in allocation of assignments or review criteria."

One senior lawyer wrote, "The firm's leaders are enlightened, but the boys under them are unruly."

Attitudes and atmosphere: In spite of their negative views of the partnership situation, most women seem relatively happy with day-to-day life at Simpson, Thacher. One midlevel associate wrote, "[The firm] prides itself on doing things 'properly,' and inappropriate behavior (even by a partner) would not be tolerated at all." Another noted that the firm is "not a macho culture, no screaming, yelling, no excessive sports-bonding." Most women reported feeling relatively comfortable around their colleagues and that instances of discrimination are very rare and generally subtle.

Nevertheless, some women reportedly feel excluded from the male cliques that they perceived exist at Simpson, Thacher. A senior associate believed, "The men don't 'buddy' with women the way they do with each other—go to the gym together or grab a lunch or sneak out for a golf game on a summer afternoon."

Several other women perceived that the firm's cafeteria is "a male bastion" and that women "don't feel comfortable in there." One respondent commented that, in her opinion, the "club" consists primarily of members of the firm's executive committee, "star [mergers and acquisitions] partners and those they admit. Even women who would fit into the 'club' find it difficult to get their foot in the door." A corporate associate remarked that, in her estimation, the male partners "freely socialize in and out of the office with male associates" and that the exclusion of women from the camaraderie places them "at a distinct disadvantage."

Another respondent dubbed Simpson, Thacher "a men's club." One senior lawyer suggested, "The firm's leaders are enlightened, but the boys under them are unruly." One junior associate noted that on multiple occasions "people (attorneys and support staff) have assumed I was a paralegal or a secretary, without ever once considering that I might be an attorney."

The partners who responded painted a brighter view, writing that women are "integrated into all departments and given responsibility," and that if a person works hard, "has a good attitude, and does good work, [she will] receive confirmation of that value on a regular basis." And an associate said that there is no "boys' club" at Simpson, Thacher and that "women are treated with the same respect given to men."

A junior attorney wrote, "What personal life? I cannot imagine having the responsibilities of childcare and having this job."

Balancing work & family/personal life: Life at Simpson, Thacher is a tough grind, but unless they are in the corporate department, those with "good organizational skills and the emotional maturity to draw some lines" need not be entirely swallowed by work. Accomplishing this, as one litigator observed, "generally requires good assignments and a willingness to say, 'Screw you, I'm going home.' " She also suggested that the firm recently lost "a couple of terrific male attorneys [who left for] new jobs that allow them to spend more time with their families." She hoped that "those visible defections by men will open the firm's eyes" in a way that perhaps women have not been able to, and "force them to make some changes that will benefit women, too."

According to another associate's opinion, "The firm puts its head in the sand when it comes to the fact that in our society today it is women who bear the brunt of 'keeping the home fires burning.' " One respondent observed that there is a "sense" at Simpson, Thacher that "face time" is important, making it uncomfortable for attorneys to leave at a reasonable hour.

In the corporate department, the schedules are particularly demanding and "often leave very little time for any life outside work," opined one senior associate. A junior attorney lamented, "What personal life? I cannot imagine having the responsibilities of childcare and having this job. I can barely get dressed in the morning and drag myself in here, much less exercise, eat right, or have any sort of hobby. Every single time I make plans, I know there is at least a 50-percent chance I will have to cancel them."

Although some men try to be understanding, in the assessment of one associate with kids, "they all have full-time mothers/wives and nannies at home!" Another mother wrote that she has been able to strike a reasonable balance, but is "quite unhappy with the quality of assignments" she has been given. The firm reportedly provides off-site emergency childcare.

A couple of lawyers praised the firm for its efforts to support attorneys' personal lives. One new associate remarked that it appeared that "if you are valued, the firm will make some adjustments, like the four-day workweek." Another associate reported that the central assigning system is the "most essential resource for associates" in that it allows the associate to advise the central assigning partner, rather than the partner looking for assistance, that she has too much work.

"[The firm] likes lip service sensitivity, [but] it is not at all 'liberated.'"

Flexibility of work arrangements: Several associates believed that part-time is available for one year following the birth of a child, a limitation that one associate found "not very realistic."

Another associate commented that extensions of this period are sometimes granted on a case-by-case basis. Part-time reportedly "means 60 percent of a full-time associate's average annual billable hours—so it is pretty much full-time (or more) by most standards."

A partner reported that several partners, including men, take advantage of such arrangements. One respondent who had worked part-time for a period did not believe that her arrangement harmed her prospects at the firm. A senior associate disagreed and reported that although part-time is technically available, there is a concern that "most of the women who do it would say that it has not worked out that well because they were expected to be 'flexible,' but that flexibility only went one way—for the benefit of the firm."

In the opinion of a litigator, despite the firm's formal position that "part-time work or maternity leave only slows you down in advancement, [many] women who take advantage seem dissatisfied and often leave shortly thereafter." Most associates believed that "chances for advancement are clearly limited" by the choice to go part-time, and several suggested that part-timers suffer a loss of credibility and respect that, according to one, can never be recaptured. An associate reported that the firm appears to offer some flextime arrangements, whereby attorneys work one day per week at home. But two other associates were concerned that such options are "not openly discussed," leading one to believe that "they are disfavored by the senior attorneys." One respondent summed up by observing, "[The firm] likes lip service sensitivity, [but] it is not at all 'liberated.'"

A senior lawyer noted that, notwithstanding its perceived lack of flexibility on part-time, "the firm can be very compassionate at times and make you proud."

"This is not a place where we discuss gender or political issues. It's work, work, work."

Diversity: Respondents gave mixed reviews to the firm's commitment to diversifying its workplace, yet by one account, the firm achieves more on this front than on gender issues. As seems typical of many large firms, the minority attorneys are reportedly concentrated primarily in the most junior classes at the firm.

Several associates were anxious that the firm does not seem serious about achieving diversity, with one remarking that, in her opinion, the issue "only comes up when it's time to tally up the minorities so that we can present an image of concern via percentages." Another associate believed that the firm shows no "support or lack of it—although certainly there are individuals here at all levels who are not open-minded about alternative lifestyles."

Several associates noted that the firm accomplishes less diversity with respect to personality. A litigator commented that, in her estimation, there is "no effort to encourage diversity in personality." One associate was concerned that "[a] very loud, aggressive woman would have trouble fitting in."

According to a partner, the firm "values people for their contribution to the firm and there is little concern for what people do outside of the firm." An associate agreed, saying, "This is not a place where we discuss gender or political issues. It's work, work, work."

"There are talented women jammed on all rungs of the ladder below equity partner, but [few] have made it to the top."

Women in leadership positions: There are reportedly no women in the top strata of power players at Simpson, Thacher, a perception born out by the large majority of women who replied negatively to this question. The real power at the firm reportedly lies in the firm's all-male executive committee. According to one lawyer, the firm has no women "in meaningful leadership roles." She added, "There are talented women jammed on all rungs of the ladder below equity partner, but [few] have made it to the top." Several associates perceived that the women partners do not always get the respect they should.

One reported that the women partners lack power and are, in her opinion, subject to heavier criticism than men, "mostly regarding their lack of ability or their way of dressing (yes, how they dress!)." She sensed that overall, women are not "valued or respected as partners."

A partner agreed with many of these opinions, writing that there are "too few female partners (and we are too junior) to be in positions of real power. Female partners are subject to more scrutiny and criticism than male partners."

Many associates expressed anger at what they perceived as women partners' lack of support. Most associates expressed the concern that the female partners "do not try to reach out to female associates in any organized fashion," as one put it, and that as a result, associates "don't feel a sense of solidarity with the women partners." A midlevel associate believed that because they do not mentor, the partners "are resented by the female associates. There is a perception that the female partners, rather than extending a hand to help us up the ladder, are even more likely to push for the *status quo*."

Simpson Thacher & Bartlett No. of Responses: 18	Strongly agree	Agree	Disagree	Strongly disagree
Women's prospects for advancement at the firm are as strong as men's	1	3	6	8
I am satisfied with the firm's family and personal leave policies	3	6	6	1
There are women in positions of power and influence in the firm		4	6	8
Women are as likely as men to receive desirable work assignments	6	4	4	3
Women attorneys feel they can discuss family obligations openly	1	9	4	1
Women are as likely as men to be mentored by senior attorneys	2	2	5	9
Women attorneys enjoy a high level of job satisfaction	1	6	7	4
Women in the firm are supportive of their women colleagues	2	5	7	4
Firm management is receptive to the concerns of women attorneys		5	8	3

SKADDEN, ARPS, SLATE, MEAGHER & FLOM LLP

Rating: 47

Skadden, Arps, Slate, Meagher & Flom LLP
919 Third Ave.
New York, NY 10022
212-735-3000

No. of Attorneys: 585
No. of Women Attorneys: 192
No. of Partners: 130
No. of Women Partners: 23
No. of Survey Responses Received: 36

Respondent Profile: 4 partners, 31 associates, and 1 counsel responded. Practice areas included litigation, corporate, mergers and acquisitions, and employee benefits.

Summary: Skadden, Arps, Slate, Meagher & Flom, home to several heavy-hitting women partners, is not a firm for the weak-kneed, according to most. Opportunities for advancement are said to be equitable for women, except perhaps in litigation. The firm's environment is tough and relentless. Those who are unmarried and childless appear to fare best, because meeting responsibilities outside of the firm is nearly impossible, and part-time arrangements, by some accounts, result in less interesting work. The four partners who responded were overwhelmingly positive. Associates' opinions were often mixed, sometimes evenly split.

Advancement: Despite the large volume of responses, a fair degree of consensus emerged that if one is willing to work like a "slave" throughout one's years as an associate, women's prospects for partnership equal those of men, except perhaps in the firm's litigation-oriented departments. By all accounts, the hours at Skadden are grueling and of critical importance to advancement. "Making partner here is not that easy," commented an intellectual property associate. "It requires committing your life and soul to your work." Several associates observed that while it can be done, women face an uphill battle in securing partnership, even if they do put forth equal effort.

Mentoring is vital to partnership, and the firm reportedly sponsors a formal program to pair new lawyers with senior associates and partners. Although one associate commented that the women partners are "the worst mentors to other women," she praised them for the example they set.

"Many midlevel female associates [apparently] 'opt out' of the partner track when they have babies. Many of us in New York City have financially successful spouses who can support such a choice," wrote a trusts and estates associate. A partner agreed: "Women do not advance as well as men to the stage where partnership selection occurs." She added that the firm recognizes the high attrition rate and has started a study "to determine why this is occurring and what we can do about it." Virtually all associates agreed that the likelihood of women advancing in litigation is worse.

A senior associate stated that, in her estimation, the factors essential to promotion include "a combination of long, long hours, aggressiveness, and ass-kissing." In a junior associate's experience, the key difficulties for women include "the difficulty of breaking into the 'boys' club' that is the litigation partnership," the "lack of mentoring for mid-level associates," and "women choosing to devote time to family."

Not surprisingly, the partners had a different spin on advancement. One partner described the firm as a meritocracy. She added that women "who do quality work will be provided with every opportunity for advancement, just as men are." Another partner commented that Skadden has "a number of women at the firm who are 'heavy hitters,' either because of their role in management or their rainmaking or deal-making ability." A mergers and acquisitions partner contended, "Joe Flom [the founding partner], who is very progressive in outlook, set the tone for the firm—open and fair."

Another partner noted, "The great thing about Skadden is that at the 'dollars and cents' level, there is *total* equality. Women are compensated at the highest tiers of compensation and they are very fairly treated."

> *"While Skadden is very likely a meritocracy, one's 'merit' may be judged on how tough you are... It's not a place for wimps."*

Attitudes and atmosphere: Skadden is not a firm for the faint of heart, according to most. A senior associate wrote that one must be "very tough-skinned."

An employee benefits attorney described the environment similarly: "While Skadden is very likely a meritocracy, one's 'merit' may be judged on how tough you are... It's not a place for wimps."

One first-year associate wrote that she and her fellow junior associates "have experienced...jokes about sex, weird looks when wearing certain arguably nondowdy clothing, etc." She further observed that women "doing *really* corporate work (mergers and acquisitions) experience an 'old boy' thing—cigar smoking, suspender-wearing, testosterone-pumping culture." But another corporate associate reported that a male partner had taken an interest in her "in a manner that wasn't professional," and when she reported it to her supervisors, they assured her that she did not have to work with him again.

Several reported that, in their estimation, the "boys' club" is alive and well at the firm. A junior associate noted that this does not only affect women: "There's a very high sports-orientation and even male associates who have little interest in sports have less to share in terms of social interaction with the male partners."

The men try, commented one litigation associate, but "some departments are worse than others because there are few women partners and it's a constantly male-dominated atmosphere." According to a litigator, there are several male partners who have "general problems working with women." Another litigator reported that in her department, "women are either patronized and treated like 'daughters' [or] disregarded completely and given no respect."

While things seem to get tougher for those who stick it out, junior associates appear to enjoy a kind of honeymoon here. One first-year associate wrote that she feels "*very* comfortable" and has "no complaints whatsoever." A first-year litigator agreed: "Women are treated equally to men" adding that her experience "has been positive." A few senior associates shared the views of the first-years. One commented that the firm is "very conscious of the equal treatment of women and has made a big effort to keep women partners in the positive media spotlight."

The partners' comments differed markedly from those of the associates. According to one, there is no gender discrimination and the firm has "an informal, relaxed atmosphere where people generally feel free to dress as they wish and speak out in matters that concern them." She added, "Now and then, there seems to be a 'boys' club' issue—especially with regard to summer associates, but we have instituted many women's-only programs within the last several years [and there now may be a] 'women's club' issue." A mergers and acquisitions partner described the firm as "a wonderful place to work." At a social level, she reported, the firm is "very close-knit. Skadden is like family."

Attorneys reportedly "can be requested to be on-call virtually around the clock."

Balancing work & family/personal life: Skadden's women were in overwhelming agreement that balancing a partnership track with a thriving family life is nearly impossible. A litigator suggested, "The only reason more men are able to make partner, be successful, *and* have a family is that they have wives at home who care for their children."

The hours are brutal across the board, according to respondents. One litigator reported that she finds the hours "to be late as a general rule (leaving before 8 p.m. feels early) and in 1996 I billed over 3,000 hours." A corporate finance partner with children observed, "The most difficult aspect of being a woman lawyer is the effect on family life." She reported that her hours have averaged 2,500 during the past few years. A first-year associate added, "[You] have to get the work done, even if you hold the baby while doing your mark-up." Attorneys reportedly "can be requested to be on-call virtually around the clock."

Several associates commented that while the firm is sensitive to crises, it is less responsive to run-of-the-mill family obligations. One attorney commented that there is "sensitivity to family issues like house floods, deaths, etc. But if I need to go to my husband's school concert, forget it!"

The burdens are also heavy on the unmarried who, in the eyes of the firm, lack a valid excuse to make room for personal time. One lawyer commented that the demands of the private lives of single women "are not respected."

Because of the pressure and the hours, "many of the women in the firm who do become partners are unmarried or have no children." Thus, one associate noted, "there are virtually no women to look to to determine if it is possible for women attorneys to sustain a satisfying personal and family life while remaining 'on track.'"

According to one partner, however, a "growing number of women here have become partners—admittedly on a delayed track—after having children and going out on maternity leave, etc., as associates." The firm does offer emergency backup childcare.

On the brighter side, a few women at the firm either have it all or feel as if they could. One senior associate with a young child said that mothers do not have to be on the "mommy track" if they don't want to be. A single associate revealed that hope springs eternal: "I don't have a satisfying personal/family life at the moment, but I think I could work it out." One woman partner wrote that her "social life is very, very full," that she has traveled the world, participated on charitable boards, renovated an apartment, dated, and just got engaged.

> *One associate remarked that if an attorney spends too many years on a part-time schedule, she is "likely to be perceived as 'stale' by the firm."*

Flexibility of work arrangements: Part-time exists at Skadden, but goes very much against the grain of the firm, according to most. Of the part-timers who responded to the survey, one declared she "is happy with the arrangement," and is off partnership track. Another part-timer wrote her partner supervisor "encourages part-time for mothers because he knows he'll lose you otherwise—or he'll be paying you for 60 hours a week when you don't have that kind of availability." She continued, "Most (but *not* all) people in the firm are accommodating, even though it's inconvenient" and acknowledged that she is "off partnership track for the time."

Although one full-timer characterized the firm as "extremely generous with part-time arrangements," others did not regard part-time arrangements

as available for the asking. Part-time "mostly works as 'flextime' or work-at-home time, rather than constituting a true 'part-time' arrangement, [as a result of] the demands of the clients and the nature of the work," in the words of one lawyer. A junior associate noted that part-time work arrangements are "not widely advertised to the junior associates and seem to be more a perk offered senior female associates who have already paid their dues in excessive hours."

Another litigator commented that part-timers must be prepared to be "very aggressive defending" their reduced schedules. One associate complained that the part-timers in her department frequently switch days and hours without notice, "leaving the rest of us to deal with their 'fires.'"

Several associates noted that part-timers make sacrifices in terms of the level of work they do. "The work is considered second-rate," observed one senior associate. A corporate attorney agreed: "[Part-timers] get less-respected work."

Working part-time is also said to place partnership out of reach. Part-time attorneys can advance to counsel status only if they bill 1,500 hours a year and cannot advance to partner, according to one associate. Another associate commented, "It seems more equitable to advance an outstanding part-time attorney to counsel, of counsel, or special counsel." One associate remarked that if an attorney spends too many years on a part-time schedule, she is "likely to be perceived as 'stale' by the firm."

> *"...it has been fascinating to see that this Jewish firm is far more tolerant of women than WASPy firms."*

Diversity: Most respondents give Skadden very high marks when it comes to diversity. According to several associates, the firm's tradition of tolerance dates back to its founding in the 1940s, "when the 'white-shoe' firms shunned" Joe Flom. Because the firm's founders, as one associate put it, "were rejects from the Wall Street law firm clubs" of the era, they made a commitment to ensure that attorneys would not be judged on the basis of race, ethnicity, personality, or political leanings. One associate noted that the "nonconformist feel" of the firm is "the main thing I like about [it]."

A few gay respondents wrote that they have never encountered negative reaction to their sexual orientation. One reported that the pictures in her office of her lover "haven't received a smirk or even a pointed comment."

A few litigators noted that while the firm may be tolerant of many forms of diversity, it embraces a rigid notion of what it take to be a good lawyer. One associate wrote, "Litigation is most comfortable with women who are like the men—aggressive, loud, combative. There is really no place for different styles."

Several respondents noted that despite its generally welcoming ethos, the firm has attracted relatively few minority attorneys.

A few associates commented that the firm is largely Jewish. One said that she is "in the minority being a non-Jew. However, it has been fascinating to see that this Jewish firm is far more tolerant of women than WASPy firms."

While most respondents thought Skadden was home to a comfortable mix of political views, one first-year associate commented, "The firm seems most comfortable with women who are willing to operate on men's terms and less welcoming toward outspoken (or even not-so-outspoken) feminists."

"[The] power women [are] accessible, concerned about women's issues and associate issues."

Women in leadership positions: Skadden includes a small number of very powerful women, including one of the firm's highest-paid rainmakers and the head of the New York office. Three women reportedly sit on the firm's policy committee. These partners, by most accounts, are extremely well-regarded both within the firm and in the legal community at large.

While the firm is largely run by white men, there is little dispute that at least a few key female players carry considerable influence. Among the first generation of women partners, however, "none have attained such positions while at the same time raising children," in the words of one lawyer. An associate added that the new generation of women partners includes several who are married and have children, although "it remains to be seen whether they will become the new power elite."

Most associates thought the firm's more powerful women had made considerable efforts to mentor and assist those coming up the ranks. One associate commented, "[The] power women [are] accessible, concerned about women's issues and associate issues." She added that the women have had "several informal meetings, meals, and programs for women at the firm concerning work environment, attrition rates, other issues. The power women are a big part of these programs." Another associate wrote that a group of female partners "promote, from a networking standpoint, the interests of other women."

Women litigators, however, took a dimmer view of the assistance, or lack thereof, they have received from their female higher-ups. One observed, for example, that the group includes "no women of power, [nor is there] mentoring between women. Rather, there is a sense of competition, and women must make a strong effort to meet and bond with other women."

Several initiatives are now underway to remedy what appears to be a perceived deficiency in women's ability to form professional networks that will lead to business. A partner reported, "Several new mentoring initiatives have recently begun and women partners have started to include women associates in special marketing programs aimed at women clients."

Skadden, Arps, Slate, Meagher & Flom No. of Responses: 36	Strongly agree	Agree	Disagree	Strongly disagree
Women's prospects for advancement at the firm are as strong as men's	9	13	7	4
I am satisfied with the firm's family and personal leave policies	4	14	8	4
There are women in positions of power and influence in the firm	20	11	1	1
Women are as likely as men to receive desirable work assignments	15	11	3	3
Women attorneys feel they can discuss family obligations openly	2	12	12	5
Women are as likely as men to be mentored by senior attorneys	11	11	9	3
Women attorneys enjoy a high level of job satisfaction	5	11	10	4
Women in the firm are supportive of their women colleagues	5	19	4	1
Firm management is receptive to the concerns of women attorneys	3	14	10	2

SONNENSCHEIN NATH & ROSENTHAL

Rating: 1

🔨🔨🔨🔨🔨

Sonnenschein Nath & Rosenthal
8000 Sears Tower
Chicago, IL 60606
312-876-8000

No. of Attorneys: 203
No. of Women Attorneys: 68
No. of Partners: 111
No. of Women Partners: 21
No. of Survey Responses Received: 10

Respondent Profile: 7 partners, 2 associates, and 1 counsel responded. Practice areas included corporate, estate planning, environmental, and litigation.

Summary: This was the only firm in which partners so significantly outnumbered associates in responding to our survey. And they almost unanimously painted Sonnenschein as a collegial and supportive firm where women are offered equal opportunities for advancement and career development. It is characterized as the best firm in Chicago with regard to alternative work arrangements, although some perceived a need to improve its promotion of women to leadership positions.

Advancement: Sonnenschein, Nath & Rosenthal is reportedly making few partners all around, but most respondents thought that women who stuck it out full-time enjoyed prospects for progress equal to those of men. One partner, for example, observed, "Currently I don't perceive that the prospects for advancement are very good for anyone, but I don't think that women are more impacted than men for advancement to partnership."

An associate perceived that the likelihood for women to advance depends on the assumption that "the firm is making [anyone] partners." One associate anointed Sonnenschein the best law firm in Chicago for women, saying that it sponsors "all-women outings with clients so that women associates can build relationships with clients."

A corporate partner commented that advancement, assignments, reviews, etc., are "as 'gender-blind' as I could imagine." She said that she frequently staffs deals with all women, and "never has issues internally or with clients." According to another partner, women's opportunities at the firm are "unlimited" and although women have traditionally had to look to men as mentors, the proliferation of women within partnership ranks means this is no longer always the case. According to another partner, "Women are now 'making rain,' the key for advancing the ultimate mile!"

Despite the generally positive outlook, a minority of attorneys identified several factors that may hinder women's advancement at Sonnenschein. One partner remarked that prospects in the litigation group, among others, were dimmer because, in her estimation, in some parts of the firm "a little bit of a 'macho' attitude exists." A litigation associate said that, in her perception, women "are hampered by the lack of the sort of strong relationships with senior partners [with] power and [the] inclination to go to bat for them at crucial moments." Those women who do succeed, in her opinion, "achieve this by finding niches in the work of senior male rainmakers in which they make themselves necessary/indispensable by virtue of administrative and briefing skills."

Although advancement to partnership is said to be relatively egalitarian, rising through the partnership ranks is, in the opinion of some, more difficult for women than for men. One partner commented that prospects for women are not at all good as far as advancement to management is concerned, because "women, (particularly more junior partners) do not seem to be mentored by the more senior men to the extent junior men are, although there are certainly individual deviations from that."

Relationships are "a little formal, never inappropriately familiar, very respectful of gender, race, religious, and ethnic differences."

Attitudes and atmosphere: Many respondents had positive comments about the atmosphere at Sonnenschein, and no significant complaints were voiced. One partner reported that women at the firm enjoy "the best of both worlds" in that they have easy working relationships with male colleagues, as well as "frequent close personal friendships and support" from their female peers. A partner who had worked at several different law firms described it as "the best I've experienced on women's issues" and added that the firm's management is receptive to the issues facing female attorneys, including recruitment, mentoring, and balancing.

Recruiting efforts have apparently paid off: Of the 1997 class of summer associates, a majority are women, according to a junior associate.

Discrimination and harassment are reported to be unheard of at the firm, and men and women interact freely. According to one respondent, relationships are "a little formal, never inappropriately familiar, very respectful of gender, race, religious, and ethnic differences." She commented that the level of respect evident between colleagues is a product of "strong firm leadership and support of what Sonnenschein calls 'citizenship' within the firm."

According to one partner, the firm places a heavy emphasis on getting work done. Although occasional crises may be greeted with sympathy, in her opinion, "women (or men) who are unreliable because of childcare issues will not be treated well."

The firm values "a happy, well-rounded lawyer and is extremely sensitive to the demands of family, parent care, children, and illness on a lawyer's life."

Balancing work & family/personal life: Summing up the views of most respondents, one partner remarked, "The firm is as committed to personal/family life as our large, demanding clients permit us to be." The billable hours requirement is reportedly 2,000 per year but, according to several lawyers, working hours are getting longer and one perceived that "there has been explicit pressure from the top on this lately." The firm's practice is, according to an estate planning partner, "serious, hardworking, demanding, stressful."

Billing and business development pressures are substantial, a partner acknowledged, noting that the "more senior and independent a woman becomes in her practice, the easier it becomes to balance work and family." Most respondents said Sonnenschein's commitment to flexibility is evidenced by its receptivity to part-time work, flextime, generous maternity leaves, telecommuting, and its flexible partnership track.

According to a partner, the firm values "a happy, well-rounded lawyer and is extremely sensitive to the demands of family, parent care, children, and illness on a lawyer's life." And one respondent reported that the firm "provides subsidized emergency childcare."

Nonetheless, working parents have it tough. One partner who has children observed that between "commuting, working and family responsibilities" she doesn't "have enough time for business development, which is pretty much a requirement here." Another partner wrote that when she entered professional life she expected to have to work really hard to have it all. Although she raised her children during "an era when it was not considered acceptable to use childcare needs or a parenting commitment as an excuse," her colleagues did not complain when she disappeared for a few hours to take a child to a doctor's appointment or to attend a school assembly. Today, she wrote, parents can be more open about their family commitments, and the firm remains accommodating.

> *One partner commented that the firm is "generous with granting (unpaid) leaves for things like working on a political campaign or writing a novel."*

Flexibility of work arrangements: The firm is viewed by its attorneys as perhaps the best in Chicago with respect to alternative work arrangements. Sonnenschein lawyers have tried virtually every conceivable schedule, including part-time, flextime, and telecommuting. Such arrangements may be structured on a percentage or hourly basis. Part-timers working 60 percent or more of full-time hours can choose whether to remain on partnership track, although some perceive that the timing of any partnership decision may be delayed because of the part-time stint. The firm apparently has part-timers working at the associate, counsel, and income partner levels, though it appears that part-time may not be available to equity partners. Arrangements, according to a partner, are "flexible and designed to meet the needs of the firm and the individual." Both men and women have managed to make such arrangements work.

All three attorneys who reported having taken advantage of the firm's alternative work schedules reported that they were pleased with their experience. One wrote that she works approximately 80 percent (or 1,500 hours) a year and the firm has been "terrific and accepting of this status, very generous on compensation, great work assignments, etc." Another part-timer reported that she has worked a reduced schedule for years and has "never been asked to work more or been judged unfavorably because of my schedule."

Most full-time respondents had positive impressions about part-time options, and full-time partners reported that part-timers need not consider themselves off partnership track.

Several respondents commented that the firm offers generous maternity and paternity leave. One partner commented that the firm is also "generous with granting (unpaid) leaves for things like working on a political campaign or writing a novel."

One partner appended the firm's written part-time policy to her survey. It states that the firm "views the accommodation of the needs of its lawyers through alternative work arrangements to be in the firm's interest in promoting job satisfaction and employee retention." The policy also affirms that alternative work arrangements may be structured "any number of ways," and describes various types of arrangements that have been successful in the past. Finally, it clarifies that part-time arrangements may be on or off-track, that there is no fixed limit to the use of alternative arrangements, and that compensation and benefits questions will be determined on a case-by-case basis.

Respondents described Sonnenschein as a place that is deeply committed to diversity.

Diversity: Although some believed the firm has experienced some difficulty attracting and retaining minority attorneys, respondents described Sonnenschein as a place that is deeply committed to diversity. According to a partner, at her prior firm "gays were quietly eased out," whereas at a recent Sonnenschein gathering, "there was a publicized

and accepted, open subgroup meeting for gay attorneys, which garnered no comments (or even raised eyebrows)." She attributed this openness to the firm's "long tradition of social liberalism." Another partner wrote that she was attracted to the firm because of its openness to diversity, and that she has not been disappointed: "Women and minority groups have organized to coordinate marketing and other initiatives and are supported by the firm." The firm encompasses "political radicals on both ends of the spectrum," according to one partner, and has done *pro bono* work "on both sides of controversial issues (in different representations)," according to an associate.

Despite its success in achieving diversity along many axes, the firm is, according to a partner, "still working on growing a critical mass of attorneys of color." One associate agreed that, in her opinion, the firm "has had some trouble hiring and keeping minority attorneys." Nevertheless, a respondent who identified herself as a member of a racial minority group reported that she has found tremendous support at the firm.

One partner observed the male leadership "denies there's a glass ceiling, but acknowledged that if the senior women think there is, that is at least an issue that must be addressed."

Women in leadership positions: Women are reportedly not part of the firm's executive committee, and several respondents commented that the firm still has "a way to go" in terms of promoting women to leadership positions. Although a woman sits at the helm of the firm's corporate practice group, in one partner's opinion, this does not constitute real power. Women also serve on the firm's legal development, finance, and limited partner review committees.

Nevertheless, all respondents reported that women are gradually climbing the ladder, and several women partners have achieved considerable stature. One partner observed that while the firm's senior women "perceive a glass ceiling," the male leadership "denies there's a glass ceiling, but acknowledged that if the senior women think there is, that is at least an issue that must be addressed."

Because power at the firm, according to this partner, "boils down to who controls the clients," the women partners—"with strong support from the firm"—have launched a business development initiative. This drive includes regular meetings among women partners from different firm offices, consultations with in-house and outside marketing specialists, seminars focusing on women entrepreneurs, business meetings with potential women clients, and social events with clients revolving around "theater nights instead of hockey tickets."

Sonnenschein Nath & Rosenthal No. of Responses: 10	Strongly agree	Agree	Disagree	Strongly disagree
Women's prospects for advancement at the firm are as strong as men's	7	1	2	
I am satisfied with the firm's family and personal leave policies	8	2	3	1
There are women in positions of power and influence in the firm	5	1		
Women are as likely as men to receive desirable work assignments	7	2	1	
Women attorneys feel they can discuss family obligations openly	7	3		
Women are as likely as men to be mentored by senior attorneys	6	2	2	
Women attorneys enjoy a high level of job satisfaction	6	2	1	
Women in the firm are supportive of their women colleagues	7	3		
Firm management is receptive to the concerns of women attorneys	6	3	1	

STEPTOE & JOHNSON LLP

Rating: 45

◣◣◣

Steptoe & Johnson LLP
1330 Connecticut Ave. NW
Washington, DC 20036
202-429-3000

No. of Attorneys: 213
No. of Women Attorneys: 57
No. of Partners: 95
No. of Women Partners: 13
No. of Survey Responses Received: 12

Respondent Profile: 4 partners and 8 associates responded. Practice areas included litigation, environmental, energy, and transactions.

Summary: Despite its congenial atmosphere and supportiveness of those seeking to juggle work and home life, the partnership door at Steptoe is apparently shut pretty tightly for both men and women. On a brighter note, the number of part-time lawyers, which includes partners, is sizable, and part-timers gave these options high marks.

Advancement: Respondents were split right down the middle regarding women's chances of promotion to partner. One associate claimed that, given the odds against *anyone* making partner, those who opt to take time off for family or other reasons or who work a reduced schedule may fall behind in an already uphill race.

Most respondents thought the criteria for partnership at Steptoe & Johnson—"quality as lawyers, business prospects, [and] contributions to the firm"—were, in themselves, gender-neutral, but that women with families both "opt out of the partnership sweepstakes" of their own initiative and are at risk of being perceived as less qualified to merit promotion. To succeed, one must be willing to put "family issues in the background," in the view of a junior associate.

Women who do make it are those who have "stayed the course and have aggressively pursued it," and who are in growth areas for the firm. Others get channeled into "reasonably secure alternative career moves (to counsel status)" that allow "super senior associates to remain at the firm," according to one respondent. By two accounts, these moves are becoming increasingly common for the firm's women.

As far as assignments, mentoring, and reviews go, women are reportedly treated equally in the eyes of a solid majority of respondents. One associate, however, feared that women "are held to a higher standard of work quality, intellect, personality fit, and dedication than men."

> *For associates, Steptoe & Johnson is said to be "very comfortable as long as you don't expect to be made partner..."*

321

Attitudes and atmosphere: Descriptions of Steptoe & Johnson's environment for women ranged from satisfactory to very comfortable. Several respondents reported that they are unaware of any manifestations of gender discrimination. The presence of women at all levels in the firm hierarchy has created a climate wherein women are fully involved in firm life, according to several respondents.

At the partnership level, there is reportedly collegiality and an understanding of the extra demands on women with children. According to an associate, however, it appears as if those women elevated in the past "had to become 'one of the boys' " in order to make partner. For associates, Steptoe is said to be "very comfortable as long as you don't expect to be made partner (true for men as well as women)," as one midlevel associate put it.

Female and male colleagues are said to enjoy positive relationships. According to several respondents, women at the firm are neither nurtured nor coddled.

An associate commented that while women receive no special support, they are "treated with respect and asked to make the same sacrifices as men are." According to a junior associate's perception, however, many of the male partners see themselves as father figures for female associates. She added that this could work to her advantage insofar as these men "try to teach me and look out for my best interests." It raises the question, however, of whether they will stay supportive once she and her colleagues begin to progress in the firm.

One associate was concerned that a group of young male partners has created "a bit of a 'boys' club,' " but added that their clubbiness takes place after hours and off the premises and does not stem from unfriendliness toward women. One partner reported, "[A] small club of men dominates," although lip service is paid to democracy. One associate agreed, expressing her anxiety that the firm has no mechanism through which women associates can raise their concerns, apart from the associates committee "where they don't seem to come up."

> *One associate with children reported that when significant family issues arose for her, the firm was very accommodating.*

Balancing work & family/personal life: The firm does a good job of trying to support attorneys faced with the very difficult task of balancing family life with the "long hours, travel, and last-minute flexibility" required. Most partners are said to be sensitive to the fact that lawyers have extra demands on their time. Generally, the importance of family is recognized, wrote one partner, "but workaholism leaves little free time."

The firm is said to offer generous and flexible maternity leave, and provides backup childcare for emergencies. According to one partner, the firm gets high marks on family issues "for a big firm, as long as attorneys don't abuse special arrangements."

One associate with children reported that when significant family issues arose for her, the firm was very accommodating. Another associate with children commented that, at 80 percent, her hours are "regular and low enough" to enable her to spend quality time with her children. She added that when emergencies such as a sick nanny arise, the firm has been flexible.

Part-time is used at the associate level and by at least three partners, and has also been taken advantage of by men.

Flexibility of work arrangements: Part-time is said to be fairly widely used at Steptoe, but respondents seemed to perceive it in widely varying ways. According to Steptoe's written part-time policy, attorneys are permitted to reduce their schedules down to approximately 80 percent of minimum billable hours. As a practical matter, however, on a case-by-case basis, the firm has approved part-time arrangements entailing hours as low as 55 percent. Part-time is used at the associate level and by at least three partners, and has also been taken advantage of by men. The firm also reportedly has a female attorney who works primarily from home. A part-time partner remarked that her arrangement has worked fairly well and that when she has been "over budget," it has been a result of client, rather than firm, demands.

One associate reported that last year a partner went on an 80-percent schedule but billed "much more than 100 percent of hours." She added, "Even if you can negotiate such a deal, the day-to-day maintenance of it is a constant struggle."

Another associate with children, who is on an 80-percent schedule, finds it "an ideal balance of work and home." She reports that, with the exception of occasional nights and weekends, her schedule is generally regular and is respected by her supervising attorneys.

While there are tradeoffs in terms of assignments, salary, and the duration of the road to partnership, part-time is said not to constitute an absolute or permanent barrier to promotion. Some part-timers choose to delay their consideration for partnership but, according to one associate, it is not clear if this is expected for those who work part-time.

Although part-time is "not looked down on," by one account, there is apparently pressure for reduced-hours attorneys to take on amounts of work that tend to stretch their hours. In the opinions of some, however, part-time is available only selectively. A partner said an attorney can reduce her hours if she had small children, but thereafter, if she's not a workaholic, she may be perceived as not being serious about the practice of law. One associate believed that part-time is available only in certain practice groups and only to those "who have proven themselves invaluable."

Several respondents observed that there is no mold for attorneys here and that the environment is very tolerant.

Diversity: A clear picture of diversity at Steptoe & Johnson did not emerge, because most associates wrote little or nothing in response to this question. One partner maintained that the firm is diverse, commenting that there are conservative Republicans and very liberal Democrats, as well as "married, single, women with significant-other roommates, etc.—a real cross section of personal situations and styles."

The firm is a welcoming environment for second-career attorneys. There are reportedly few openly gay lawyers at Steptoe. Several respondents observed that there is no mold for attorneys here, and that the environment at the firm is very tolerant. One associate remarked that the firm has sought to improve the diversity of its attorney pool and has been "moderately successful."

The firm's senior-most females were described as "very powerful [and] highly regarded both inside and outside the firm."

Women in leadership positions: Apparently, a handful of Steptoe & Johnson's women are real power brokers. Women reportedly sit on the firm's executive committee and head several other committees, including compensation. The firm's senior-most females were described as "very powerful [and] highly regarded both inside and outside the firm." The relatively recent appointment of a woman partner from Steptoe as United States Trade Representative has led to "recognition of the fact that women partners are important," as one respondent observed.

A partner wrote, "Women's issues are clearly advanced by the partners," but that it is not clear the extent to which more junior women are "helped concretely" by their female superiors. Another partner commented that younger women "may not be aware of all the senior women have done and do."

One respondent was concerned that the women in power "share values/ problems of the ruling men," and an associate feared that the women partners do not appear to help promote opportunities for other women. She added that, in her opinion, the women partners suffer from the attitude of having arrived where they are "the hard way, so why should they help you." According to one associate, the women partners are "very busy," making mentoring difficult to come by. There are reportedly no firm-sponsored female-bonding events, leaving it up to individuals to seek role models among the female partnership.

Steptoe & Johnson No. of Responses: 12	Strongly agree	Agree	Disagree	Strongly disagree
Women's prospects for advancement at the firm are as strong as men's	3	3	5	1
I am satisfied with the firm's family and personal leave policies	3	8	1	
There are women in positions of power and influence in the firm	5	5	2	
Women are as likely as men to receive desirable work assignments	5	3	2	1
Women attorneys feel they can discuss family obligations openly	3	4	2	1
Women are as likely as men to be mentored by senior attorneys	4	5	1	1
Women attorneys enjoy a high level of job satisfaction	2	3	7	
Women in the firm are supportive of their women colleagues	2	6	3	1
Firm management is receptive to the concerns of women attorneys	3	4	2	1

STOEL RIVES LLP

Rating: 36

♟♟♟

Stoel Rives LLP
900 SW Fifth Ave.
Suite 2300
Portland, OR 97204
503-224-3380

No. of Attorneys: 156
No. of Women Attorneys: 36
No. of Partners: 98
No. of Women Partners: 22
No. of Survey Responses Received: 7

Respondent Profile: 4 partners and 3 associates responded. Practice areas included business, labor and employment, trusts and estates, environmental, and corporate.

Summary: Our small sample of respondents, more than half of whom were partners, characterized Stoel Rives as a collegial and relatively stress-free firm where women have an equal shot at partnership. Described as a trailblazer in hiring and promoting women lawyers to positions of power, Stoel Rives, in the opinion of some respondents, has retreated from this progressive tradition on the diversity front. The firm's flexible work arrangements, although available and enjoyed by several partners, are perceived to be out of reach at the associate level.

Advancement: For women who stick it out, prospects at Stoel Rives are reportedly as good as for men, if not better. "Compared to other firms I know, we are light-years ahead," wrote one partner. Several respondents made comments to the effect that highly respected male business and trial lawyers at the firm have mentored women and that women are now playing these roles as well. Advancement criteria for men and women are reported to be uniform, and assignments and reviews are apparently handled impartially.

Attrition at the associate level is high, reportedly as a result of the reluctance of many attorneys to put in the long hours required for partnership. In recent years, however, men have also left, "wanting more family or personal time," reported one respondent.

According to one associate, "Superstars at the firm are frequently women," although she perceived that those who are not in the top 10 percent must put in tremendous hours.

> *"[The] types of concerns you seem to have in mind are virtually nonexistent here."*

Attitudes and atmosphere: Perceptions regarding the comfort level for women at Stoel Rives varied between associates and partners, although most expressed satisfaction with the firm's atmosphere. It was reportedly the first large firm in Portland to hire women attorneys during the 1960s and, thus, has long experience with a gender-integrated workplace. Women attorneys work in all practice areas, and the firm has a sizable number of women partners.

Although one partner claimed that the "types of concerns you seem to have in mind are virtually nonexistent here," a couple of associates disagreed, characterizing social events and "retreat free-time activities" as definitely male-oriented." One associate suggested that when groups of women attorneys try to get together, there is a "backlash."

Nevertheless, it was clearly the majority view that discrimination does not exist and that women are very conformable at the firm.

> *"This impact on family life appears to be more keenly felt when it is Mom who is away rather than Dad."*

Balancing work & family/personal life: Although hours are relatively reasonable, sustaining a life outside the firm remains challenging, especially for associates. "No Portland law firm bills East Coast hours, so the basic expectation is lower," according to one partner.

However, according to some respondents, the expectation is not low enough. Although the firm has, in the words of one partner, "always had a broad range in the number of hours lawyers devote to practicing law," of late, some respondents perceived that the firm has been stepping up pressure on attorneys to increase their billables. One corporate partner commented that the "needs of clients and competitive pressure in a practice like this do not always end at 5 or 6 p.m."

In addition to getting their work done, women are apparently expected to be involved in client development and in nurturing business relationships. Nonetheless, according to one partner, "If you 'want it all,' this is one of the better places to practice." She explained that the firm sees an advantage in supporting new parents "on the theory that those lawyers, once back in full-time practice, will be valuable members of the firm." Balancing work and family in this climate is tough and may also require, in the words of one partner, "passing on the high-stress, travel-intensive large business or trial work."

Associates were considerably less optimistic about the potential for striking a balance between work and personal life. One opined, "There's not a partner (male or female) at the firm with whom I work that appears to have the type of satisfying personal/family life that I seek. Those who have a personal/family life appear to be extremely pressured to fit it in with work." Another associate perceived that seeking any accommodations for family life "hurts both men and women. Until men ask for it, women fall behind by comparison."

Another associate was concerned that "this impact on family life appears to be more keenly felt when it is Mom who is away rather than Dad." She further perceived that to progress at Stoel Rives, "one must act like the men in devotion to work vs. family. Not always an option!"

Senior partners appear to have an easier time of it. One partner with kids wrote that she tries to "ignore" the mounting pressure for billables, and that the heaviest pressure comes from clients, not the firm.

An associate wrote that she would not take advantage of part-time options for fear that she would be "viewed as not having the commitment to the firm."

Flexibility of work arrangements: Respondents expressed radically differing viewpoints regarding the practicality of part-time work at Stoel Rives. The picture that emerged suggests that part-time and other alternative arrangements are more readily available at partnership than at associate level. One partner wrote, "Yes, Yes, Yes," in response to this question and added that she works four days per week.

Another respondent related that one partner has taken three maternity leaves of three to four months' duration and worked half-time for six months due to a child's illness. She has also worked at an 80-percent level "in various combinations," including four-day weeks. Currently, she works a five-day schedule with "flexibility for school events" and other activities with a half-afternoon off per week and no weekends or evenings at the firm.

Another respondent reported that a partner worked part-time for three of her associate years in order to raise her children. She made income partner as a part-timer and was promoted to capital partner a year after returning to full-time work. According to the firm's policy, she reported, "a part-time partner with enough years and experience under her belt can become a capital partner."

Some respondents questioned the practicality of such arrangements. One partner perceived that part-time arrangements are made available only from time to time and almost exclusively when they involve new mothers. She added that part-time stints can extend into leaves of absence of four to six months, and that leaves of up to two years have occasionally been allowed. She cautioned, however, that, in her estimation, the "economic impact of these leaves and part-time arrangements on the firm and the impact on career development is a source of ongoing concern and discussion."

An associate commented that she was not aware that such part-time options existed and that, in any event, she would not take advantage of them for fear that she would "be viewed as not having the commitment to the firm." Another associate expressed the concern that, despite the existence of part-timers in the partnership ranks, "part-time status seems to impact getting to be account head, working for better clients, etc."

Although part-time is apparently available for limited periods to associates who are beyond entry level, an associate said that, in her opinion, "Individual partners informally discourage it and it can delay partnership consideration."

Another associate concurred, suggesting that part-time and other alternative work arrangements are rare and "a complete career-killer if taken advantage of (partnership track would be forever lost)."

"The attitude [as I perceive it is]: 'We just hire and promote the best candidates, and if they happen to be white males with stay-at-home-wives, so be it.' "

Diversity: The partners and associates were split on their assessments of diversity at Stoel Rives. The partners concluded that, because the city of Portland as a whole boasts little ethnic diversity, the firm is "probably *the* most tolerant/supportive firm in Portland on ethnic, political, or life style matters." One partner explained that the firm has a long tradition of tolerance of diverse politics, and "to some extent," diverse personalities. Acknowledging that, in her opinion, "our track record with minorities is not as good," she nevertheless contended that the firm has been a leader with respect to women. In the mid-1980s, when other major firms had two or fewer female partners, Stoel Rives had several.

Associates were more cynical on this topic. According to an associate, "Partners are human; they support those who are like them (predominantly male and white) because it validates their interests, choices, and sacrifices they have made." Another associate said that, in her opinion, in response to the firm's attention in past years to diversify its hiring, "there has been a backlash." She reported that although Stoel Rives embraces those with wide-ranging political views, hobbies, and personalities, in her opinion, it lacks a commitment to diversity with respect to race, gender, and sexual orientation: "The attitude [as I perceive it is]: 'We just hire and promote the best candidates, and if they happen to be white males with stay-at-home-wives, so be it.'"

> *In contrast to many firms, partnership ranks at Stoel Rives include several women who reportedly wield true power.*

Women in leadership positions: In contrast to many firms, partnership ranks

at Stoel Rives include several women who reportedly wield true power. There is a woman managing partner in charge of the firm's Portland office "who is highly regarded," according to one respondent, and other women in the firm play management roles and "head up major clients." Women also reportedly lead or co-lead several subgroups. In the opinion of one partner, "Not surprisingly, some of the most successful women are single, no kids." Nevertheless, these women, in her view, "tend to be sympathetic to family issues and equity issues."

One associate took a dimmer view, suggesting that the firm does include women who are powerful but that these women "do not appear committed to improving and modifying the old-boy culture." Another associate remarked that, although the influential female partners "are all very accessible to women," in her estimation, none of them has "made a stand for women or on women's issues."

Stoel Rives No. of Responses: 7	Strongly agree	Agree	Disagree	Strongly disagree
Women's prospects for advancement at the firm are as strong as men's	1	3	3	
I am satisfied with the firm's family and personal leave policies	4	1		1
There are women in positions of power and influence in the firm	4	3		
Women are as likely as men to receive desirable work assignments	1	6		
Women attorneys feel they can discuss family obligations openly		3	3	1
Women are as likely as men to be mentored by senior attorneys	3	2	1	1
Women attorneys enjoy a high level of job satisfaction	1	5	1	
Women in the firm are supportive of their women colleagues	2	5		
Firm management is receptive to the concerns of women attorneys	1	4	2	

SULLIVAN & CROMWELL

Rating: 30

Sullivan & Cromwell
125 Broad St.
New York, NY 10004
212-558-4000

No. of Attorneys: 317
No. of Women Attorneys: 70
No. of Partners: 90
No. of Women Partners: 4
No. of Survey Responses Received: 19

Respondent Profile: 2 partners and 17 associates responded. Practice areas included corporate, estates and personal, litigation, banking, and mergers and acquisitions.

Summary: Sullivan & Cromwell, an hospitable firm for women lawyers, is said to be a model of meritocracy for women who can sustain the frenzied pace. Despite the overwhelming hours, the firm reportedly recognizes its lawyers' responsibilities outside of work. Some associates were in the dark about part-time options, although a partner claimed they've been available for a decade. Senior women received distinctly mixed reviews.

Advancement: A large majority of respondents described Sullivan & Cromwell as a meritocracy. Women who have the stamina and determination to make it through eight years of hard work and intense pressure are said to be on as strong a footing for partnership as men. In a first-year associate's estimation, women are treated "equally as well, or as poorly, as male associates at S & C." She commented that those who "can survive the intellectual rigors and the demanding hours can flourish. Regardless of gender, you simply have to be tough."

During the last round, three out of eight partners promoted by S & C were women, according to a partner who added that this was a "very high percentage in relation to the representation of women at the firm."

Several associates reported that they were very satisfied with the quality of the assignments they have received. According to a first-year corporate attorney, gender does not play a role "in the allocation of assignments for junior associates." An associate reported receiving "more responsibility than many of my male peers on account of proven capabilities." Another associate, however, said that, in her opinion, "it's difficult to tell whether prejudice operates at high levels with regard to assignments."

Mentoring at S & C, on the other hand, received mixed reviews. According to one junior litigator, there is "little mentoring of *anyone* at S & C, male or female." Another associate said that, in her opinion, "[Women are] less likely to be mentored and, therefore, less likely to advance to partnership." A midlevel associate believed that mentoring was more available from men than women because "it seems sometimes like women partners are too busy working [to take part in] mentor-type relationships." According to partners, however, mentoring opportunities are meted out equally.

> *If you accept that the "demands of New York practice are never a 'comfortable fit,' " S & C is a "comfortable" place to work.*

Attitudes and atmosphere: Respondents were, on the whole, overwhelmingly pleased with the firm's work environment. According to one junior corporate associate, if you accept that the "demands of New York practice are never a 'comfortable fit,' " S & C is a "comfortable" place to work.

S & C has managed to steer clear of virtually all manifestations of gender discrimination, according to most. In the words of one partner, it is "well-understood that the firm does not tolerate any discrimination or other conduct that would make S & C an uncomfortable place for women." One associate observed that the positive tone set by the firm is enhanced by the women partners who "play a big part in the partnership and are good role models." A senior associate recalled that over the years, "occasional instances of inappropriate remarks," when reported, resulted in the offending party being "condemned roundly and the women supported."

Several associates commented on the collegial and supportive relationships that they enjoy with their male counterparts. A junior associate said that she has "always been treated respectfully by both male partners and associates and shares numerous wonderful friendships and working relationships" with male colleagues. Another junior associate reported that one of her male colleagues immediately rose to her defense to "correct a client's assumption that I was merely a 'witness' rather than a lawyer."

Several lawyers were less enthusiastic about the atmosphere at S & C. A corporate associate believed there is, in her opinion, "a bit of a 'boys' club' in certain corporate practices." Another stated that women "prepared to 'do business' by the boys' rules are fine." Yet another claimed that, in her opinion, some men have become "lecherous" at firm outings.

On a more subtle level, a litigator reported that, in her estimation, "women appear to get more 'document'-type assignments [and] less court time." Another litigator feared that two areas of the firm—litigation, which she perceived to have a " 'boys' club' atmosphere," and project finance, where, she asserted, women do not get staffed on deals—are "difficult areas for women to work."

> *"S & C is a service-oriented firm, specializing in complex matters, and is not naturally designed to accommodate flexible schedules."*

Balancing work & family/personal life: Unpredictable and voluminous hours required by S & C reportedly pose a serious challenge to those seeking to sustain a personal life, but no consensus emerged as to the firm's role in alleviating these conditions. Several lawyers conceded that the firm's hours are grueling and variable, but attributed this to the nature of the beast. One partner summed up the views of several by writing, "S & C is a service-oriented firm, specializing in complex matters, and is not naturally designed to accommodate flexible schedules." Nevertheless, she added, the firm has, in her view, "shown great flexibility."

Several lawyers praised the firm for its sensitivity toward family responsibilities. One partner noted that the firm has a "work environment which has traditionally recognized that we all have families." Lawyers are "encouraged to seek a balanced life style, to take vacations, etc., since the work can be very demanding," in the words of a junior associate. She added that male partners are *"extremely* sensitive to family responsibilities," which apparently manifests itself in their bringing their own children to the office on weekends.

Several associates were less upbeat about their ability to strike a healthy balance between work and home. One lawyer said she perceived the firm to be "generally still run from a male perspective," because the belief system is that "clients are only satisfied if the project that came in the door today is completed by tomorrow." This attitude, in her view, is "self-perpetuating, since most women who stay long enough to become partner view the world from a similar perspective."

A midlevel associate said her experience was similar: "[The] unpredictability and length of the working hours" make family life "nearly impossible unless you are more senior than a fifth-year." In short, one "cannot come into work and *expect* to leave at any given time," in the words of a senior associate.

According to a junior corporate associate, "[The] work demands 100 percent of your time and commitment [which is]

not exactly family-friendly for *any* of the lawyers." The chance of achieving some sort of balance varies from "somewhat to very difficult," with the general practice and litigation groups being "*very* demanding" on one's time, according to a midlevel lawyer.

> *Part-time options are reportedly available on a case-by-case basis and do not appear to be not widely used.*

Flexibility of work arrangements: Part-time options are reportedly available on a case-by-case basis, and associates perceived that they were not widely used at S & C. Such arrangements have been officially available to associates for 10 years, according to a partner, who added that these options are "encouraged for associates as a means of addressing work/family issues." She added that several women currently work part-time in arrangements "that appear to be successful."

Several associates were in the dark about the firm's policies in this area. A midlevel associate reported that she only knew about part-time arrangements through word of mouth, adding that the firm's policy book states, "Part-time work will only be considered for women with children." Nevertheless, the one part-timer responding to the survey stated that she does not have children. And the firm stated its part-time policy was *not* limited to women with children.

Associate respondents gave widely varying responses about the feasibility and professional consequences of going part-time. On the positive side, a senior woman lawyer reportedly "works four days a week and is still considered and acknowledged to be the best at the type of work she does," according to a first-year associate. Another junior associate observed that partners "seem to make an effort to keep part-time women involved/staffed on deals."

Shortcomings associated with going part-time were attributed to client demands, incompatibility of certain practice areas, and a perceived lack of cultural acceptance within S & C. According to a junior lawyer, the clients, who "expect lawyers to be on-call 24 hours a day, seven days a week," not the firm, are the source of the difficulty in making part-time arrangements work. A securities lawyer reported that she had not exercised part-time options "because such a schedule would not be compatible" with her practice.

As to the effects of going part-time on partnership prospects, one midlevel litigator wryly remarked that she could not tell whether exercising such an option "hurts your chances, because you have no chances anyway."

S & C has reportedly led the way "in promoting equal benefits for and social integration of gay lawyers and their partners..."

....

Diversity: S & C, which has reportedly adopted a *laisez faire* approach towards diversity, is home to lawyers with a wide range of political leanings and personalities, yet few racial minorities. The firm has taken some affirmative steps, such as requiring diversity training and issuing formal policies to accept and respect life style and background diversity, according to a partner.

Although S & C shows no signs of any racial or other prejudice, according to a corporate associate, "the firm is overwhelmingly white and conservative." Another respondent had a distinctly different impression, reporting, "[The] name plates on the wall read like the United Nations," and concluding, "[The firm] must be doing something right."

S & C's political affiliations and beliefs are said to span the spectrum. One respondent who described herself as "a staunch Republican" reported that she has "found many who agree and disagree with my stances..." On the flip side, a respondent who described herself as very liberal also noted she is vocal about her politics.

As for sexual orientation, S & C has reportedly led the way "in promoting equal benefits for and social integration of gay lawyers and their partners, and in providing all lawyers the opportunity to pursue their political or other opinions in *pro bono* activities." The firm includes "several gay partners and a Gay and Lesbian Group."

"Several women partners go out of their way to assure that women associates are receiving interesting work and are happy at the firm."

....

Women in leadership positions: Several associates had nothing but praise for their senior colleagues. They said the senior women partners were highly regarded and strong. A first-year corporate associate reported that several women partners "have unimpeachable reputations within the firm." Another associate described the firm's senior women as "very supportive of other women at S & C" and said that "several women partners go out of their way to assure that women associates are receiving interesting work and are happy at the firm."

The senior women were also praised for hosting "formal and informal get-togethers for the female associates." In addition, junior female associates are also reportedly assigned a female senior associate mentor. One woman partner in particular was cited by a first-year associate as having "taken an active role in ensuring that women at the firm continue to be treated as equals and with respect," including making herself approachable on gender issues and taking "the lead in the summer program in recruiting women."

An equal number of associates were less enthusiastic about the efforts of the firm's senior women. One observed, "We need more women partners, obviously—and more pointers from existing partners on how to survive in the system." Another said that, in her perception, "there is definitely not enough" woman-to-woman mentoring. An associate agreed that the most senior women are "too busy to mentor." A midlevel associate said that she had observed that, although one woman partner "has been trying to promote flexible work arrangements, [a] few other female partners actually oppose such efforts." According to another midlevel associate, the "most talented and dynamic female I know is perceived as 'difficult' by male colleagues." She is, however, "an excellent mentor."

Sullivan & Cromwell No. of Responses: 19	Strongly agree	Agree	Disagree	Strongly disagree
Women's prospects for advancement at the firm are as strong as men's	6	8	3	1
I am satisfied with the firm's family and personal leave policies	9	8	1	
There are women in positions of power and influence in the firm	5	5	6	3
Women are as likely as men to receive desirable work assignments	11	4	4	
Women attorneys feel they can discuss family obligations openly	5	5	6	1
Women are as likely as men to be mentored by senior attorneys	7	5	5	1
Women attorneys enjoy a high level of job satisfaction	4	10	3	1
Women in the firm are supportive of their women colleagues	7	9	1	1
Firm management is receptive to the concerns of women attorneys	6	5	2	1

SUTHERLAND, ASBILL & BRENNAN LLP

Rating: 16

◣◣◣◣

Sutherland, Asbill & Brennan LLP
999 Peachtree St., NE
Atlanta, GA 30309
404-853-8000

No. of Attorneys: 128
No. of Women Attorneys: 32
No. of Partners: 68
No. of Women Partners: 8
No. of Survey Responses Received: 12

Respondent Profile: 4 partners, 7 associates, and 1 respondent who did not identify her position responded. Practice areas included litigation and tax, among others.

Summary: With a cadre of influential, senior women setting the tone, women lawyers are said to feel right at home here. Sutherland, Asbill & Brennan is apparently a thoroughly pleasant workplace, receptive to the concerns of women lawyers, and sensitive to the burdens of those seeking to juggle work and family life. Respondents disagreed on the practicality of the part-time policy, however, especially on whether it marginalizes such workers and whether it will affect partnership prospects.

Advancement: Respondents' perceptions of women's advancement potential at Sutherland varied, though an overwhelming majority were positive. An associate seemed to sum it up best, commenting, "[The] legal profession unfortunately is not yet an 'even playing field' for women, but I believe that the ground is more even here than at other firms." The partners who responded tended not to perceive a "difference in prospects based on sex," in the words of one. According to another, "Women are, to some extent, more likely to advance to partnership. Some of this is basically self-selection: We work very hard to ensure that our work-product is equal to or better" than the men's. She added that the presence of women in positions of authority at client companies "has made even the less progressive aware of women as business-getters."

Associates emphasized that mentoring is critical for advancement, and that women must look to the women partners to provide the support they need. A first-year litigator wrote, "Getting a mentor is very important to one's success here, as is working with a number of partners. You need someone to champion your 'cause,' and you need exposure to a lot of the partners who will someday vote on your entrance into the ranks, if that is your goal." She added that most female partners are "very supportive and encouraging of young female associates."

A midlevel litigator agreed that many of the women partners are "active in mentoring women associates, as are most men partners." A senior litigator concluded that women are as likely to advance as men, that assignments and reviews are handed out impartially, and that the factors central to promotion are "business development ability and track record, specialization in a useful or important area, and quality of work product." An associate in a smaller department commented that for those who "take the initiative to go after work and mentoring," chances for advancement are good. She added that she has developed mentoring relationships with more than one partner and has never felt that she has "been 'shortchanged' in the way of quality work assignments due to gender."

A few associates were critical of the firm with regard to mentoring and business development opportunities for women lawyers. One respondent feared that the firm's emphasis on business generation puts women at a disadvantage because they are excluded from "the kinds of mentoring relationships that lead to clients accepting the associate as a substitute for the partner, and to partners giving the associate the business. The vast majority of female associates serve partners' needs for work, and it stops there." One litigator remarked that women are "beginning to make inroads on advancement to partnership." She added that, in her opinion, the "influence of gender on those decisions" depends on the lawyers with whom one works.

According to several respondents, the interactions between men and women at the firm at all levels are "easy and informal."

Attitudes and atmosphere: Virtually all respondents spoke highly of the atmosphere here. The firm's leadership was praised as "receptive to women's concerns," as exemplified by the formation of a women's issues committee several years ago. The firm has a relatively large number of women, particularly in the litigation department, and a number of women partners who are assertive and enjoy "influence throughout the firm," as one partner put it.

According to several respondents, the interactions between men and women at the firm at all levels are "easy and informal." One associate wrote, "As a woman, I feel no discomfort in walking into any conversation." She added that she has "made friends of both sexes and I think that is the common pattern." A midlevel associate commented that the firm is "more of a 'family' firm than most of the other big firms in Atlanta; most of the attorneys, male and female, are very involved in family activities and not very interested in 'good old boy' activities."

Several partners commented that the firm's management takes a hard line on gender insensitivity at all levels. One reported, "Partners have been told to change their behavior, as have associates."

Although they found the firm very comfortable on a daily basis, several associates perceived segregation of the sexes on a social level. One senior associate remarked, "The personal friendships where the firm's business really gets done are still among men." A litigator agreed: "There is some tendency to overlook women in making social or business development plans." According to a junior litigator, "There will always be a 'boys' club' in every large firm but there are enough women here who look out for each other and take an interest in a young associate's professional development to counteract at least some of the disadvantages of being left out of [it]. On a professional level, the male partners seem to be very fair."

> *A partner described the firm as "probably as sensitive to family issues as any large commercial practice firm."*

Balancing work & family/personal life: Several respondents lauded Sutherland for its sensitivity to outside responsibilities. One attorney characterized the firm as "probably the healthiest large firm environment one could hope for." A partner described the firm as "probably as sensitive to family issues as any large commercial practice firm."

The firm's billable requirement—1,800 hours per year—is reportedly among the lowest in Atlanta. Several respondents commented that the firm offers great flexibility in terms of hours. One remarked, "It is okay to leave for a school play, for example, as long as you don't leave a client hanging." A partner agreed that time management is left up to the individual attorney, "so leaving to care for sick children, to keep appointments, or to hear your 4-year-old give the weather report during circle [time] on her gold star day (as I often do) is not a problem."

One associate reported that family commitments are "accepted and appreciated," and that "children frequently come to visit Mom or Dad, and toddlers get lots of attention." Another associate commented that she has been able to schedule work around family needs and has never been asked to "unschedule a vacation" and that, for these reasons, she "would not leave this firm for another large firm unless some extraordinary circumstances arose."

Achieving the balance requires help, one partner commented, noting, "There are a few excellent schools and day-care facilities near our office, but many people prefer in-home assistance." One partner commented, "More and more of our young married male associates are coming to grips with the problems inherent in long hours and a family." She added that attorneys' ability to sustain family life often depends on the people with whom they work and how assertive they are. One associate suggested that women can discuss family obligations, "but probably can't get by with too many requests for 'leniency.' The only form of 'mommy track' is part-time."

> *The firm is "fairly flexible and whatever deal an attorney can negotiate for herself or himself is what is acceptable."*

Flexibility of work arrangements: Part-time arrangements are reportedly available and utilized, but some characterized them negatively. Attorneys may reportedly work on part-time schedules for a maximum of two years, a restriction that one senior associate described as the firm's way of discouraging reduced schedules. Part-time is "available although not encouraged as permanent arrangements," reported one partner, adding that the firm is "fairly flexible and whatever deal an attorney can negotiate for herself or himself is what is acceptable." An associate faulted the part-time policy as, in her opinion, "ill-conceived and not particularly useful for women looking for long-term solutions."

Respondents were split on whether the firm marginalizes part-time workers and were uncertain about its effect on partnership prospects. One associate praised the firm for resisting "the urge of some to treat our part-time lawyers as unimportant" by, for example, rejecting a proposal to put part-timers in paralegal offices. Another associate believed, however, "Satisfaction of part-time attorneys varies tremendously, and there is an undercurrent of feeling that part-time attorneys are not accorded equal respect." Another associate was concerned that the impact of part-time status "on ultimate partnership decisions is unclear, since many of these arrangements are fairly new."

One partner reportedly took a six-month leave after the birth of a child and "returned to the firm with no loss of time towards partnership." Another partner reported that her hours "vary depending on both work and family obligations" and that she has not been "penalized for these variations."

> *According to a senior associate, "Differences are respected and tolerated by the great majority of attorneys here."*

Diversity: Although lacking in racial diversity, Sutherland is reportedly home to lawyers of diverse political leanings and personality types. According to the opinion of one associate, "The firm is expanding its diversity, but like other firms, especially in the South, it is mostly filled with heterosexual WASPs." A partner suggested, "The firm needs to continue its efforts to attract more minority attorneys."

In terms of personalities and politics, the firm is reportedly diverse. The firm encompasses women "from prim and proper, to 'soccer mom,' to relaxed and easy-going, liberal, and conservative," wrote one associate. A partner remarked that the firm has "women attorneys of varying backgrounds and ethnic and religious heritage: African-American, Indian, Jewish." She added that the firm covers "the spectrum of political activity, although we do not have many on the far right."

An associate commented that "*pro bono* activities of all sorts are supported." According to a senior associate, "Differences are respected and tolerated by the great majority of attorneys here. I have always felt this to be one of the firm's greatest strengths." A litigator agreed that the firm "encourages independent thinking and diversity" and reported that she has always "felt very comfortable being myself here."

> *"The one weak spot in the situation [for women at the firm] is the lack of a 'critical mass' of women partners, especially in positions of power."*

Women in leadership positions: Although the lone woman on Sutherland's executive committee just ended her term, women have other committee posts and one woman chairs a firm committee, according to respondents. The percentage of women in the partnership is "small but growing," as one lawyer put it. A senior associate observed, "The one weak spot in the situation [for women at the firm] is the lack of a 'critical mass' of women partners, especially in positions of power." She added, however, that the number of women partners "has almost doubled" during her years at the firm, and she is optimistic that women will continue to make inroads, as a result of the firm's recognition of "the need for improvement in this area."

According to another associate's perception, "Women are not generally in the highest positions of power in the firm. As a result, policies that affect primarily women are not as accommodating as they could be (for example, part-time). Some female partners exercise leadership skills but not generally to promote the quality of life of women in particular." An associate commented that, in her estimation, the firm has just one woman "intellectual powerhouse, who is especially supportive of young associates." According to several respondents, the more influential women in the firm have worked well together and have actively sought to support the younger women in the firm.

According to a partner, "Women are generally perceived as tough when they do the same things men do that go unremarked." She added, "On the whole," however, women lawyers are "looked at as individuals, not just women lawyers."

Sutherland, Asbill & Brennan No. of Responses: 12	Strongly agree	Agree	Disagree	Strongly disagree
Women's prospects for advancement at the firm are as strong as men's	5	5	2	
I am satisfied with the firm's family and personal leave policies	4	6	2	
There are women in positions of power and influence in the firm	3	5	3	1
Women are as likely as men to receive desirable work assignments	6	6		
Women attorneys feel they can discuss family obligations openly	4	7	1	
Women are as likely as men to be mentored by senior attorneys	4	5	2	1
Women attorneys enjoy a high level of job satisfaction	3	8		
Women in the firm are supportive of their women colleagues	8	4		
Firm management is receptive to the concerns of women attorneys	5	4	2	

TESTA, HURWITZ & THIBEAULT LLP

Rating: 60

↖↖

Testa, Hurwitz & Thibeault LLP
High Street Tower
125 High St.
Boston, MA 02110
617-248-7000

No. of Attorneys: 196
No. of Women Attorneys: 74
No. of Partners: 53
No. of Women Partners: 7
No. of Survey Responses Received: 6

Respondent Profile: 6 associates responded. Practice areas included securities, corporate, and litigation.

Summary: Our respondents, all associates, painted Testa, Hurwitz & Thibeault as a young firm that poses few, if any, barriers to women's advancement and offers a largely hospitable environment. That said, they also agreed that sustaining a life outside of the firm is nearly impossible. Part-time options are regarded with some suspicion, and senior women are few and far between.

Advancement: Testa, Hurwitz & Thibeault was founded in 1973, so it did not inherit the hidebound traditions and cultures of other firms surveyed. Women were nearly unanimous that those who stick it out for the duration of the eight- to nine-year partnership track enjoy chances equal to men, although they believed that, as a result of family obligations, few women are around to be considered for promotion.

Respondents also agreed that "allocation of assignments is very even-handed and fair," as one lawyer put it. A corporate associate commented that lawyers are "given equally challenging and high-profile work and equal amounts of responsibility on transactions." The key factors for partnership, in a first-year associate's estimation, include "service to the firm, team-player mentality," and "service to clients."

Women do not stay at the firm because "family life and work is perceived as incompatible," in the opinion of one respondent. Women lawyers are said to be "less willing to sacrifice everything for this job, which is what is required." Another associate agreed: "Women are more likely to be fed up with the lack of control working at a big firm brings."

Thus, although the firm is populated by many junior women associates without children, there are fewer and fewer women "up the ladder." This year, for the first time, one respondent reported, an associate who had a baby and cut back to part-time will be up for partner, and there are apparently "lots" of part-time women in the senior associate ranks. As a result, "The test will come in the next three years," in the view of one lawyer.

Several factors were cited as disadvantages by those who believed women may find it more difficult than men to succeed even if they are willing to make the necessary sacrifices. One lawyer opined that lack of mentoring is the source of women's difficulty in being promoted. "Because of the lack of female mentors," she commented, "women receive no guidance and women do not and cannot form the type of collegial relationships with male partners as do male associates." Another associate, however, thought that the "nonexistent" mentoring hindered both men and women. Although incoming associates are assigned mentors, it appears that these relationships do not always take off.

In the opinion of one associate, women are viewed as "not 'inspiring confidence' to an adequate degree," a perception that is rooted in "gender difference in communicating and interacting." Furthermore, she estimated, "Arrogance and blind devotion are two very necessary traits to advancement, which, from my perspective, more men in this job possess."

According to one associate, although there are few women partners at present, "the firm seems committed to changing that."

"Male associates frequently golf and do other social activities with the male partners, while women are [not usually] invited on such informal, non-firm-sanctioned outings."

Attitudes and atmosphere: Most respondents reported that they feel comfortable at Testa, Hurwitz, although some had reservations. One lawyer believed, "The lack of a woman in firm management and leadership leads to...a lack of understanding in terms of what being an active member of the family entails." A litigator observed that the firm's practice is "so male," which she characterized as "emotionless, calculating, etc."

One associate commented that she sees "little stuffiness of [an] 'old boys' attitude among partners (with notable exceptions) [and] several strong senior women." Overall, however, she concluded that the firm is *much* better than my old firm."

A first-year associate wrote that the number of women at her level makes the firm "very comfortable" and added that the men "are very aware of being polite and of not saying or doing anything that could be construed as harassment." She further noted that "secretaries are given enormous respect."

Although women are treated hospitably within the firm, some felt less than welcome at certain social activities. One corporate associate wrote that although she has never witnessed discrimination or harassment, "Male associates frequently golf and do other social activities with the male partners, while women are [not usually] invited on such informal, non-firm—sanctioned outings."

The firm's few women partners are said to be "too busy with their families to interact socially as are senior as well as junior female associates." According to another associate, social interactions within the firm are "primarily great," although the firm includes some " 'men's men' who seem to have trouble with women working alongside them and with women's different ways of dealing with opposing counsel and clients."

> *"It's hard to have energy for meaningful emotional interaction at the end of the week (if there is an end!?)."*

Balancing work & family/personal life: Balancing work and family is "virtually impossible" at the firm because of the working hours and pressure, which are very "intense." Although one associate concluded that many people "work it out, but it's not easy," several others complained bitterly. A second-year associate feared that there is "no ability to exercise any significant control over one's life as an associate," which leads to "depression and burn-out."

Another lawyer commented, "[A handful of] women attorneys have small children (but many men do)." A first-year associate wrote that her husband is very understanding, "but I see very little of him, and he has had to take over most of my half of domestic responsibilities." The firm, she added, "basically doesn't care what you have planned—work comes first, and if a partner needs you here, you have to be here."

Another associate agreed: "It is not encouraged to have priorities outside the firm." She added there is a perception that women "find it more difficult to give up other aspects of their lives, i.e., relationships, family, nonwork-related commitments." She was concerned that young male associates "who are willing to work 15 hours every day are the ones who advance" and the ones who receive mentoring and praise.

A single associate believed that there are no women with primary childcare responsibility in the litigation department and that "it is very difficult to maintain a satisfying personal life—the

hours are long and the work is intellectually and emotionally demanding." She continued, "It's hard to have energy for meaningful emotional interaction at the end of the week (if there *is* an end!?)."

> *Some respondents were apprehensive about the use of part-time schedules. Most associates reported that they did not know anyone who actually worked part-time.*

Flexibility of work arrangements: Part-time options exist at the associate and partner levels, although respondents, primarily junior associates, expressed reluctance to use them. One respondent was of the view that part-time arrangements are available for "people who have been here for a number of years." To the firm's credit, those who go part-time for less than a year are apparently "still considered on [the] same track for partnership," according to another lawyer.

Some respondents were apprehensive about the use of part-time schedules. Most associates reported that they did not know anyone who actually worked part-time. One respondent feared that part-time is "more acceptable" at the partner level than at the associate level because of "a certain 'earning your stripes' mentality that takes some of the legitimacy from doing it as an associate."

With respect to both parental leave and part-time work, one associate observed, "Women here are concerned that their chances for partnership will be affected by use of such policies." Another associate speculated that part-time "would probably mean 40 hours a week here!"

The firm reportedly provides emergency day-care service that is "frequently used and appreciated," as well as "substantial family leave for attorneys of both genders." A number of men are said to have taken advantage of paternity leave.

"...there is no racial and ethnic diversity at all."

Diversity: Testa, Hurwitz is said to provide a welcoming, open environment for gays and assertive women, but a lonely one for minority attorneys. One associate commented that the firm is a comfortable home for attorneys of varying political persuasions and diverse lifestyles, but "there is no racial and ethnic diversity at all." She added that despite suggestions from herself and others on "numerous occasions," she has seen "absolutely no effort to make changes in this area." According to the 1997 National Directory of Legal Employers, there are seven minority attorneys at Testa.

The firm evidently takes a hands-off approach to its lawyers' personal lives. According to one associate, the firm's approach "is to take *no* position on personal lives and for the most part it works." Another associate agreed that the firm has adopted a "purposefully apolitical stance," with the result that, "as much as there are people with diverse politics, personalities, etc., unless you know the people personally, you are unlikely to be aware of people's diversity."

Some respondents reported that there are several gay women at the firm. One lawyer noted that the firm offers full benefits for "families, which includes domestic partners of either gender," with whom the attorney has lived for one or more years. One associate observed

that there are "many (most) women with very strong, assertive personalities, many self-identified feminists," which, she noted, is positive in that these women "serve as a support group for each other in this stifling male environment."

One associate described the "very few" women holding power in the firm as "quite unapproachable" and lacking "any interest in promoting the quality of life or opportunities for women."

Women in leadership positions: Most respondents believed that few if any women wield significant influence in the firm and that the firm does not have enough female partners, period. Although there is a woman hiring partner, several departments reportedly do not include any women partners or women even nearing partnership. In the corporate department, however, there are apparently lots of senior associate women, a "good sign," in the words of one respondent.

Although one partner "who is part-time and has three children, has been instrumental in pursuing part-time schedules for women associates with children and in promoting the idea of a 'back-up' day care center," most female partners are perceived to do little on behalf of other women in the firm.

One associate described the "very few" women holding power in the firm as "quite unapproachable" and lacking "any interest in promoting the quality of life or opportunities for women." She added that, in her opinion, the firm "tries to be 'up with the times,' but in reality, the culture of the firm does not follow suit."

Testa, Hurwitz & Thibeault No. of Responses: 6	Strongly agree	Agree	Disagree	Strongly disagree
Women's prospects for advancement at the firm are as strong as men's	1	4		1
I am satisfied with the firm's family and personal leave policies	3	3		
There are women in positions of power and influence in the firm		2	3	1
Women are as likely as men to receive desirable work assignments	3	2	1	
Women attorneys feel they can discuss family obligations openly		1	5	
Women are as likely as men to be mentored by senior attorneys	1	1	2	2
Women attorneys enjoy a high level of job satisfaction		2	4	
Women in the firm are supportive of their women colleagues	3	1	2	
Firm management is receptive to the concerns of women attorneys	1	2	3	

TROUTMAN SANDERS

Rating: 8

🔨🔨🔨🔨🔨

Troutman Sanders
600 Peachtree St.
Nations Bank Plaza
Suite 5200
Atlanta, GA 30308
404-885-3000

No. of Attorneys: 213
No. of Women Attorneys: 62
No. of Partners: 95
No. of Women Partners: 12
No. of Survey Responses Received: 13

Respondent Profile: 2 partners, 10 associates, and 1 counsel responded. Practice areas included litigation, real estate, labor, and corporate, among others.

Summary: Troutman Sanders, a relaxed firm with "great people," reportedly offers its women attorneys an atmosphere noted for its lack of clubbiness, in contrast with some of its Atlanta peers. Despite the small number of women partners and women in positions of power, the number of women making partner in recent years is on the upswing, and respondents were unanimous in assessing women's chances for advancement as excellent. Some fear, however, that the firm's alternative arrangements may be impractical.

Advancement: The number of women staying around for partnership consideration and those making partner in recent years has substantially increased, according to respondents, creating an anticipation that the underrepresentation of women in partnership ranks will soon disappear. Some suggested that women, many with families, have tended to leave the firm in larger numbers for in-house counsel positions, or to leave the law entirely, but respondents were unanimous that those who do stay at the firm on full-time status have equal chances for promotion.

An associate wrote that the firm has equal numbers of male and female associates and that they appear to advance at the same rate. One junior associate remarked that she was "impressed by the fact that both women up for partnership this year were pregnant at the time they were made partner." According to a partner, the shift indicates that "the firm has come to reflect society's increased flexibility with respect to the role of women." A junior associate wrote that because many of the firm's leaders are "relatively young, and because the women who are 'top' partners are great attorneys, for the most part, it does not matter whether you are male or female, as long as you perform well in your job."

Two associates noted that assignments and mentoring are available for women on an equitable basis. A midlevel litigation associate reported that she had been assigned to cases in a gender-neutral way and had received as much experience taking depositions and handling hearings as the men in her section. A lawyer reported that despite her perception that the firm lacks a "formal" mentoring program, she has found her own mentors, "none of whom are women."

"[It is] very possible to maintain my femininity and still prove my intellectual capabilities."

Attitudes and atmosphere: All respondents spoke favorably of the atmosphere at Troutman. An associate remarked that while many Atlanta firms are "dominated by the 'boys' club,' " the firm distinguishes itself from its peers by fostering "an atmosphere where women are respected and accepted as equals." She added that the environmental group is 50-percent female and that women have taken a strong leadership role.

A midlevel litigator said, "I actually feel very fortunate to have had the luck to work at a firm with such great people." A junior associate remarked that it is "very possible to maintain my femininity and still prove my intellectual capabilities." The one counsel noted that a mothers' group meets quarterly to discuss issues of shared concern.

A couple of respondents believed that there were undercurrents of inequality. A partner held the opinion that there are a few "senior male partners (who are becoming decreasingly powerful) who are uncomfortable with women as equals."

Several associates were concerned that the firm's partners organize golf outings that, in their experience, do not tend to include women and that can "make client development more male-oriented," as one partner put it.

One senior corporate attorney said she perceived that many clients are uncomfortable because she is a single woman and that they "prefer to work with a male attorney." Another associate reported that poor treatment by clients does occur, but "has decreased over the years, and the male attorneys stand up for the women in such situations."

"Partners and other attorneys are very understanding about childcare issues."

Balancing work & family/personal life: Respondents generally agreed that Troutman is family-friendly and supportive of outside commitments. One partner remarked that she is usually able to juggle work, client, and bar activities with family concerns. She noted, "Partners and other attorneys are very understanding about childcare issues," adding that clients "are equally as understanding." The other partner observed that "women generally seem able to work out a schedule suiting their individual needs," but said that, in her opinion, achieving a satisfying balance often means foregoing partnership opportunities as a result of having to reduce one's workload.

An associate was concerned that Troutman offers "little flexibility in crunch situations, but otherwise, the firm seems amicable to family needs." Another associate wrote that although management "expects the associates to work hard, the firm wants the associates to have a family life." A junior associate asserted that Troutman's family-friendly orientation is a "deeply embedded part of the firm's culture."

One associate commented that the firm does not have a "mommy track." She added that, in her estimation, having a family would be "extremely difficult to do while maintaining my current levels." A couple of associates commented on the lack of childcare in the building, although one reported that the topic has been discussed. A childless associate commented that despite an absence of "major pressure about billing hours," there is still "major pressure to get the work done, which requires late nights, weekends, and very unpredictable hours," which, in her view, "seems an unacceptable life style for a mother."

> *"A woman associate does not know until she's leaving for maternity leave whether she may go part-time, which is a little late to find another job if she has decided full-time is not an option."*

Flexibility of work arrangements: The firm's part-time policy is apparently *ad hoc*, and experiences with part-time arrangements vary, according to respondents. One associate observed, "Part-time work and other options are in their infant stages of development, and it is too early to tell how they will play out over the long-term." A litigator said, in her opinion, "A woman associate does not know until she's leaving for maternity leave whether she may go part-time, which is a little late to find another job if she has decided full-time is not an option."

A litigation associate reported that, in her estimation, some on reduced hours "may be passed over for the more exciting assignments, probably due to a fear that they won't be available in emergencies."

According to one partner, part-time schedules are available "on a limited basis, although this is increasing annually." She added that the minimum hours available for more junior associates is 1,500 per year, "still a fairly hefty load." In contrast, an associate reported that there are now about 10 part-timers, and opined that the more there are, "the more the firm will likely have to limit part-timers in the future."

Apparently, there are no part-timers at the partnership level, although some work a "reduced schedule (8:30 a.m. to 6:30 p.m., Monday through Friday)." According to the counsel, when part-time set-ups are negotiated, "the firm has been able to work out a variety of arrangements with women, but these have all come about as a result of the efforts of individual women articulating what their particular desires are."

> *"Atlanta is very much a segregated city, and it is difficult to recruit and to keep black attorneys."*

Diversity: Most respondents observed that the firm's lawyers are largely mainstream. With regard to race, the predominant view was that the firm lacks diversity. One respondent, who characterized diversity at the firm as "sad," reported that there are only three African-American woman lawyers. Another lawyer said that, in her opinion, "Atlanta is very much a segregated city, and it is difficult to recruit and to keep black attorneys."

Although most respondents concluded that the firm was working hard to recruit more minorities, they agreed that

Troutman "seems to embrace people with strong personalities, regardless of political leanings, etc." Another associate characterized the firm as "fairly liberal—as far as the Southeast goes [with] room for social butterflies and wallflowers."

A corporate associate observed that there are no openly gay attorneys. She added, "It's the South—lawyers down here tend to be somewhat more conservative in demeanor."

Women partners "are very active in the firm's committees and in the legal community at large."

Women in leadership positions: A woman heads up the associate review committee, and she drew high praise from respondents. She is "perceived with a great deal of respect by her male partners, even though she also keeps a flexible schedule in order to participate in her kids' car pools," according to a litigation associate. A midlevel associate commented that this woman "has played a strong role in promoting part-time work for working mothers."

Women also apparently head several small practice groups and other firm committees, including the hiring committee. A senior litigator noted that the women partners "are very active in the firm's committees and in the legal community at large." Several respondents attributed the lack of powerful women to lack of seniority, rather than conscious exclusion.

Nevertheless, many respondents did not perceive the senior women as a whole as "advancing the interests of women" at the firm, as one associate put it, especially women with children.

A litigator commented on the absence of women partners who are also mothers of school-age (or younger) children. One respondent was concerned that the senior women "have not historically played a role in promoting the opportunities and quality of life for women within the firm." She added that as she herself has become more senior, she has "much more sympathy and understanding for the reason they have not done so. Their time is fully committed to practicing at the level required and meeting their obligations to their family." A trend in the other direction, however, may be starting, because the senior women have "organized firm-sponsored lunches with the women in the firm to begin to form some support networks among the women."

Troutman Sanders No. of Responses: 13	Strongly agree	Agree	Disagree	Strongly disagree
Women's prospects for advancement at the firm are as strong as men's	6	6		
I am satisfied with the firm's family and personal leave policies	6	5	1	
There are women in positions of power and influence in the firm	6	7		
Women are as likely as men to receive desirable work assignments	9	3	1	
Women attorneys feel they can discuss family obligations openly	5	6	2	
Women are as likely as men to be mentored by senior attorneys	8	4	1	
Women attorneys enjoy a high level of job satisfaction	6	5	2	
Women in the firm are supportive of their women colleagues	7	6		
Firm management is receptive to the concerns of women attorneys	5	7	1	

VENABLE, BAETJER and HOWARD LLP

Rating: 5

◂◂◂◂◂

Venable, Baetjer and Howard LLP
1800 Mercantile Bank and Trust Bldg.
Baltimore, MD 21201
410-244-7400

No. of Attorneys: 123
No. of Women Attorneys: 35
No. of Partners: 73
No. of Women Partners: 12
No. of Survey Responses Received: 7

Respondent Profile: 1 partner, 5 associates, and 1 counsel responded. Practice areas included litigation, corporate, and environmental.

Summary: Venable is a hospitable and discrimination-free workplace that offers women a fair shot at partnership as well as family-friendly policies. Hours are reportedly manageable, and alternative work options appear to be an accepted part of firm culture. Women partners are genuinely respected and considered by most to be experts in their fields.

Advancement: Respondents almost unanimously expressed confidence that women's chances for partnership at the firm were on par with their male colleagues. Several respondents observed that, although women advance equally to the nonequity partnership tier, they feared that progress toward share partnership is more likely to be stalled because, in the words of the one partner, "business development is a major factor and fewer women are successful rainmakers." Several respondents noted that the partnership includes women who have worked part-time, as well as some who still have part-time arrangements.

While one associate contended that the firm adjusts partnership tracks to reflect reduced experience during part-time years, a few respondents reported that one long-term part-time woman was made partner along with her class. One associate recalled that when she asked the managing partner of the firm's D.C. office whether her part-time arrangement meant that she would advance more slowly, his response was, "Why should it?" In the words of the associate, "That said it all."

A junior litigation associate acknowledged that she had chosen the firm in part because of its efforts to advance women and the availability of a part-time partnership track. She added that many women at Venable continue on a full-time basis "and manage to juggle both family and work." Several associates noted that they have received good mentoring, mostly from male partners.

One litigator believed that women are not likely to advance "as quickly as men," at least in her department. She wrote that, in her experience, progress is easier for those who are single and childless, and as much like one "of the guys as possible." That said, however, she

351

pointed out that Venable is "a good place to be a female lawyer" and that "the firm works hard at equality and succeeds as much as a large organization can."

A litigator observed that while the firm's attitudes toward part-time work and family leave are conducive to equal opportunity, in her estimation, "client development and bar activities and networking opportunities are still less available due to external attitudes about female attorneys."

An associate reported having encountered no discrimination whatsoever and said that "such behavior would not be tolerated."

Attitudes and atmosphere: Most respondents spoke very favorably about the atmosphere. A corporate lawyer observed that the firm is filled with women attorneys and has a large number of female partners. According to a midlevel associate in the D.C. office, the firm is "very proud of its emphasis on placing women in leadership positions and has won awards for its efforts."

Another associate wrote that she has not witnessed gender discrimination in the litigation practice group, but has "heard that this is not so true in corporate." A litigator said that, in her opinion, "there may still be subtle remnants" of discrimination that need to be corrected. In contrast, an associate said she had encountered no discrimination whatsoever and declared that "such behavior would not be tolerated." And the partner agreed that any "subtle issues of gender discrimination are dealt with promptly," and that firm management has a "conscious commitment to place women in leadership positions."

One respondent reported that the only vestige of a "boys' club" is the tendency for the men "to play golf with each other and with clients." Most respondents noted that social interactions within the firm are generally gender-neutral. One senior litigator reported, "Working here is a blast."

"[The firm] is sensitive to the needs of working mothers to maintain reasonable, regular working hours."

Balancing work & family/personal life: The firm is said to be unusually supportive towards those seeking to strike a healthy balance between work and home. At 1,800 hours per year, the firm's billable requirement is not outrageous and most lawyers—both men and women—reportedly value family time. Venable does not emphasize "face time," according to one associate, who added that if one is not busy, he or she "can feel free to go home." A senior associate concluded that the firm "is as good as it gets in a profession like ours." A respondent who is a mother concurred, "[The firm] is sensitive to the needs of working mothers to maintain reasonable, regular working hours."

An associate without children described the firm as very sensitive to "the importance of having a life outside the office." One respondent wrote that while the time demands are heavy, the firm is "very good about honoring vacations and other personal/family commitments."

Several associates asserted that while the firm is generally supportive of lawyers' outside commitments, they perceived considerable variation depending upon practice group and supervising partners.

One associate reported that the firm offers "a generous maternity leave policy, allowing up to three months' leave with full pay."

"Venable is a leader in alternative work arrangements for women."

Flexibility of work arrangements: Venable reportedly offers great flexibility with regard to work arrangements. The three part-timers who responded expressed satisfaction with their own arrangements. A partner who has no children wrote that several years after being promoted, she reduced her workload to 60 percent "as a matter of personal preference." She added that this arrangement has worked well for a number of years, and she expects it to continue.

One associate said her part-time status is "scrupulously respected." She has "never felt like anything but a valued part of the firm." She further noted that her days change in accordance with her schedule, an arrangement that is made viable by a flexible nanny. "Sometimes I'll work seven days straight if we're busy," she said, "but then I'll take a week off and recoup the time." While she personally has had "great luck" with part-time, she added that, in her estimation, "not all other people have."

According to a senior associate with kids, "Venable is a leader in alternative work arrangements for women." She reported that she has worked a four-day-per-week schedule for some time, and that, although she occasionally must come into the office on her day off, her supervising partners have worked hard to arrange a reasonable workload for her.

Several respondents noted that the firm has promoted part-time associates who have never worked full-time and that these lawyers have remained part-time once they reached partnership. A litigation associate wrote that the part-timers include "several highly respected women partners and associates" who retain high esteem among colleagues—male and female. One woman partner was reportedly granted a leave of absence "for several years to be with her children," and an associate has reportedly been granted part-time status to write a book.

The firm is very tolerant, a partner maintained, but no one has been very vocal about issues such as homosexuality.

Diversity: According to one lawyer, the firm "has actually won awards for diversity." Another respondent observed that, in her opinion, the firm has had problems retaining women and people of color: "[They] often choose to go elsewhere after short service with the firm," she observed, which to her, likely reflects that "support on an ongoing basis is probably weak."

The firm is said to take no particular stance toward the sexual orientation or political views of its lawyers. The partner said, "Such issues are seldom discussed." The firm is very tolerant, she maintained, but no one has been very vocal about issues such as homosexuality. An associate agreed that the firm includes lawyers of "many personalities," but politics "and life styles are not particularly discussed."

Although it is perceived those with the most influence in the firm are men, several respondents predicted that this was bound to change.

Women in leadership positions: Several women have attained positions of significant responsibility and "many are very well-compensated," according to one partner. One respondent reported that several women occupy what she perceived to be "second-tier leadership roles." Another respondent said that a woman "[with three] kids and a *great* attitude" heads the firm's associates committee. Although it is perceived that those with the most influence in the firm are men, several respondents predicted that this was bound to change eventually as the number of women in the partnership increases. Most respondents said that the more prominent women in the firm are highly respected. The partner wrote that the women partners are "generally viewed as experts in their field."

One respondent was decidedly cynical, saying that, in her estimation, it is "hard to imagine a woman at the top tier of firm leadership" and that she doubts that "a woman wielding 'real power' would be accepted."

Venable, Baetjer and Howard No. of Responses: 7	Strongly agree	Agree	Disagree	Strongly disagree
Women's prospects for advancement at the firm are as strong as men's	3	3	1	
I am satisfied with the firm's family and personal leave policies	4	2		
There are women in positions of power and influence in the firm	4	3		
Women are as likely as men to receive desirable work assignments	4	2		
Women attorneys feel they can discuss family obligations openly	2	1	1	
Women are as likely as men to be mentored by senior attorneys	4	2	1	
Women attorneys enjoy a high level of job satisfaction	3	2	1	
Women in the firm are supportive of their women colleagues	3	4		
Firm management is receptive to the concerns of women attorneys	4	2		

VINSON & ELKINS LLP

Rating: 23

Vinson & Elkins LLP
2300 First City Tower
1001 Fannin
Houston, TX 77002
713-758-2222

No. of Attorneys: 335
No. of Women Attorneys: 83
No. of Partners: 173
No. of Women Partners: 28
No. of Survey Responses Received: 15

Respondent Profile: 5 partners and 10 associates responded. Several respondents did not indicate their practice areas. For those who did, they included litigation, labor and employment, tax, environmental, and public financial.

Summary: Vinson & Elkins, which fosters a generally supportive working environment for women, is said to have recently introduced a partnership track for those working part-time and appears to be a generally family-friendly firm. A large majority viewed women's prospects for advancement positively; a minority questioned the distribution of plum assignments.

Advancement: Three of five partners and seven of 10 associates thought women at V & E had as favorable prospects for advancement as men. Those who were pessimistic about women's opportunities attributed their view, in large part, to what they perceived to be inferior work assignments. According to one associate, although women "generally receive comparable assignments," she believed that there are "still some men who think women can't have a family and be a partner in the law firm." A litigator wrote that, in her experience, "Women generally are not given the same level of mentoring or high-profile assignments as men are given."

A partner commented that although prospects for women's advancement have "improved greatly from what they were three or four years ago" and the firm has "made a much greater effort to see that women are given more opportunities that lead to the type of experience necessary to become a partner," in her view, "[there] are still problems." In the litigation department, in her opinion, "Men still get opportunities to do more complex projects and are still given greater responsibility sooner...Women get the writing assignments, while men start getting courtroom work."

A midlevel associate commented that, in her opinion, women are "somewhat less likely" to make partner because of their life style choices. Although the firm is "open" to promoting women, according to this associate, advancement may come "at a high personal price (i.e., family and personal time)." A partner commented that partnership "is a long, hard road, requiring long hours and a focused effort to make partner and to sustain a profitable practice at the partnership level. Many do not find it worth the struggle."

It is perceived that opportunities for advancement vary by department and depend upon the partner for whom one works. The labor and employment department, for example, was reported by one midlevel associate to be at least half women. Her perception is, "Women at the firm have at least as good of a chance (if not better) to make partner and to be appointed to firm-wide committees," although she thought that her experience might be "atypical."

A midlevel associate in the project finance practice area said she has received excellent work, the "opportunity to develop 'niche' expertise (which is a factor to be considered in the partnership equation), detailed reviews and evaluations of my performance, and realistic appraisal[s] of my prospects." One partner observed that few women have advanced in V & E's business groups, but noted that the firm is trying to rectify this.

> *"There are no women attorneys in charge of complex litigation, although there are women who are as qualified as men heading these cases."*

Attitudes and atmosphere: The overall perception of the environment at V & E was very positive, although several respondents observed that the comfort level depends upon the department, with the level being higher in departments with more women. One associate said, "Traditional areas for women lawyers," such as labor and environmental law, include a number of women attorneys

and partners. Similarly, she observed, "women are accepted and respected" in the insurance defense department. Yet, in her estimation, in the other two litigation sections, "which do more complex litigation, there are few women and very few women partners." In her opinion, "There are no women attorneys in charge of complex litigation, although there are women who are as qualified as men heading these cases."

According to a partner in the environmental department, there is no discrimination at the firm and "management will not tolerate any if it comes to light."

Another partner observed that although "some men work better with women than others," the tone set by the firm's leadership is "excellent." One partner declared that she was aware of no gender discrimination during her decade-long stint at V & E.

Comfort levels among associates seemed to vary across departments, although most reported that they find the firm hospitable. A public finance associate wrote that she is very much at home and feels valued for her "unique contributions." Another associate remarked that the firm's leaders actively promote women and observed that "there are only a certain few lawyers who might want to have a 'boys' club.'"

According to one associate, while women are welcomed overall, she has observed that "references are still made about women's moods ('wrong side of the bed,' 'hormonal imbalance,' etc.). There is still a 'boys' club,' but the 'sisterhood' is rising." One associate reported that the firm sponsors a "Women in the Law" series of speakers and luncheons for women attorneys and clients.

Shouldering outside responsibilities is reported to be most difficult in the corporate areas, where hours are least predictable.

Balancing work & family/personal life: Partners appeared to be more optimistic about the ability to strike a balance than associates, more than one of whom cautioned against drawing firm-wide conclusions on this question. One partner pointed out that, in her experience, "Sometimes sensitivity can backfire. I notice that women do not get assigned to projects and cases that might require a lot of travel. Everybody, men and women, should be given choices. Men should not automatically assume women can't travel because of family considerations." Like most, she regards the firm as family-oriented. Despite occasions when striking the balance between work and mothering feels overwhelming, this partner observed, "Most of the time, you can balance work and family with planning and organization and a supportive spouse."

A tax partner said that while "many lawyers tend to be perfectionists in all things," this does not work when balancing work and family, and "adjustments to the level of perfection and delegation ability are critical. Those who can't don't make it." An environmental partner said that, in her assessment, "women feel guilt more acutely than men over family issues. All the 'sensitivity' in the world will not correct a tilt in favor of a lawyer who works constantly and is hugely profitable."

Associate respondents emphasized their perception that one's ability to strike a healthy balance is heavily dependent upon one's practice area. Shouldering outside responsibilities is reported to be most difficult in the corporate areas, where hours are least predictable. In one associate's perception, firm-wide attorneys are encouraged to bill from 2,300 to 2,600 hours per year to be in line for partnership. Another associate commented that, in her estimation, promotion requires working "60 to 80 hours a week, and the expectation is that work comes first—even to the point of cutting short a family vacation."

One associate described the firm as "sensitive to women's needs, but not always able to make problems go away." A litigator believed that she has seen "evidence of other women being placed on the 'mommy track,'" but an associate who is also a mother noted that this need not be the case. She reportedly has continued to work full-time, is on partnership track, and has "been encouraged to seek the arrangement that gives me the most satisfaction." She added that the firm "does not want me to leave because of work-family conflicts."

"[Part-time is] not a good deal based on hours expected, pay offered, and lost time for partnership."

Flexibility of work arrangements: Vinson & Elkins has recently introduced a partnership-track, part-time policy that extends the period prior to partnership consideration. One partner commented, "The policy seems fair to me. After all, if you are not working full-time, you do not have the same experience level as others in your class." According to an environmental partner, part-time arrangements remain available, in her experience, "only in certain cases" and "only if the section supports a woman's decision. The long-term viability of these arrangements remains to be seen."

V & E has reportedly offered for some time and continues to maintain nonpartnership-track, part-time alternatives. A partner in the project finance division reported that three women in her department work part-time for child-rearing reasons: "Two of the three have now gone to full-time, nonpartnership track of 40 hours per week after years of part-time." The policy is available to partners on paper, but respondents believed that none have yet taken advantage of it.

One part-time associate reported that her arrangement has worked well: "I am responsible for my own clients and am treated with respect by the partners and other associates in my section." An associate in the project finance department observed that the new policy allowing associates to remain on partnership track "has been well-received" by the partnership and the associates.

According to some associates, however, part-time and promotion do not mix. A litigator wrote that those she has spoken to feared that part-time is "a fast track to derailing a promising career. In other words, other lawyers will assume that you can't balance your career and family." A midlevel associate said it was her perception that part-time is not "viable if you want to make partner" and "not a good deal based on hours expected, pay offered, and lost time for partnership."

Vinson & Elkins was reportedly one of the first employers in the city to offer benefits to same-sex domestic partners.

Diversity: V & E has few lawyers of color, but is said to be quite diverse in other respects. One partner reported that the firm "has the most eclectic group of attorneys imaginable—strong personalities are not only approved of, they are encouraged." She noted that the firm has attorneys who are active in the Democratic and Republican parties and in gay and lesbian organizations, although she said that, in her assessment, the firm does not have "as many attorneys from ethnic minorities as we would like, but it's not because we are not trying."

A partner reported that there are two partners who are women of color, and that V & E has its own political action committee that supports "all sides, from the most liberal to the most conservative." Vinson & Elkins was reportedly one of the first employers in Houston to offer benefits to same-sex domestic partners.

Associates who responded to this question tended to focus on the lack of racial minorities at the firm. One associate observed that V & E has "only a few minority women." According to another's perception, "Women attorneys of diverse backgrounds seem to have a more difficult time excelling."

"A few women have powerful positions, but not at the highest level."

Women in leadership positions: Just a handful of women reportedly hold positions of influence at V & E. A junior associate commented that, in her assessment, "a few women have powerful positions, but not at the highest level." The one woman previously on the firm's management committee—"where the real power at Vinson & Elkins is," as one partner remarked—was reportedly not reelected this year. Another partner predicted that the lack of real power held by women may change, "but it will take another decade."

Only about 15 percent of the firm's partners are women, and according to another partner, six of these were elected just this year. She added that two women hold positions of real power—the former management committee member and the head of the firm's appellate section, who is also the mother of two young children and is "very well-respected by our partners and the legal community as a whole." According to an associate, "Some of the busiest and most well-known partners are female."

Vinson & Elkins No. of Responses: 15	Strongly agree	Agree	Disagree	Strongly disagree
Women's prospects for advancement at the firm are as strong as men's	5	5	4	1
I am satisfied with the firm's family and personal leave policies	7	6	2	
There are women in positions of power and influence in the firm	4	6	4	
Women are as likely as men to receive desirable work assignments	7	5	1	2
Women attorneys feel they can discuss family obligations openly	6	3	4	1
Women are as likely as men to be mentored by senior attorneys	6	4	3	1
Women attorneys enjoy a high level of job satisfaction	4	7	2	
Women in the firm are supportive of their women colleagues	7	7	1	
Firm management is receptive to the concerns of women attorneys	6	6	2	

WEIL, GOTSHAL & MANGES LLP

Rating: 54

Weil, Gotshal & Manges LLP
767 Fifth Ave.
New York, NY 10153
212-310-8000

No. of Attorneys: 360
No. of Women Attorneys: 106
No. of Partners: 116
No. of Women Partners: 17
No. of Survey Responses Received: 13

Respondent Profile: 1 partner and 12 associates responded. Practice areas included litigation and corporate. Several respondents did not identify their practice areas.

Summary: Weil, Gotshal & Manges appears to foster a comfortable atmosphere for its women lawyers, but reportedly does not offer them much more. According to respondents, women experience an uphill battle in terms of advancement, and the firm has a blind spot when it comes to lawyers seeking to juggle responsibilities of work and home. On a positive note, the firm gets an "A" for effort in the area of diversity.

Advancement: Slightly fewer than half of all respondents (including one partner) observed that women are less likely to make partner than men. Asked if women's prospects are equal, the partner responded that, in her estimation, "No...women don't get mentored often, and often have to fend for themselves more than men." She emphasized that "bringing in business!" is vital to advancement. A corporate associate agreed that advancement is based on "rainmaking abilities and/or the attachment of large clients of the firm to the particular attorney."

According to a senior associate, advancement demands "a very ambitious, aggressive, proactive personality." A litigator observed that women are "scarce" in the senior associate ranks and that the only way the picture on advancement will change is through improved mentoring and "an understanding that women (more than men) have to choose between family and career."

A senior associate was concerned that those women who stick it out for the full partnership track believe they are required to "meet an extra, higher, but unspoken mark." A first-year associate observed that women are less likely to advance, and remarked that "the men seem to eat together, stop by each others offices, but do not interact socially with the women as much."

Another junior-level litigator believed that few women partners have children and that many who do "had their kids once they 'made it.' " A corporate associate said that although women's chances for partnership were equal to those of men, they are "close-to-nonexistent" for nearly everyone. Another respondent observed "a lack of partnership opportunities for both sexes" in her department.

A handful of associates painted a brighter picture of women's opportunities. A corporate associate commented, with several others concurring, that the allocation of assignments is equal. In the litigation department, women have historically advanced more slowly than men, according to one litigator's impression, though she predicted that "now, since there is a feeling that there should be more women partners, it will probably be easier for women than for men, at least for awhile" in that department.

> *The firm, overall, is a "very good place for women who are willing to take on the demands of large firm practice."*

Attitudes and atmosphere: The firm won high ratings in terms of the atmosphere it offers women on a daily basis. According to one associate, Weil, Gotshal is comfortable because it "is very politically correct and encourages that attitude among the attorneys as well as its staff." She added that the firm has held mandatory diversity training workshops to heighten sensitivity to these issues.

One senior associate attributed the firm's sensitivity to diversity issues to the firm's "strongly Jewish culture and the resultant identification with 'outsiders' in the larger culture." She reported that there is "no 'monolithic patriarchy' within the firm but the clients are another (worse) story." Another senior associate perceived the firm to be as comfortable as any big New York firm could be, "given the fact that our revenues are derived from business with

predominantly white males over 50, i.e., Fortune 500 legal departments." The firm is gender-neutral for the most part, which "is pretty impressive" for a firm of this size, as one associate put it.

Not all respondents were completely satisfied on this front. A partner wrote that, in her view, comfort levels vary by department and that "corporate doesn't lead the way." She further charged that, in her estimation, there is a "boys' club" comprised of midlevel partners and that the older partners "are actually more civilized and thoughtful on women's issues."

A first-year associate reported her impression of "a definite 'boys' club'" during her short time at the firm. Another junior lawyer believed the existence of "all-male sports pools, etc." creates an exclusive atmosphere. Yet an associate said that Weil, Gotshal is a "very good place for women who are willing to take on the demands of large firm practice."

> *The firm's partners, "act as if they owned you with respect to your availability to work late hours or weekends."*

Balancing work & family/personal life: According to the opinion of one partner, Weil, Gotshal is "not a family firm—anyone who wants a family life goes elsewhere." The firm's clients, she observed, "are totally insensitive to family responsibilities, so we are too." A corporate associate portrayed hours at the firm as "very long, we work under tight deadlines, and there is no childcare available (on the premises or off)." The firm's partners, in her opinion, "act as if they owned you with respect to your availability to work late hours or weekends."

As to the "mommy track," several respondents did not believe it existed. As one remarked, these "are two words that do not exist," although another feared that "mommy track comments are still made by male associates with respect to female colleagues who go on maternity leave, and there is generally speculation as to whether such person will return to work or stay home with the child."

She admitted, however, that the firm is "tolerant" of long maternity leaves. A senior associate suggested that for those willing to forego partnership who "otherwise work hard" and are smart, there are possibilities for enjoying a personal/family life. But she believed, "you will be a permanent second-class citizen."

One litigator reported, "When you're working with a 'nice' partner, you can make family a priority at times." One single litigator wrote that although the hours are very long, she has never had difficulty taking time off for personal and family events. Another commented that "most of the pressure" seems to be "self-imposed because I know a number of attorneys that work reasonable hours."

> *The availability of part-time schedules depends on practice group and "how much the attorney is liked by the partners."*

Flexibility of work arrangements: Most respondents do not perceive part-time arrangements at Weil, Gotshal as practical. There is a concern that part-time arrangements are *ad hoc* and, according to several respondents, it is their perception that they cannot lead

to partnership. A part-timer suggested that she was "made aware that I am not on the partnership track," though she thought that when part-time works, "it's wonderful."

In the opinion of a corporate attorney, the availability of part-time schedules depends on the practice group and "how much the attorney is liked by the partners." The structured finance and derivatives groups, according to this respondent, "will [rarely] entertain the idea but general practice groups will." She added that, in her estimation, part-time does not appear to be available at partnership level and that women and men desiring more time with their families tend to become of counsel rather than partners.

A senior associate was concerned that having any obligations outside of the office is "deemed to show 'lack of commitment' to the firm and the client," though this rule applies to men and women alike. She added that, in her mind, very few women associates at the firm have children and most either wait for partnership before becoming mothers or leave the firm once kids enter the picture.

> *A litigator who praised the firm for being quite vocal about its commitment to diversity, believed that it "has not demonstrated this commitment through advancement to partnership."*

Diversity: Most respondents agreed that the firm is committed and vocal about diversity, but, as with many firms, has not achieved in practice what it preaches. Diversity is reportedly a "hot topic," according to the partner, who added that Weil, Gotshal tries to demonstrate a commitment, though in her opinion, it "sometimes gets lost."

Several respondents commented that the firm's diversity committee has held diversity training, which is apparently mandatory for all attorneys. One litigator reported, "Many minority and lesbian women have joined the firm," although another, who praised the firm for being quite vocal about its commitment to diversity, believed that it "has not demonstrated this commitment through advancement to partnership."

One associate reported a "large Orthodox Jewish contingent" and a "gay and lesbian support group," which led her to believe that "WGM is supportive of women and minorities." The numbers of minority attorneys still remain "abysmally low," in the estimation of one associate.

The firm is reportedly supportive or at least impartial towards its attorneys' sexual orientations. One lesbian commented that she brings her partner to firm events where she is "always graciously welcomed." In contrast, a partner perceived that such practices are permissible, yet still "raise eyebrows" among at least some attorneys.

> **"To have power here, you must inherently be an aggressive power seeker—it's that kind of place."**

Women in leadership positions: Opinions varied as to which women, if any, wield power at Weil, Gotshal. "There are precious few women who have clout at our firm," in the opinion of one senior associate. A junior associate wrote that she had heard that there was a powerful woman in the tax department, but suggested that "in a firm of [our size], I guess that's not saying much."

A midlevel associate explained that there is a perception that the "real power, regardless of titles, lies [with] five or six senior partners who are the principal rainmakers of the firm (all of whom are men over 50). However, the co-chair of the hiring committee is a woman, and the vice-chair of the hiring committee (who is in charge of minority recruitment and retention) is also a woman and both seem to be outspoken on gender and diversity issues and... well-respected by their partners."

A senior associate observed, "To have power here, you must inherently be an aggressive power seeker—it's that kind of place."

Respondents were generally enthusiastic about the efforts of senior women to support their junior colleagues. The sole ostensible powerful woman department head has thrown her weight behind other women, according to the partner. More generally, the efforts of senior women to "take part in special programs designed to mentor women on such things as developing business" are appreciated, according to a senior associate.

One associate remarked that there are women here "who are leaders in their fields and are well-respected in that regard." One litigator characterized the senior women as excellent lawyers and said approvingly, "Because most of them have families, I think female associates look upon them as role models or models of how life can be here at the firm."

In contrast, another associate wrote that her perception of some of the senior women is that they are "aggressive, ambitious, ruthless, and *not* good role models."

Weil, Gotshal & Manges No. of Responses: 13	Strongly agree	Agree	Disagree	Strongly disagree
Women's prospects for advancement at the firm are as strong as men's	3	4	3	3
I am satisfied with the firm's family and personal leave policies	3	6	2	1
There are women in positions of power and influence in the firm		7	4	2
Women are as likely as men to receive desirable work assignments	5	5	3	
Women attorneys feel they can discuss family obligations openly	1	7	4	1
Women are as likely as men to be mentored by senior attorneys	4	2	4	2
Women attorneys enjoy a high level of job satisfaction	3	5	2	1
Women in the firm are supportive of their women colleagues	3	7	2	
Firm management is receptive to the concerns of women attorneys		5	2	

WHITE & CASE

Rating: 57

White & Case
1155 Avenue of the Americas
New York, NY 10036
212-819-8200

No. of Attorneys: 282
No. of Women Attorneys: 77
No. of Partners: 84
No. of Women Partners: 10
No. of Survey Responses Received: 16

Respondent Profile: 5 partners and 11 associates responded. Practice areas included tax, litigation, and corporate.

Summary: Women lawyers considering White & Case would be wise to head to the firm's tax department, a group that offers favorable opportunities for advancement and appears to be amenable to part-time arrangements. Outside of this haven, attorneys were concerned about a range of challenges, including a thriving "boys' club" and uphill battles to partnership.

Advancement: Although four out of five partners were optimistic about women's chances to advance at W & C, associates were split right down the middle.

"Very few women have made partner," reported one associate, although she emphasized her belief that this was due more to "personal choices about family life than to firm chauvinism." Nevertheless she suggested, "The firm needs to recognize this as a *problem* and not just accept it as a foregone conclusion."

According to one partner's opinion, women "have to work harder to demonstrate commitment, aggressiveness, and client skills." She noted, however, that in recent years, "the firm has had the good fortune to attract a number of highly talented women associates who have excellent prospects for advancement." Another partner noted that mentoring is key and without it, in her

opinion, partnership is unattainable for associates of either gender. Another partner said that, in her opinion, advancement "has a lot to do with being in the right practice area at the right time."

Several associates perceived that patterns of advancement vary across practice groups. According to one associate's experience, women do better in the "support" attorney fields such as tax and trusts and estates. A tax lawyer noted that she was encouraged by the recent promotion to partnership of a woman who had two children while she was an associate.

A corporate associate claimed that, in her opinion, "There are many deserving, capable, hard-working senior women associates who are passed over repeatedly for partnership." One midlevel associate characterized women partners as "really men in disguise."

Several associates suggested that the only barriers to women's advancement were work/family related. One litigator perceived that women are less likely to advance because they are "less likely to devote their lives to the practice," but emphasized that her comment was "not a criticism of the firm, [which] judges all associates on the basis of their competence as lawyers, plus the amount of time put in." She added that in terms of mentoring and assignments, her opportunities have been equivalent to those of male associates.

A corporate attorney declared that, in her opinion, firm leadership "has shown no interest in making W & C a comfortable place for women."

Attitudes and atmosphere: The atmosphere at White & Case is clearly not comfortable to some respondents. One junior associate recalled having "been referred to as 'girlie' by a male peer." She added that she is working on one deal with another male associate who, in her opinion, receives "all of the substantive assignments," while she is stuck with document review. A midlevel associate said that, in her estimation, "The 'boys' club' is alive and well. One partner here never works with women at all, and everyone is aware of his preference and accepts it. He is also known to take his boys off to men-only lunches. I find this repulsive." A corporate attorney declared that, in her opinion, firm leadership "has shown no interest in making W & C a comfortable place for women."

The prevalence of poor treatment appears to depend upon the practice group. A partner wrote that in certain departments "there is a perception that men get preferred work or are more likely to 'bond' with the partners through after-work activities." A tax attorney reported that she believes that she has been accorded responsibility equal to that delegated to males, yet noted that "women in other departments may have a different experience."

According to a corporate partner, efforts have been made to eliminate problems that may have existed in certain areas. Measures taken include sponsorship of several meetings of women attorneys to discuss issues such as mentoring, work assignments, and work and family.

Several respondents were more positive about the environment at the firm. A tax attorney described a culture that is "very respectful of everyone." A litigator observed that her colleagues, male and female, "like each other, for the most part," and that "men and women socialize equally." A corporate partner opined that the firm's attorneys "are not discouraged from showing their individuality (within bounds)," and need not "fit a particular mold for success."

"No allowances are made for women on account of [the] likelihood they are shouldering more family responsibilities."

Balancing work & family/personal life: The firm reportedly expects long hours and constant availability, not unlike most, if not all, of its competitors. Although those who are prepared to trade in their chance at partnership for a less hectic schedule can do so, at least for a while, "women with partnership ambitions cannot," in one partner's opinion.

A project finance associate characterized the personal life one can sustain at the firm as "not satisfying. If you want to establish and maintain a good reputation and work in interesting areas, you have to pull in the hours, sacrificing your personal life." One partner wrote that, in her opinion, "no allowances are made for women on account of the likelihood they are shouldering more family responsibilities."

On the other hand, one midlevel associate stated that for those off partnership track, balancing work and personal life is "not difficult at all." She explained that for her, "personal/family life has always come first and I've made that pretty clear. This may have affected my 'standing' here. However, I accept that consequence fully."

Several respondents praised the firm's provision of emergency childcare and the sensitivity of individual attorneys.

> *"[No one] really knows what 'firm policy' is and whether part-time work is an option. In general, people seem to be afraid to ask."*

Flexibility of work arrangements: Part-time is reportedly available, but, in some respondents' assessment, only for those prepared to abandon all hope for partnership. In one partner's opinion, the "nature of the practice frequently does not encourage it." When part-time status is granted, it is reportedly done on an *ad hoc* basis.

According to an associate's experience, "Very little information is available from the 'powers that be' concerning part-time," and as a result, in her opinion, no one "really knows what 'firm

policy' is and whether part-time work is an option. In general, people seem to be afraid to ask."

No partners reportedly work on part-time schedules. One partner explained that no partner had yet asked for a reduced schedule, though she believes "the partnership would be receptive to this" if it were requested. Another partner disagreed. In her opinion, "W & C is a long way from making a part-time woman partner or permitting a partner to choose part-time hours."

The viability of part-time apparently varies considerably by practice area, with the tax department being particularly amenable to such arrangements. A tax associate reported that her request for more flexible working arrangements was "met with support from all of the (male) partners for whom I work."

A project finance attorney, in contrast, said that, in her opinion, if you "want to work in the big, exciting, and more challenging areas, you will not advance if you can only work part-time." A corporate attorney opined that part-time is possible only for "senior female attorneys with specialized knowledge."

> *Several respondents noted that the women at White & Case are more diverse than the men, "who tend to be white."*

Diversity: Most respondents concluded that the firm is accepting of diversity and that the spectrum of attorneys has broadened considerably as a function of W & C's large international practice and its foreign attorney program.

A partner observed that if "your skills are good, your individuality will be appreciated [as long as] you get along with others and are not eccentric in a bad way." Another partner wrote that, in her opinion, the firm is "not particularly diverse, although it is improving." She suggested that the firm "must begin to view diversity as something other than a recruiting issue before real improvement can happen." She expressed a concern that diverse personalities don't quite fit in well with the firm's culture.

Several respondents noted that the women at White & Case are more diverse than the men, "who tend to be white," in the words of one. An associate reported that "two deserving, highly intelligent, hard-working women" were recently made partner, one of whom is "openly gay, [while] the other is African-American and the mother of two small children (born since she came laterally to the firm)."

One associate believed that none of the three or four lawyers at the firm, who, in her opinion, wield "real power" were women.

Women in leadership positions: Respondents were evenly split on whether women hold powerful positions at White & Case. Apparently, no woman holds a seat on the firm's management committee, and the only examples given of women in positions of authority either involved women who held posts in the past or women in foreign offices. One associate believed that none of the three or four lawyers at the firm who, in her opinion, wield "real power" were women. One partner observed that many lawyers lack "an understanding that men and women bring different skills to the table" and added that no women hold leadership positions, partially because, in her opinion, "all of the men in positions of power represent a certain personality—which is very aggressive."

One partner observed that not everyone (herself included) strives for power. "Obtaining and maintaining power," she noted "is time-consuming and nerve-wracking." Moreover, she observed, "It probably is difficult to obtain." She contended that a woman who sought power "and fought for it" could get it, but "she would have to fight harder" than a man.

Virtually all associates believed that the women partners have done little to advance other women, or to draw attention to women's concerns. One associate wrote that she wished "to be quite clear there is *no* effort" by most women partners "to promote the opportunities or quality of life of the women." A dissenting associate, however, reported that some women partners "have made efforts in promoting advancement of both women in general and women with children."

White & Case No. of Responses: 16	Strongly agree	Agree	Disagree	Strongly disagree
Women's prospects for advancement at the firm are as strong as men's	2	7	5	1
I am satisfied with the firm's family and personal leave policies	2	10	2	1
There are women in positions of power and influence in the firm		7	6	2
Women are as likely as men to receive desirable work assignments	7	5	1	1
Women attorneys feel they can discuss family obligations openly	2	6	5	3
Women are as likely as men to be mentored by senior attorneys	5	7	2	2
Women attorneys enjoy a high level of job satisfaction	1	9	4	1
Women in the firm are supportive of their women colleagues	2	11	2	
Firm management is receptive to the concerns of women attorneys		6	5	2

WILLKIE FARR & GALLAGHER

Rating: 39

Willkie Farr & Gallagher
One Citicorp Center
153 E. 53rd St.
New York, NY 10022
212-821-8000

No. of Attorneys: 309
No. of Women Attorneys: 92
No. of Partners: 88
No. of Women Partners: 7
No. of Survey Responses Received: 13

Respondent Profile: All of the respondents were associates. Practice areas included primarily litigation and corporate, and two smaller departments.

Summary: Willkie is hospitable to women and discrimination-free, but the dearth of senior women has led to what some characterized as a mentoring vacuum. Despite grueling hours, the firm provides lawyers some flexibility in juggling work and family. Part-time arrangements are satisfactory to some, feared as career-killers by others.

Advancement: Although a reasonable majority of respondents contended that women have an equal chance to make partner at Willkie, even some of them added negative comments. As one associate observed, if a woman is a "superstar" and forgoes having children "she has a chance at making partner." Because there are only seven women partners at the firm, some respondents perceived that "many female associates do not receive the type of mentoring that male associates receive."

Another litigator commented that treatment of women is equal to men on a day-to-day basis, yet, in her opinion, the fact that "there are so few women partners and senior associates is obviously troubling." One litigator said, "It takes a fair amount of luck to make partner, and bringing in lots of business doesn't hurt." A lawyer in a smaller department wrote that women's partnership prospects are not equal and added, in her assessment, "this is still an old 'boys' club.' "

A corporate attorney wrote, "Women are given choice assignments and mentored equally with men." Another respondent reported, "[One of my] closest mentors is one of the male executive committee members whose advice is invaluable to my professional development." According to another corporate associate, however, "Assignments appear to be given based upon past experience, so who you worked for initially is crucial and appears to be somewhat arbitrarily determined."

> *Most respondents reported that they find Willkie very hospitable and that they are aware of no discrimination.*

Attitudes and atmosphere: Most respondents reported that they find Willkie very hospitable, and that they are aware of no discrimination. A midlevel litigator reported that she has never felt left out or marginalized as a woman. Another agreed that the firm is, for the most part, a comfortable place to work, although, in her assessment, the corporate department "is apparently more of a 'boys' club' " than litigation. A litigator suggested that there are several male partners who "are perceived as preferring to work with pretty, young women." Whether she shared this apprehension, "the perception alone," prevalent among junior associates, in her opinion, "is extremely troubling." A midlevel litigator remarked that, in her estimation, the attitude toward women who take maternity leave is condescending—"basically, you take yourself out of the running." Another attorney reported that some partners in the firm had openly voiced the view that having children before making partner sounds the "death knell" for a lawyer's career.

Some lawyers were more positive. A real estate lawyer wrote that the firm's leadership is very supportive of women, and that the firm recently held a cocktail party for women partners and associates. A senior litigator reported that the firm makes "a strong effort [to] further women's careers."

> **"A 'mommy track' exists—any woman who works part-time is on it."**

Balancing work & family/personal life: Respondents said the hours here are "brutal," in the words of one, and are for some, "consistently grueling," making life at Willkie essentially typical for a New York law firm. An unmarried litigator sensed, "It is difficult for anyone who wasn't married when they arrived to sustain a satisfying personal life." One respondent noted that although the firm is "understanding of family responsibilities," the hours are "killer [for those who] want to have it all."

Some respondents were relatively upbeat about their ability to strike a balance. One corporate attorney noted that the firm culture "encourages attorneys to leave the office if they are in 'down-time' " and reported that there is no preoccupation with "face time." An unmarried corporate lawyer wrote that women at the firm do seem to "make things work," and that there are many who have children and continue working full-time. A litigator with a child wrote that she has managed to strike a successful balance with the help of a husband who "understands the problems I face." She added that, in her opinion, "a 'mommy track' exists—any woman who works part-time is on it."

According to one litigator's opinion, "Choosing to have a child is viewed as extremely negative by the partnership" and a sign of lack of commitment and loyalty. She observed that the firm "does not yet seem to have appreciated that we are losing a significant portion of the talent pool because women perceive that there is no future if one wants both a career and a family."

One respondent reported that women have taken generous nine-month maternity leaves (three months paid, six months unpaid). The firm has a backup childcare arrangement.

Willkie "has gone to great lengths to make part-time work beneficial to the part-timers and the firm."

Flexibility of work arrangements: Most respondents perceived that part-time was available, but only at the cost of relinquishing one's hopes for partnership. A litigator opined that a woman seeking to join the partnership "could never work part-time without sacrificing her goal." One associate wrote that, in her opinion, part-timers have been passed up for partner even when they have been "more than competent" and would have received promotion if they were willing to shift to full-time. (According to the firm, only one part-time associate has been passed up for partnership.) She added, however, that some women with children here work part-time and, in her opinion, "appear to be very happy with a permanent associate status."

A litigator suggested that in her department, "part-time positions have been mostly a flop," because the firm "still views lawyers as 'all or nothing' propositions." She asserted that, in her opinion, Willkie should be "working a little harder and more creatively to utilize these talented individuals in a manner that achieves both sides' interests."

A couple of part-timers expressed satisfaction with their arrangements. One, who stated that she does not want to make partner, said she works four days per week and leaves each day at 6 p.m., "which is pretty good for a big firm." Another respondent reported that, although she initially worked far more than her scheduled hours, when she complained that she was unable to complete all her assignments satisfactorily, "the firm was *very* accommodating."

The success of part-time arrangements apparently varies across departments. One respondent suggested, "[According] to the grapevine, there never will be any [part-time partners]." One part-timer said she thought that while no partner would be permitted to work part-time "officially," a flexible, unofficial reduced workload might be viable.

Two respondents noted that the firm is currently in the process of developing a more structured part-time program. One senior litigator perceived that Willkie "has gone to great lengths to make part-time work beneficial to the part-timers and the firm."

The firm is attempting to improve on the diversity front, and some strides have been made in recruitment.

Diversity: "[Willkie] is more diverse than many other firms of its size and nature in the sense that it does not hire from strictly Ivy League colleges/law schools or have a predominant religious persuasion," one associate wrote, an assessment shared by other respondents.

Most other associates noted that the firm is attempting to improve on the diversity front, and that some strides have been made in recruitment for the summer and entering classes, changes that should ultimately filter into the higher ranks. One associate wrote that women of "different backgrounds are actively recruited and mentored." Another commented that the firm "encourages all associates to be themselves."

Women partners "appear to be on the fringes of the partnership..."

Women in leadership positions: There is one woman on the firm's executive committee, and respondents agreed that she is the only woman who is perceived to have real power in the firm. One associate believed that she was "appointed at the request of the women partners" and another suggested that her appointment "took lots of lobbying." Characterized as well-liked and intelligent, respondents noted she is "interested in the concerns of women at the firm" and is working "quietly to improve women's issues."

Another associate remarked that, apart from the executive committee member, the other women partners "appear to be on the fringes of the partnership and do not play roles of any importance." She added that the women partners have made an effort by organizing meetings of women attorneys to "promote and discuss women's issues and opportunities." Another associate noted that the women partners are perceived "as having succeeded on the partner track because they made sacrifices many of us would not have made (family postponement until after age 35, etc.)." She added that she has been mentored by a woman partner but that, as a group, the partners could "do more internally to get to know/nurture the associates on an individual basis, and to support a more widespread part-time program."

Willkie Farr & Gallagher No. of Responses: 13	Strongly agree	Agree	Disagree	Strongly disagree
Women's prospects for advancement at the firm are as strong as men's	2	6	3	2
I am satisfied with the firm's family and personal leave policies	6	3	1	1
There are women in positions of power and influence in the firm	2	6	4	
Women are as likely as men to receive desirable work assignments	7	4		
Women attorneys feel they can discuss family obligations openly	2	4	4	2
Women are as likely as men to be mentored by senior attorneys	5	5	2	1
Women attorneys enjoy a high level of job satisfaction	2	5	3	2
Women in the firm are supportive of their women colleagues	5	7	1	
Firm management is receptive to the concerns of women attorneys	4	3	3	

WILSON SONSINI GOORICH & ROSATI

Rating: 52

Wilson Sonsini Goorich & Rosati
650 Page Mill Rd.
Palo Alto, CA 94304
415-493-9300

No. of Attorneys: 374
No. of Women Attorneys: 107
No. of Partners: 97
No. of Women Partners: 15
No. of Survey Responses Received: 5

Respondent Profile: 2 partners and 3 associates responded. Practice areas included securities and corporate.

Summary: A relatively young firm, Wilson, Sonsini received some positive and some mixed reviews, though from only five respondents. While both partners gave the firm high marks on advancement, mentoring, and allocation of assignments, associates were often more negative in their perceptions. The work is demanding, flexibility in work assignments is perceived as "not commonplace," and senior women were given lukewarm praise, at best.

Advancement: Partners and associates had distinctly different perceptions of women's opportunities at Wilson, Sonsini. According to a partner, advancement is merit-based and "mentoring and allocation of assignments are *not* influenced by gender." Both male and female partners, she added, "have contributed to my career development, assisted me in bringing in new clients as I develop my own practice, and 'share credit' in a fair manner."

Another partner commented that as more women become partners, woman-to-woman mentoring "has grown stronger over the last 10 years," although she admitted that "the number of women advancing to partnership is not as high as I would like."

All of the associate respondents were less sanguine about their chances for advancement. An associate maintained,

"Women are viewed as just as capable as men and are just as likely to advance if they work as hard as men do." In her perception any discrepancy in advancement is due to the fact that women "have other priorities in life besides work and, therefore, don't work quite as hard as men."

Another respondent reported that despite the trend toward more women making partner, in her opinion, some partners are "determined to keep WSG & R as a 'boys' club.' " She also expressed frustration at seeing such partners "handing out tickets to hockey and basketball games, as well as good deals and clients, to guys who are definitely not 'stars' at the firm."

Another associate commented that, in her estimation, the low numbers of women at all levels of Wilson, Sonsini is "surprising given the relative youth of the firm." She observed that its clients are "high-tech firms already dominated by men," and she has "encountered very few women in positions of authority in companies that are firm clients." In her perception, because "like tends to attract like," she feared the absence of women clients "could hamper a woman attorney's chances at rainmaking, deal-making, and partnership."

Respondents unanimously agreed that the firm was responsive to the concerns of women attorneys.

Attitudes and atmosphere: One partner commented that "law firms in general can be difficult places for women to work," and that Wilson, Sonsini is no exception. A couple of respondents described the firm's atmosphere as "relaxed" and said they hadn't experienced or observed any gender discrimination. Respondents unanimously agreed that the firm was responsive to the concerns of women attorneys.

One associate remarked that while the firm is an "okay place for women, it's odd being one of so few." Another associate observed that the partners in the firm's corporate practice are "predominantly men, as are most of the venture capitalists and entrepreneurs." She said that she is frequently the only woman in meetings of 15 to 20 people, but observed that "this speaks more about the lack of women in *all* areas, not just law."

The balance "seems impossible, especially if you are both ambitious and family-oriented—forget it!"

Balancing work & family/personal life: Although nestled in the suburbs, the atmosphere at Wilson, Sonsini is by no means sleepy or laid-back. All associates agreed that given the pressures of hours and the demands of clients, meeting the needs of children while working at the firm could be a formidable challenge. One remarked, "Work hours are long. I think it would be extremely difficult to do this job if you have kids—[whether] you are male or female."

Another said that, to her, the balance "seems impossible, especially if you are both ambitious and family-oriented— forget it!" Yet another said she had sensed that the families and personal lives of women partners could suffer because of "client demands for 24-hour attorney on-call services."

Both partners were more positive, with one describing the firm as "both demanding and supportive." She reported that during one partner's maternity leave, other partners and associates volunteered to cover her clients and projects. Following her return from maternity leave, the partner was treated the same as before she had a child. Because law is not a "9-to-5 job," she added, "it's a juggling act—long hours and demanding (but very interesting) clients."

"These [part-time] options are not impossible, but given the 'high-intensity' nature of the practice, they are difficult to do successfully over any extended period of time."

Flexibility of work arrangements: There is anxiety that part-time at Wilson, Sonsini is not something to bank on. According to a partner, "These options are not impossible, but given the 'high-intensity' nature of the practice, they are difficult to do successfully over any extended period of time."

Another partner wrote that, in her opinion, "some women have worked part-time, with limited success." Although she asserted that the firm is "willing to be flexible concerning part-time arrangements for associates," other survey respondents were in agreement that such arrangements are perceived as "not commonplace."

According to one respondent, "Maternity leave is a given" and "paternity leave for one to two weeks is average."

"Really good lawyers do well here, no matter what their background."

Diversity: According to a partner's perception, there are "very few women of diverse backgrounds at this firm." In her view, the firm "has not demonstrated a commitment to diversity," but rather focuses on merit. "Really good lawyers do well here, no matter what their background," she said. According to another partner, "Background, political leanings, life styles, etc., seem pretty irrelevant. Ability to do the work, good judgment, productivity, and client skills are the most important factors."

An associate observed, "I think that out of [nearly 400] lawyers, there is only one openly gay lawyer in the entire firm." Another associate perceived that "the firm makes a lot of effort on the race front, more than the gender front." (And the 1997-1998 National Directory of Legal Employers certainly bears out the first part of her opinion: 13 African-Americans, 37 Asians, and 11 Hispanics.)

"The positions of power within the firm are still predominantly held by men."

Women in leadership positions: The major power players at Wilson, Sonsini are men, as far as three of the five respondents were concerned.

A partner commented that, in her assessment, "the positions of power within the firm are still predominantly held by men." An associate said she believes that "women are not seen as powerful at the firm." A partner reported, however, that two of the firm's four hiring partners are women.

As for the more influential women at the firm, one associate commented that they "tend to abandon other women as they reach success and don't act as mentors." In another associate's opinion, however, things could be worse. She remarked that some of her friends work at another Bay Area firm where women partners have a "reputation of sabotaging or destroying women associates," a situation worse than at Wilson, Sonsini, where there is simply "a lack of women altogether."

Wilson, Sonsini, Goorich & Rosati No. of Responses: 5	Strongly agree	Agree	Disagree	Strongly disagree
Women's prospects for advancement at the firm are as strong as men's	1	1	3	
I am satisfied with the firm's family and personal leave policies	1	4		
There are women in positions of power and influence in the firm		2	3	
Women are as likely as men to receive desirable work assignments	3		2	
Women attorneys feel they can discuss family obligations openly	1	2	1	1
Women are as likely as men to be mentored by senior attorneys		3	1	1
Women attorneys enjoy a high level of job satisfaction	1	1	3	
Women in the firm are supportive of their women colleagues	1	2	1	
Firm management is receptive to the concerns of women attorneys	1	4		

WINSTON & STRAWN

Rating: 71

Winston & Strawn
35 West Wacker Dr.
Chicago, IL 60601
312- 558-5600

No. of Attorneys: 324
No. of Women Attorneys: 137
No. of Partners: 235
No. of Women Partners: 26
No. of Survey Responses Received: 20

Respondent Profile: 3 partners and 17 associates responded. Practice areas included litigation, environmental, corporate, and labor and employment.

Summary: Many respondents perceived that women are routinely ignored and excluded socially, and that they are apparently slighted with regard to assignments and offered little mentoring or other support. So, it is no surprise that women lawyers who choose to raise families while working at Winston & Strawn are said to face even greater obstacles, especially in light of the unsatisfactory part-time options. The firm's saving grace seems to be the environmental department, which got more favorable reviews and is home to a couple of well-respected women partners.

Advancement: Advancement is perceived to be an uphill battle for women at Winston & Strawn. A large majority of respondents believed that women were far less likely to be promoted to partnership than men, and gave just about every explanation in the book in an attempt to explain why. Simply stated, women must be "better than men" to make partner, in the opinion of one respondent. Advancement is "rare" for women, in her estimation, and even more unlikely for mothers, whose prospects are said to be "severely hindered." Even if a woman can succeed in handling the demands of family life, according to a senior associate, there is a concern that the "male leadership is suspicious of any woman's 'commitment' once she has children." Hence, according to

another associate's estimation, any woman "who might want a family thinks about leaving prior to any such decision." Another lawyer reported that, in her opinion, few women are around when partnership decisions are made, and for those who do try to juggle family with the "grueling nature of the practice," the balance tends to be "tenuous, at best."

An associate characterized senior men as supporting their subordinates by channeling good work to male associates and establishing strong professional relationships with them. Among women, in the opinion of many, there is said to be little mentoring and little support.

Advancement is perceived to be particularly difficult in the corporate and litigation practice areas and more attainable in the environmental department, which has a "good track record" for promoting women. Other support departments, such as estate planning, labor, and benefits, are also said to be more friendly to women, because the "life style is more manageable" and there are more women in the senior ranks. The bigger departments were characterized by one respondent as lacking "female mentorship and role models and are by their very nature male-oriented."

In a corporate associate's opinion, "There are really no prospects for advancement for women" in her department. For corporate attorneys with children, she maintained that "your chances of becoming a partner are *zero!*" She added it was her speculation that, to be promoted in the corporate department, "it helps significantly if you play golf."

It is easier for women to secure the mentoring they need to rise to the lowest partnership rung in at least one associate's opinion, but the partnership "appears to do little to assist women beyond this point." Another associate agreed that it is becoming *easier* for women to rise to income partner level because the firm feels a need to rectify the discrepancy in numbers of male and female partners.

That said, in the opinion of one environmental partner, assuming women "do not have children or work part-time, and assuming that they are better than most of the men in their class, they will make partner at Winston."

According to a respondent's opinion, the "boys' club" is concentrated in the senior ranks of the partnership.

Attitudes and atmosphere: Winston & Strawn is a "boys' club," according to many associates, and the atmosphere is perceived to be disadvantageous to women, both socially and professionally. Although an associate commented that the firm is more comfortable than one would expect, given what she characterized as "its outside perception as a 'white male, Republican' breeding ground," others disagreed.

A senior associate suggested that there are, in her opinion, "a great many" senior lawyers who will not voluntarily work with women and who assign women "lesser quality" work.

A few departments within the firm are reportedly hospitable for women, and some individuals seem to experience the surroundings very differently than others. The environmental department, for example, is reportedly dominated by women, and as a small department, is "removed from much of the atmosphere of the rest of the firm," according to an associate. The labor/employment group also includes well-respected women, including three partners "who sort of lead the way for the rest of us." A first-year corporate associate reported that she was "surprised to find no 'boys' club' in the corporate department," and added that she has received as much mentoring as her male counterparts.

In another respondent's opinion, the "boys' club" is concentrated in the senior ranks of the partnership and the situation is "gradually changing as more women enter the partner ranks." Another associate agreed, adding that the firm's women are "working hard to assert themselves."

> *"I never see my husband and my cat is developing neurotic behavior from spending so much time alone—I cannot imagine trying to have a child."*

Balancing work & family/personal life: "Brutal" hours make "sacrifice" the watchword at Winston & Strawn, in one respondent's opinion. There is reportedly no "mommy track," and "only those without children are truly successful within the eyes of the firm and how it rewards and views attorneys," in one associate's estimation. Those hoping for promotion are advised to bill between 2,200 and 2,600 hours per year.

The pressure is reportedly the worst in the litigation and corporate departments. A corporate associate quipped, "I never see my husband and my cat is developing neurotic behavior from spending so much time alone—I cannot imagine trying to have a child." The most difficult aspect of the job, she added, is that "I can never plan any family activity because of the constant pressure of being available for whatever emergency a partner might have at 5 p.m. on a Friday." Another corporate associate said that, in her opinion, "[The] personal, physical, and psychological costs of being an associate in the corporate department are too high and onerous" to allow attorneys to shoulder much else.

Female associates should "beware of what a leave can do to your evaluation," an associate cautioned. She added that a partner once demanded to know "why her husband could not sit for her children" on a Saturday when she was wanted for work. "Another partner," she recounted, "wanted to know the exact day of my return from a leave taken because one of my parents had passed away—he left four messages in my voice mail regarding this!"

A few respondents contended that as difficult as it is, maintaining a semblance of balance is possible. A midlevel litigator explained, "It's a matter of setting firm personal priorities and making them known to others." One associate commented that she has sustained a satisfying family life by accepting the compromises she has made "and will have to make at work as a result." An environmental partner commented that the firm is "trying," as evidenced by a two-day women's seminar held last year, "which addressed topics such as marketing, rising in the firm, and balancing home life."

Winston & Strawn offers no childcare assistance—as one respondent remarked, "That's what wives are for—don't you know?" Nevertheless, Winston noted they offer childcare flexible accounts.

> *In the corporate department, part-time makes sense only if "you are a kamikaze."*

Flexibility of work arrangements: Part-time arrangements are available on a case-by-case basis in most departments, but the costs are perceived to be very high, according to most respondents. In the opinion of one associate, other lawyers "openly snicker and resent women with alternative work arrangements." Those who choose part-time options risk being "written off" and invariably receive less desirable work assignments, in the opinion of several respondents. Another partner maintained that, in her opinion, the combined "problems of reduced pay, [being taken] 'off track,' and [receiving] lesser quality work" make the option unrealistic. Those on part-time schedules may also face heavy pressure from the partners with whom they work, "who will push the individual to produce and be available as needed."

In the corporate department, part-time makes sense only if "you are a kamikaze," in the words of one respondent.

Working on a part-time schedule long-term reportedly precludes advancement— "You can kiss possible partnership good-bye," in the estimation of one lawyer. Although a partner claimed otherwise, many respondents agreed that no attorney who has ever gone part-time has subsequently made partner, including those who later returned to full-time work. It appears they are wrong—a spokesperson for Winston confirmed that there are currently two women part-time partners who were part-time associates.

A couple of associates were slightly more optimistic. A corporate associate commented that while some attorneys seem happy with their arrangements, "part-time means 40 hours a week." A first-year associate predicted that part-time is "slowly becoming acceptable," though the hours remain long.

According to a respondent, Winston & Strawn's women are a more eclectic and interesting group than the firm's men.

Diversity: Although a sizable portion of respondents left this question blank, those who did comment reported that although the firm as a whole is relatively conservative, Winston & Strawn's women are a more eclectic and interesting group than the firm's men. A minority woman reported that the firm is "a comfortable place in this regard," but added that she has seen "no large efforts to increase diversity." In another associate's opinion, although "political, social, and gender diversity are relatively embraced," racial diversity remains "an issue." Another associate characterized diversity as a "nouvelle concept at the firm."

As for life styles, just one associate commented, saying, "I have no idea—no one talks about that, really."

One partner reported that the firm recently held "diversity training for every person at the firm and rolled out a new workplace harassment policy to demonstrate management's zero tolerance of harassing behavior."

"[The] women role models at this firm (at least in litigation) are few and far between..."

Women in leadership positions: A woman partner reportedly heads the environmental group and is a member of the firm's executive committee, but that's virtually it in terms of powerful women at Winston & Strawn, respondents believe. With the exception of the environmental group, which has lower hours and offers a more manageable life style, women have reportedly not advanced to posts of power within the firm. An associate observed that, in her opinion, the income partners "do not look happy and do not seem to have the same support and opportunities—i.e., business introductions/referrals—as other younger partners." A litigation associate agreed that her department is "quite a few years behind" and that the " 'buzz' just keeps working against women." One

---

associate wrote, "There are no female attorneys in positions of power" and wryly added, "That would be too progressive."

Although several environmental partners, including the executive committee member, are said to promote the opportunities and welfare of women within the firm, many respondents commented that the more senior women partners at the firm are not perceived as role models. One associate wrote that the executive committee member is "extremely well-respected by the entire firm, has considerable power, and goes out of her way to help other women. But, she's unique. No other woman has this degree of respect and power."

In stark contrast, a corporate associate commented that, in her opinion, the firm's top women "are, as a whole, perceived as insensitive workaholics, as are most of the male partners in power here." Another associate believed, "[The] women role models at this firm (at least in litigation) are few and far between. Those women who are successful have precious little else in their lives except work."

Those who have made partner without having "sacrificed family entirely" had, in the opinion of one respondent, "strong political connections." According to one associate's perception, the lack of support from woman-to-woman is "sad" and "results from a combination of exhaustion and concentrating on staying alive that prevents female attorneys from helping each other as much as it is needed in a place like W & S."

Winston & Strawn No. of Responses: 20	Strongly agree	Agree	Disagree	Strongly disagree
Women's prospects for advancement at the firm are as strong as men's		5	11	3
I am satisfied with the firm's family and personal leave policies	1	8	9	1
There are women in positions of power and influence in the firm	1	7	9	3
Women are as likely as men to receive desirable work assignments	3	6	8	3
Women attorneys feel they can discuss family obligations openly	1	4	9	3
Women are as likely as men to be mentored by senior attorneys	2	5	7	4
Women attorneys enjoy a high level of job satisfaction		7	9	3
Women in the firm are supportive of their women colleagues	5	7	8	
Firm management is receptive to the concerns of women attorneys	2	5	9	3

WOLF, BLOCK, SCHORR and SOLIS-COHEN

Rating: 63

Wolf, Block, Schorr and Solis-Cohen
Packard Building
12th Fl.
Fifteenth & Chestnut Sts.
Philadelphia, PA 19102
215-977-2000

No. of Attorneys: 156
No. of Women Attorneys: 43
No. of Partners: 86
No. of Women Partners: 15
No. of Survey Responses Received: 16

Respondent Profile: 6 partners and 10 associates responded. Practice areas included litigation, corporate, and labor.

Summary: Under new management, Wolf, Block is described as a firm in flux, whose main priority is pulling in business. The pressure to make rain seems to affect both associates hoping to advance and partners seeking to hold onto their seats. The perceived impracticality of selective part-time arrangements, and some lingering elements of a "boys' club," may contribute to some women's dissatisfaction.

Advancement: Advancement sounds like a tense issue at Wolf, Block, Schorr and Solis-Cohen, seemingly because many respondents believe it is so closely tied to having a considerable book of business.

Atypically, the six partners who responded were split evenly on the question of women's prospects for advancement, while six out of nine associates were relatively optimistic.

One associate believed that only one of Wolf, Block's women partners is a "senior" partner. She characterized the others as being at the "lowest level" of a partnership pecking order that may consist of as many as six distinct tiers. Nevertheless, this associate added that, in her estimation, if a woman "survives the prescribed number of years," which she claimed was recently increased from seven to nine, she is "very likely to make partner because of the political imperative."

Besides the difficulties in attracting business, respondents attributed women's poor prospects for advancement to inadequate mentoring and to perceptions that women lawyers are not adequately aggressive. According to an associate, although women are rewarded for good performance, they are still "more likely to be perceived as reticent or lacking confidence or presence if they are not aggressively confident in manner."

One associate reported that the mentoring is "nonexistent" and the assigning process highly political. She added, "Women are outside the 'good-old-boys' club' that dictates who works with whom." Attrition of women lawyers, in the view of some respondents, exacerbates the problem. In one associate's opinion, women "drop like flies before partnership" because the firm offers little flexibility with regard to part-time arrangements.

Other associates expressed a distinctly rosier view. One partner reported that prospects are good, pointing to her own advancement. One associate wrote, "[Women] certainly have the same opportunity as men to progress to partnership. The allocation of assignments has nothing to do with gender." She added, "Evaluation criteria are not only the same, but are also applied evenly. A woman is looked at as an attorney—not just as a woman."

One partner stated that women are as likely to advance as men, as long as they are "team players." Other partners thought women were at a disadvantage. One reported that women "have not advanced as frequently or as far," and attributed this to "unequal allocation of assignments (fewer important ones); lack of mentoring for women; and women's generally greater concern with family responsibilities." Another attributed the problem to the firm's failure to delegate women to handle client relations. "Women do *not* have the same advancement chances as men," she wrote, claiming that "there is a greater likelihood that client relations will be turned over to a male, thereby resulting in him receiving greater compensation/earlier promotion to partner."

> *"Despite [the firm's] efforts—it is a 'boys club.' For a woman to enter, she must do something extraordinary!"*

Attitudes and atmosphere: Some respondents reported that Wolf, Block is free of overt discrimination and comfortable, but others were concerned that the firm retains certain elements of a "boys' club." Wolf, Block was vindicated by the Third Circuit's decision dismissing a very public discrimination suit. In the aftermath of the suit, a partner reported, "[Wolf, Block] has tried hard...to address inequality. Despite these efforts—it is a 'boys' club.' For a woman to enter, she must do something *extraordinary!*"

One associate believed that to "the extent that any human being is comfortable at Wolf, Block, it's not that much worse for women, but it definitely [is] worse. Since new management took over, nobody is very comfortable, because everyone knows his job is on the line, partner or associate."

Several respondents reported satisfaction with the firm's atmosphere. According to one labor lawyer, women are given "equally complex assignments and are treated as important members of the team. I do not feel that there is an all-boys network. I am included in the lunches out of the office, the hallway chatter, and the 'inside loop' just as the male lawyers are included."

And a partner described Wolf, Block as "perhaps the least overt 'boys' club' law firm at which I have worked."

However, others reported that, in their view, women lawyers are left out of the loop socially. One respondent observed that women can be treated equally, "as long as they do all the same things men have been doing for decades: work long hours and leave your children with caretakers (or a stay-at-home spouse) for lengthy periods." She added, however, "Even if you do all these things, don't expect to be asked out to lunch with the guys, or be invited out for drinks with the guys, etc., which is where the real bonding goes on..."

> *"It is acceptable to leave the office in time for family dinner— work can be done from home in the evening."*

Balancing work & family/personal life: Respondents were in some disagreement as to whether the firm helps or hinders women lawyers in maintaining a healthy balance. Women lawyers must keep billable hours up, as well as devote considerable time to nonbillable and client development activities, all of which compete for time outside the firm.

With that said, several respondents reported that the firm is understanding of attorneys' outside commitments. One partner, acknowledging that she is more productive at work if "nonwork activities are also scheduled on a regular basis," reported that her partners "have always been understanding of family obligations," and that many partners make family a priority. "It is acceptable," she wrote, "to leave the office in time for family dinner—work can be done from home in the evening."

The firm reportedly has arranged "fantastic" emergency childcare. One associate stressed that her colleagues were conscious of family responsibilities and that they arranged schedules accordingly in order to avoid conflicts with childcare responsibilities.

Some lawyers find balance more difficult to maintain. One married partner wrote that sustaining a home life is *"difficult, difficult, difficult.* To succeed here, the firm must be number one. The attitude that pervades the firm is that you are a lawyer first and whoever else last."

Another partner asserted: "Billable hours are important, and 'Johnny's' school play [and] honor roll assembly do not peacefully coexist with billable hours." One associate said her impression was that the firm "loves the 'I-can-do-it-all' woman..."

> *"[Part-time arrangements are] only given if they love you. Otherwise they can easily replace you."*

Flexibility of work arrangements: Part-time arrangements are reportedly available, but respondents perceived them to be options only for a select group of associates, and only at the cost of any prospect of advancement within the firm. One part-timer who made a lateral move into the firm was already on a part-time schedule when she came and was allowed to continue that arrangement "without any pressure" to change her schedule.

Full-timers seemed to view part-time options here in a considerably different light. One associate reported that there is a perception that part-time arrangements are "only given if they love you. Otherwise they can easily replace you." According to a partner, "Suggesting this type of alternative probably limits any ability to advance." An associate wrote that part-time "is okay if you've got full-time childcare at home so that you are on-call full-time, because [the firm will] want to be able to call you whenever they want and know you'll be available."

Another respondent perceived part-time as "a real career killer." Supposedly, as she recalled, a senior associate who "wanted to work part-time was allowed to cut back to four days a week and was promptly given all the junk work in the department after having been a 'star' associate. (She left.)"

"The ultimate nondiscriminatory firm: They really don't care about your background, political leanings, personality, and life style, as long as you bill enough hours and you don't cross the wrong person."

Diversity: Several respondents commented that they chose to join Wolf, Block because the firm embraces a variety of personalities and doesn't require its attorneys to conform to any particular mold. One lawyer characterized it as "the ultimate nondiscriminatory firm: They really don't care about your background, political leanings, personality, and life style, as long as you bill enough hours and you don't cross the wrong person." Another respondent noted that the firm is "tolerant of great diversity in the political activities, sexual orientation, gender, ethnicity, race, religion, etc., of all personnel."

Several respondents reported that the firm makes efforts to maintain a supportive environment for attorneys of diverse backgrounds. Several noted, however, that the firm, in their experience, is "sorely lacking in racial/ethnic diversity for both women and men," as one put it. An associate reported that the firm "tries to get all types of minorities," and an associate who is active in hiring wrote that she "knows the firm is committed to hiring women and other minorities." One partner concluded that the firm "is not opposed to diversity, but has not been able to attract many non-white males and keep them for long."

One woman on the firm's executive committee was characterized as "...the only woman of power or any seniority" in a firm of 156 lawyers.

Women in leadership positions: Respondents were almost evenly split on whether there were women in positions of influence and power at Wolf, Block. Many of our respondents reported that a woman who recently joined a branch office was appointed to the executive committee. She was characterized by one lawyer as "...the only woman of power or any seniority" in a firm of 156 lawyers. Another concluded that she "will be a very positive influence for women."

One associate summed up the positive view of women's leadership at the firm, reporting that there are two female department heads, "and some bright, well-respected female partners. Typical 'women's issues' are being examined and resolved more and more over time."

"[The firm's] culture is obsessed with billable hours and is very male-dominated."

Miscellaneous: Very mixed results point to a situation best illustrated by the ambivalent comment of one associate: "There are some very good people, men and women, at Wolf, Block who will be personally hurt by this review. But these few people do not have much influence on the overall culture, which is obsessed with billable hours and which is very male-dominated. I really wouldn't recommend Wolf, Block to any woman."

Wolf, Block, Schorr and Solis-Cohen No. of Responses: 16	Strongly agree	Agree	Disagree	Strongly disagree
Women's prospects for advancement at the firm are as strong as men's	3	6	4	2
I am satisfied with the firm's family and personal leave policies	5	4	3	3
There are women in positions of power and influence in the firm	1	6	4	4
Women are as likely as men to receive desirable work assignments	5	6	2	2
Women attorneys feel they can discuss family obligations openly	4	4	6	1
Women are as likely as men to be mentored by senior attorneys	2	3	7	3
Women attorneys enjoy a high level of job satisfaction	2	5	5	3
Women in the firm are supportive of their women colleagues	4	8	1	
Firm management is receptive to the concerns of women attorneys	3	4	2	4

Appendix

PRESUMED EQUAL: WHAT AMERICA'S TOP WOMEN LAWYERS REALLY THINK ABOUT THEIR FIRMS

PO BOX 687, FRANKLIN LAKES, NJ 07417

April 11, 1997

Dear Colleague:

We write to ask your assistance with the publication of the second edition of *Presumed Equal: What America's Top Women Lawyers Really Think About Their Firms*, a project initiated by the Harvard Women's Law Association. You may remember the uncertainty and anxiety that characterize the search for summer and permanent employment at law firms. Often, the questions women law students most want answered are not addressed in firm recruitment brochures and are difficult to raise during interviews. In response to these concerns, *Presumed Equal* seeks your participation in filling out an anonymous written survey aimed at gathering information about women's experiences with regard to career advancement, work and family, firm attitudes and atmosphere, and overall job satisfaction at individual firms.

As many of you are aware, the first edition of *Presumed Equal*, distributed on law school campuses and in cities across the country, provided an inside look at how large law firms compare in terms of the opportunities and quality of life they offer to women attorneys. Covered in the *Wall Street Journal*, *Washington Post*, *Los Angeles Times*, and the *New York Post*, the findings contained in *Presumed Equal* also served as an impetus for reflection and reform at many of the firms surveyed. Numerous survey respondents contacted us to say that, in response to *Presumed Equal*, their firms had held special meetings and convened task groups to address the concerns raised by women in the survey. Our goal in the second edition is to follow up on our earlier findings and to monitor the pace of women's advancement within private legal practice. We have also expanded our coverage to include a substantial number of new firms.

We ask that you complete the enclosed survey and mail it back to us **no later than May 19, 1997**. The success of this project will depend almost entirely upon the willingness of women attorneys to reach out to today's law students by sharing information and insights on their experience in law firms. In responding, we ask you to be as candid as possible and to share any information that you think might possibly be of interest to women law students or to other women in the profession. The more information, anecdotes, and thoughts you can give us, the more *Presumed Equal* will have to offer both to law students, and as a tool for change in the legal profession.

In compiling the second edition of *Presumed Equal*, we wish to take any necessary steps to ensure the confidentiality of all respondents. To that end, while it is essential that you indicate the firm with which you are associated, in filling out the survey we urge you to leave out information that might allow your comments to be traced back to you individually.

If you have any questions concerning the survey itself or this project, please do not hesitate to contact us at 202-319-8638. Thank you very much for your participation. We look forward to reading about your experiences and insights. We aim to have the survey results compiled for dissemination this October in a book that will contain anecdotes, views gathered from the survey, and response rates tallied for each of the firms covered. If you would like to pre-order a copy call 1-800-227-3371.

Suzanne Nossel & Elizabeth Westfall
Co-Editors, *Presumed Equal*

PRESUMED EQUAL ANONYMOUS SURVEY
PO BOX 687, FRANKLIN LAKES, NJ 07417

Firm Name:_____City:_____

Your Position: Partner_____   Associate_____   Year_____   Counsel_____

Practice Area (optional):_____   Family Status (optional):_____

1. ADVANCEMENT. Please describe your perception of the prospects and patterns of advancement for women at your firm. Are women as likely as men to advance to partnership? In your view, what factors are central to the advancement of women within the firm? (Please comment on mentoring, allocation of assignments, review criteria, reasons for attrition, etc.)

2. ATTITUDES AND ATMOSPHERE. Is your firm a comfortable place for women to work? Why or why not? What manifestations, overt or subtle, are there of gender discrimination? (Please comment on social interactions between men and women, dress code, "the boys' club," the tone set by firm leadership, etc.)

3.a WORK AND FAMILY. Are part-time and other alternative work arrangements considered to be legitimate and viable options for women at the firm? Why or why not? Are such arrangements available at partnership level? (If you have taken advantage of such policies, please describe your experience.)

3.b How easy or difficult is it for women attorneys in your firm to sustain a satisfying personal/family life? (Please comment on working hours, pressure, availability of childcare, "the mommy track," sensitivity of the firm to family responsibilities, etc.)

4. DIVERSITY. Is the firm a comfortable and supportive environment for women attorneys of diverse backgrounds, political leanings, personalities, and life styles? To what extent does the firm demonstrate a commitment to diversity? (Descriptions of personal experiences are appreciated.)

5. FIRM LEADERSHIP/ADDITIONAL COMMENTS. Are there women in positions of real power in the firm? How are these women perceived? Have they played a role in promoting the opportunities and quality of life of women attorneys? Please comment on any other issues of relevance to the status of women in your firm.

PLEASE CHECK ONLY ONE BOX	STRONGLY AGREE	AGREE	DISAGREE	STRONGLY DISAGREE
Women's prospects for advancement at the firm are as strong as men's				
I am satisfied with the firm's family and personal leave policies				
There are women in positions of power and influence in the firm				
Women are as likely as men to receive desirable work assignments				
Women attorneys feel they can discuss family obligations openly				
Women are as likely as men to be mentored by senior attorneys				
Women attorneys enjoy a high level of job satisfaction				
Women in the firm are supportive of their women colleagues				
Firm management is receptive to the concerns of women attorneys				

Please use additional pages to add your comments on any issues that you think are or should be of concern to women contemplating employment at your firm. Thank you very much for your participation.